AF600524

TEACHING RACE IN PERILOUS TIMES

SUNY series, Critical Race Studies in Education

Derrick R. Brooms, editor

TEACHING RACE IN PERILOUS TIMES

JASON E. COHEN, SHARON D. RAYNOR
AND
DWAYNE A. MACK

Published by State University of New York Press, Albany

Printed in the United States of America

For information, contact State University of New York Press, Albany, NY
www.sunypress.edu

Library of Congress Cataloging-in-Publication Data

Names: Cohen, Jason E., 1975- editor. | Raynor, Sharon D., editor. | Mack, Dwayne, 1968- editor.
Title: Teaching race in perilous times / [edited by] Jason E. Cohen, Sharon D. Raynor, Dwayne A. Mack.
Description: Albany, NY : State University of New York Press, [2021] | Series: SUNY series, critical race studies in education | Includes bibliographical references and index.
Identifiers: LCCN 2020022021 | ISBN 9781438482255 (hardcover : alk. paper) | ISBN 9781438482279 (ebook)
Subjects: LCSH: Race—Study and teaching (Higher)—United States. | Racism—Study and teaching (Higher)—United States. | Race awareness—Study and teaching—United States. | Race relations—Study and teaching (Higher)—United States. | Multicultural education—Study and teaching (Higher)—United States.
Classification: LCC HT1506 .T43 2021 | DDC 305.80071/173—dc23
LC record available at https://lccn.loc.gov/2020022021

10 9 8 7 6 5 4 3 2 1

CONTENTS

ACKNOWLEDGMENTS ix

INTRODUCTION 1
Jason E. Cohen and Sharon D. Raynor

PART 1. AFFECT AND AUTHORITY IN THE CLASSROOM

CHAPTER 1
On Native American Erasure in the Classroom 23
Scott Manning Stevens

CHAPTER 2
Multiple Pedagogies Required: Reflections on Teaching Race and Ethnicity in the Intercultural and Intergenerational Classroom 41
Felicia L. Harris

CHAPTER 3
"Black Rage": Teaching Gender, Race, and Class in the Wake of #BlackLivesMatter and #SayHerName 63
Emerald L. Christopher-Byrd

CHAPTER 4
Can the White Boy Speak? Coming to Terms with the Color-Blind Li(n)e 79
Douglas Eli Julien

PART 2. SCHOLAR-ACTIVISM: TEACHING FOR SOCIAL JUSTICE

Chapter 5
Technologies of Discrimination: Structural Racism beyond Campus 101
Jason E. Cohen

Chapter 6
Teaching from the Tap: Confronting Hegemony and Systemic Oppression through Reflection and Analysis 135
Kerri-Ann M. Smith and Paul M. Buckley

Chapter 7
"I Never Touch Race": Teaching Race in Online Spaces with Future Indiana School Leaders 155
Rachel Roegman and Serena J. Salloum

Chapter 8
Scaffolding for Justice: Deploying Intersectionality, Black Feminist Thought, and the "Outsider Within" in the Writing about Literature Classroom 183
Shane A. McCoy

PART 3. PRECARIOUS INSTITUTIONS, PRECARIOUS APPOINTMENTS

Chapter 9
Institutionalizing (In)Equality: The Double-Edged Sword of Diversity Requirements 205
Daniel J. Delgado and Keja Valens

Chapter 10
"Survival Is Not an Academic Skill": Life behind the Mask 231
Sharon D. Raynor

CHAPTER 11
Reflections from a Precariously Employed Carpetbagger: A Canadian's Experience Teaching in the South 255
Stephen W. Sheps

CHAPTER 12
Undocumented Learning Outcomes and Cyber Coyotes: Teaching Ethnic Studies in the Online Classroom 273
Erin Murrah-Mandril

PART 4.
HISTORICIZING THE MOMENT, HISTORICIZING THE CURRICULUM

CHAPTER 13
A Du Boisian Approach to Making Black Lives Matter in the Classroom (and Beyond) 299
Derrick R. Brooms and Darryl A. Brice

CHAPTER 14
The Racial Oracle Has a History 319
Mark William Westmoreland

CHAPTER 15
The Death of the Black Child 343
Tasha M. Hawthorne

AFTERWORD: TEACHING RACE WITHIN CRIMINAL JUSTICE 365
Chyna Crawford

CONTRIBUTORS 373

INDEX 381

ACKNOWLEDGMENTS

From Jason E. Cohen: This book has been too long in the production, as many works are, in part for our volume because of the complexity we encountered in our work of assembling a group of teachers and scholars whose work would stand out, not only for its remarkable intellectual contributions but also for the very diversity across the landscape of higher education that we have pulled together in this collection. My first acknowledgment consequently goes out to each one of our contributors. I learned so much in the process of building this book, and I am grateful to each of you individually and collectively for showing me how dynamic and generous our field can be. Thank you to Olivia Ernst for her enthusiasm and accuracy in preparing the index. In particular, to my coeditors Sharon D. Raynor and Dwayne A. Mack: you are models of intellectual rigor, curiosity, caring, and imagination. Thank you. Sharon sat down with me over coffee and we talked through an early version of this chapter, which, alongside conversations with Dwayne, lent this book an early shape. In the early stages of writing, Stephanie Browner's keen advice, generous temperament, and sharp eye were invaluable. Chad Berry gave me the chance to write my chapter and assemble this volume during his time as dean, and, in addition, he showed me the lived meaning of reconciliation and restoration, for which I express deep gratitude. Keja Valens read a full draft with critical eyes and, along with Matthias Rudolf, talked me through questions of equity and justice with acuity and scotch. At Berea, Verlaine McDonald gave me courage to write when she told me that I was telling a story that remained too-often silent. Kennaria Brown encouraged me to live and teach better through her honesty and sincerity. Keith Bullock and Andrew Baskin each in their own ways gave me well-timed words of wisdom, and Linda Strong Leek showed me how powerful it can be to stand by principled decisions, even when they may not be widely appreciated.

Recently, the loss of Steve Pulsford has given new gravity to this project: he and I talked through the politics of race and asked how to teach humanely and yet critically over many evenings, and just as I lament the loss of his complicated mind, so, too, I regret that he cannot see this work in print. In the final emailed note I received from him, he asked salient questions that have resonated with me as this collection moves to press: "How might we take account of the US in 2020, of systemic police racism and brutality, of Trump, and the politicization of coronavirus? These things seem linked. It seems to me they are in almost anyone's view fundamental failures of democracy and government and of a culture that one might hope would show more caring about human life." I hope this book begins to speak to that caring in ways that we can stand by and continue to speak for.

My father, Alan Cohen, asks me nearly every time we speak when my book will appear, and this one has become the book I think of as defining my scholarship over the last decade, so thank you for your persistence, love, and high expectations, Dad. They have paid off. Liz and Larry Weiss, Danielle Weiss, and Brian Cohen are all my constant cheerleaders and enthusiasts. You make me smile, and I am honored by your love. Without Ellis and Meghan, I wouldn't be able to focus on any of this or see its importance for the future of our schools, our teaching, our lived experiences, or our communities, especially in the wake of the coronavirus pandemic of 2020. My work in this book is dedicated to you two, with love.

From Sharon D. Raynor: To my family, especially my parents, Louis and Katie, who always supported my desire to teach and to serve others; I want to acknowledge and thank them for always encouraging me to fight for those who could not fight for themselves. To my siblings and family members Cassandra, Jerry, Tosha, Marquitta, Amanda, Vanessa, Shironda, and Alex, who are educators in various environments in which teaching race is paramount to their survival and success; I appreciate their inspiration and those late-night chats that keep me motivated. To my beloved niece-daughter Amaris, who keeps me young and reminds me that her generation will fight the good fight and survive to tell the story. To my former student Janelle Martin, who continuously dares to dream and who is never afraid to defy anyone's perception of her. To my former student and friend Markiest Waller, who was there at the beginning of my career as an educator. He epitomizes how true grit and determination can break through the walls of prejudice and racism. To the new generation of activists in the #BlackLivesMatter, #MeToo, and #SayHerName movements, who are also my students and colleagues, I want to express my personal gratitude to you for sticking to your convictions and always fighting for justice and equality. Being a part of this book project was welcoming and, at times, therapeutic, so I especially want to thank my dear friend Jason for asking me to be a part of this journey and for the many conversations and absolute honesty that allowed us both to better manage life in this educational vortex.

INTRODUCTION

JASON E. COHEN AND SHARON D. RAYNOR

> Not long ago you are in a room where someone asks the philosopher Judith Butler what makes language hurtful. You can feel everyone lean in. Our very being exposes us to the address of another, she answers. We suffer from the condition of being addressable.
>
> —Claudia Rankine, *Citizen*

> When we claim to know and to present ourselves, we will fail in some ways that are nevertheless essential to who we are. We cannot reasonably expect anything different from others in return.
>
> —Judith Butler, *Giving an Account of Oneself*

TEACHING: A MOMENT OF RECOGNITION

In 1960 Robert Penn Warren interviewed James Baldwin, who touched on, among other topics, the revolutionary conditions that were emerging through the parallel rise of new expressions of African American racial pride alongside glaringly bald forms of racial threat. Asked about the status of hope for better race relations in that moment, Baldwin imagined both its challenge and potential power: "In order to accommodate me, in order to overcome so many centuries of cruelty and bad faith, and genocide and fear, all the American institutions and all the American values, public and private, will have to change. The Democratic party will have to become a different party, for example."[1] Baldwin goes on to call that vision "almost impossible to imagine in this country," one defined by "a world in which race would count for nothing."[2] How far we have still to come to overcome the racial calculus Baldwin entertains. Perhaps it remains unsurprising that the concerns for equity, justice, and responsibility Baldwin raised over a generation ago have remained just as urgent to scholars and teachers of race now, even if the tactics used to address them—or the forms of that address, whether political, cultural, pedagogical, or pursued by other means—have shifted over the decades. Baldwin suggests that, in effect, we would have to find new ways of addressing and configuring our relations to race, new ways of identifying its contours both in public and private discourse. In order to generate a foundational shift, Baldwin's piece suggests, we need to become responsible for the potential identities we take up in response to the social and educational changes that equity and justice demand in relation to race.

We as teachers and scholars have taken the persisting urgency of discourses informed by race as the central condition motivating the work in this collection. That singular motivation underlies our shared concern for teaching race today; more importantly, it also points to the very heart of the perilousness our volume identifies as our call to arms. These perilous times have lasted for decades: no single presidency or event marks their onset. Rather, the perils we discuss in the chapters that follow are not new, even if the agents, moments, and audiences might be. Nevertheless, these perilous times, our perilous times, demand our renewed and refocused attention as teachers and scholars. We define the perilous times of this collection, therefore, according to several forms of persistent danger that inform discussions of race in our moment as it sits in a historical trajectory of racial discourse. The perils of teaching race we confront in these pages include the rising frequency and fear of death not only in classrooms but on the streets. Rates of fatal encounters have risen in surprising ways: not only in confrontations with police or other gun deaths but, as these chapters reveal, through encounters with the seemingly benign or even beneficial elements of our engineered world, including water. All of those deaths are deeply driven by the social, institutional, and structural dynamics of race. Our strongest marker of peril, however, lies in a racial understanding of the death of citizens whose bodies are black and brown. In that light, today's fatality rates for black and brown persons are higher than they have been since race-based civic unrest became coupled with the progressive deregulation of firearm possession alongside the strengthening of police protections from prosecution through legislation and judicial precedent, both of which crystallized during the late 1960s.[3] In addition to the perils of teaching race we find reflected in the world, we also consider the perils propagated by institutional imbalances and threats for our students and ourselves on campus. Finally, we consider the perils of the very continuity of the racially motivated dynamics, whether physical, cultural, or ideological, that continue to shape our classrooms as spaces that have inherited racial oppression and division from the formation of the modern university over a century ago. Given this combined core of lasting perils, coupled with a renewed form of attention to a long-standing set of conditions, our collective engagement in teaching race in perilous times remains as sensitive to historical forms of teaching as it is to more contemporary instances. Sadly, the perilous times have already lasted far too long, and just as Baldwin called for a change in institutions, we see that same call for change across institutions, social dispositions, syllabi, canons, and academic cultures in this collection as a moment to take responsibility for our current perils by responding to them forcefully.

The essays in our volume have converged on one point: each essay articulates a call to see our national conversations about race include a moment of self-recognition and recognition of others, a moment of teaching and learning, a moment that acknowledges the urgency of seeing race through a lens that focuses us on the lasting significance of public debates today, as well as those that have been conducted historically. We take it as central to address the tension identified in our epigraphs, one adopted from Judith Butler's investigation of the ethics involved in our accounts of ourselves. Her inquiry signals, on the one hand, the limits implicit in every attempt to acknowledge ourselves and others and, on the other, the call to listen to others as they provide theirs. Butler's insistence that "we cannot reasonably expect anything different" than a necessary kind of failure or shortcoming in such accounting points, ultimately, to ourselves. We know we will fail in our attempts to describe ourselves to ourselves or to others. Likewise, we know others will fail in their multiple attempts. But neither of those inherent tensions lets us off the hook. This collections suggests many lines along which we must therefore engage in telling about and listening to our many selves along with those of our students, even if we are bound to retell the story another time, in another voice, or after yet another small disappointment or even smaller triumph.

In this light of telling, listening, and accounting, what we learn during the current moment, this collection maintains, is always informed by its historical emplacement. Our historical and social arcs point back from the present to our many and diverse past experiences, and it informs the ways in which, as Claudia Rankine noted in her retelling of Judith Butler's position in our first epigraph, that we "suffer from the condition of being addressable." These perilous times, punctuated by hate speech and violence aimed at populations from Black, Jewish, LGBTQ+, Indigenous, and immigrant and resident Hispanic and Latinx people, both dramatize the continuity of these behaviors with past moments of social discord and, at the same time, punctuate our moment with virulent eruptions. By noting this continuity across punctuated moments, we frame the discussions of each teachable moment with which our volume grapples through a comparative lens.

This volume emerged from a series of conversations among the editors about this perilous moment for teaching race that we inhabit. As Jason E. Cohen's chapter describes in detail, after tweeting a student's name, I—Jason Cohen—began to address the fallout that my words caused. I needed to take an account both in public and in private of the racist effects of those words. That account, however, occurred not only through my initiative, and those several forms of accounting generated the energy behind this collection. The events my chapter details began in December 2011; in the spring 2012 term, Sharon D. Raynor shared a semester's fellowship with me. Over the course of that semester, we considered how to understand the radical and strange powers of social media platforms to connect or alienate us from one another. One of the consistent fires in which our friendship was forged was the heat generated by confronting those new forms of connection and estrangement, whether because we were institutional strangers during our fellowship period or because of our discussions about the shifting contours of my recently emerged social media crisis. We never mentioned the Jewish philosopher Emmanuel Levinas, but our discussions did engage in considering the ways in which the call to "see the face of the Other," as Levinas describes an encounter with a stranger, became more complicated by technological as well as institutional forms of mediation.[4] Thus, when Dwayne Mack approached me later in the spring 2012 semester to tell me about his anger and disappointment in my actions, I was ready to listen, to see the pain in his eyes. We decided to approach that moment by collaborating on a scholarly collection that would engage us in shared work on questions of how to address race in our moment. That mutual work of overcoming became the kernel of this collection. Dwayne, as a historian of race in America, also saw the importance of considering our gender imbalance and urged me to find an additional editor who would be able to speak from a frame outside of male discourse; Sharon thankfully obliged by accepting our invitation, and her voice has proven invaluable to shaping our present work for the better.

In the process of assembling in this collection, a series of interventions focused on how race enters into and works in the classroom, we considered the socially constructed category of race as well as the ongoing processes and phenomena that ground the racial subject in both structural and experiential forms of interpretation. The racial self thus situates one's relations to society, one's own being, external and historical markers, and institutional forces that, as Sherry Ortner suggests, include "the ensemble of modes of perception, affect, thought, desire, and fear that animate acting subjects. But I always mean as well the cultural and social formations that shape, organize, and provoke those modes of affect, thought, and so on."[5] The work of pulling together this collection thus became parallel with the work of redefining our relationship to ourselves and our socially constructed positions as voices speaking to and about racial subjects.

The double position of the racial subject that Ortner describes, one who stands in relation to individual perceptions and to social formations, has informed our understanding of how the embodied subjects of the teacher and student circulate in the classroom. As Du Bois writes, "there is almost no community of intellectual life or point of transference where the thoughts and feelings of one race can come into direct contact and sympathy with the thoughts and feelings of the other."[6] That problem that we found articulated by Levinas and described further by Du Bois was one profoundly reified in the classroom: Where else could one encounter the other intimately, if not in the classroom? And yet that challenge of seeing the other in the encounter persists.

Perhaps because of that persistence, the critical literature about pedagogies of race, while it has been informed by insights and frameworks driven by powerful methods and approaches drawn particularly from the social sciences, remains grounded in much of the same foundational critical literature today that it has called upon for the last three decades. The work of bell hooks, Paulo Freire, Frantz Fanon, and scholars of critical race theory has been represented in this collection not only because they continue to have a lasting and relevant impact on the discourses of race in the classroom and beyond, but also because their texts and approaches continue to inform the work in social sciences that has evolved from these shared foundations. Thus, when scholars in this volume engage with

George Yancy's provocation in "White Self-Criticality," or the emergent literature on white fragility, we also frame these responses as a part of the long conversation stemming from the interventions in white identity that bell hooks first articulated in the early 1990s.[7] The decade-long engagement by Eduardo Bonilla-Silva, Kristin Haltinner, and others on questions of colorblindness as a form of social and educational erasure;[8] the structural and institutional implications of public policy and private beliefs regarding race;[9] the gendered (female) and racially coded work of teaching that occupies scholars of educational practice and curricular theory[10]: all of these discourses share the common roots established by Freire, hooks, Fanon, and other scholars our contributors represent in this volume as being relevant to contemporary discourse alongside more recent scholars of race, society, and pedagogy.

At the same time that the vectors of race continue to track in new directions, the resilience of open dialogue also demands that we approach anew those issues of race which have, for a very long time, presented themselves both in the classroom and around its edges. When, in 1963, James Baldwin spoke before a room full of teachers, he urged them to persist in an approach that rings in its opposition to voices of moderation. As Baldwin wrote, "Now if I were a teacher in this school, or any Negro school, and I was dealing with Negro children, who were in my care only a few hours of every day and would then return to their homes and to the streets . . . I would teach [each child] that he doesn't have to be bound by the expediencies of any given Administration, any given policy, any given time—that he has the right and the necessity to examine everything."[11] While the questions and problems persist, the present volume suggests that our approaches have evolved.

How to teach race, how (as Baldwin wrote) to "examine everything," gives voice to an unparalleled concern for teachers and scholars today, in classrooms across the landscape of American higher education, classrooms in which identity politics have entered the conversation, whether through intentional practices or unwelcomed intrusions. What, in Butler's and Rankine's language, more "addressable" condition can one imagine than the classroom? What more intimate location for meditations on vulnerability and the need for persistence in our inquiries into Baldwin's "everything" that we must examine, including race? The essays in this collection explicitly maintain that teaching in the humanities and humanistic social sciences remains the crucial locus of a meditation on race because of the complexity and urgency of the problems tied to these concerns. Perhaps, we suggest, identity politics can usefully be complicated by reflecting on the interdependent challenges of teaching, curricular selections and requirements, institutional demographics, the career paths individual scholars pursue, shifting modes of content delivery (now often distant and mediated by technology), and the evolutions of our disciplines, all of which are affected by the discourses and politics of race.

Such debates, we also suggest, do not stop at the threshold of a classroom or remain within the gates and sidewalks of a campus. At least since Thomas Jefferson built the University of Virginia on the backs of slave labor; at least since the US Supreme Court's 1954 decision in *Brown v. The Board of Education of Topeka* to overturn the "separate but equal" doctrine of *Plessy v. Ferguson* (1896); at least since Emmett Till's body was found lynched and mutilated in Mississippi in 1955; at least since the fatal campus riots of 1968–70 from Kent State to Columbia and beyond; at least since the explosive reactions to Rodney King's beating in 1992 bled onto campuses from California to Michigan; at least since James Byrd was lynched by dragging in 1998; at least the kidnapping and murder of Matthew Shepard also in 1998; at least since President Obama signed into legislature the Matthew Shepard and James Byrd, Jr., Hate Crimes Prevention Act as an anti–hate crime bill in 2009; at least since the Emanuel AME Church shooting in Charleston, South Carolina, in 2015; at least since the Charlottesville, Virginia, marches reverberated across large and small campuses in 2017; at least since membership in hate groups was at a twenty-three-year high in 2020; at least since George Floyd, Breonna Taylor, Rayshard Brooks, and Ahmaud Arbery were killed in painfully close succession and gave rise to further shockwaves of unrest; at least since too many more and too many other moments that we cannot commemorate individually, the national politics of race have shaped and been shaped by the implications of civic activism on campus and beyond. In the 2016 elections, while the hometowns of victims of racial violence, including Trayvon Martin, Tamir Rice, Laquan McDonald, Eric Garner, Rekia Boyd, Sandra Bland, Aiyana Stanley-Jones, Freddie Gray, Charley Leundeu Keunang, Ezell Ford, Michael Brown, Akai Gurley, and Alberta Spruill, among too many others, became fodder for political slogans and campaigns. Tub-thumping diatribes continued to support police and security and ultimately, in a nationally televised debate, included an endorsement by the future president of the use of force in response to civic activism and protest.[12] How then should we revisit race in the classroom in light of these eruptions, rather than trying to cover over repeatedly uneven handling of these events on the national stage today as well as in historical contexts?

Yet, engaging with a counterfactual possibility for a moment, what would change if debates engaged with policy regarding racial justice or affirmative action were suddenly more equitable, balanced, and productive? Baldwin's suggestions would nonetheless powerfully echo the problems that attend to treating race as an issue of national policy and legislation. Even Baldwin's admonitions to progressive technocrats ring with a contemporary interest in the problems of data-driven decisions to shape policies over issues that are rarely as cut-and-dried as the numbers would indicate. As Baldwin chides, "One of the reasons we are so fond of sociological reports and research and investigational committees is because they hide something. As long as we can deal with the Negro as a kind of statistic, as something to be manipulated, something to be fled from, or something to be given something to, there is something we can avoid, and what we can avoid is what he really, really means to us."[13] The nebulous something that Baldwin so clearly resents in national responses to race also presents a line of retrenchment against cynicism. Rather than succumbing to accepting the handouts as "something to be given to," Baldwin holds that a response to racial injustices should not happen only on the national stage of legislation; it should happen at other locations where there can be no simple motive to appease or suppress. More potent responses to racially motivated language and actions must be more complex, more personal, and more revealing than policy or legislation would allow. The present collection contends across its chapters that a critical response to cultural and personal identity politics can happen at key educational sites—namely, at the level of the student, classroom, and institution—that provide models for the local interventions that remain as formative and powerful today as they were for James Baldwin.

The attention this collection gives to the student, classroom, and institution responds programmatically to that neglect. Indeed, the language of utility and outcome-driven educational models promoted by the tech sector, including charter management organizations supported by philanthropic initiatives for school privatization as disparate politically as the Chan Zuckerberg Initiative, Bill and Melinda Gates Foundation, Eli and Edythe Broad Foundation, and Walton Family Foundation.[14] Such philanthropic organizations' apparently liberal interest in educational alternatives for ailing public schools finds strange bedfellows with initiatives advocated by conservative think tanks like the Heritage Foundation that favor preprofessional and technical educational models in STEM and affiliated fields across the pure and applied sciences at the expense of an engagement with race in the liberal arts context.[15] In both of these models, originating from seemingly unrelated motivations on the political left and the political right, the discourses of race and inequality are treated instrumentally as subordinate to the utility of the education, its outcomes for markets and jobs, and its apparent use-values, rather than for the broader civic implications of education as a platform for social change. In short, we demonstrate the need for a robustly critical view of identity politics in the classroom today because the national discourse on these topics has dried up as the weight of political capital shifts away from the concerns for racial equity and tips instead in the direction of a promotion of a utilitarian and class-segmented view of education. For those who can afford it, the humanities remain available, whereas broad swaths of society have begun to shunt such reflections toward preprofessional preparations, where conversations about race, alongside other more humanist concerns, have very little purchase on a student's or scholar's attention.

The present volume contends that a critical and sustained attention to the discourse of race in the collegiate classroom may begin to address a historically imbalanced treatment of race as a national concern. The chapters advocate civic activism in the classroom; we include discussions relevant to the weakening of affirmative action by addressing general education curricula as well as institutional admissions criteria; we examine structural racism in the classroom by writing about curricular innovations in *what* and *how* material is presented to students; we address new potentials for understanding race opened by hybrid learning platforms; we respond to accusations of insularity and irrelevance leveled at the liberal arts by showing how to teach materials that address the socially urgent questions; and we unpack the rhetoric of "illegal immigrants" in relationship to African American, Native American, Latinx, immigrant, and non-traditional-aged student populations.

The collection is divided into four major sections: (1) Affect and Authority in the Classroom; (2) Scholar-Activism: Teaching for Social Justice; (3) Precarious Institutions, Precarious Appointments; and (4) Historicizing the Moment, Historicizing the Curriculum. In the first section, the chapters ask us to consider, individually and collectively, how the emotional and affective charges of racialized contexts, events, and reactions come to bear on our authority as teachers. In classrooms where race and racial discourse take a central position, these chapters suggest that the ways in which teachers recognize the emotional and cognitive dimensions of these topics can give great power to the material, as well as making it more immediately accessible to students who may or may not be well prepared to be confronted with these highly contentious topics. In the section's opening chapter, "On Native American Erasure in the Classroom," Scott Manning Stevens examines the classroom dynamic that frequently distinguishes an introductory course in Native American studies through the productive tension between dominant white and Native discourses, one that crosses national boundaries not only among Indigenous nations but also among global nation-states. For instance, Mohawk legal scholar Patricia Monture-Angus pointed out that she was frequently held responsible for the feelings experienced by white students when they learned about the conquest and settling of the Americas. If she were to accept responsibility for her students' feelings of guilt, then she would be forced to silence herself and ignore the aspects of legal history she wished to study in the first place. Stevens's chapter names three key strategies for dealing with the range of majority-student responses to a critical engagement with US history as Indigenous history and consider how to incorporate these strategies in our teaching.

Felicia L. Harris's chapter follows on the heels of Stevens's by considering how to teach the single most highly stigmatized word in our language today. Her chapter, "Multiple Pedagogies Required: Reflections on Teaching Race and Ethnicity in the Intercultural and Intergenerational Classroom," offers an application of classroom strategies using "reality pedagogy." Her work grows out of the personal experience of being judged by her students while addressing such charged material; it reveals not only how to handle such classroom experiences, but also how the affective force of these discussions themselves demand conscientious strategies to frame them productively. Returning in an affective key to the problems and questions raised by the Black Lives Matter movement, Emerald L. Christopher-Byrd's chapter, "'Black Rage': Teaching Gender, Race, and Class in the Wake of #BlackLivesMatter and #SayHerName," examines the link between rage and a passion for justice, a passion that bell hooks has suggested does not necessarily come from the context of love. This chapter explores how anger serves as a pedagogical tool in examining not only individual responses to events, but more systematically in regard to institutional violence and discrimination against Black men and women. Ultimately, Christopher-Byrd's chapter questions the political role that emotions may serve as responses to structural forms of violence against black bodies. In the section's final chapter, "Can the White Boy Speak? Coming to Terms with the Color-Blind Li(n)e," Douglas Eli Julien examines problems of colorblindness and white fragility in the classroom. As a white male teaching from an anti-racist perspective, his chapter demands that we assess where we are headed as teachers and ask what comes next after race surfaces in our classrooms. He argues that the task in the twenty-first century to unlearning racism always also involves an attempt to disrupt the narrative refusal of "they, them, and others." By framing his chapter through repeated references to Derrida's key text, "The Truth that Wounds," the chapter turns critical theory into a direct interlocutor. Using this dialectical approach, Julien approaches lyric and prose pieces including Kate Chopin's "Désirée's Baby," Langston Hughes's "Cora Unashamed," and Toni Morrison's "Recitatif" through the lens of Derrida's radical critique of racial discrimination. The powerful result develops a sustained and multivocal discussion of the twenty-first-century problem of colorblindness, as it updates Du Bois's concern with the color line nearly a century ago.

The volume's second section turns attention to the role of teachers as scholar-activists of race, and as we see throughout, the focus here is on the historical trajectories of those efforts to marry activism with teaching, but also further, to think about the futures of scholarly activism and, along with them, the futures of race across our institutions. Coeditor Jason Cohen's chapter, "Technologies of Discrimination: Structural Racism beyond Campus," engages in a wide-ranging discussion of how social media and technology have shifted the discourses of race on campus and beyond. His chapter argues that the landscape of our institutions must be considered in terms of the lived experiences of race on campus; it culminates in a series of institutional principles that, rather than advocating a direct approach or type of action, asks us to consider our dispositions toward race and racial discourse as an intervention itself. In a turn toward public engagement in the classroom, "Teaching from the Tap: Confronting Hegemony and Systemic Oppression through Reflection and Analysis," the chapter by Kerri-Ann M. Smith and Paul M. Buckley, takes as a case study the water crisis in Flint, Michigan, in order to examine the ways in which students gain an understanding of how the roles of institutions, government agencies, and government officials have collided, beginning in the "post-racial" Obama era. By engaging tools relating to information literacy, critical race theory, and environmental justice, the authors explain how they use reflection on contemporary and historical crisis to determine the transformative nature of the projects they designed for their courses.

Drawing on the field of education leadership, Rachel Roegman and Serena J. Salloum, coauthors of the section's third chapter, " 'I Never Touch Race': Teaching Race in Online Spaces with Future Indiana School Leaders," discuss the process of preparing educators to address cultural mismatches between students from diverse backgrounds and the educators in their schools. This chapter addresses the unique challenges of online and hybrid teaching both authors face in preparing future Indiana school leaders to be culturally responsive—to support academic achievement of all students, to affirm students' home cultures, to empower parents and communities from diverse neighborhoods, and to advocate for marginalized voices and greater social change. The section concludes with Shane A. McCoy's contribution, "Scaffolding for Justice: Deploying Intersectionality, Black Feminist Thought, and the 'Outsider Within' in the Writing about Literature Classroom." McCoy's work takes up the problem posed in *Pedagogy of the Oppressed*, in which Paulo Freire contends that education should aim to condition young students to understand how "a culture of domination" has produced a professional class afraid of disrupting the status quo. McCoy's chapter links an interest in activism to the volume's earlier concerns for affect by examining students' affective relationship to engaging with Black feminist thought. The essay suggests ways to teach a social-justice-oriented lens for reading, writing, and intervening in systemic inequalities.

The volume's third section considers race in relationship to a rising social condition not only of our students but also of employment in the university: precariousness. Contingent appointments and positions, contingent funding and programming, and contingent populations in our student bodies all signal the ways in which the conditions of precariousness govern a growing percentage of our institutions and, accordingly, shape their actions. This section opens with a chapter by Daniel J. Delgado and Keja Valens, "Institutionalizing (In)Equality: The Double-Edged Sword of Diversity Requirements," focused on the problems of diversity requirements at the institutional level from two distinct and complementary disciplines. The chapter considers how diversity requirements, particularly in general education curricula, function as part of scholarly, pedagogical, and institutional commitments to teaching diversity, especially in majority-white, middle-tier institutions. In so doing, the authors raise questions about how diversity requirements can reinforce, and how they can challenge, racial and ethnic inequality and, as a result, draw populations from the precarious margins toward central institutional positions. Further, they ask about the incidental costs and benefits of requiring diversity measures for students and faculty as well as for institutions. The second chapter in this section, coeditor Sharon D. Raynor's narrative of transformation, "Survival Is Not an Academic Skill: Life behind the Mask," skillfully examines the evolution and movement she has pursued in her academic career in response to the same forces of precarity that have been drawn to the surface across the volume. As a Black female academic in a Historically Black College and University (HBCU) context, Raynor reveals how negotiations of academic spaces both within the classroom and, more structurally, within a larger institution require strategies that mirror the imaginary and metaphorical worlds of racial discourse found in literature. Her chapter assesses the academic landscape based on professional negotiations of what bell hooks names "belonging." Her tale of negotiating a career as a Black female literature professor across several institutions and in several positions, far from being serendipitous, provides a methodical approach to navigating the academic world and, like the concepts dominating discussions of "race" itself, moves between the prosaic and the metaphorical in its understanding of how institutions respond to faculty of color.

For Stephen W. Sheps, a precarious appointment has become normal. In the time since this collection was first assembled, Sheps has in fact been pushed out of the academy. That non-permanent academic status allows Sheps's chapter to examine his unique relationship to teaching race, one that works to resist the forces of compliance built into structures of review, promotion, and continuing employment on which the academy has traditionally relied. His chapter, "Reflections from a Precariously Employed Carpetbagger: A Canadian's Experience Teaching in the South," reflects on the challenges posed by limited-term and adjunct employment as an underlying condition of teaching race. Both precariously employed and living far from home, he addresses the challenges of coming up against the real, lived experiences of race and racialization in the South. His chapter suggests how his precariousness informs his teaching practice, and indeed, how it provides an unanticipated space to think critically about these matters. The section concludes with a chapter by Erin Murrah-Mandril, "Undocumented Learning Outcomes and Cyber Coyotes: Teaching Ethnic Studies in the Online Classroom," which discusses the process of creating an online version of her university's Introduction to Mexican American Studies course. The course is designed for a Hispanic-serving institution where most students who enroll in the class are Mexican American, many of whom have spent several years if not their entire life in Texas, a conservative state known historically for its discrimination against Mexicans and Mexican Americans. Picking up on hybrid pedagogical formats introduced earlier, her course is taught in an online context as well. This chapter addresses how to model critical discourse about races and provide students with strategies to critique racism in the world around them. How, it asks, can instructors and instructional designers incorporate the unwritten outcomes of an ethnic studies course within a technical apparatus that is disembodied and highly regulated? It concludes that in an online course, the role of the teacher recedes to the periphery while student's writing becomes more central, which leads to the possibility of more open dialogue between teacher and writer, but it also acknowledges the risk of students being less challenged to push beyond their own preconceived and comfortable notions of race.

In the fourth section, we examine the long trajectories of race in the classroom through the texts that have been foundational to critical race pedagogy since W. E. B. Du Bois began to shape an awareness of Black consciousness and its relationship to racialized social powers, laws, and institutions over a century ago. His voice, like those other voices that have crossed the intervening years, provide a platform from which our contributors suggest we may better consider how to situate our work historically in the classroom as we teach for social and individual change. To that end, the section opens with Derrick R. Brooms's and Darryl A. Brice's chapter, "A Du Boisian Approach to Making Black Lives Matter in the Classroom (and Beyond)," which uses an autoethnographic inquiry into the experience of teaching as Black male professors whose sociology courses focus on race and racism. Brooms and Brice show how to incorporate experiences and perspectives from the Black Lives Matter movement in three key ways: first, by grounding teaching within a historical methodology; second, by engaging students in critical conversations about and within Black communities; and third, by asking students to develop writing that connects past and current realities, from Dred Scott to Ferguson, Missouri. Brooms and Brice pursue a Du Boisian method to raise Black consciousness and suggest its urgency for our work in the classroom in our moment. "The Racial Oracle Has a History," Mark William Westmoreland's chapter, continues to build on the long-standing relevance of historical models for teaching. His chapter raises concerns about the lack of historical awareness regarding how the modern concept of race developed over the last few hundred years and offers strategies to fill that gap. Westmoreland's chapter asks particularly how one's social position affects the lens through which one understands race. The strategies his chapter develops represent a sustained effort to frame a racial way of knowing, a racial epistemology, as a pedagogical tool crucial to seeing racialized identity and community formation as deeply rooted factors in the everyday life of our students and, of course, ourselves.

Black community remains at the center of the section's third chapter, Tasha M. Hawthorne's "The Death of the Black Child," which focuses on the ways in which the Black Lives Matter movement carries a legacy of literary representations of Black homicides into the contemporary moment by considering the continued tragedy of lost lives in Black communities across the nation today. From the lynching depicted in Ida B. Wells's *Red Record* (1892) to Emmett Till's horrifying murder in 1955 to seven-year-old Aiyana Stanley-Jones's 2010 death by police gunfire, Hawthorne's chapter shows how lifeless Black bodies have long been offered up for public consumption. The chapter uses these literary and cultural texts to show students and teachers how to navigate the topics in a multicultural classroom, tracing how texts, activists, students, and critics interact in a complex cultural exchange centered on the image of the Black body drained of life.

In each of these chapters, and across each section, the argument for a sustained and patient engagement with historical materials undergirds treatments that emphasize the importance of seeing each new day's current events as urgent for ourselves, our students, and our institutions. Perhaps, as we have suggested implicitly across these chapters and explicitly as a recurrent thread within several of them, the platform and contents of social media and digital cultural channels more broadly—whether presidential or private, popular or subterranean—will provide us with durable historical artifacts; or perhaps, as other chapters have suggested, we should consider our historical relationships to race as an antidote to all that overly hasty work. In either case, the processes and practices of engaging in historically relevant critiques of race and its social power are growing in importance, particularly as we have observed just a few of the myriad ways in which cultural amnesia about racial inequality seems to be mounting. We hope to have offered a space in which the remembrance and commemoration of racial struggles remains urgent even as public discourse about the historical contexts for these conversations has too often begun to wane in richness and depth, if not in frequency.

NOTES

1. Stephen Drury Smith and Catherine Ellis, eds., *Free All Along: The Robert Penn Warren Civil Rights Interviews* (New York: New Press, 2019), 255.

2. Drury Smith and Ellis, *Free All Along*, 255–56.

3. See, for recent data, Frank Edwards, Michael H. Esposito, and Hedwig Lee, "Risk of Police-Involved Death by Race/Ethnicity and Place, United States, 2012–2018," *American Journal of Public Health* 108, no. 9 (September 2018): 1241–48. Homicide was the first leading cause, followed by accidental death, among Black men in their twenties. For this same group, suicide, HIV, and cancer also ranked above police death (the sixth-ranked cause of death), which nevertheless outpaced pneumonia and flu and diabetes, among others, as causes of fatality among young Black men. Historically, violence has more closely tracked with gun laws and their enforcement, which have risen since the 1990s after decreasing in the decades following the 1960s. For historical trends, see Ryan K. Masters, Robert A. Hummer, Daniel A. Powers, Audrey Beck, Shih-Fan Lin, and Brian Karl Finch, "Long-Term Trends in Adult Mortality for U.S. Blacks and Whites: An Examination of Period- and Cohort-Based Changes," *Demography* 51, no. 6 (2014): 2047–73, https://doi.org/10.1007/s13524-014-0343-4.

4. Emmanuel Levinas, *Totality and Infinity: An Essay on Exteriority*, trans. Alphonso Lingis (Pittsburgh, PA: Duquesne University Press, 1969), 76–78; see also Levinas, "Signification and Sense," in *Humanism of the Other*, trans. Nidra Poller (Urbana: University of Illinois Press, 2003), and especially on the ethics of seeing the face of the other, see 33.

5. Sherry Ortner, "Subjectivity and Cultural Critique," *Anthropological Theory* 5, no. 1 (2005): 31–52; quoted in Karida L. Brown, *Gone Home: Race and Roots through Appalachia* (Chapel Hill: University of North Carolina Press, 2018), 201.

6. W. E. B. Du Bois, *The Souls of Black Folk* (New York: Penguin, 2002), 145.

7. See, for instance, George Yancy, ed., *White Self-Criticality beyond Anti-Racism: "How Does It Feel to Be a White Problem?"* (New York: Lexington Books, 2015); see also George Yancy, *Black Bodies, White Gazes: The Continuing Significance of Race* (New York: Rowman and Littlefield, 2008); and Robin DiAngelo, *White Fragility: Why It's So Hard for White People to Talk about Racism* (New York: Beacon, 2018); for a response to DiAngelo, see Marcia Nichols and Jennifer Wacek, "Frangible Whiteness: Teaching Race in the Context of White Fragility," in *Teaching with Tension: Race, Resistance, and Reality in the Classroom*, ed. Philathia Bolton, Cassander L. Smith, and Lee Bebout (Evanston, IL: Northwestern University Press, 2019).

8. See Kristin Haltinner, ed., *Teaching Race and Anti-Racism in Contemporary America: Adding Context to Colorblindness* (New York: Springer, 2014); Eduardo Bonilla-Silva, *Racism without Racists: Color-Blind Racism and the Persistence of Racial Inequality in the United States* (Lanham, MD: Rowman and Littlefield, 2006).

9. For recent discussions, see Eduardo Bonilla-Silva, "Toward a New Political Praxis for Trumpamerica: New Directions in Critical Race Theory," *American Behavioral Scientist* 63, no. 13 (2019): 1776–88; and Joe R. Feagin, *The White Racial Frame: Centuries of Racial Framing and Counter-Framing*, 2nd ed. (New York: Routledge, 2013).

10. See, among others, Kirsten T. Edwards and Maria del Guadalupe Davidson, eds., *College Curriculum at the Crossroads: Women of Color Reflect and Resist* (New York: Routledge, 2018); and to emphasize the gendered forms of this racially differentiated discourse, see also Stephen D. Hancock and Chezare A. Warren, *White Women's Work: Examining the Intersectionality of Teaching, Identity, and Race* (Charlotte, NC: Information Age Publishing, 2017).

11. James Baldwin, "A Talk to the Teachers," *Saturday Review*, December 21, 1969. Reprinted in *Collected Essays*, ed. Toni Morrison (New York: Library of America, 1998), 685–86.

12. The *Washington Post*'s politics blog, "The Fix," published an annotated version of the September 26, 2016, presidential debate with clear references to the debate over how to respond to racial tensions in politics as well as on the streets. See Aaron Blake, "The First Trump-Clinton Presidential Debate Transcript, Annotated," *Washington Post*, September 26, 2016, https://www.washingtonpost.com/news/the-fix/wp/2016/09/26/the-first-trump-clinton-presidential-debate-transcript-annotated.

13. James Baldwin, "In Search of a Majority: An Address," in *Collected Essays*, 215–21, quotation at 219.

14. For a discussion of the role philanthropic organizations have played in privatizing education through charter management organizations, see Sarah Reckhow, *Follow the Money: How Foundation Dollars Change Public School Politics* (New York: Oxford University Press, 2012); Megan Thompkins-Strange, *Policy Patrons: Philanthropy, Education Reform, and the Politics of Influence* (Cambridge, MA: Harvard University Press, 2016); and Andrea Gabor, *After the Education Wars: How Smart Schools Upend the Business of Reform* (New York: New Press, 2018).

15. The Chan Zuckerberg Initiative is supporting education particularly by funding a network of schools they consider "Innovation Labs." Comparatively, the Brookings Institution and Heritage Foundation both maintain pro-STEM and professional training positions in their policy papers. For the Chan Zuckerberg priorities, see https://www.edinnovationlab.com. The Heritage Foundation's platform centers on "expanding choice," understood through deregulation and privatization, as characterized here: http://www.heritage.org/education.

BIBLIOGRAPHY

Baldwin, James. *Collected Essays*. Edited by Toni Morrison. New York: Library of America, 1998.

Blake, Aaron. "The First Trump-Clinton Presidential Debate Transcript, Annotated." *Washington Post*. September 26, 2016. https://www.washingtonpost.com/news/the-fix/wp/2016/09/26/the-first-trump-clinton-presidential-debate-transcript-annotated.

Bonilla-Silva, Eduardo. *Racism without Racists: Color-Blind Racism and the Persistence of Racial Inequality in the United States*. Lanham, MD: Rowman and Littlefield, 2006.

———. "Toward a New Political Praxis for Trumpamerica: New Directions in Critical Race Theory." *American Behavioral Scientist* 63, no. 13 (2019): 1776–88.

Brown, Karida L. *Gone Home: Race and Roots through Appalachia*. Chapel Hill: University of North Carolina Press, 2018.

Butler, Judith. *Giving an Account of Oneself*. New York: Fordham University Press, 2005.

DiAngelo, Robin. *White Fragility: Why It's So Hard for White People to Talk about Racism*. New York: Beacon, 2018.

Drury Smith, Stephen, and Catherine Ellis, eds. *Free All Along: The Robert Penn Warren Civil Rights Interviews*. New York: New Press, 2019.

Du Bois, W. E. B. *The Souls of Black Folk*. New York: Penguin, 2002.

Edwards, Frank, Michael H. Esposito, and Hedwig Lee. "Risk of Police-Involved Death by Race/Ethnicity and Place, United States, 2012–2018." *American Journal of Public Health* 108, no. 9 (September 2018): 1241–48.

Edwards, Kirsten T., and Maria del Guadalupe Davidson, eds. *College Curriculum at the Crossroads: Women of Color Reflect and Resist*. New York: Routledge, 2018.

Feagin, Joe R. *The White Racial Frame: Centuries of Racial Framing and Counter-Framing*. 2nd ed. New York: Routledge, 2013.

Gabor, Andrea. *After the Education Wars: How Smart Schools Upend the Business of Reform*. New York: New Press, 2018.

Haltinner, Kristin, ed. *Teaching Race and Anti-Racism in Contemporary America: Adding Context to Colorblindness*. New York: Springer, 2014.

Hancock, Stephen D., and Chezare A. Warren. *White Women's Work: Examining the Intersectionality of Teaching, Identity, and Race*. Charlotte, NC: Information Age Publishing, 2017.

Levinas, Emmanuel. "Signification and Sense." In *Humanism of the Other*, translated by Nidra Poller, 9–45. Urbana: University of Illinois Press, 2003.

———. *Totality and Infinity: An Essay on Exteriority*. Translated by Alphonso Lingis. Pittsburgh, PA: Duquesne University Press, 1969.

Masters, Ryan K., Robert A. Hummer, Daniel A. Powers, Audrey Beck, Shih-Fan Lin, and Brian Karl Finch. "Long-Term Trends in Adult Mortality for U.S. Blacks and Whites: An Examination of Period- and Cohort-Based Changes." *Demography* 51, no. 6 (2014): 2047–73. https://doi.org/10.1007/s13524-014-0343-4.

Nichols, Marcia, and Jennifer Wacek. "Frangible Whiteness: Teaching Race in the Context of White Fragility." In *Teaching with Tension: Race, Resistance, and Reality in the Classroom*, edited by Philathia Bolton, Cassander L. Smith, and Lee Bebout, 239–54. Evanston, IL: Northwestern University Press, 2019.

Ortner, Sherry. "Subjectivity and Cultural Critique." *Anthropological Theory* 5, no. 1 (2005): 31–52.

Rankine, Claudia. *Citizen: An American Lyric.* New York: Greywolf Press, 2014.

Reckhow, Sarah. *Follow the Money: How Foundation Dollars Change Public School Politics.* New York: Oxford University Press, 2012.

Thompkins-Strange, Megan. *Policy Patrons: Philanthropy, Education Reform, and the Politics of Influence.* Cambridge, MA: Harvard University Press, 2016.

Yancy, George. *Black Bodies, White Gazes: The Continuing Significance of Race.* New York: Rowman and Littlefield, 2008.

———, ed. *White Self-Criticality beyond Anti-Racism: "How Does It Feel to Be a White Problem?"* New York: Lexington Books, 2015.

PART I

AFFECT AND AUTHORITY IN THE CLASSROOM

Historicizing the Moment, Historicizing the Curriculum

CHAPTER 1

ON NATIVE AMERICAN ERASURE IN THE CLASSROOM

SCOTT MANNING STEVENS

This thing of darkness we acknowledge *ours*.

—paraphrase of Shakespeare's *The Tempest*, V.1.275–76

There is a current trend among high school and college students wishing to force their schools and universities to drop offensive mascots, change school seals and crests, and pull down statues of morally dubious forebearers. One thinks of the student-led movement to force Amherst College to retire its old mascot, "Lord Jeff," a character representing Lord Jeffery Amherst, the British colonial general who suggested Native Americans be given blankets infected with smallpox, or the school crest of Harvard Law School, which was based on the coat of arms of the family of Isaac Royall Jr., who endowed the first law professorship in the eighteenth century with wealth derived from the slave trade.[1] More recently we have seen student activists take it upon themselves to remove offending icons, such as the "Silent Sam" statue of a Confederate soldier on the grounds of the University of North Carolina at Chapel Hill in the late summer of 2018.[2] Over the summer of 2020, following the massive public demonstrations sparked by the police murder of George Floyd, the efforts to remove statues of Confederate leaders and those of Columbus have made it impossible to avoid the debates around commemoration and general education concerning our nation's violent history.

From the perspective of institutions of higher education, these actions speak to an elusive goal of moral purity that seems to place the offending idea, person, or event outside of the student's immediate culpability. It is a wish to disassociate completely with any such moral or ethical blot and make emphatically clear "this is not of me." While motivated in part by a desire to force institutions to face their pasts, such desires to purge institutional histories of inconvenient truths are just as likely to serve the moral narcissism encouraged by the self-fashioning phenomena of social media. It seems everyone wants to be on the side of the angels, except for that considerable hoard who embrace the machismo of open bigotry, racism, sexism, and a general lack of human decency. While this latter portion of the population holds considerable political sway over the nation, college students can cocoon themselves in a sense of self-righteousness. But these same students are often far less rigorous in undertaking the self-examination required of those who wish to acknowledge the moral legacy of the United States as regards Native America.

We less often hear of students organizing on a campus to force its administration to acknowledge that the university or college sits on Native American land, nor do they demand that Native communities be justly compensated for those lands. This is as seemingly impossible as repatriating oneself back to Europe or one's ancestral homeland because you realize the entire enterprise of the conquest of the Americas was wrong from its inception. In some cases recently, faculty and students have pushed their schools to institute a "land acknowledgment" that expresses awareness of the fact that the school occupies land which originally belonged to a local Native nation. But too often such acknowledgment statements are treated as ends in themselves and not the beginnings of much more difficult conversations. Only certain historical mistakes may be redressed—or even contemplated for that matter—but those wrongs committed against the Indigenous people of the Western Hemisphere are not usually among them. Perhaps there is some sincere but obscure feeling of collective guilt about the conquest of Native America, but there is little to nothing suggested in the way of reparations or other forms of social justice. The social problems of this country are profoundly complex given the legacies of slavery and structural racism or economic and gender inequalities, but the issue of Native America surely deserves its own discourse within the history of the United States.

We must consider when addressing Native American issues in an American college classroom that most students have never heard, discussed in a classroom setting, the most pressing issues confronting today's Native American communities. The depressing reality is that the average American student does not learn much about Native America at school after fourth grade. That means, beyond nine or ten years old, students almost never revisit the subject of Native American history while being formally educated. Because of the persistence of the "vanishing Red Man" trope, Native people are presumed absent and consigned to the distant past. Add to this the fact that possible Native American presence in the classroom often goes unrecognized because Indigenous students may not fit a stereotypical phenotype or other notions characterized as "Indian." We have been written out of the curriculum for most young adult students, and the hard truths of genocide, land dispossession, forced assimilation at boarding schools, or the involuntary sterilization of Native women will never confront these students unless they choose at some point in their college education to study various aspects of Native American history and culture. Nor will they likely think of our nations as diverse and contemporary communities given that, since their childhoods, we have been consigned to the past.[3]

While one portion of our students demands institutional purity, the other half is openly annoyed or angry upon learning about the violent and racist foundations of the nation they smugly inhabit—not so much angry that it happened, but angry to be reminded of it. Fed a steady diet of the "American dream" with a master narrative of "freedom, equality, and opportunity for all," they cannot fathom why this remnant of the original Americans will not simply "get with the program" or "get over it" and just be American. What little exposure they may have had to Native American cultures as children was likely firmly imbedded in the national mythology of Pocahontas and John Smith, Squanto and the first Thanksgiving, or Sacagawea and Lewis and Clark. A side glance to the Trail of Tears may or may not occur at some point in their education, but the reality of institutionalized ignorance concerning Native America is overwhelming. One result of the absence of Native Americans from school curricula is that tremendous pressure is then transferred to museums to be the unique institutional source of knowledge production on this topic. School field trips and visits with families may be the only time students are asked to learn about Native America outside of the classroom, and museums are taken to be authorities on this issue. The same issues regarding the national narrative and the presence of Indigenous perspectives occur here, as in schools, and only more recently have institutions such as the National Museum of the American Indian been created to address some of those problems.[4] Even as such institutions attempt to critique earlier misperceptions, they meet resistance from settler audiences and federal funding agencies. Many Indigenous scholars and other scholars of color in this and other settler-dominated societies will recognize this feeling of hostility aimed at instructors and institutions who critique the master narrative.

Maori law scholar Ani Makaere wrote of the difficulties she faced when teaching the colonial history of Aotearoa (New Zealand) to her Pākehā (non-Maori) students: "Their ignorance meant that it was left to me to teach them history that they should have been exposed to as a matter course while at school. But what made it much worse was that the students appeared to hold me responsible for the guilt that they felt at learning about what their ancestors did to mine. Complaints to the Dean that Pākehā students were being made to feel culturally unsafe in class were not uncommon."[5] Likewise, the late Canadian Mohawk scholar Patricia Monture-Angus wrote that she refused to silence herself on the topic of Indigenous history "for the sole purpose that the oppressor will not feel badly," going on to say that "trying to force me to be responsible [for their feelings] is a powerful tool intended to silence."[6] When non-Indigenous students note that neither they nor their more recent immigrant ancestors caused any direct harm to Native Americans, and so why should they care, I ask them if they have benefited from dispossession of Native peoples. I also remind them that to Native Americans this history has a daily effect on our lives now.

But I do not wish to draw attention to these issues without offering some strategies for correcting a bad situation. Short of the necessary major educational reform at all levels of schooling in the United States, I believe there are several key concepts that non-Natives can learn and integrate into their teaching across a variety of disciplines. In the rest of this essay I shall name several of these key concepts and provide a general explanation of them and some thoughts about how we might apply them to our classroom experiences. First among these concepts is one whose articulation has evolved within my lifetime as a scholar; that is the notion of *settler colonialism*. This term came about in the work of Australian scholar Patrick Wolfe and Canadian scholars Daiva Stasiulis and Nira Yuval-Davis in the early 1990s. The term was used to distinguish between models of colonialism practiced by primarily European countries in the eighteenth, nineteenth, and twentieth centuries—but in some cases beginning even earlier. The distinction lies between *extractive colonialism* and *settler colonialism*. The extractive model meant that certain nation-states, whether constituted as kingdoms, empires, or republics, sought to control regions in remote parts of the world in order to extract their natural resources and labor and enrich the metropole, or capital city, back in the colonizing state. Such was the case in much of Africa during the nineteenth century, when European powers scrambled for control of African territories so they could exploit their wealth and natural resources, which included human labor. Colonial control was achieved more through administrative and military means and less through European emigration to these territories.

On the other hand, a settler colonial model focused on gaining possession of territory so that it could be resettled by the colonial powers after the Indigenous populations were vanquished and removed. Patrick Wolfe identified "the settler colonial tendency that [he termed] the logic of elimination."[7] In the Anglophone world, this is most apparent in the modern nation-states of Australia, Canada, New Zealand, and the United States. In each of these former British colonies the emphasis was on the permanent acquisition of Indigenous lands and the gradual replacement of the Native population with a settler population. All of these nation-states, which at one time were composed of populations that were 100 percent Indigenous, now have Indigenous populations of approximately 10 percent or less of the general population. The settler colonial story is a replacement narrative that seeks to consign the Indigenous population to the past through a process of extermination, removal, assimilation, and erasure. Settler colonialism is not, as Evelyn Nakano Glenn reminds us, an event that occurred in the past "but an ongoing structure."[8] In her work, Glenn makes clear that settler colonialism not only dispossessed Indigenous peoples of their lands and sought to exterminate them and their cultures, but it also "transplanted certain racialized and gendered conceptions from the *metropole* [or colonizing country]" and "transformed them in the context of and experiences in the New World."[9]

Because of the radical demographic shifts that settler colonialism imposes, there can be no progress toward a *post*colonial existence. Unlike extractive colonialism, which can be thrown off or exhausted, the settler colonial state, by its demographic composition, can maintain a state of permanent colonial hegemony. Students in the United States learn of the struggle for independence from Great Britain, but that does not make us a postcolonial society; rather, settlers determined to cut their allegiance to the metropole and form a new independent colonizing nation-state. Such euphemisms and slogans as the "Empire of Liberty" or "Manifest Destiny" provide cover for the United States' imperial ambitions—made clear through the Louisiana Purchase, Indian Removal, the Mexican War, the Indian Wars, the acquisition of Alaska, and the annexation of Hawaii and other territories in the Pacific and the Caribbean. The average American student is trained not to examine these expansions too critically, and attempts to do so are frequently interpreted as unpatriotic. I agree with those who contend that if a high school or college student were taught American history *as* settler colonial history we would have a vastly better educated body of citizens in regard to a more complex and accurate study of American history and the issues of social justice.[10]

For our students to understand more fully the systemic aspects of settler colonialism in the United States, they would need to be introduced to juridical and legislative history that has allowed for and continues to protect the supremacy of the settler colonial nation-state. No elementary school, and very few high schools, will have introduced students to the legal relationship between the United States and Native Americans that was formulated in the early nineteenth century through several landmark Supreme Court cases, which form the basis of this nation's federal Indian policy. Primary among those laws and treaties are the three cases that make up the so-called Marshall Trilogy. If instructors in social studies, history, or civics were to incorporate these three cases in US history, they would be introducing students to a framework of legal decisions which affect Native American life to this day.

Settler colonialism depends on the dispossession of land from the Indigenous inhabitants, and this can be accomplished by military conquest, removal, and treaties, but the legal justification of any of those means lies within the introduction of the Doctrine of Discovery into US constitutional law. This doctrine, based on a series of late fifteenth-century papal bulls, supported the preemptive right to territorial title of Christian polities over the non-Christian and "non-civilized" peoples they "discovered." In its papal formulation it was originally dictated to settle contests between Christian kingdoms claiming lands along the African coast, but after contact with the Americas it was applied here. Chief Justice John Marshall, through tortuous legal logic, applied the Doctrine of Discovery to US law in his landmark decision in the case of *Johnson v. McIntosh* in 1823. In that case two settlers had purchased the same piece of land, one from its Indigenous inhabitants and the other from a federal land agent. The court ruled that the Piankeshaw Nation did not have the right to sell their land to a private individual but that only a federal land agent could sell it on behalf of the government, which claimed preemptive title to the land based on the Doctrine of Discovery. Christian civilization was purported to trump "pagan savagery" when it came to land tenure. In Marshall's mind, the English Crown bore preemptive territorial rights to the lands it discovered according to the doctrine. And so, when Giovanni Cabota "discovered" Newfoundland in 1497 on behalf of the English Crown, future British claims on the island were made under the authority of the Doctrine of Discovery. That authority to claim foreign lands remained with the British even after their break with Rome in the 1530s, in Marshall's opinion, and would transfer to the leaders of the thirteen colonies when they wrested their independence from Britain. This is the short version of the argument but a variety of readily accessible essays exist to guide students through Marshall's logic.[11] The fact that the Doctrine of Discovery was even cited in the 2005 *City of Sherrill v. the Oneida Indian Nation* decision shows how durable this legal fiction has remained in upholding settler claims against Indigenous peoples in the United States.

If we are attempting to expand our students' knowledge of Native American history as an integral part of the history of the United States, we will have to make clear what is distinctive about the Indigenous cultures of the contemporary US. We can start with the numbers: the US Census of 2010 recognized some 5.22 million Native Americans, roughly 1.6 percent of the entire population; among that Native population are 573 federally recognized "tribal nations."[12] Those Indigenous nations (it should be noted that most Indigenous nations reject the term "tribe," which is the federal government's designation) represent considerable cultural, linguistic, and regional diversity; from Maine to Southern California and from Washington State to Florida. And as nations they have cultures every bit as diverse as the many cultures of Europe or Africa; what binds us together is that we share one overwhelming common experience, that of the continued dominance of the settler colonial state that encompasses our nations.

Another aspect of our ongoing position as nations within the United States is our oft-contested "sovereignty." For students living far from Native American communities this notion of sovereignty is usually as unfamiliar as it is surprising. To students who grew up in proximity to Native American reservations or in states with large Native American populations, they will likely have heard of the issue of "tribal sovereignty" from members of the majority population and frequently in the context of conflict. This is usually around hunting and fishing access, local taxation laws, and casinos. I have had numerous aggrieved white students query why Native peoples get special treatment and perks from the government. Their assumptions lie in their ignorance of any Native American history or in an understanding of the status of Native peoples under US federal law. The fact that many of these perceived "perks" were meant to compensate for land cessions and are the result of treaties made between the US government and specific Native nations is completely unknown to them. If one were to object that this seems a very specialized field of study, I would counter by pointing out the absurdity of studying the history of any settler nation and not accounting for the continuing place of the Indigenous peoples of that same country. I am not expecting American students to have to learn about all ethnic minorities or indigenous nations in other countries, but I certainly expect Americans to learn about Native Americans, just as I would expect Australians to learn about the Aboriginal cultures of that nation.

All American students should be obligated to know some basic facts about Native American and US history. Among those basic facts is the United States' treaty relationship with Native nations. Beginning in 1788 with the Treaty of Fort Pitt between the US and the Delaware Nation, the federal government made over 360 treaties on a nation-to-nation basis with the Indigenous nations of this continent. Congress ceased making treaties with Native peoples after 1871, the early period of the Indian Wars, after which they planned to enforce the federal government's will by military conquest and containment on reservations. Though hundreds of treaties have been broken and ignored, some still carry the force of law when revisited by contemporary federal courts. Laws governing Native American hunting and fishing rights off reservation territories are frequently the result of existing treaties—as was famously the case with the Boldt Decision of 1974, which honored the Indigenous nations of Washington State's claim of access to 50 percent of the salmon stock of that state, as guaranteed by nineteenth-century treaties. When the majority settler population is ignorant of such treaties it often leads to conflict. Likewise, tax codes differ for Native communities on reservations because of our different relationships to state and federal authorities and services. Though I might not expect the average student to understand the finer points of the state and federal tax codes vis-à-vis Native Americans, I do ask them to have a working understanding of Native American sovereignty.

We should begin by considering definitions of the word *sovereignty* through the language of the law, political science, and a quotidian sense of the term. As the Oxford English Dictionary defines *sovereignty*, it has a complex field of meaning. It can mean preeminence in respect of excellence in a field, or supremacy in respect of power or authority, or the supreme power of a ruler, like a king, or "the supreme controlling power in communities not under monarchical government; absolute and independent authority." This last definition is a transferal of the idea of monarchial sovereignty onto a community and is most like the definition as it's used to understand so-called tribal sovereignty. When the Marshall Court made its landmark decision regarding the status of Native American polities in *Cherokee Nation v. Georgia* (1831), Marshall infamously defined Native polities as "domestic, dependent, nations." In so ruling, the court denied that Native nations were either foreign or independent states but did acknowledge that they were nations—going on to claim that their relationship to the United States was that of a "ward to its guardian." This precedent-setting ruling effectively established one aspect of the fraught definition of the terms pertaining to notions of "tribal sovereignty" under US law.

Treaties between the federal government and Native nations continued to underscore our "nation-to-nation" status until 1871. If sovereignty consists in the authority to self-govern within the boundaries of our established communities, this has been only partially realized over the last two centuries. But aside from strictly political notions of sovereignty, one of the greater parts of this concept lies within the notion of cultural sovereignty. The nation-state has exerted tremendous energy to reduce the cultural sovereignty of Native nations. Through displacement, education, and the law, both federal and state governments have managed to attack Native sovereignty across a range of areas including religion, language, gender norms, habitations, and food ways. One frequently hears of Native demands for greater religious, linguistic, or food sovereignty as a means of preserving that which is culturally unique about them. Indigenous sovereignty, regardless of our status as "domestic dependent nations," was weakened in the past through such legislation as the Religious Crimes Code of 1883, meant to suppress all non-Christian Indigenous religious practices; the creation of government-run boarding schools, meant to implement the forced assimilation and language loss of Indigenous children; and the alienation of Indigenous peoples from their traditional diets and shift to government-approved agricultural practices or government-supplied commodity foods. Each of these actions has been extremely detrimental to Indigenous cultural identity and health—political sovereignty without our respective cultural identities would have little meaning.

To a great extent Native American sovereignty is defined by the constant testing of its power and its limits. Marshall's designation "domestic dependent nations" clarified nothing in that 1831 ruling. Justices Thompson and Story, in their dissent to Marshall's majority opinion in *Cherokee Nation v. Georgia*, did find the Cherokee Nation to be a foreign nation according to established legal definitions. Unfortunately, their opinions did not carry the day and we are left with a legacy of what Audra Simpson has termed "nested sovereignty."[13] Meaning, a level of autonomy which exists within the confines of another sovereignty, much, as Tsianina Lomawaima reminds us, in the manner that a US state's sovereignty exists within the larger sovereignty of the nation-state.[14] Native intellectual and political theorists frequently warn about taking a too narrowly political view of sovereignty, which according to one is ultimately a European concept of governance based on the coercive power of the state, and one Indigenous people should not wish to replicate outright.[15] Beyond semantic differences, what is clear is that Indigenous nations within the United States value immensely the sovereignty we retain and remain vigilant against its erosion by the United States.

Majority-society students learn little to nothing about the destructive attacks on Native sovereignty perpetrated by state and federal authorities, and yet Native communities face their effects every day. The pernicious habit of placing Native Americans into the United States' distant past means that students never have to confront these acts as contemporary social justice matters. Native American history, when taught at all, may strike them as a litany of abuses suffered in the past but ultimately remote from them. There exists a wealth of materials to help instructors clarify these complex contemporary issues, many written by Native scholars, but until state standards and curricular reform recognize Native American history as an integral part of US history, they will have little cause to avail themselves of these resources. One can reasonably expect more advanced high school and college students to grasp the main points about settler colonialism and Native sovereignty when these are incorporated into their American history or social studies curricula. Likewise, younger students need to be taught more about contemporary Native nations—including those in their regions or state. While some states do not have federally recognized Native American reservations, there are no states without a

Native American population today. If significant Native populations are absent, then teach students what became of them and explain where Native populations live today. In many cases an Indigenous nation from a state with no reservations has been relocated to the West. In all cases this aspect of US society must be acknowledged.

One strategy I recommend for teachers of students from elementary school through college is to acknowledge Native American contributions across fields, from popular culture to the fine arts, from scholarship to political activism. The presentism of our culture means that students often engage ethnic differences outside of the classroom through film, television, music, and social media. They may be more likely to know the YouTube comedy of the 1491s than the name of Tecumseh, or the actress Irene Bedard instead of the author Zitkála-Šá, but an awareness of contemporary Native Americans is better than not knowing the names of any. One of the findings of Shear's important study on the representation of Native America with K–12 education is that references to Native nations and historically important individuals fall off precipitously once history courses reach the Civil War. References thereafter are few and far between, with almost no significant figures from the twentieth and twenty-first centuries.[16] If searching for a relatively simple means of including Native people in US history or social studies classes, choosing the major events of the twentieth and twenty-first centuries and inquiring how Native America was involved or affected by these events is a straightforward plan.

Native Americans served in both world wars and in World War I they were not yet counted as US citizens. In both of those wars Native-language speakers served a vital intelligence role as code talkers, employing the very languages that the government had attempted to extinguish through boarding schools and forced assimilation. Students should know that Native Americans continue to serve in the armed forces in a greater proportion to our populations than other ethnic groups in the United States. Upon sharing this fact one could easily engage students in a discussion of how and why this might be, considering the usually antagonistic relationship between Native Americans and the US government. One might also consider including Depression-era legislation, which is commonly referred to as the "Indian New Deal." Often this legislation was meant to halt previous deleterious government policies and allow for greater autonomy on reservations. Such relief was short-lived, though, given postwar federal legislation that sponsored the termination and relocation policies of the 1950s and 1960s. Such policies dissolved federal recognition of over one hundred tribes and attempted to shift Native populations to large cities with further hopes of assimilation, then termed *detribalization*.

Those policies contributed directly to Native American struggles during the civil rights era, and just as African Americans and Latinx Americans organized and demanded their civil rights, so did Native Americans. Unified by common grievances over the centuries, organizations such as Indians of All Tribes, under the leadership of Richard Oakes (Mohawk, 1942–72), would gain national attention through the occupation of Alcatraz Island in 1969, which lit the spark for subsequent actions by groups such as the American Indian Movement (AIM). The early 1970s were a time of tremendous social upheaval in the United States and Native Americans were at the forefront of this. Actions such as the Trail of Broken Treaties in 1972 and the occupation of Wounded Knee in 1973 raised public awareness of the cultural, economic, and political plight of Native Americans like nothing else before them. It was in this atmosphere of political activism that some of the damage done by termination was rolled back, as in the Menominee Restoration Act of 1973—the result of Menominee activism led by Ada Deer. Other actions would lead to the admission by Indian Health Services that their forced sterilization program had sterilized between 25 and 50 percent of Native American women in the years 1970–76.[17] Similarly, the American Indian Religious Freedom Act of 1978 returned the civil liberties protections for Native religious practice that had been denied us since 1884. Contemporary students are almost wholly ignorant of any of these Native American issues from the latter half of the twentieth century.

Besides the continuing struggles for our cultural and political sovereignty are the equally urgent struggles by Indigenous communities on behalf of the environment. Pollution and climate change have affected Native communities living in remote and fragile ecosystems from the Arctic to the Sonoran Desert. The degradation of water resources and deforestation are having catastrophic effects on Native and non-Native communities alike. Many students share a deep concern about the coming environmental disasters and would likely have an interest not only in Indigenous environmental activism but also in the alternatives Indigenous environmental practices offer to the wholesale exploitation of the world's resources by global capitalism. Understanding the custodial relationship toward the environment espoused by many Indigenous cultures and other concepts, such as "seven generations sustainability," would help our students see the virtues of consulting and partnering with Indigenous peoples on these challenges. Likewise, Potawatomi scholar Robin Kimmerer has promoted the study of traditional ecological knowledge (or TEK) alongside scientific ecological knowledge (or SEK) to better understand how and what Indigenous people contribute to environmental studies.[18]

The dramatic protests that took place at Standing Rock in 2016 showed the nation the urgency of protecting resources for our communities—even as big oil and corporate powers would ultimately prevail. Native Americans have led in this struggle to raise consciousness about the dire situation with the environment and with hope that an increased understanding of what is at stake will reach the majority population. Social media played a significant role in the Standing Rock protests and the call to action, which drew participants from hundreds of Native nations and the majority population. Continued activism against the Keystone Pipeline and the monitoring of other sites of ecological risk remain dependent on social media since corporate mainstream media has consistently failed to cover such news. Social media groups such as the Indigenous Peoples Major Group for Sustainable Development and the Indigenous Environmental Network have created sites for sharing information about a large variety of environmental issues and actions being led by grassroots Indigenous groups and their allies.

The internet has of course provided a huge amount of information never before available for the study of Indigenous issues, including government documents, critical essays, maps, statistics, and the like. But it has also allowed for a cacophony of opinions and misinformation to compete with genuine resources. Students become increasingly more reliant on Google searches alone and usually do not possess the knowledge necessary to assess the accuracy of Wikipedia entries on Native American topics. Teams of scholars have created various educational sites to assist instructors and the interested alike. One such site was created under the auspices of the Newberry Library in Chicago, an independent research library with vast holdings in Native American archival materials. The site, Indians of the Midwest, is a collaboration between the Newberry Library and the National Endowment for the Humanities, whereby a team of both Native and non-Native scholars, led by Dr. Loretta Fowler, created a resource for teachers in that region looking for reliable information and course materials on the subject of Native America.[19] Though no site can be definitive, Indians of the Midwest provides an instructive template for scholars who might wish to undertake such a project in other regions of the United States. Likewise, the National Museum of the American Indian has created a teaching resource site based on its collection and the field of experts to which it has access. Their site, Native Knowledge 360°, bills itself as the museum's "national initiative to inspire and promote improvement of teaching about American Indians."[20] Besides online resources the site allows interested educators to apply to participate in workshops developed to aid in the instruction about Native American cultures at a variety of educational levels. Their continued use of the term *American Indian* is indicative of their relationship to the federal government, which still uses the term in their official correspondence, as well as the title of the museum itself. Other similar resources exist in varying degrees at the state and regional levels but with no uniformity or universal availability. The thrust of such projects is on the whole a hopeful sign that this material will find its way into the classroom and someday form a rudimentary knowledge of the Indigenous peoples of this country. Otherwise, if the curricular disregard for Native American cultures continues, across disciplines, then we and the contributions of our respective cultures remain marooned in the past. Our erasure in educational curricula and thus contemporary consciousness only results in Indian removal all over again. This time, no Trail of Tears, no forced relocations, just utter institutional and social silence.

NOTES

1. See Jess Bidgood, "Amherst Drops 'Lord Jeff' as Mascot," *New York Times*, January 27, 2016, https://www.nytimes.com/2016/01/27/us/amherst-college-drops-lord-jeff-as-mascot.html; and Steve Annear, "Harvard Law School to Ditch Controversial Shield," *Boston Globe*, March 14, 2016, https://www.bostonglobe.com/metro/2016/03/14/harvard-law-school-ditch-controversial-shield-with-elements-from-slave-owning-family/UIYgbyviFdwwGKjexZgWqN/story.html.

2. Jesse James Deconto and Alan Blinder, " 'Silent Sam' Confederate Statue Is Toppled at Chapel Hill," *New York Times*, August 21, 2018, https://www.nytimes.com/2018/08/21/us/unc-silent-sam-monument-toppled.html.

3. Sarah Shear, R. Knowles, G. Soden, and A. Castro, "Manifesting Destiny: Re/presentations of Indigenous People in K–12 U.S. History Curriculum," *Theory & Research in Social Education* 43, no. 1 (2015): 68–101.

4. See Scott Manning Stevens, "Collectors and Museums: From Cabinets of Curiosities to Indigenous Cultural Centers," in *The Oxford Handbook of American Indian History*, ed. Frederick Hoxie (Oxford: Oxford University Press, 2016), 475–96.

5. Ani Mikaere, *Colonising Myths—Maori Realities: He Rukuruku Whakaaro* (Wellington, NZ: Huia Publishers, 2011), 98.

6. Patricia Monture-Angus, *Thunder in My Soul: A Mohawk Woman Speaks* (Halifax, NS: Fernwood Publishing, 1995), 63.

7. Patrick Wolfe, "Settler Colonialism and the Elimination of the Native," *Journal of Genocide Research* 8, no. 4 (December 2006): 387.

8. Evelyn Nakano Glenn, "Settler Colonialism as Structure: A Framework for Comparative Studies of U.S. Race and Gender Formation," *Sociology of Race and Ethnicity* 1, no. 1 (2015): 57.

9. Glenn, "Settler Colonialism as Structure," 60.

10. See Mikal Eckstrom and Margaret Jacobs, "Teaching American History as Settler Colonialism," in *Why You Can't Teach United States History without American Indians*, ed. Susan Sleeper-Smith, Juliana Barr, Jean M. O'Brien, Nancy Shoemaker, and Scott Manning Steven (Chapel Hill: University of North Carolina Press, 2015), 259–72.

11. See Robert Miller, "The Doctrine of Discovery, Manifest Destiny, and American Indians," in Sleeper-Smith et al., *Why You Can't Teach United States History without American Indians*, 87–100; and Joseph Heath, "The Doctrine of Christian Discovery: Its Fundamental Importance in United States Indian Law and the Need for Its Repudiation and Removal," *Albany Government Law Review* 10 (2017): 112–56.

12. Bureau of Indian Affairs: https://www.bia.gov/bia.

13. Audra Simpson, *Mohawk Interruptus: Political Life across the Borders of Settler States* (Durham, NC: Duke University Press, 2014), 116.

14. K. Tsianina Lomawaima, "Federalism: Native, Federal, and State Sovereignty," in Sleeper-Smith et al., *Why You Can't Teach United States History without American Indians*, 274.

15. See Taiaiake Alfred, "From Sovereignty to Freedom: Towards an Indigenous Political Discourse," *Indigenous Affairs* 3 (2001): 22–34.

16. Shear et al., "Manifesting Destiny," 81.

17. Erin Blakemore, "The Little-Known History of the Forced Sterilization of Native American Women," *JSTOR Daily*, August 25, 2016, https://daily.jstor.org/the-little-known-history-of-the-forced-sterilization-of-native-american-women.

18. Robin Kimmerer, "Native Knowledge for Native Ecosystems," *Journal of Forestry* 98, no. 8 (August 2000): 4–9.

19. https://publications.newberry.org/indiansofthemidwest.

20. https://americanindian.si.edu/nk360.

BIBLIOGRAPHY

Alfred, Taiaiake. "From Sovereignty to Freedom: Towards an Indigenous Political Discourse." *Indigenous Affairs* 3 (2001): 22–34.

Annear, Steve. "Harvard Law School to Ditch Controversial Shield." *Boston Globe*, March 14, 2016. https://www.bostonglobe.com/metro/2016/03/14/harvard-law-school-ditch-controversial-shield-with-elements-from-slave-owning-family/UIYgbyviFdwwGKjexZgWqN/story.html.

Bidgood, Jess. "Amherst Drops 'Lord Jeff' as Mascot." *New York Times*, January 27, 2016. https://www.nytimes.com/2016/01/27/us/amherst-college-drops-lord-jeff-as-mascot.html.

Blakemore, Erin. "The Little-Known History of the Forced Sterilization of Native American Women." *JSTOR Daily*, August 25, 2016. https://daily.jstor.org/the-little-known-history-of-the-forced-sterilization-of-native-american-women.

Deconto, Jesse James, and Alan Blinder. " 'Silent Sam' Confederate Statue Is Toppled at Chapel Hill." *New York Times*, August 21, 2018. https://www.nytimes.com/2018/08/21/us/unc-silent-sam-monument-toppled.html.

Eckstrom, Mikal, and Margaret Jacobs. "Teaching American History as Settler Colonialism." In *Why You Can't Teach United States History without American Indians*, edited by Susan Sleeper-Smith, Juliana Barr, Jean M. O'Brien, Nancy Shoemaker, and Scott Manning Stevens, 259–72. Chapel Hill: University of North Carolina Press, 2015.

Glenn, Evelyn Nakano. "Settler Colonialism as Structure: A Framework for Comparative Studies of U.S. Race and Gender Formation." *Sociology of Race and Ethnicity* 1, no. 1 (2015): 54–74.

Grande, Sandy. *Red Pedagogy: Native American Social and Political Thought*. Lanham, MD: Rowman and Littlefield, 2004.

Kimmerer, Robin. "Native Knowledge for Native Ecosystems." *Journal of Forestry* 98, no. 8 (August 2000): 4–9.

Lomawaima, K. Tsianina. "Federalism: Native, Federal, and State Sovereignty." In *Why You Can't Teach United States History without American Indians*, edited by Susan Sleeper-Smith, Juliana Barr, Jean M. O'Brien, Nancy Shoemaker, and Scott Manning Stevens, 273–86. Chapel Hill: University of North Carolina Press, 2015.

Mikaere, Ani. *Colonising Myths—Maori Realities: He Rukuruku Whakaaro*. Wellington, NZ: Huia Publishers, 2011.

Monture-Angus, Patricia. *Thunder in My Soul: A Mohawk Woman Speaks*. Halifax, NS: Fernwood Publishing, 1995.

Shear, S. B., R. Knowles, G. Soden, and A. Castro. "Manifesting Destiny: Re/presentations of Indigenous People in K–12 U.S. History Curriculum." *Theory & Research in Social Education* 43, no. 1 (2015): 68–101.

Simpson, Audra. *Mohawk Interruptus: Political Life across the Borders of Settler States*. Durham, NC: Duke University Press, 2014.

Stevens, Scott Manning. "Collectors and Museums: From Cabinets of Curiosities to Indigenous Cultural Centers." In *The Oxford Handbook of American*

Indian History, edited by Frederick Hoxie, 475–96. Oxford: Oxford University Press, 2016.

Wolfe, Patrick. "Settler Colonialism and the Elimination of the Native." *Journal of Genocide Research* 8, no. 4 (December 2006): 387–409.1.

CHAPTER 2

MULTIPLE PEDAGOGIES REQUIRED

Reflections on Teaching Race and Ethnicity in the Intercultural and Intergenerational Classroom

FELICIA L. HARRIS

Have you heard the imperative "fail faster"? It is a mantra that has been embraced by a range of authors, artists, creative tinkerers, and entrepreneurs to refer to the process of failing as necessary to improve and, ultimately, succeed. A paradoxical idea, it was introduced in Samuel Beckett's *Worstward Ho*: other iterations of the phrase include "fail fast, fail often" and "fail better."[1] The notion that failure is inevitable is a truth that those who have answered the call to teach are intimately familiar with. However, failing inside the classroom is a specific type of failure that can have lingering consequences for both teacher and student. The failure of educators has a certain type of weight, paired with a responsibility to address and correct, unlike the failures of tech tinkerers, who can simply scrap their projects and start over with a clean slate. The teaching cannot simply be scrapped and started over, and the learning must forge on. In lieu of the luxury to fail fast and fail often, educators are met with the pressure to rarely fail, particularly within the context of the present dangers that mark the perilous times described in detail within this volume.

When educators fail, our failures are both personal and public, occurring with several pairs of eyes credulously searching for the appropriate answer or action. Inevitably, in today's hypervisible classroom, the mistakes of some educators are more likely to be broadcast and criticized than others. While errors within commonplace subjects, such as algebra or composition, may be easily corrected and forgotten, those who teach contentious subjects, such as race and ethnicity, may find their failures rising through the ranks of administrative offices or circulating online in the form of a viral hashtag. Jason Cohen's chapter in this volume offers an exemplary case study of the perils of our unbounded roles as educators within and beyond the classroom. Although Cohen's misstep was on Twitter and not behind the podium, his viral display of racial insensitivity resulted in lasting consequences and change for himself and his institution.

The notion that a misstep of one word or one phrase in less than 140 characters can influence the trajectory of our careers is menacing. As a result, educators may find themselves choosing to avoid this specific failure at any cost (*"Fail never!"*), even if it means forgoing critical engagement with teaching and learning about subjects that significantly impact the lives and well-being of our students. Sadly, an education that conveniently circumvents the complexities of the social world in order to avoid criticism is an ultimate failure to our students, who are increasingly interested in and exposed to critical race issues in their everyday lives, whether it be through national media attention, viral social media posts, or casual dialogue with friends or classmates. A body of educators without stories of "lessons learned" to share with those following in their footsteps fails educators who aspire to approach this sort of critically engaged teaching in an informed manner.

In this chapter, I share my experience of failure in my initial efforts to teach race and ethnicity during my first year of teaching at the college level. Although I was eager to create a space where transformative teaching and learning about race could transpire, I lacked the appropriate pedagogical framework to make that vision a reality. Through my narrative, I explore how blind confidence and lack of preparedness led to self-doubt and abandonment of ambitious and radical teaching practices. However, through continued dialogue with students and an active engagement with scholarship on teaching, I adopted a new outlook on pedagogies for race and ethnicity that enabled me to return to teaching about race in a meaningful way. I share my experience with the hope that my lessons learned will help other educators learn from my mistakes and replace fear of failure with an eagerness to achieve the opposite: success.

YOU DON'T OWN THE N-WORD: A CASE STUDY ON FAILURE

Starry-eyed and way too naive, I tore into the challenge of my first semester as a tenure-track assistant professor of communication studies at the University of Houston–Downtown, an urban commuter campus in the heart of the most ethnically and racially diverse city in the United States. Reeling from five years of graduate education at a predominantly white institution in the Southeast, I had high hopes for what I would be able to accomplish in my classroom, particularly when it came to discussions on race and ethnicity. During my initial campus visit in April 2015, I could hardly contain my excitement while peering around, amazed at the sight of a campus that boasted ranges in race, ethnicity, language, culture, and age beyond my wildest dreams. My institution's commitment to a diverse student body and minority education is evident through its designation as a minority-serving and Hispanic-serving institution[2] and average undergraduate student age of twenty-seven years old.[3] During my first semester of teaching, my students hailed from far-off places like Mali, Sri Lanka, and Colombia, with ages ranging from eighteen to sixty-five. The diversity on campus mirrors the fast-growing city of Houston, predicted soon to become the third-largest city in the nation. Shortly after my arrival, I found great comfort in the words of a speaker who proclaimed that Houston, and our university, represented the future of the United States. I could have never anticipated that within the next year the nation's political climate would change to one where many of the identities embraced in my institution's diversity would be under scrutiny and attack.

As I outlined my course objectives and lesson plans for my first fall semester, I relished the idea that my students of color would not be "the only" in my classroom—that whoever they were, they would most likely, and easily, find a version of themselves passing through the halls or even behind the podium. As a young educator, I still have burned into my memory the moments when, in the classroom, it felt like the color of my skin was screaming louder than any discussion being had. I had often experienced the heightened visibility (or invisibility) that comes with being one of the few or the only when race or Otherness surfaces as the focal point of a conversation. As a student at a predominantly white institution, I would feel eyes move in on me whenever race was vaguely mentioned, lingering for a moment before darting awkwardly to other landing places in the room: the clock, the instructor, some faraway spot on the wall just to the left of my head, scratch paper on the table, and then, ultimately, back to me. For years, I fluctuated between being the voice of the entire Black race and getting into shouting matches with students who were determined to invalidate my experiences and perspective once they were no longer deemed useful to their own understanding, or when my contributions did not confirm what they thought to be true about the world.

It was during those crucial moments—as opposed to during lectures or office hours, or while completing assignments—that I assessed the credibility of my instructors. Was my professor the type of person who allowed tension to simmer to the point where I stormed out of the room? Were they the type to reel it in and divert the conversation, leaving pivotal questions that arose unanswered? Or would they intervene and facilitate a learning opportunity that was transformative for all involved? As a result of this tension, in the more than ten years I spent as a college student, I charged out of classrooms quite a few times. Only once did an instructor follow up with me.

Consequently, it was through these vulnerable moments that I learned how to critically interrogate notions of race—using my lingering, unanswered questions to fuel a passionate research agenda that centered my experiences of Blackness and Otherness inside and outside of the classroom and my discipline.[4] My research is informed by cultural studies, media studies, critical theory, and Black feminist thought and is built upon understanding systems of power and how they are maintained in society. Such theoretical frameworks underpinned my philosophy as an aspiring educator. Anchored in these philosophical positions is a commitment to deconstructing ideas of race and Otherness that are haphazardly accepted as "true" and appropriate. If knowledge is created and sustained within classroom settings, and if knowledge is power, I reasoned, then systems of power are created and sustained within the context of the classroom as well. How could I teach in such a way that students would cultivate a natural propensity toward questioning their "truth"? Rarely had my instructors gone *there*, and that is what I was committed to doing in my new position in the classroom. After years of wearing the mask that Sharon Raynor expertly describes in her chapter in this volume, I had found an institution that would allow me to take the mask off and engage in the honest dialogue I had craved as a student.

The first time I went *there* was a disaster. I was teaching an entry-level course on public speaking and had racked my brain over ways to make my teaching more engaging and insightful. As a media studies hire, I figured it would be fitting to incorporate YouTube videos as discussion starters to complement lecture topics. And, as a scholar who interrogates issues of race, class, and power, I chose timely videos that explored these issues through blunders in public speaking. Research has shown that popular culture and media can be used inside the classroom to facilitate transformative learning experiences around diversity and equity issues, particularly when students are given the opportunity to engage in a guided discussion of relevant social issues.[5] Alas, we were pulling double duty, learning the skills of public speaking while using a critical lens to examine the world.

On one particular morning, we were learning about the powerful role of language in public speaking and I ambitiously decided to go *there*: we were going to discuss "the n-word."

I had read *just* enough literature to know that teaching this particular word could present a challenge, and I developed what I thought was a foolproof plan.[6] I selected two videos highlighting the use of the n-word in different contexts: President Obama's use of the n-word to talk about race relations during a podcast interview, and Cornel West's response to President Obama's use of the word in a CNN segment, during which he turned the n-word into an adjective to describe President Obama.[7] I prefaced the videos with a trigger warning and planned to follow with a moment of silent reflection before facilitating the discussion. I was prepared to do what the best college teachers do.[8]

While the clips played on the projector, I carefully watched my students. Eyes widened, hands covered open mouths; some students laughed and others dutifully took notes. While observing the range of emotions, I noticed that Jeremy, an older, Black male student, was growing increasingly upset. I tried to make eye contact with him, to read him and see how he was responding to the subject matter, but he was engrossed in the screen. As the second clip came to an end, and before the lights were up, he started to speak out passionately.

"Not yet!" I interrupted with a knowing smile. Prior to this moment, he and I had built a pretty decent rapport. It was not uncommon for him to stay after class and pick my brain, asking questions about the lecture content or pitching ideas for his assignments.

"I know you all have several thoughts, so let's take a moment to process what we've just watched. As you look over your notes, think about some of the questions I asked before we started the videos." I directed my comments to the entire class and waited for about a minute or so before opening up for discussion. The tension of the silence was almost intolerable.

"Okay." I looked in Jeremy's direction. "What did you all think?"

He glared toward the front of the room and avoided my eyes. I had lost him. While others around the room perked up, he did not even bother to raise his hand. However, a student who could physically pass as a white man, but who I knew to be Latino and very bright, did. I called on him.

About a minute into the discussion, Jeremy began to loudly pack up his belongings. A moment later, he was walking out of the room. The brief discussion, which had started off lively and engaging, came to a halt and all eyes were on me for our next move. I looked out into the room full of Black and Brown and seemingly white students. It was an ideal reflection of diversity and we were unpacking *the n-word*. Silently, I recounted the past ten minutes or so. Where had I gone wrong?

"Hang on just a moment," I told the class as I headed toward the door. In the hallway, I caught up with him. "What's wrong? Why are you leaving?" I asked.

"How are *you* going to let *him* talk about *that* word?" he asked me. "I've been called that word my entire life and you told me to be quiet and you let *him* speak first!"

I was stunned. I knew what he was implying—how could I let a *white* man launch our discussion? The pain in his face was palpable. I tried to recall the words I had always hoped to hear from a professor in a moment like this, words that would have prevented a younger version of myself from leaving a classroom feeling defeated.

"Listen." I softened my voice. "I know this is a difficult conversation to have, but you don't *own* that word. You're not the only person who has an experience with that word." I reminded him that this was the sole point of the lecture: to talk about language and how it affects different people and why. I assured him that his perspective was valuable and that he needed to be heard, even if he was upset. Then I explained that his classmate's perspective was equally valuable and worthy of being heard, with the overarching goal of sparking dialogue that helps us all go deeper in our learning. Ultimately, he concluded that he was too upset to have that conversation and it would be best for him to leave. I conceded.

As he walked away, I found myself frozen in the moment, embodying the ghosts of professors past. When I returned to the classroom, I repeated to the class what I had said in the hallway: This is why language matters. This is why the words we use have power. Words can create adverse reactions for different people, draw on different experiences, and result in various consequences. I reminded my students that this was the privilege of being in a college classroom: to have reactions and conversations about difficult topics in a space where we can learn from one another without storming out of the room.

But I wanted to. I wanted to walk out of there and go straight to my office, shut the door, and cry.

WHAT GETS BROUGHT INTO THE CLASSROOM

Failing in front of the classroom forces you back to the drawing board in haste, analyzing every lesson plan, each learning outcome, and the pedagogical framework used to prepare for your time there. After my experience teaching the n-word, I was in turmoil over the potential that I had caused a student to feel what I had often felt as a college student. In retrospect, I was painfully aware that the critical framework I had acquired to examine social phenomena in the material world had not adequately prepared me to engage in dialogue that leapt off the paper and into the confines of the classroom.

Furthermore, this failure exposed me to the dynamic that intergenerational and intercultural diversity introduced to teaching and learning about race and other contentious topics. After our conversation in the hallway, I learned that there were a number of factors that contributed to Jeremy's decision to leave the room. One was that he believed I was too young and naive an instructor to introduce language he felt was inappropriate for a classroom setting. Another was his assumption about the racial composition of the room and who should have been "allowed" to speak and in what order. At the same time, the students who remained behind almost too easily dismissed the moment of conflict, making it known that they perceived Jeremy to be hyperemotional and the topic "not that big of a deal." Although I felt that I had approached the lesson with sound pedagogy, the range in student responses troubled me, and I deemed the experience a teaching failure. As a result, I found myself reflecting on my role and responsibilities as a college professor and questioning my ability for the rest of the semester. My feelings of failure revealed that in my role as an "Other," I would still need to do the work of creating effectual learning spaces and opportunities in a classroom setting where students were vastly different from me and from one another.

This type of diversity is often encountered in urban schools, and I found myself drawn to a popular text in urban education, *For White Folks Who Teach in the Hood . . . and the Rest of Y'all Too*, by Christopher Emdin.[9] Emdin's central premise is that educators who teach students from communities that differ from their own should adopt new lenses and frameworks in order to engage urban youth of color. Although Emdin's primary audience is typically those who teach in primary and secondary education settings, his argument that educators must create a learning environment conducive to how students view the world (and view learning in itself) is useful for those taking on the highly personal, highly experiential subject matter of race and ethnicity. Emdin's reasoning was a useful introduction for thinking critically about pedagogies in the context of the college classroom and, in particular, with a nod to teaching race and ethnicity. My failure taught me that effective pedagogy needs more than "soundness"; teaching practices must be rooted in the context of the dynamics of our classrooms and our students. As an example, Shane McCoy's chapter in this volume details the need for techniques such as *scaffolding for justice* as he teaches introductory literature. My deep dive into pedagogies exposed me to a range of pedagogical concepts, including culturally relevant pedagogy, feminist pedagogy, critical pedagogy, andragogy, and more.[10]

In his text, Emdin discusses "reality pedagogy," a dialogic approach that accounts for the lived experiences that students carry into the classroom.[11] This particular approach seems to encompass the underlying premise of each of the aforementioned pedagogies and has various implications for the changing nature of college classrooms in the United States, which are steadily diversifying in age, race and ethnicity, nationality, and breadth of experiences tethered to those multiple and fluctuating identities.[12] Whereas culturally relevant pedagogy invites educators to become more aware of culture and its impacts on the learning process, reality pedagogy asks educators to view students as individuals who are influenced by their cultural identity, as opposed to equal to it.[13] In other words, it pushes back on assumptions that are often implicit when adopting teaching practices for certain *groups* of students (i.e., Black, Latinx, poor, adult, etc.) and calls for a continual understanding of students as unique individuals. This practice embraces the dynamic view of culture that Ladson-Billings called for in a remix of her widely used theory, noting that scholars must understand the "heterogeneity of cultural experience."[14] As a result, the primary goal of reality pedagogy is "meeting each student on his or her own cultural and emotional turf."[15]

In this approach, the classroom structure becomes decentralized and the teacher learns alongside students, who are empowered as experts in their own learning. While I had initially found myself overjoyed at the thought of being in such a diverse classroom, I had not understood the amount of effort required to attend to the individuality of such a diverse body. Furthermore, I was simply unprepared. In *Teaching to Transgress*, bell hooks explores this very dilemma: "When I first entered the multicultural, multiethnic classroom setting I was unprepared. I did not know how to cope effectively with so much 'difference.' . . . Despite progressive politics, and my deep engagement with the feminist movement, I had never before been compelled to work within a truly diverse setting and I lacked the necessary skills. This is the case with most educators . . . This is why so many of us stubbornly cling to old patterns."[16] As hooks suggests, I realized that the first step necessary to create the learning environment I'd hoped for was to abandon teaching as usual and embrace new styles. Likewise, I realized that best practices for certain *groups* of students would not suffice when student bodies straddle the boundaries of many. In her reflections, hooks echoes the thoughts of Paulo Freire, who acknowledges that oftentimes individuals with hopes of liberation subconsciously emulate the oppressive conditions that have structured their thinking.[17] In the face of a truly progressive student body, I had been forced to rely upon pedagogical practices of old that did not achieve the transformative, inclusive learning opportunity I so desperately wanted. The commonplace pattern of posing questions, showing a video, pausing for reflection, and launching into discussion was not the approach needed by that particular student body, hence the catalyst for my great learning moment.

Emdin's emphasis on teacher and students working side by side to co-construct learning through co-teaching and peer-to-peer teaching encouraged me to rethink my approach to teaching race and ethnicity in such a way that I avoid taking the lead on race because, in spite of my years researching and acquiring the language necessary to explore the subject matter in depth, I am not the expert in the room, not on race anyway. I do not believe any one person is. As hooks argues, although academic training encourages teachers to assume they are "right," we must be open to admitting what we do not know.[18] It is imperative for educators who teach race to acknowledge that there are even more gray areas than we typically encounter.

Ultimately, we must accept that students will have some sort of experience—perhaps even lingering psychological trauma or a heightened emotional understanding—of race and ethnicity that gets brought into the classroom. For example, being Black and hearing the n-word had a meaning to Jeremy that was not accessible to the rest of the class. This is a type of knowledge and way of knowing that, as educators, we cannot know until we meet and begin to learn from our students. As a result, race and ethnicity cannot be approached in the same manner as the more established lines of our core disciplines, such as English, mathematics, or psychology, because the boundaries of knowledge and scholarship for teaching on race and ethnicity are less determined; they are instead sometimes productively spread and sometimes distorted by a range of disciplinary and personal vantage points.

Whereas students who enroll in a course such as advertising may be willing to acknowledge that they do not know much about the subject and with an eagerness to acquire whatever insight an instructor has to offer, students who enroll in my course on race, ethnicity, and communication, for example, tend to begin with quite a different disposition: they *know* about race and ethnicity and have various levels of willingness and excitement about unpacking that knowledge in a room full of others. That is a fact for any college course being taught in the United States. However, this truth becomes even more significant for teaching and learning when we account for intercultural and intergenerational classrooms like those at universities similar to the University of Houston–Downtown, where lived experiences, those that ground what students know and bring into the classroom, are even more varied.

RACE, ETHNICITY, NATIONALITY . . . AND AGE?

In my classrooms in Houston, and at other institutions throughout the United States, traditional and nontraditional students often sit alongside international students or students who are first-generation American citizens, for whom the concept of race and ethnicity in the US may be altogether daunting, as they did not grow up with similar lived experiences or understanding of the material reality of race as some of their peers.[19] If a student identifies as a non-Black or non-white person of color, they may self-censor and privilege the perspectives of students who are members of those groups, or simply feel less inclined to engage in classroom discussion at all. Likewise, students who belong to those groups may feel the need to dominate conversations that they perceive as applying solely to them. This tension was a factor in my initial foray into teaching the n-word, during which Jeremy felt that he should have the largest share of the conversation because he was a Black man, and my international or first-generation American students took the heated debate in stride. All too often, discussions of race tend to home in on "Black" and "white" in a way that serves as a great disadvantage to understanding the complexity of race and ethnicity in America.

However, in recent years, I have witnessed students express a desire to understand how this spectrum of racial and cultural difference and experience operates in the US in a more nuanced way. I initially noticed the shift in my classroom in the fall after my initial foray into radical teaching practices during the 2016 presidential debate season. Around this time, Donald Trump publicly and repeatedly espoused comments disparaging large groups of Black *and* Brown people, referring to them as criminals, drug dealers, and rapists.[20] In class, the word *stereotype* moved beyond popular discussions of Black men wearing hoodies or white men in trench coats to a deeper exploration of how several different groups of people are often perceived in the United States. At times, almost every student in my classes could identify a moment when one of the nation's leading candidates for the highest office had gone viral for making hateful remarks about groups of people sharing their race, ethnicity, or nationality. Under the Trump administration, the problem of whiteness and white patriarchy entered into national discourse as a threat to many people living in the United States, many of whom aspire to achieve the "American dream." The widespread disdain for Trump created a disposition among students to explore the concept of Otherness along multiple gradients of race, ethnicity, nationality, cultural experiences, and more.

The initial tension and trauma that the Trump administration brought into my classroom created space for a sense of inclusion that bell hooks describes as necessary for radical pedagogy. In this form of pedagogy, everyone's presence must be acknowledged and valued, and widespread contributions are essential resources, eliminating the notion that only the professor is responsible for what happens in the classroom.[21] The sheer amount of critical reflection and engagement was a relief. However, it also revealed what my pedagogy had been lacking: the requirement of every student's contribution and the unplanned teaching that happens as a result.

In the semesters since my public failure, I have taught students who run the gamut of experiences: a Latino student whose family members had been harassed, deported, and in one circumstance, murdered; a student from Mali who could not bear to talk about racialized violence due to her experiences with conflict in her hometown in Africa; an Asian student who grew up being referred to as "chink" while struggling to live up to expectations of being a model minority; and yet another Black male student, this one a bit older than Jeremy, who recounted having family members lynched, raped, and harassed during the Jim Crow era. In addition to the large number of first-generation students recently matriculating from high school, several of my students have had twenty-plus-year careers; bought and sold businesses; served combat tours in the military; and are caregivers for husbands, wives, parents, and children.

Chances are, most of us who teach on college campuses will be able to recount a similar breadth in the backgrounds of our students. However, prior to my arrival at UHD, and among the many institutions that I have visited or attended, I had never experienced this breadth in a single classroom at one time. The vast range in the ages and experiences of my students introduces an interesting and nuanced dynamic into our learning about race and ethnicity. As the fairly young Black woman in the front of the classroom, I have learned that my experiences with the n-word and other forms of racially charged language or experiences could, more often than not, be quite different from most of my students', and that my students' experiences would also be—again, more often than not—vastly different from one another's.

While I was still reveling in the triumph of increased engagement across race, ethnicity, and nationality, a conversation with my mother drove home the need for my pedagogy around race and ethnicity to be inclusive of differences in generational experiences as well. Around the same time that I transitioned into my role as a college professor, she decided to return to college full-time. Born in the late 1950s, my mother did a short stint in the air force before becoming a military wife and mother of four children. After she divorced my father, she took a few classes here and there at local colleges and ultimately went on to become the owner of a small cleaning company in a rural college town. As an entrepreneur, and after supporting me through college and attending several commencement ceremonies, she decided it was time to earn her bachelor's degree, that highly lauded "piece of paper," as she describes it. During my first year of teaching, I would often share with my mother just how similar her experiences were to those of many of my students at UHD.

One day, my mother called after a classroom discussion had turned toward Black activism. She was perturbed. "*These* kids," she exclaimed, "have no idea what it was like!" Apparently, the conversation on activism had escalated when passionate, younger students were taken aback by her disinterest in current political movements. My mother, who has fair skin, green eyes, and freckles, was raised in a small Texas town in the 1960s and 1970s. On several occasions, she has shared stories about how she wore a big Afro and a wristband in solidarity with the Black Power movement in spite of being told that she was too white (light) to be Black and too Black to be white. Her argument was that, while millennials were just now waking up to the reality of ignorance, hatred, and blatant racism, she had spent hours upon hours expending energy in this same fight decades ago with little, and not hardly enough, visible change in race relations. The passion and initial negative response of her classmates had overwhelmed her in the moment. She felt that she did not have the energy, and her professor had not created the space for her, to clearly articulate the knowledge and understanding that decades of "real-world" experience as a Black woman living in America had afforded her.

"I just let them have it," she concluded. "I bet I won't ever speak up in that class again." When we hung up the phone, I was deflated. I had tried, to no avail, to get her to understand how important it was for her to speak up. As her daughter, I knew what she could contribute to her classmates' learning and, as a college professor, I could see the learning opportunities she would miss by shutting down. Her classroom experience took me back to the failure in my own. Later in my first semester, Jeremy—who I found out was a returning student in his forties—shared with me his horrific experiences with the local jail (which just happened to be outside of our classroom window), racial profiling, a contentious history with Southern white men and their use of the n-word, and more. Although we had gotten along well in the moments leading up to our explosive conversation on the n-word, it was likely because our lessons had yet to tap into this particular area of knowledge, which had significantly shaped his life. Had I failed to create the safe space necessary for him to contribute to his learning, his classmates' learning, and even my own?

In the same way that campuses are encountering an increasingly racially and ethnically diverse student body, intergenerational classrooms are a phenomenon that educators should be prepared to face more frequently. It is no secret that older adults are settling into retirement early, becoming more interested in gaining new skill sets, and finding themselves on college campuses for the first time in a long time, or for the first time ever.[22] According to the National Center for Education Statistics, adults over the age of twenty-five accounted for nearly one-half of students enrolled part-time at public four-year institutions in fall 2015. Furthermore, this same group accounted for 11 percent of students enrolled full-time, a number that is projected to continue growing.[23] Certainly, there is much to learn from the knowledge and experiences of such students—like Jeremy and my mother—in the context of the classroom and, as a result, new teaching practices are needed to pair the directed learning experiences that younger students require with the learner-centered approach that adult learners may crave.

Students born in the 1950s and 1960s in the United States will undoubtedly approach learning about race and ethnicity in different ways than their younger counterparts, who tend to be optimistic, open-minded, and publicly and socially engaged with issues they find meaningful.[24] This was a point of tension often observed in both my mother's classroom and my own. Beyond merely gaining new skill sets, adult learners benefit from scenarios in which they believe that what they are learning is needed and can be immediately applied to their current living situations, and when they can use their life experiences to make sense of new information.[25] Complicating lessons on race and ethnicity, however, some older students have lived through the Jim Crow era, the violent desegregation of public schools, and the assassination of civil rights pioneers such as Dr. Martin Luther King Jr., Malcolm X, and President John F. Kennedy. They watched riots unfold in Los Angeles in the aftermath of the Rodney King beating and then, a few years later, debated the intricacies of interracial dating during the trial of O. J. Simpson. These students may have been taught not to talk about race in "mixed company," as even the words we use to describe race and ethnicity have continued to fluctuate in levels of political correctness. They may cringe or hesitate at the use of the word "Black," vividly recounting its political trajectory and opting for other terms, such as "African American," "Afro-American," or "Negro." As one student explained to me, they may simply need a moment or two to process the newfound language they are being given to describe experiences and knowledge they have possessed their entire lives.

Ultimately, the mental labor that it takes to learn, or relearn, about race and ethnicity can be overwhelming and, in the worst-case scenarios, may result in students shutting down, walking out, or questioning, "Why are we talking about race, anyway?" The opportunity, albeit a challenge, in the intergenerational and intercultural classroom becomes helping students understand that, while a clear racial hierarchy privileges whiteness on one end of the spectrum and penalizes Blackness on the other, within that range is a vast array of discussions to be had about experiences tethered to race, ethnicity, nationality, and culture. Along this spectrum, there is much to share with and learn from every individual in the room at any given time. Taking an approach to teaching that encourages students to co-construct their learning in a way that centers and explores commonality among their individual experiences, as opposed to the expertise of the teacher, assists in creating the safe space necessary to have such dialogue.

WHAT FAILURE TAUGHT ME

During this transformative era of teaching race and ethnicity, I have learned that it is not my responsibility to *lead* the discussion on race, as I would in my advertising course, but rather to serve as an expert facilitator. In this way, expertise is most useful when, as we learn about the experiences of our students, teachers provide the language and lenses through which they can gather insight about their world. The processes of *learning from* and *teaching to* happen simultaneously. I have also learned that the role of a facilitator is not always to tie discussions up into nice, neat bows. It is more likely that learning will lean toward the exact opposite: messy and unfurled, leaving behind unanswered questions. Although I may not be leading the discussion, it is my responsibility to raise difficult questions and let them linger in the air, perhaps uncomfortably, while offering a safe space to interrogate ignorance of others' lived experiences in a way that society, fear, previous experiences, and political correctness will not allow.

In the classroom, this requires teachers to commit to transparency and honesty about what we know and what we do not know. As bell hooks explains, there is a greater need to explain philosophy and intent in a transformed classroom than in a "normal" setting.[26] In my experience, an admission to students that, as their teacher, I do not know hardly enough to be considered an "expert" on race and ethnicity allows them to be receptive to the idea that they, too, could stand to learn just a little bit more. At the same time that I admit my ignorance, I position myself as a critical scholar with interests related to race, ethnicity, and power. In addition, I share examples of my research and the work of other scholars with students to emphasize that my knowledge and my way of knowing do not exist in silos and will not be privileged in our learning. I explain that the way I view the world will filter the examples I choose in class and how I teach. But, and most importantly, I encourage students to seek out and share their own course-related material that represents their experiences and perspectives in the classroom discussion.

This form of co-teaching is one that Emdin posits as a way to reduce the tension that arises when there is a cultural misalignment between teachers and students.[27] It requires teachers to be transparent about the teaching process and its challenges, by exposing students to the larger contexts that influence teaching decisions. This approach shows students that there is something bigger influencing how I make decisions in the classroom—my course material, my language, and even my storytelling—and that *something* may serve as a blind spot or a tunnel focus that I am unaware of. Through doing this, I advise them that a failure to contribute their own "bigger picture" and simply relying upon my expertise will be a waste of a learning opportunity for us all. This reiterates hooks's notion that what happens in the classroom is a shared responsibility.[28]

Simply put, I've learned to begin with my students and to end with a judgment call. I routinely ask questions such as "What's important *to you*?," "What does this mean *to you*?," or "How does this resonate *with your experiences*?" Occasionally, I will ask students to put their thoughts in writing during moments of reflection, but most often we talk as a class or in small groups. Breakout groups are particularly useful as they allow each student the opportunity to speak with group members, collectively deciding among themselves on the most important point to bring to the attention of the class. As students discuss, I take notes, being mindful to connect what they deem important with key course concepts. As one might imagine, in communication studies courses my classroom conversations are particularly vulnerable to current events related to race and ethnicity, and I am diligent about creating organized opportunities to go *there*.

Whether I am allowing students to discuss a current event, a media artifact, or a tough concept explored in our text, one such organizing mechanism I employ is to place time limits on open discussion before we begin. That way, students have clear parameters for when we must move on (for the sake of classroom management) and are less likely to take the endings as dismissive or somehow undermining their contributions. Oftentimes, I enlist the help of a student as timekeeper, so that it is not me who brings a piqued discussion to an end. Another organizing mechanism is to offer a guide for the discussion, including clear parameters about the topics that are *not* to be discussed in the span of the class meeting. The sole goal of these strategies is to allow students to go *there* on their own, while I assist in unpacking their knowledge and curiosity in a productive way.

So far, this conglomeration of multiple pedagogies has been working for me. I have seen a turnaround in the way that I am able to tackle difficult conversations about race, ethnicity, identity, class, power, and more in the classroom. Most importantly, I have taken away from my public failure that classroom composition is just one component of being able to effectively teach—and learn—about race and ethnicity. The opportunities for dialogue are certainly vast, but the challenge becomes creating a safe space that encompasses mutual respect for different levels of comprehension and a common language for learning alongside each other, as opposed to privileging one vantage point. However, this dynamic must be recreated every semester, acknowledging that every classroom is different and no ordinary blueprint will suffice.[29] In this regard, I find that Emdin's charge to educators to optimize flexibility for students to contribute to their learning while avoiding a grand narrative should be revisited and put into practice for every class or lecture in which race and ethnicity becomes a focal point.

Although my campus can be classified as "urban," there is no one culture to refer to when developing a pedagogy for teaching race and ethnicity. Similar to what is occurring in college classrooms across the country, the notion of a "traditional" or "nontraditional" group of students has disappeared. In turn, there is no singular approach to exploring this often-precarious subject matter in the classroom. Multiple pedagogies are required.

The bottom line is, when it comes to how we individually conceive and experience race and ethnicity, we are all the "only." No one person has the same understanding, although certainly groups may have shared collective histories or similar experiences. By no means am I suggesting that instructors completely overhaul their teaching styles or pedagogical approaches that have been otherwise effective; rather, consider that, for this particular subject matter, it is imperative to radically shift our approach to teaching in such a way that it leaves room to account for—while not silencing, privileging, or exhibiting—the varied lived experiences and knowledges that students have regarding race and ethnicity. And, although I am sure there is much I have yet to learn, I share my experiences here with hopes that they may inform others' understanding of the need for new teaching practices in regard to this subject matter and, if at all possible, to prevent another promising teacher from experiencing the mental angst that comes along with "failing fast."

NOTES

1. Samuel Beckett, *Worstward Ho* (New York: Grove, 1983), n.p.

2. "College Scorecard: University of Houston–Downtown," US Department of Education, https://collegescorecard.ed.gov/school/?225432-University-of-Houston-Downtown, accessed January 23, 2018.

3. *University of Houston Downtown Fact Book 2016–2017* (Houston, TX: UHD Office of Institutional Research), https://www.uhd.edu/administration/institutional-research/Documents/Fact Book 2016--2017.pdf.

4. Felicia Lynne Harris, "Connecting the Dots: Touching the Interstices of Media Culture, Society and Self" (master's thesis, University of Georgia, 2012).

5. Elizabeth J. Tisdell, "Critical Media Literacy and Transformative Learning: Drawing on Pop Culture and Entertainment Media in Teaching for Diversity in Adult Higher Education," *Journal of Transformative Education* 6, no. 1 (2008): 48–67.

6. See Randall Kennedy, "Who Can Say 'Nigger'? And Other Considerations," *Journal of Blacks in Higher Education* 26 (1999): 86–96; Emily Bernard, "Teaching the N-Word: A Black Professor, an All-White Class, and the Thing Nobody Will Say," *American Scholar* 74, no. 4 (2005): 46–59.

7. See Nick Gass, "Obama Uses the N-Word in Podcast Interview," *Politico*, June 22, 2015, http://www.politico.com/story/2015/06/obama-n-word-marc-maron-interview-119272; "Cornel West Reacts to Obama's Usage of the N-Word," *CNN*, June 22, 2015, http://www.cnn.com/videos/world/2015/06/22/obama-podcast-n-word-cornell-west-intv-wrn.cnn.

8. A nod to the introductory text on pedagogy that was provided to all new faculty at my institution during new faculty orientation. See Ken Bain, *What the Best College Teachers Do* (Cambridge, MA: Harvard University Press, 2011).

9. Christopher Emdin, *For White Folks Who Teach in the Hood . . . and the Rest of Y'all Too: Reality Pedagogy and Urban Education* (New York: Beacon, 2016).

10. Gloria Ladson-Billings, "But That's Just Good Teaching! The Case for Culturally Relevant Pedagogy," *Theory into Practice* 34, no. 3 (1995): 159; Frances L. Hoffmann and Jayne E. Stake, "Feminist Pedagogy in Theory and Practice: An Empirical Investigation," *NWSA Journal* 10, no. 1 (1998): 79; Barry Kanpol, *Critical Pedagogy: An Introduction* (Westport, CT: Greenwood, 1999); Stephen Pew, "Andragogy and Pedagogy as Foundational Theory for Student Motivation in Higher Education," *InSight: A Collection of Faculty Scholarship* 2 (January 2007): 14–25.

11. Emdin, *For White Folks.*

12. Joseph P. Williams, "College of Tomorrow: The Changing Demographics of the Student Body," *U.S. News & World Report*, September 22,

2014, https://www.usnews.com/news/college-of-tomorrow/articles/2014/09/22/college-of-tomorrow-the-changing-demographics-of-the-student-body.

13. Gloria Ladson-Billings, "Toward a Theory of Culturally Relevant Pedagogy," *American Educational Research Journal* 32, no. 3 (1995): 465–91; Emdin, *For White Folks*, 27.

14. Gloria Ladson-Billings, "Culturally Relevant Pedagogy 2.0: a.k.a. the Remix," *Harvard Educational Review* 84, no. 1 (2014): 74–84.

15. Emdin, *For White Folks*, 27.

16. bell hooks, *Teaching to Transgress: Education as the Practice of Freedom* (New York: Routledge, 1994), 41.

17. Paulo Freire, *Pedagogy of the Oppressed* (New York: Bloomsbury, 2018), 45.

18. bell hooks, *Teaching Critical Thinking: Practical Wisdom* (New York: Routledge, 2009).

19. Donald Mitchell Jr., Tiffany Steele, Jakia Marie, and Kathryn Timm, "Learning Race and Racism While Learning: Experiences of International Students Pursuing Higher Education in the Midwestern United States," *AERA Open* 3, no. 3 (2017), https://doi.org/10.1177/2332858417720402.

20. Katie Reilly, "Donald Trump: All the Times He's Insulted Mexico," *Time*, August 31, 2016, http://time.com/4473972/donald-trump-mexico-meeting-insult.

21. hooks, *Teaching to Transgress*, 8.

22. Kelly Holland, "Why Americas Campuses Are Going Gray," *CNBC*, August 28, 2014, http://www.cnbc.com/2014/08/28/why-americas-campuses-are-going-gray.html.

23. "Characteristics of Postsecondary Students," National Center for Education Statistics (NCES), US Department of Education, https://nces.ed.gov/programs/coe/indicator_csb.asp, accessed June 16, 2017.

24. "Millennials in Adulthood," *Pew Research Center's Social & Demographic Trends Project*, March 6, 2014, http://www.pewsocialtrends.org/2014/03/07/millennials-in-adulthood.

25. Malcolm S. Knowles, Elwood F. Holton III, and Richard A. Swanson, *The Adult Learner: The Definitive Classic in Adult Education and Human Resource Development*, 8th ed. (New York: Routledge, 2015).

26. hooks, *Teaching to Transgress*, 42.

27. Emdin, *For White Folks*, 87.

28. hooks, *Teaching to Transgress*, 8.

29. hooks, *Teaching to Transgress*, 10–11.

BIBLIOGRAPHY

Bain, Ken. *What the Best College Teachers Do*. Cambridge, MA: Harvard University Press, 2011.

Beckett, Samuel. *Worstward Ho*. New York: Grove, 1983.

Bernard, Emily. "Teaching the N-Word: A Black Professor, an All-White Class, and the Thing Nobody Will Say." *American Scholar* 74, no. 4 (2005): 46–59.

"Characteristics of Postsecondary Students." National Center for Education Statistics (NCES), US Department of Education. Accessed June 16, 2017. https://nces.ed.gov/programs/coe/indicator_csb.asp.

"College Scorecard: University of Houston–Downtown." US Department of Education. Accessed January 23, 2018. https://collegescorecard.ed.gov/school/?225432-University-of-Houston-Downtown.

"Cornel West Reacts to Obama's Usage of the N-Word." *CNN*, June 22, 2015. http://www.cnn.com/videos/world/2015/06/22/obama-podcast-n-word-cornell-west-intv-wrn.cnn.

Emdin, Christopher. *For White Folks Who Teach in the Hood . . . and the Rest of Y'all Too: Reality Pedagogy and Urban Education*. New York: Beacon, 2016.

Freire, Paulo. *Pedagogy of the Oppressed*. New York: Bloomsbury, 2018.

Gass, Nick. "Obama Uses the N-Word in Podcast Interview." *Politico*, June 22, 2015. http://www.politico.com/story/2015/06/obama-n-word-marc-maron-interview-119272.

Harris, Felicia Lynne. "Connecting the Dots: Touching the Interstices of Media Culture, Society and Self." Master's thesis, University of Georgia, 2012.

Hoffmann, Frances L., and Jayne E. Stake. "Feminist Pedagogy in Theory and Practice: An Empirical Investigation." *NWSA Journal* 10, no. 1 (1998): 79–97.

Holland, Kelley. "Why America's Campuses Are Going Gray." *CNBC*, August 28, 2014. http://www.cnbc.com/2014/08/28/why-americas-campuses-are-going-gray.html.

hooks, bell. *Teaching Critical Thinking: Practical Wisdom*. New York: Routledge, 2009.

———. *Teaching to Transgress: Education as the Practice of Freedom*. New York: Routledge, 1994.

Kanpol, Barry. *Critical Pedagogy: An Introduction*. Westport, CT: Greenwood, 1999.

Kennedy, Randall L. "Who Can Say 'Nigger'? And Other Considerations." *Journal of Blacks in Higher Education* 26 (1999): 86–96.

Knowles, Malcolm S., Elwood Holton III, and Richard A. Swanson. *The Adult Learner: The Definitive Classic in Adult Education and Human Resource Development*. 8th ed. New York: Routledge, 2015.

Ladson-Billings, Gloria. "But That's Just Good Teaching! The Case for Culturally Relevant Pedagogy." *Theory into Practice* 34, no. 3 (1995): 159–65.

———. "Culturally Relevant Pedagogy 2.0: a.k.a. the Remix." *Harvard Educational Review* 84, no. 1 (2014): 74–84.

———. "Toward a Theory of Culturally Relevant Pedagogy." *American Educational Research Journal* 32, no. 3 (1995): 465–91.

"Millennials in Adulthood." *Pew Research Center's Social & Demographic Trends Project*, March 6, 2014. http://www.pewsocialtrends.org/2014/03/07/millennials-in-adulthood.

Mitchell, Donald Jr., Tiffany Steele, Jakia Marie, and Kathryn Timm. "Learning Race and Racism While Learning: Experiences of International Students Pursuing Higher Education in the Midwestern United States." *AERA Open* 3, no. 3 (2017). https://doi.org/10.1177/2332858417720402.

Pew, Stephen. "Andragogy and Pedagogy as Foundational Theory for Student Motivation in Higher Education." *InSight: A Collection of Faculty Scholarship* 2 (January 2007): 14–25.

Reilly, Katie. "Donald Trump: All the Times He's Insulted Mexico." *Time*, August 31, 2016. http://time.com/4473972/donald-trump-mexico-meeting-insult.

Taylor, Paul, Kim Parker, Rich Morin, Eileen Patten, and Anna Brown. "Millennials in Adulthood." Washington, DC: Pew Research Center, 2014. http://www.pewsocialtrends.org/2014/03/07/millennials-in-adulthood.

Tisdell, Elizabeth J. "Critical Media Literacy and Transformative Learning: Drawing on Pop Culture and Entertainment Media in Teaching for Diversity in Adult Higher Education." *Journal of Transformative Education* 6, no. 1 (2008): 48–67.

University of Houston Downtown Fact Book 2016–2017. Houston, TX: UHD Office of Institutional Research, 2017. https://www.uhd.edu/administration/institutional-research/Documents/Fact Book 2016--2017.pdf.

Williams, Joseph P. "College of Tomorrow: The Changing Demographics of the Student Body." *U.S. News & World Report*, September 22, 2014. https://www.usnews.com/news/college-of-tomorrow/articles/2014/09/22/college-of-tomorrow-the-changing-demographics-of-the-student-body.

CHAPTER 3

"BLACK RAGE"

Teaching Gender, Race, and Class in the Wake of #BlackLivesMatter and #SayHerName"

EMERALD L. CHRISTOPHER-BYRD

During the summer of 2015 I introduced a new course, Gender, Race, and Feminism. The intent of the course was to guide students to learn and demonstrate how social categories function to create and justify systems of advantage and disadvantage in society. While I was teaching the course, the Charleston shooting occurred and the story of Rachel Dolezal[1] broke the news. Students arrived to my class crying, some angry and others expressing their own individual experiences with racism and sexism. Some appeared to be physically overwhelmed and simply turned and asked me, "Professor, how do you feel?" At this moment I was confronted with being both an object and an agent of pedagogical practices. As a black woman teaching at a predominantly white institution, I spent an immense amount of time and energy suppressing my rage and distancing myself from my students. This functions as a continuation of pedagogical practices instilled to extend a hierarchal divide. This inevitably does a disservice to students, as I am not immune, nor is any instructor, to what happens in the world. It is at this point that I asked, and continue to ask, myself and my students, "What does our rage at injustice mean if it can be silenced, erased by individual material comfort?"[2]

Each semester I taught the course, further events led to more intense classroom discussions. In 2016, police officers killed more than 250 black Americans.[3] For those deaths, rarely were officers held judicially accountable. While each day brings a new social media spotlight on institutional and social racism, during 2016 the United States also witnessed one of the most contentious presidential campaigns and elections in modern politics. During the many conversations leading up to the election, gender, race, class, sexuality, and nation were both hypervisible and contentious. These conversations have been further aggravated with the confirmation of the forty-fifth president of the United States, Donald Trump. The political agenda of the forty-fifth presidential administration has resulted in a divisive sociopolitical environment. Although social media was saturated by coverage of protests and outrage around institutional violence, elected officials and political contenders have skirted around gender, class, and race relations in the United States or merely used them as political strategies for garnering electoral votes. At a time when the United States is experiencing a resurgence of white supremacist organizations and viral racial attacks, conversations have reemerged around the use of rage as a tool for social justice. Students are coming to classrooms wanting to know not only about theory but also how to apply that theory to action. Students are looking to transform their society utilizing the tools given in the classroom. Moreover, students have expressed physical and emotional distress as a result of the current sociopolitical climate. Whereas black rage has been taught to be repressed and suppressed, the following sections offer an analysis of the functions and manifestations of black rage in American society. Throughout my course I examine the various dimensions of rage as articulated by Shermaine Jones, rage as a moral imperative, as a philosophical principle governing behavior and conduct, and as a political strategy.[4] These functions become critical when exploring resolutions for racial injustices and inequalities. This chapter explores how reinterpreting historical moments, particularly by making bodies of knowledge produced by women of color, allows for a reinterpretation of rage.[5] Moreover, this chapter will demonstrate how rage can be used as a pedagogical tool to simultaneously destroy and construct.

BLACK RAGE AS A PEDAGOGICAL TOOL

With few exceptions, students are subjected to disciplinary pedagogy that defines black rage as "untutored anger [and] undisciplined emotion that cannot be contained."[6] Reinterpreting historical figures and contemporary events through texts and writings by women of color serves to offer students an expansion of rage. Therefore, I utilize black rage as a catalyst for the development of critical consciousness. Coming into critical consciousness by acknowledging rage moves students into growth and change while recognizing that rage is a necessary component of resistance. Writings from black feminists, Chicana studies, Latina testimonies, queer women of color, Native women, and Asian American women, to name a few, provides students with perspectives and knowledges that the "traditional" (i.e., white) canon of knowledge often excludes. Students are thus exposed to insights that challenge dominant interpretations of racial and social injustices. This becomes even more imperative because queer black women founded the Black Lives Matter movement and black women founded the Say Her Name movement. Though discussing black rage as a whole is imperative to understanding the experiences of black men and women in the United States, it is also important to note that oftentimes the voices and rage of black women are silenced due to the intersection of white supremacy and patriarchy.

In the anthology *All the Women Are White, All the Blacks Are Men, But Some of Us Are Brave*, the authors articulate the tradition of race being viewed as a discourse between men and feminism as a discourse between women, specifically white women. It is in this articulation and observation that the business of race fails to incorporate an analysis of gender. Historically and presently, when race is explored through the prism of gender, it is seen as "derailing the more important political discussion [of race], not adding a necessary dimension."[7] For this reason, exploring black rage through the necessary dimension of gender allows for a transformative articulation of black rage that closes critical gaps in vision and strategy. Specifically, women of color developed "intersectional analyses within social movement settings."[8] Presenting students with the multiple narratives of intersectionality through works by women of color demonstrates the ways in which this alliance of women engendered movements by calling attention to the intersections of race, class, gender, and sexuality in lived experiences.[9]

For instance, the Combahee River Collective (CRC) produced groundbreaking works analyzing the experiences of black women. The CRC sought to develop an analysis and practice that would address the interlocking oppressions of racism, sexism, heterosexuality, and class.[10] There was a need to develop politics that were "antiracist, unlike those of white women, and antisexist, unlike those of black and white men."[11]

Members of the CRC sought to transform society into one that would permit all people to live in full dignity. The anthology *This Bridge Called My Back: Writings by Radical Women of Color* features writings that demonstrate the use of affect by women of color before it became popularized by mainstream feminist thought. These writings provide a dimension of analysis for students that opens a different kind of critical literacy and knowledge. Although women of color have utilized affect in their writings for decades, overwhelmingly women and gender studies courses focus on affect as a theory without the narratives that exemplify the lived reality of affect for women of color. Affect has effectively been morphed and commodified and then situated as a generalized feminist theory absent of an intersectional analysis of race and gender. Moreover, courses focused on race overwhelmingly discuss affect in terms of race without an analysis of intersecting identities. Utilizing writings by women of color exposes students not only to affect theory but also to the implications of affect theory on women of color with intersecting identities. This literature allows students to take up work to build alternatives in addressing inequalities in radical ways, such as the use of rage.

Further, examining works by women of color provides a genealogy of intersectionality prior to Kimberlé Crenshaw coining the term in 1989. Women of color have analyzed the implications of intersecting identities, specifically the ways in which these impact lived experiences. Crenshaw extended these ideas by demonstrating the political and legal implications for women with intersecting identities. These political and legal implications directly impact the lived experiences discussed by women of color. Crenshaw's use of intersectionality marks all the ways women of color are erased in policy formation and the ways barriers for those marginalized are written into policy. While studying texts by women of color along with current events, students in my course explore the evolution of intersectionality from its use in identifying lived experiences and political and legal implications, to its use as a tool for analysis and a catalyst for change in social movements. Therefore, engaging students with writings from women of color allows for exposure to new forms of theories, including the literate body or embodiment of pedagogy that can begin when a student connects with the reading and writing practices of the author. It moves from the oversimplified gentrification of intersectionality to an exposure of the struggles of ideas by women of color and how these struggles are connected to their communities. The interaction that can happen between student and theory is a feminist practice that raises questions about the relations between body, consciousness, and theory.[12] This opens the possibility of cultural recognition rather than a blind acceptance of "the way things are."[13] For students of color, this approach allows exposure to writers that potentially relate to their positionality. While it is constructive to understand rage as an effective tool for healing, tapping into that rage might also result in feelings of fear. It forces students to confront past and present social conditions of black Americans, thereby forcing them out of ambivalence. These emotions have the potential to change one's relationship to the world. Rather than being ashamed of that rage, rather than attempting to silence or repress it, students can use that rage as a catalyst for the development of critical consciousness.

Throughout the course, students practice applying theory to current events as well as situated self-reflections. For instance, students practice deconstructing and disrupting their own textual knowledge of racial injustices through the use of metanarratives of women of color and through their own personal writings. One assignment, the politics of location paper, requires students to write a short autobiographical paper using gender, race, class, or sexuality (or other forms of identity) as the prism of ordering their thoughts. Students employ course readings and theoretical frameworks learned in class to analyze their social location. In addressing how their understandings of the world have formed based on their positionality, the students write their first draft at the beginning of the semester and then revisit the assignment incorporating the course material at the end of the semester. This self-reflexive activity, a hallmark of women's and gender studies, allows students to explore the impact racial injustices have had on them and/or how they may participate in the political system of white supremacy consciously or unconsciously.

In addition, the current political and racial climate plays a role in shaping students' understanding of racial and gender identity. Although the Black Lives Matter movement has been instrumental in bringing attention to racial injustice and police brutality, overwhelmingly narratives in the media focus on the experiences of black men. As noted by Crenshaw, the co-founder and executive director of the African American Policy Forum who coined the term *intersectionality*, ""Although black women are routinely killed, raped, and beaten by the police, their experiences are rarely foregrounded in popular understandings of police brutality. Yet, inclusion of black women's experiences in social movements, media narratives, and policy demands around policing and police brutality is critical to effectively combating racialized state violence for black communities and other communities of color."[14] Examining media narratives, specifically the creation of #SayHerName, along with theoretical perspectives on gender, race, and sexuality, exposes the nuanced relationships between women of color and their lived realities in the United States. #SayHerName sheds light on the ways in which the bodies and experiences of women of color are allowed in public discourse only when they serve the narrative of others.

A point stressed throughout the course is that these revelations are not meant to divide men and women of color. Rather, it is an acknowledgment that black women's bodies have been used and exploited in various ways to fit the interest of everyone but themselves. Social movements such as #SayHerName extend the concept and utilization of rage to include multiple identities. In addition to thinking about rage beyond an unadulterated and undisciplined concept, students examine rage using a gender and race frame of analysis that allows for the creation of social movements aimed at cultural, social, and political change and resistance.

THE FUNCTION AND REBIRTH OF BLACK RAGE

After the assassination of Rev. Dr. Martin Luther King Jr., William H. Grier and Price M. Cobbs published *Black Rage* in 1968. Written largely in response to the uprisings that ensued after the assassination, the authors focused on the psychic damage of racism that causes black anger. Through their analysis, Grier and Cobbs pathologized black anger by focusing on the psychological rather than the economic consequences of racism. As articulated by the authors, black rage is a reflection of the psychological tightrope formed by white oppression that black Americans must walk. Although Grier and Cobbs made a poignant argument that allowed a wide audience to see the psychological damage of racism, their approach to the subject reduced black rage to powerlessness. bell hooks argues that the assertions made by Grier and Cobbs "did not urge the larger culture to see black rage as something other than sickness."[15] Therefore, when invoked, black rage is merely seen as an inappropriate, and too often disproportionate, consequence of white supremacy.

Contrary to Grier and Cobbs's argument, black rage does not automatically suggest violence. Historical accounts of black rage might begin with Malcolm X's approach to white supremacy or "The Letter from a Birmingham Jail" written by Martin Luther King Jr.: black rage has long been utilized in various ways to confront the system of white supremacy.

However, that rage has been analyzed and even silenced by scholars and black thinkers. For instance, in *Race Matters*, Cornel West equates Malcolm X's rage with a defiance that was rooted in his love for black people.[16] In West's analysis, Malcom X's ultimate goal was to encourage other black Americans to feel the same rage in hopes that that rage would convert into black love for self. West argues that Malcolm X's dedication to black rage was debilitating for the activist. In other words, West views the use of black rage as a shortcoming of Malcolm X, and while he acknowledges that black rage was present in Malcolm X's platform and that his use of it was unprecedented, West nevertheless fails to explore how Malcolm X's rage is linked to a passion for justice.[17] By viewing Malcolm X's rage as a shortcoming, West denies the ability to use rage in multiple ways. Scholars such as West that articulate Malcolm X's rage as a shortcoming reflect an analysis of black rage as having no place in contemporary responses to racial injustices. Further, classroom settings that solely focus on the literary work by black men such as West fail to expose students to varied analysis and critiques. By contrast, hooks sees a "sacrificial mechanism" in this response from black scholars as a way of dismissing or silencing black rage in the name of attempts to garner dialogue with white leaders. In this sense, black leaders who advocate for the repression of rage are, in hooks's reading, complicit with America's long history of ignoring black Americans' rage.[18] For Malcolm X, his commitment to justice was a catalyst for his rage. Seeing it from a different perspective opens up the possibility of rage as a constructive mechanism and not a shortcoming.

In addition to Malcolm X, Rev. Dr. Martin Luther King Jr. is often described as a non-violent advocate in responding to racial injustice. If rage is seen as synonymous with violence, the work of Martin Luther King Jr. is often read to be without anger. In his "Letter from a Birmingham Jail" he states:

> We have waited for more than 340 years for our constitutional and God given rights. The nations of Asia and Africa are moving with jetlike speed toward gaining political independence, but we still creep at horse and buggy pace toward gaining a cup of coffee at a lunch counter. Perhaps it is easy for those who have never felt the stinging darts of segregation to say, "Wait." But when you have seen vicious mobs lynch your mothers and fathers at will and drown your sisters and brothers at whim; when you have seen hate filled policemen curse,

> kick and even kill your black brothers and sisters; when you see the vast majority of your twenty million Negro brothers smothering in an airtight cage of poverty in the midst of an affluent society . . . when you are forever fighting a degenerating sense of "nobodiness"—then you will understand why we find it difficult to wait.[19]

It is hard to read King's letter or to listen to many of his speeches today and not sense the anger and frustration he, and others, felt in addressing racial injustice, or more specifically, white supremacy. However, the most common approaches to teaching King's work invokes an idealized image of a "peaceful dreamer" that has essentially been whitewashed to be palatable for the masses.[20] Similarly, while King is exalted as the leader of the civil rights movement, others such as Rosa Parks have been celebrated for their involvement in resisting segregation laws of the Jim Crow era. However, primary school education often results in an abridged history of Parks' involvement in the civil rights movement. This history paints Parks as a quiet and meek figure that did not participate in the movement prior to the Montgomery Bus Boycott. However, contemporary research by women reveals the political symbolic positions King and Parks have been placed in as a maneuver for the masses to reject rage as a tool for change. Both King and Parks, as well as others, lived a life of resistance, and their passion for racial justice is reflected in their life's work. The depoliticized images of civil rights leaders such as King and Parks construct "a view of America as a postracial society."[21] Moreover, based on the political symbolic position Parks has been placed in, these images of her construct a "narrow, gendered vision" of the civil rights movement focused on a "not angry" ideology that serves the political interests of those who proclaim the United States is a post-racial and post-sexist society.

Having a great love for black people and a commitment to addressing racial injustices can in fact incorporate the use of rage as a catalyst for change. Black men and women are often conditioned to equate rage with violence and, as such, something that needs to be repressed. For instance, throughout history when white men and women in the United States respond to perceived tyranny, they are applauded and their rage is justified. Oftentimes, these "riots" are labeled as "rebellions." However, when black men and women respond to perceived racial injustice, their actions are characterized as "violent" or "resisting authority." It is for these reasons the term *uprising* is used. as it suggests that those participating are active agents in their response to the moment and their concerns should be taken seriously. In the wake of uprisings after the assassination of Dr. King, the acquittal of the officers who physically assaulted Rodney King,[22] and the uprisings in Ferguson, Missouri, and Baltimore, Maryland—to name a few—mass media has framed black rage with what bell hooks names "the underclass, with desperate and despairing black youth who in their hopelessness feel no need to silence unwanted passions."[23] As such, white Americans do not hear black rage as justifiable.

When our students learn that black rage is akin to violence and destruction, the frustration felt by black Americans often goes ignored. The analysis of black rage as unjustifiable is rooted in the political system of white supremacy. Part of the colonizing of black Americans' minds and bodies has included teaching black Americans to repress rage. Moreover, black Americans have been taught to avoid making white Americans the target of the anger that might be felt due to racism.[24] This embedded ideology becomes internalized and perpetuated in the black community as well. This furthers the importance of using rage as praxis while exploring the theoretical underpinnings of rage. Students thus gain a more nuanced understanding of rage as a catalyst for social change. For instance, black Americans were told to suppress their rage in order to survive slavery and the Jim Crow era. However, regardless of behavior, actions, or attire, racial violence still occurred, and therefore the roots of this violence should be explored on a deeper level. While it is often argued that overt racist systems of slavery and Jim Crow no longer exist, black Americans continue to live in a society where black men and women are murdered by white Americans as a way to express whites' rage. During the semester I created the course that focuses on social categories that justify systems of inequality, the 2015 mass shooting in Charleston, South Carolina, occurred. That shooting illustrates the corporeal vulnerability of black men and women as a result of white rage. Dylann Roof, a twenty-one-year-old self-proclaimed white supremacist, opened fire in the Emanuel African Methodist Episcopal Church. Roof published a personal manifesto online that detailed his racial hatred, and photos depicted him with white supremacist symbols. It was Roof's rage about race that led him to the shooting. Yet mass media covered the matter as Roof being mentally ill. Few media outlets addressed the concern around white rage as a marker for violence against black Americans. Rather than denouncing white supremacy, many news outlets focused on the alleged mental health issues of Roof. This is not the only incident throughout history that demonstrates the way in which white Americans kill black Americans to express their rage. Not only are there incidents in which this is the case, but it is often read as acceptable or condoned, whereas there is no place for black rage. The use of social media with the circulation of memes—iterations of discrimination under the guise of free speech—is a part of a toxic digital ecosystem that normalizes discrimination and perpetuates violence against men and women of color.

Rage seen as a factor of white supremacy is an embedded understanding among both white and black Americans. White supremacy is both an enactment and an unnamed political system that functions in the world.[25] Charles Mills conceives of white supremacy as a support of racial hatred. This unnamed political system of white supremacy is a racial contract, "not a contract between everybody, but between just the people who count, the people who really are people."[26] Charles Mills conceived of the racial contract as a conceptual bridge with white Americans and political philosophy on one side and non-whites (Native American, African American, third- and fourth-world people) and discussions of imperialism, colonialism, and racism, among others, on the other side. The failure of the US population to effectively name and acknowledge the role of white supremacy as Mills conceives it, in all facets of black Americans' experience, allows for the continued perpetuation of racist discourse and the repression or dismissal of black rage.

hooks extends Mills's notions of white supremacy with the phrase "imperialist white supremacist capitalist patriarchy."[27] The phrase describes a concept or a worldview that captures the interlocking forms of discrimination that impact lived realities, a complex of identities and structures that Jason Cohen's chapter also remarks on. These interlocking forms operate simultaneously and allow for a comprehensive understanding of realities without looking through one lens. The political system of an imperialist white supremacist capitalist patriarchy is rooted in history and has recently become more evident, despite claims for a post-racial society. After the fatal shooting of Trayvon Martin and the subsequent acquittal of George Zimmerman, black rage entered a new era. Black Americans once again witnessed another injustice fueled by perceptions of race. Following the death of Martin, black America witnessed the fatal shooting of Michael Brown by a white police officer in Ferguson, Missouri, in 2014; the death of Freddie Gray from injuries he sustained from an arrest and while in police custody in Baltimore, Maryland, in 2015; and the deaths of Alexia Christian, who was fatally shot after being handcuffed and put in the back of a police cruiser, and Meagan Hockaday, who was shot and killed by police officers when they responded to a domestic disturbance, to name a few. The Black Lives Matter and Say Her Name movements grew out of a response to state violence. The deaths of black men and women in the last several years demonstrate that no matter the behavior, location, or attire of a black man or woman, interlocking forms of domination in the form of state officials and vigilantes still permit the systemic killing of black men and women. Today black rage is focused on institutional racism and, at its best, black rage radically critiques the system of racism held up by an imperialist white supremacist capitalist patriarchy. Seeing black rage and its manifestations through a process of learning allows students to see the ways in which black rage critiques social and political institutions that are built and supported by an imperialist white supremacist capitalist patriarchy, thereby causing black Americans to live in an unjust society. While witnessing viral racist attacks, the rise in white supremacist organizations, and the systematic deaths of black men and women by the state, black individuals and their allies have lost whatever apathy they once had.

As an educator I strive to expose students to knowledge beyond that of scholarly textbooks. My goal throughout my course is to teach an oppositional worldview different from that of oppressors. Using rage as a pedagogical tool enables students to critically and analytically see the world and themselves through a different lens. While there are those that purport to know which affective response is most effective in addressing racism and injustice, history and contemporary events can and have shown the potential and efficacy of rage as a tool for addressing racial injustices and responding to the construction of an imperialist white supremacist capitalist patriarchy in the United States. Understanding the ideology behind rage and its multiple functions allows for rage to be used as a pedagogical tool. Viewing it as a tool, students are able to see various iterations of resistance and responses to racial and gender injustice without discounting moments based on mass-mediated labels that dismiss rage as an instrumental component of progress.

THE FUTURES OF BLACK RAGE

Although the 2016 presidential election and inauguration of the forty-fifth president of the United States marks a historic moment in the resurgence of resistance, the issues of race and gender injustice precede the forty-fifth president and will likely continue after his tenure. There is a larger history of black rage in the United States that shifts based on the sociopolitical climate of the time. This chapter is focused largely on the Black Lives Matter and Say Her Name movements. The future of black rage will undoubtedly continue with these movements, but it has also been used in reflecting on the progress of movements that don't explicitly use race as a frame of analysis. For instance, in 2017 Alyssa Milano, a white American actress, encouraged people on Twitter to tweet #MeToo: "If all the women who have been sexually harassed or assaulted wrote 'Me too' as a status, we might give people a sense of the magnitude of the problem."[28] Milano's tweet resulted in the hashtag #MeToo, and within days, millions of men and women began to share their stories of sexual assault and harassment. However, the phrase "Me Too" was created in 2006 by Tarana Burke, an African American activist. Burke created the phrase in an effort to bring attention to sexual abuse in marginalized communities. The pervasiveness of sexual abuse in the United States has resulted in a resurgence of rage among women. As a result of the viral hashtag, a movement was created. This movement began to hold high-profile men such as Harvey Weinstein, Bill Cosby, and Kevin Spacey, to name a few, accountable for sexual abuse.

The viral #MeToo movement has justifiably allowed women to rage against the everyday sexism and harassment they experience. However, there is a glaring gap in the demographic of women who are able to express their rage. The stories of those who are most vulnerable, those who are the most marginalized, are rarely the stories featured on media outlets. Moreover, they are rarely the cases in which the perpetrator is held accountable. Although Milano later became aware of the history of the phrase and Burke has been credited with beginning the movement, the ability of black women and others from marginalized communities to express their rage about sexual harassment and abuse is still a work in progress. The precedent set by the Black Lives Matter and Say Her Name movements gives room for the future possibilities of movements such as Me Too.

Intentionally or unintentionally, contemporary activists have used rage as a catalyst to bring attention to social injustices. The use of rage today is a continuation of rage used by black historical figures. For some, their rage has been either silenced or deemed a character flaw. At its core, black rage presents a case of racial injustice before the nation's conscience. The deaths of Trayvon Martin, Freddie Gray, Sandra Bland, and other black men and women are both bodily sacrifices and a symbolic call to action. Their deaths serve as a symbolic function to "awaken the conscience of the nation."[29] In the current sociopolitical climate, the rage experienced and expressed by black men and women is rooted in a continued history and system of white supremacy. This is evident in the ways in which the viral murders of black men and women today have relevance when considering the words of King in his "Letter from a Birmingham Jail": "We present our very bodies as a case before the nation." It is the very bodies of black men and women that continue to set the case for responding to racial injustice and white supremacy.

Seeing black rage beyond the interpretations of violence illuminates racial injustice in different ways. Specifically, black rage demonstrates how white supremacy has upheld institutions of oppression that have participated in creating disadvantages for black men and women. The uprisings from the past and present have drawn attention to injustice and have driven people to act. Public expressions of black rage have shown others that what they are feeling is not isolated and validate their feelings.

The movement known across the country and the world as Black Lives Matter has pushed an agenda to address police violence. The Say Her Name movement has fought for the recognition of police violence against black women. When black rage is recognized and utilized, movements are formed and action is taken. Black rage is Fannie Lou Hamer stating, "I'm sick and tired of being sick and tired" at the Democratic National Convention in 1964; black rage gives room for Audre Lorde in 1981 to say, "My fear of anger taught me nothing. Your fear of that anger will teach you nothing also"; black rage announces itself in response to Pepsi's 2017 commercial that whitewashed the experiences of Ieshia Evans, black rage brought Angela Peoples to the January 2017 Women's March with a sign that read, "Don't forget: white women voted for Trump"; and black rage brings students across the country to protest racism and discrimination on their college campuses. When the uses and reasons of black rage are taught, black rage can be used as a catalyst for change. Sometimes it is just a matter of recognizing the moments that spark action.

NOTES

1. Rachel Dolezal was the president of the NAACP chapter of Spokane, Washington. In 2015 her birth parents revealed to the media that Dolezal was born white but was passing as black. Dolezal eventually revealed she was born white but identifies as black.

2. bell hooks, *Killing Rage: Ending Racism* (New York: Henry Holt, 1995), 19.

3. "The Counted: People Killed by Police in the U.S.," *Guardian*, https://www.theguardian.com/us-news/ng-interactive/2015/jun/01/the-counted-police-killings-us-database.

4. Shermaine M. Jones, "Presenting Our Bodies, Laying Our Case: The Political Efficacy of Grief and Rage During the Civil Rights Movement in Alice Walker's *Meridian*," *Southern Quarterly* 52, no. 1 (Fall 2014): 183.

5. For the purpose of this chapter, the use of rage operates as an extension of Dan T. Carter's *The Politics of Rage: George Wallace, the Origins of the New Conservatism and the Transformation of American Politics* and Carol Anderson's *White Rage: The Unspoken Truth of Our Racial Divide*. Where Carter and Anderson focus on the historic construction and integration of white rage into political institutions, this chapter interrogates the systematic upholding of white rage and the justification of its use while the devaluing, criminalizing, and disregard of black rage is upheld socially and politically.

6. Jones, "Presenting Our Bodies," 183.

7. hooks, *Killing Rage*, 2.

8. Patricia Hill Collins and Sirma Bilge, *Intersectionality* (Hoboken, NJ: John Wiley & Sons, 2016), 65.

9. Hill Collins and Bilge, *Intersectionality*, 71.

10. Combahee River Collective, "A Black Feminist Statement," in *Feminist Theory Reader*, ed. Carole McCann and Seung Kyung Kim (New York: Routledge, 1982), 106.

11. Combahee River Collective, "A Black Feminist Statement," 107.

12. Terry Threadgold, "Everyday Life in the Academy: Postmodernist Feminisms, Generic Seductions, Rewriting and Being Heard," in *Feminisms and Pedagogies of Everyday Life*, ed. Carmen Luke (Albany: State University of New York Press, 1996), 280.

13. Anneliese Kramer-Dahl, "Reconsidering the Notions of Voice and Experience in Critical Pedagogy," in Luke, *Feminisms and Pedagogies of Everyday Life*, 242.

14. The African American Policy Forum, "#SayHerName: Resisting Police Brutality against Black Women," July 2015, https://aapf.org/sayhernamereport.

15. bell hooks, *Killing Rage*, 12.

16. Cornel West, *Race Matters* (New York: Beacon, 2000), 151.

17. West, *Race Matters*, 151.

18. bell hooks, *Killing Rage*, 12.

19. Rev. Dr. Martin Luther King Jr., "Letter from a Birmingham City Jail," 1963, in hooks, *Killing Rage*.

20. Mychal Denzel Smith, "The Function of Black Rage," *The Nation*, April 1, 2014, https://www.thenation.com/article/archive/function-black-rage.

21. Jeanne Theoharis, *The Rebellious Life of Mrs. Rosa Parks* (New York: Beacon, 2015), 241.

22. On March 3, 1991, officers from the Los Angeles Police Department were engaged in a high-speed car chase that ended with a witness filming the officers repeatedly beating King. The officers were charged with assault with a deadly weapon and use of deadly force. Despite the video footage, all of the officers involved were acquitted due to the jury being deadlocked. Following the acquittal of the officers, uprisings broke out across Los Angeles, with the National Guard eventually becoming involved.

23. hooks, *Killing Rage*, 12.

24. hooks, 12.

25. Charles W. Mills, *The Racial Contract* (Ithaca, NY: Cornell University Press, 2014), 1.

26. Mills, *Racial Contract*, 3.

27. bell hooks, *The Will to Change: Men, Masculinity, and Love* (New York: Simon and Schuster, 2004), 17.

28. Alyssa Milano (@Alyssa_Milano), "If you've been sexually harassed or assaulted," Twitter, October 15, 2017, https://twitter.com/Alyssa_Milano/status/919659438700670976.

29. Jones, "Presenting Our Bodies," 187.

BIBLIOGRAPHY

Combahee River Collective. "A Black Feminist Statement." In *Feminist Theory Reader*, edited by Carole McCann and Seung Kyung Kim, 106–7. New York: Routledge, 1982.

Grier, William H., and Price M. Cobbs. *Black Rage*. Eugene, OR: Wipf and Stock, 2000.

Hill Collins, Patricia, and Sirma Bilge. *Intersectionality*. Hoboken, NJ: John Wiley & Sons, 2016.

hooks, bell. *Killing Rage: Ending Racism*. New York: Henry Holt, 1995.

hooks, bell. *Talking Back: Thinking Feminist, Thinking Black*. Boston: South End Press, 1989.

hooks, bell. *The Will to Change: Men, Masculinity, and Love*. New York: Simon and Schuster, 2004.

Jones, Shermaine M. "Presenting Our Bodies, Laying Our Case: The Political Efficacy of Grief and Rage During the Civil Rights Movement in Alice Walker's Meridian." *Southern Quarterly* 52, no. 1 (Fall 2014): 179–95.

Kramer-Dahl, Anneliese. "Reconsidering the Notions of Voice and Experience in Critical Pedagogy." In *Feminisms and Pedagogies of Everyday Life*, edited by Carmen Luke, 242–62. Albany: State University of New York Press, 1996.

Mills, Charles W. *The Racial Contract*. Ithaca, NY: Cornell University Press, 2014.

Smith, Mychal Denzel. "The Function of Black Rage." *The Nation*, April 1, 2014. https://www.thenation.com/article/archive/function-black-rage.

Smith, Mychal Denzel. "The Rebirth of Black Rage: From Kanye to Obama, and Back Again." *The Nation* 301, nos. 9–10 (2015): 28–33.

Theoharis, Jeanne. *The Rebellious Life of Mrs. Rosa Parks*. New York: Beacon, 2015.

Threadgold, Terry. "Everyday Life in the Academy: Postmodernist Feminisms, Generic Seductions, Rewriting and Being Heard." In *Feminisms and Pedagogies of Everyday Life*, edited by Carmen Luke, 280–314. Albany: State University of New York Press, 1996.

West, Cornel. *Race Matters*. New York: Beacon, 2000.

CHAPTER 4

CAN THE WHITE BOY SPEAK?

Coming to Terms with the Color-Blind Li(n)e

DOUGLAS ELI JULIEN

I have a great relationship with the blacks. I've always had a great relationship with the blacks.

—Donald Trump, TALK 1300, April 14, 2011

Here, an interpretation that surprises presupposes violence with regard to the conscious signatory of the poem: you meant what you did not know you wanted to say; you will have said more than you think or something other than you think. That is what analysis is, be it deconstructive or not. You said something you did not think you said or that you did not mean to say. It is violent, that's true.

—Jacques Derrida, "The Truth that Wounds"

I am very proud now that we have a museum on the National Mall where people can learn about Reverend King, so many other things. Frederick Douglass is an example of somebody who's done an amazing job and is being recognized more and more, I notice—Harriet Tubman, Rosa Parks, and millions more black Americans who made America what it is today. Big impact.

—Donald Trump, remarks on
Black History Month, February 2, 2017

Big impact. Well before Donald Trump's turn to politics, when in the classroom addressing issues of race, I sought a big impact and accomplished little more than confirmation of previously held beliefs. I thought myself capable of evading the trap of language Derrida exposes in "The Truth that Wounds." I sutured the wound, believing I was neither providing evidence of my own existent racial bias as Trump does nor resting in the limited, divisive logic of interpretation stemming from Trump-like comments that are by no means confined to his regime or recent history—Trump's comments, and by extension Trump, are or are not racist. I hoped to be a part of the struggle wrestling the damaging, culturally constructed concept of race to the ground, forcing it from thought and language, and rendering it simply a marker of past transgressions against a common humanity. What actually transpired was that the discussion stagnated as soon as it began. My evasion of bias and lack of vulnerability also attempted to evade the violence of interpretation. Reading through the chapters in this collection makes clear there is no one way to teach race correctly, nor is there one way to do it wrong. Thankfully, the collection also makes it clear the work of teaching race is necessary, worth it, and contributing to the education of our students. We need the violence of interpretation teaching in the era of Trump.

In other words, if I profess a necessity in aligning myself in the classroom with Derrida, including his ideas in his 1985 text "Racism's Last Word" and in his 1986 text "But Beyond . . . (Open Letter to Anne McClintock and Rob Nixon)," such an alignment entails a certain cost, including the admonishment Derrida has for his interlocutors: "Don't separate word and history!"[1] "Race" itself is an artifice and not a scientific category—it is even a relatively recent invention. This declaration, however, does nothing to deny the word's invention, persistence, or power over time. If I am aligned with Derrida in this regard, I also find myself implicitly aligned with Trump, my fellow Americans, and my students. I call to memory the concept of race in my classroom in assignments and stand in the way of locating race as simply a problem Trump and his supporters possess in this moment of history. In doing so, I must also call to memory and recognize my own participation in what was and remains a decidedly racist culture in order to effectively "call to struggle but also to memory."[2]

This volume represents a series of moments that worked and moments that did not. If I speak of the memory of past "failures," my determination here is not to speak of unprecedented success following a change. Rather, it is to insist upon a hermeneutic opening the possibility for success—an ethics of reading, discussing, and writing about race: a call to struggle. In the same manner I struggle in classroom discussions and on the page with the student who would insist that "white men are the most persecuted group in America" (this exact phrasing came from a student the first day of class after Trump's election; though perhaps not so simply stated, such a feeling emerged long before Trump and will persist beyond his term in office), I need to struggle with the student insisting that racism is located somewhere out there, over there, and in the other when they insist "Trump has created racial division in America" (another exact phrasing). I attempt to bring my students to understand the vulnerability in refusing the ability to separate the word from history. I myself remain vulnerable; remaining vulnerable means that my interpretation here and in the classroom is never closed nor completed—meaning never fully exhausted. Ethically and violently, I leave open the wound of interpretation, the existence of another reading, and the persistence of the memory. I let the other speak and the other in me speak: speaking while allowing the other to speak and speak for me—not remaining silent nor imposing silence. Teaching something to my students but also something to myself.

AN INACCESSIBLE SECRET[3]

My students' responses to race in class discussions always seemed to fit a neat, orderly pattern regardless of where my travels took me: from the public land-grant University of Minnesota to the smaller satellite of the University of Minnesota in Morris, Minnesota, to the private for-profit Brown College in the Twin Cities to the small public Bradley University to my current location in the A&M System at Texas A&M University–Texarkana. Throughout the essay, I point to students' comments and know exactly where I was and who the students were that I am quoting and paraphrasing. I am not labeling the where and when. One issue that participating in and reading through this collection makes clear is that neither the particular student demographics nor the size or prestige of university makes a significant difference; this conversation on race begs for attention across the country. The vast majority of my students across this time and space, unless offering outrage at historical figures and characters, sat in a certain nervous silence—well trained by culture to recognize the awfulness of the past but uncertain about what could be done or how to speak without indicating their own racial biases in the present. A smaller segment of students responded to issues of race feeling they themselves had transcended the terrible logic of race and cast aspersions upon the fictional characters in my American and world literature survey classes while remaining ready to extend those critiques to their classmates should their peers' language fail them. Eventually, in the midst of these two positions, what often emerged after the transcendent students had their say were two other responses. The first was the insistence that their generation, unlike the characters we study, was free from racist beliefs; as good citizens of a post-racial world, they were simply waiting for the last racist from the prior generation to die. The second took the form of a student eventually emerging and declaring, in Trump-like fashion, that he didn't understand what the fuss was all about because we are all equal: minorities are always and adequately being recognized for their accomplishments, and the student himself "has plenty of black friends." Such announcements, occurring during interactions within and beyond the classroom in modes that Felicia Harris's chapter investigates, were greeted with groans, the notion that "there is always that one guy," and regardless of efforts made to discuss more, the comment was dismissed as anomalous. This list of responses could be longer and more nuanced, but all of the classroom discussions suffered from the same complex of fears bound up with personal vulnerability and an avoidance of the violence bound up in the interpretation of racial bodies and selves. No one wanted to own any racial bias or keep the wound open other than locating bias out there in someone else, in an other.

THE OTHER IS SECRET[4]

Certainly there were breakthrough moments throughout the years, and some classes yielded more sustained discussions, but for the most part, they failed to generate a big impact and stagnated along typical lines. Discussions with colleagues over the years at these various institutions and entering into a conversation with these assembled texts embolden me now to say that anyone who has taught undergraduate students has seen this transaction and the retreat from the face of difficulty, but it is instructive to "watch" it and suggest how it could play differently. When Trump made his comments about "the blacks," the media buzzed about his comments. Looking back at some of these, I was particularly struck when watching the discussion on the now defunct-MSNBC show *Jansing and Co.* hosted by Chris Jansing: it was like watching the discussions from my classrooms throughout the years.

Jansing brought Karen Hunter and Pat Buchanan on her show to discuss the rise in popularity of Donald Trump. She began the segment talking about Trump's participation in the birther arguments against then President Obama before introducing Trump's comments. Hunter immediately performed the role of the transcendent student: "The blacks . . . oh . . . some of my best friends are blacks . . . oh, you people . . . oh, that one. Donald, [Jansing interrupts with "the"] why didn't you just say all of that?" Jansing then chimed in, reiterating the offending language with "the blacks." Hunter continued, "The blacks . . . yeah . . . the black ties . . . being in the black . . . he loves that [laughs]. No, actually, being one of the blacks, I can tell you clearly, Chris, he does not have a great relationship with the blacks." From this point Hunter discussed the Central Park jogger rapist trial and the ad Trump took out calling for the death penalty of the black youths who were later exonerated for the crime.[5]

I want to isolate Hunter's nod to the idea that this statement is racist and, by extension, so is Donald Trump—though she never explicitly says Trump is a racist. Trump, to Hunter, is behaving in bad faith referring to "the blacks" and through his actions regarding the Central Park case. However, she cannot prove with certainty that he or is not racist. No one could. The best she can do is talk around the idea that "the blacks" is a distancing rhetorical device using the definite article "the," and she should. In the classroom, this was always where I drew the line. It is an easy line to draw and feel effective in battling, at the least, racist sentiment. But this line of difference drawn as Trump often does discussing blacks, Hispanics, gays, Muslims, or groups other than whites contains something more than Trump intends and something now essential to my classroom discussions: Trump is quite correct about the distance in ways I do not presume that he intends. It does not, however, make him any less correct.

While less right about others, in relation to black-white relations in America, Trump's language also points to an actual physical distance. A Brookings Institution study about racial segregation published in 2015 pointed to a "modest decline" in black-white segregation, but

> a standard measure of segregation indicates the percentage of blacks that would have to change neighborhoods to match the distribution of whites. It ranges from zero (complete integration)

> to 100 (complete segregation). When applied to the nation's 52 largest metropolitan areas with at least 20,000 black residents most show segregation levels between 50 and 70 (see Map). While far below the nearly apartheid racial separation that existed for much of the nation's history, these are still high measures—more than half of blacks would need to move to achieve complete integration.[6]

The use of the term "the blacks" isn't merely about an attempt to distance, a potential suggestion of racism in Trump's beliefs. It points exactly to the historical racial distance and ongoing racist landscape of America. Trump's comments absolutely others black folk, a point necessary to make, but so does the society at large. This is not to exonerate Trump or his comments; rather, it seeks to prevent the wound from being sutured with the notion that it is Donald Trump alone who behaves as a racist.

We should stand behind our ethics and attack Trump for racist sentiment and rhetoric, as so many in this collection do in their classrooms. However, occupying this position alone opens the door for a stagnant classroom discussion where the order of the day is confirming prior belief, which is exactly where the discussion headed on the show. After referencing how Trump is enjoying being at the height of publicity, Pat Buchanan tackled the statement "but I don't find any malice in what he said with that statement about the black folks. I mean I'm a Catholic and if he said I have a great relationship with the Catholics, I don't think I'd take great offense."[7] One might note that Buchanan, a more careful speaker and pundit, avoided saying "the blacks" and instead offered "the black folks." Equally important though is that Buchanan moves exactly where "that guy" of the classroom would go: "Where is the offense?" Or simply, "He's not racist."

Hunter tried to insert an explanation but rested in thinly defined difference: "Oh Pat, you know it's completely different . . . it's a completely different dynamic. Gimme a break." What Hunter lacks is why it is different. It is one of power, of in-group and out-group, but it also immediately recalls our segregated society that is unequally segregated in favor of white folks. Hunter's inability to articulate anything other than difference led Buchanan to seize on the necessarily incomplete sense of bad faith:

> BUCHANAN: Well, I mean, what do you think he meant? Did he . . . dislikes them? Or . . . I mean, I don't. . . . Where's the malice in what he said?

HUNTER: No, but I mean, it's . . . It's a . . . It's a pand . . . It's a pandering . . . kind of undermining . . . uh, kind of, uh . . . you know . . . pat on the head. Well, you know. It's . . . It's that thing. You people.

BUCHANAN: Well [laughs].

HUNTER: We're not aliens. We're Americans.

BUCHANAN: [Laughs] Well maybe you're hearing something that Donald Trump really didn't say.

JANSING: Well, we will let everyone, um, make their, uh, own decision about this, but I think that you can listen to it, and it's very clear what the Donald had to say.[8]

Buchanan immediately turns to the unprovable secret. However, instead of working through the impossibility of the proof that can never be adequate, Buchanan returns to that which "Donald Trump didn't really say" and points the discussion toward deciding if he is or he isn't a racist. "That thing" Hunter could discuss is the racial segregation of America.

One can say this is why the media fails at a dialogue on race, but is it really so different than a classroom setting? In the aftermath of Trump's campaign and election, this style of conversation occurred in my own classroom multiple times with results similar to Jansing's rejoinder: the students left confirmed in their own prior decision. Since Trump's election and our seemingly ever-increasingly polarized world, the Trump folk were left believing in Buchanan and the anti-Trump in Hunter and Jansing. Ethically articulating the impossibility of knowing and then turning to the truth of racial segregation turns the discussion toward American racial bias and racism.

AN OVERABUNDANCE OF MEANING[9]

No one wants to be labeled a racist and to recognize the overabundance of meaning in our language pointing to the racism of our culture. No one wants to acknowledge racism in his or her own thought and action. Everyone knows to swear allegiance to being color-blind. Yet anyone who reads the works collected here recognizes color-blindness is far from the truth. I could simply point to my fellow authors' texts as proof. But here let me list some of the more effective pieces of evidence I use in my classroom to cut against the notion of a color-blind society. We live in a world where it is common knowledge that employers are more likely to turn away job seekers if they have black-sounding names. It is common knowledge that black men are more likely to go to prison and will serve longer terms than the smaller number of white counterparts who are convicted of the same crimes. Even in preschool, black students are punished more often and severely than their white peers. Our geographic segregation in regions and cities produces school segregation and disparate learning conditions as minorities attend the poorest school systems. The list could continue, but it hardly seems necessary. These are truths we have been aware of since the civil rights era. We are a part of these truths. Yet, as essays in this collection by Rachel Roegman and Serena J. Salloum, as well as by Shane A. McCoy, show, we swear our allegiance to a color-blind society and our own color-blindness. I recently gave a talk about race at the Texarkana Public Library, and one of the audience members complained: "You know the worst thing about people claiming to be color-blind? You can't say nothing to them. They aren't listening."

AN EXCESS[10]

As the audience member's comment suggests, we have become so certain in our color-blind belief that we actually believe our own lie and have stopped listening for an excess of meaning. Time and again researchers point to the need for implicit race bias tests to find the truth of our beliefs. This is not information bound behind the ivory towers of academia; these studies appear in mainstream newspapers and magazines—a constant reminder that we are not as color-blind as we propose. Indicative of this is a piece from *U.S. News & World Report*: "Dozens of national polls in America during the past two decades consistently show more than three-quarters of us don't believe we have a problem with racial tension in America. Fewer and fewer Americans openly admit that they're racist, these polls have shown for years. But a more nuanced study conducted by the National Opinion Research Center at the University of Chicago found that many Americans still do, in fact, harbor beliefs about racial and ethnic minorities that are based on racist stereotypes."[11] If we have reached the point of educating folks that the problem of the twentieth century was the color line, then the problem of the twenty-first century seems to be the ideology of color-blindness masking systemic institutional and cultural racism: the color-blind lie. My students always tackled issues of race, but when they did, what they arrived at was predominantly an artful dodge of "I can't believe how 'they' treated minorities." "They did" in the past stood in for a silent "we do not" in the present and a return to previously held positions. Without being called to be vulnerable to our own implicit bias and attuned to the irreducibility of meaning, the conversation stagnates.

MAKE MYSELF LISTEN[12]

What is witnessed in college classes, this implicit bias, is possibly threatened with a change in the era of Trump. BuzzFeed News, in conjunction with the Documenting Hate project, conducted the first nationwide study of its kind on reports of bullying connected to Trump's language during the campaign and the beginning of his presidency. Reporters Albert Samaha, Mike Hayes, and Talal Ansari declare that "Donald Trump's campaign and election have added an alarming twist to school bullying, with white students using the president's words and slogan to bully Latino, Middle Eastern, black, Asian, and Jewish classmates."[13] The BuzzFeed News report does not pretend to be more than it is: a bellwether of a political storm on the rise. However, Samaha, Hayes, and Ansari understand that "with so many recent examples of racist beliefs leading to violence, the verbal abuse in schools stands out not just as an example of kids testing boundaries, but as a possible window into a disturbing future." Though not conclusive or determined, it appears the college classroom will bring a different violence in the near future.

It seems the nation is divided and undergoing trauma stemming from the campaign and election of Donald Trump. The *New England Journal of Medicine* also sought to explain this and cast a wider net around the nation by reaching back to the Obama presidency specifically in terms of race, but also with the effects of nationally traumatic experiences well before Obama's election. In doing so, they pick up the threads of the BuzzFeed study and extend beyond the K–12 environment into society at large: "At the same time, events linked to the recent presidential campaign and election have given rise to fear and anxiety in many Americans. Research suggests that these events can have negative health effects on people who have been direct targets of what they perceive as hostility or discrimination and on individuals and communities who feel vulnerable because they belong to a stigmatized, marginalized, or targeted group."[14] From this, Williams and Medlock advance the notion that it is "worth examining" the health effect on the American population. However, while explicit targeting of individuals and communities may be rising, it is false to suggest that the feeling of being stigmatized and marginalized, particularly among black folk, began with Trump. Before Trump's ascension, the Pew Research Center found, "Blacks, far more than whites, say black people are treated unfairly across different realms of life, from dealing with the police to applying for a loan or mortgage. And, for many blacks, racial equality remains an elusive goal."[15] The actual numbers are alarming: 88 percent of blacks believe that changes are needed for equality while 43 percent are skeptical that a change will ever occur. Among whites, only 53 percent believe changes are necessary and only 11 percent are skeptical about the possibility of those changes. If Trump exposed racial bias and racism in the here and now, if we listen, we will hear that his rhetoric only confirms what black folks have been telling America for years. Attributing the trauma to Trump's campaign and election only points to how white folks dominate the narrative. One must remain cognizant of these numbers when discussing race in the classroom.

LETTING THE OTHER SPEAK[16]

This twenty-first-century task of reaching past the color-blind li(n)e and unlearning implicit racism is located in attempting to disrupt the narrative refusal of "they" and adopting an ethics of interpretation that allows for the violence of leaving the wound open and for something else to emerge. The first time through a new version of my American literature syllabus that added Toni Morrison's "Recitatif," I failed to recognize the discussion had stagnated as my students read and responded to Kate Chopin's "Désirée's Baby" and Zora Neale Hurston's "Sweat." It felt like we were working through a meaningful discussion of the texts and race in America. It seemed they were quick to respond both emotionally and intellectually to the texts and write freely about the problems of race. It was not until later that I realized I was not doing my duty.

This failure in duty emerged as they read and wrote about "Recitatif." My writing assignments in these introductory, general education literature classes are a mixture of writing and drawing. Students are asked to select a remarkable passage from the text and draw it as completely and detailed as possible. Their paper then becomes a discussion of the details of their drawing and how those details contribute to the meaning of the passage and the theme of the text as a whole. In this manner, they learn to close-read and explicate passages. I had just finished viewing and reading excellent drawings and papers on the concept of race in Chopin's and Hurston's work and was looking forward to seeing what they would produce in regard to Morrison's text. Instead, they found themselves at a loss, as I was with them.

Some students attempted to draw a passage without either Twyla or Roberta, but most chose to draw one of the characters as white and the other black. Most of my students could not shake the belief that they could not ever know which character was not white, or in a text actively seeking to remove racial codes, that neither is necessarily white. They spent significant time arguing for one or another race and never truly gave up the fight. The confidently color-blind class struggled to come to grips with the fact that they hold the belief that knowing the color of an individual's skin will tell them something very important about that individual. The prejudice found in that belief quickly bent toward racism the moment it became clear they favored the character they believed to be the white character. My pedagogy now searches for a means to bring a class to this reckoning well before Morrison, so it can be a sustained discussion of the twenty-first-century problem of the color-blind li(n)e.

NOT TO REMAIN TOO SILENT[17]

I came to realize that my students reacted to "Désirée's Baby" in a very personal way. They engaged with Chopin early and grappled with Désirée's question to Armand: "Look at our child. What does it mean? Tell me."[18] They wanted the answer. They reacted to the explicit racism of Armand and became angry at him for his treatment of Désirée and the slaves under his thumb. They wondered about Désirée's fate: "Does 'she did not come back again' on the last page mean what I think it means?" They reveled in the turn of the story when it is revealed that it is Armand's mother who "belongs to the race that is cursed with the brand of slavery."[19] This reading was fair and understandable but captured only the surface of the text. It was easy outrage. I needed a way to get them to truly listen to the text's insistence against purity and biological categorization. I now pair Chopin with a piece from Robert Wald Sussman: a readily accessible extract from his book *The Myth of Race: The Troubling Persistence of an Unscientific Idea* that appeared in *Newsweek* in 2014.

Prior to my inclusion of a reading on the myth of race, my students reveled in the personal "demise" of Armand in the story, yet they failed to reflect that his comeuppance is less impactful than they suspect. Championing Chopin for turning Armand on his ear, they neglected to notice that nothing is changed in the story and Chopin's own relationship with the other is much more complicated than simply Armand got what was coming to him because he belongs to the race that is cursed by slavery/society. After assigning Sussman, though Boas or Montagu would accomplish the same, the class discussions and writing shifted so that, while noting it would have been anachronistic to attribute it to Chopin, they discuss how we have known for years that race is not biological, and yet we are often writing about race, pointing to race, and speaking as if race existed as a biological category. The curse in Chopin's text that no student ever suggested should remain a curse is understood as a cultural construction in 1893 and in the present. To recognize that the divides of race based on arbitrary delineations of skin coloration still exist requires significant change beyond this pedagogical insertion; it requires further vulnerability to our own mistaken calculations in the present and requires more than we are prepared to offer—offering the silence for the other to speak, but this small change has opened the wound for interpretation.

SURPRISED TO HEAR[20]

Zora Neale Hurston's "Sweat" presents a different challenge. My students were seduced again by their disdain for a character, Sykes, cheered for another, Delia, and celebrated the end. Added to this, they were all too quick to pick up on a Richard Wright–esque critique of Hurston: the failure of the black community to stand "for one of their own" and the mistreatment of black women by black men. Students came eager to discuss how much they loved that when Sykes is calling for Delia, "She never moved, he called, and the sun kept rising,"[21] and they often drew and wrote about that passage. For them, it was a deserved end for Sykes's brutality, not to mention that he is being hoisted on his own petard because he brought the snake into their home. What they didn't hear in

Hurston's story is something Hurston may not have intended: Delia Jones's precarious position has as much to do with a man named Sykes as it does the white power structure that manipulates her work and life, and that blame is too easily cast upon the black men in the story.

They missed that the same inaction they see in the crowd on Joe Clarke's porch (they talk a good game of what they would do to Sykes and for Delia but do nothing) belongs with them, if they would listen to themselves and others. They turned away from the ending and how it is perceived by Delia, took their own disdain for Sykes and the men on Joe Clarke's porch, and made it all ok. They neglect to see "his one open eye shining with hope. A surge of pity too strong to support her bore her away from that eye that must, could not fail to see the tubs . . . She waited in the growing heat while inside she knew the cold river was creeping up and up to extinguish the eye which must know by now that she knew."[22] Filled with desire to see Sykes punished, students were pleased by the obvious. They missed that Delia, in her inaction, is no better than the crowd on the porch. Though this is not, I do not think, what Hurston had on her mind when writing the narrative, I now ask them to consider the Pew Research Center Survey on American views on race and inequality referenced earlier about the need for change in views about race.

I ask them to consider how taking Sykes out of the action would change the world for Delia. Certainly, he won't be around to mercilessly beat her and spend her money on other women, but the basic socioeconomic conditions at the beginning of the story remain unchanged. It is a twilight before a change that doesn't happen. The white community will abuse Delia, she will continue to do nothing to change that, and the students sitting in judgment also are inactive in the present along with the Pew survey respondents. No longer slave labor as it is in Chopin's work, Hurston seems to see an equivalency in her description of Delia's work: "She squatted in the kitchen floor beside the great pile of clothes, sorting them into small heaps according to color, and humming a song in a mournful key, but wondering through it all where Sykes, her husband, had gone with her horse and buckboard."[23] Putting her in the kitchen suggests typical house labor for slaves, and as she squats between the piles of cotton humming, we are hearkened to the work of the fields, but our focus unnecessarily goes all to Sykes.

Now I ask my students to take the risk of considering Sykes's position outside the domestic violence. Sykes is horrible to Delia. Hurston could free her of him if she chose to do so, but instead she has Delia declare it "too late for everything but her little home," which she refuses to leave. At the risk of reducing the violence of domestic abuse, I ask them to consider Hurston's presentation of Delia as free to do as she pleases, just as we are free in the way we react to race. She does stand up to Sykes in the very beginning of the text when she defends herself, holding the iron skillet in a "defensive pose."[24] What made her lose her "habitual meekness" is the question I ask my students.

They usually determined she had simply had enough. They now consider what the fight was about. It wasn't simply a fight and Sykes was wrong. What Sykes wants out of his house is the white folks' clothes: "Ah done tole you time and again to keep them white folks' clothes outa dis house."[25] My students are quick to see the inequity in the relationship between Delia and Sykes and are beginning to recognize the inequity in white and black folks. The church is Delia's defense, but Sykes argues that it brings her no true deliverance, calling her "one of them amen-corner Christians—sing, whoop, and shout, then come home and wash white folks' clothes on the Sabbath."[26] In doing so, Sykes diagnoses the economic disparity in the community between white and black but also portends Delia's own inconsistent moral and ethical choices. These inconsistent choices also belong in the present in the wage gap between white and black Americans.

SOMETHING THAT APPRISES OR SURPRISES[27]

As mentioned earlier, it was when my course hit "Recitatif" for the first time that I realized the discussion had been stagnant all along. Responding to how the reading went, a student quickly raised their hand and asked, "So who was white and who was black?" Another student answered immediately for them by pointing to the text: "One of the things she said was that they never washed their hair and they smelled funny. Roberta sure did. Smell funny, I mean."[28] The responding student was certain that Morrison tells us that Roberta is black in this moment. Even when I provided Morrison's own comments that "The only short story I have ever written, 'Recitatif,' was an experiment in the removal of all racial codes from a narrative about two characters of different races for whom racial identity is crucial,"[29] the student was not swayed. Morrison was mistaken. In each class thereafter, at least one student, usually more, would suggest that there are mistakes that make it clear who is white and who is black. Critics often begin with the same game. It refers back to itself. For the reader, racial identity is crucial. We are all taught something in the moment: our own racial bias.

There are, throughout the text, these slippages between racial codes that become a rich discussion of the wound of racism and interpretation. The reveal in the story is not an answer to who is white and who is black; rather, it answers where the reader's racial biases exist. I still have students who try to draw Twyla or Roberta as black or white, but many are now coming to the conclusion that the other's secret remains a secret—something inaccessible. Having been asked to consider that race is not biological or pure and that we all participate in race and racism, they suture the text less. Morrison's "Recitatif" becomes a narrative seemingly written as a companion to Derrida's "The Truth that Wounds." In every turn of the text, the hermeneutic is revealed.

However, it is not just in the intentional removal of racial codes that "Recitatif" resonates with the hermeneutic. While my students were reading for all the ways to determine the race of the two girls, they neglected to notice the litany of references to the ways the unexamined world taken as normal and determined is neither normal nor determined. They begin to pick up on some of them now, usually: "I am left-handed and the scissors never worked for me."[30] This seem innocuous, but much like the idea that Twyla and Roberta are the only two without "beautiful dead parents in the sky,"[31] my students are more apt to pick up on the idea that the girls are put in places and situations where they don't exactly fit: "Things are not right. The wrong food is always with the wrong people. Maybe that's why I got into waitress work later—to match up the right people with the right food."[32] Morrison seemingly goes out of her way to point to the imbalances of society and the notion that "things are not right." My students are beginning to listen to the other, to allow themselves to be surprised, and to resist suturing the wound, where space is opened for the other to speak and the other in them to speak.

Morrison writes toward this idea of suturing wounds with belief when Twyla and Roberta run into each other later in life. They begin to question the learned behaviors of their youth and why they didn't get along at the Howard Johnson but wanted to see each other now. Twyla narrates: "We went into the coffee shop holding onto one another and I tried to think why we were glad to see each other this time and not before. . . . Two little girls who knew what nobody else in the world knew—how not to ask questions. How to believe what had to be believed."[33] The students are less willing to rest in the belief of what had to be believed and are more apt to recall just a page later that that idea is more than critiqued and the reason for not being together might best be boiled down to racial perception:

> "Were you on dope or something that time at the Howard Johnson's?" I tried to make my voice sound friendlier than I felt.
>
> "Maybe, a little. I never did drugs much. Why?"
>
> "I don't know; you acted sort of like you didn't want to know me back then."
>
> "Oh, Twyla, you know how it was in those days: black-white. You know how everything was."
>
> "But I didn't know. I thought it was just the opposite. Busloads of blacks and whites came into Howard Johnson's together. They roamed together then: students, musicians, lovers, protesters. You got to see everything at Howard Johnson's and blacks were very friendly with whites in those days."[34]

Just as Twyla wonders about the opposite, I wonder and my students wonder. The election of Donald Trump is seen as not a new threat per se, and I do not want to be so dismissive as to declare it to be "just the opposite." In fact, this collection suggests that the threat is quite real. However, the threat from racial bias and racism in America is anything but new and my students and I are coming to that recognition together.

What we are required to do in our teaching of and about race is to interpret: the stories, actions, and cultural milieu surrounding race in America. This interpretation must open the wound of a racist past and present without comfortably suturing the wound opened by the literature and responses to the literature. There is a great deal more said than what was intended as a natural function of language. Teaching and analyzing requires an ethics of reading and responding, that's true.

Saying we are in an era of Trumpian identity politics extends too much credit and discredit to one person. We are in an era of racial identity politics that we cannot possibly understand if we resist a call to struggle, to memory, and refuse to both remain silent and listen with and to one another at the same time. As much as I desire to align myself with Derrida, Chopin, Hurston, and Morrison against Trump, I recognize my place in both spaces and profess accordingly. My own classroom has served as a reminder that I was saying, and always will be saying, something that I did not think I said. By listening carefully and refusing to provide or allow sutures to the violence of interpretation, I hope to continually hear that which I did not recognize in myself and others and hope I instill the same practice in my students so the word *race* shall never be separated from history and memory; the promise, as it turns out, is in these memories.

NOTES

1. Jacques Derrida, "But Beyond (Open Letter to Anne McClintock and Rob Nixon)," *Critical Inquiry* 13 (Autumn 1986): 159.

2. Derrida, "But Beyond," 160.

3. Jacques Derrida, "The Truth that Wounds," in *Sovereignties in Question: The Politics of Paul Celan*, trans. Thomas Dutoit (New York: Fordham University Press, 2005), 164. Derrida responds, "There is in every poetic text, just as in every utterance, in every manifestation outside of literature, an inaccessible secret to which no proof will ever be adequate," when asked by Evelyne Grossman about the proofs of interpretation (and lack thereof). This section plays with the notion of an inability to prove racism and racist sentiment as well as the inaccessible secret of racial bias as it manifested in my classrooms.

4. Derrida, "The Truth that Wounds," 165. In continuing his response to Grossman's question about proof, Derrida offers, "One will never be able to 'prove'—what we call 'prove'—that someone is in bad faith. This stems from the fact that the other is secret. I cannot be in the other's place, in the head of the other. I will never be equal to the secret of otherness. The secret is the very essence of otherness." This section initially considers the difficulty with proving the racism of an other as an inaccessible secret while maintaining the utterances still point to an accessible secret: the historical racial divide in America.

5. Such Is Life Videos, "Donald Trump: I Have a Great Relationship with the Blacks," YouTube video, April 15, 2011, 05:21, https://www.youtube.com/watch?v=3qrP-9MGio8.

6. William H. Frey, "Census Shows Modest Declines in Black-White Segregation," Brookings Institution, December 8, 2015, https://www.brookings.edu/blog/the-avenue/2015/12/08/census-shows-modest-declines-in-black-white-segregation.

7. Such Is Life Videos, "Donald Trump," remarks at 3:32.

8. Such Is Life Videos, "Donald Trump," remarks at 4:46.

9. Derrida, "The Truth that Wounds," 165. Derrida further develops the idea of hermeneutic interpretation in relation to the secret: "There is in all texts . . . a secret, that is to say, an overabundance of meaning, which I will never claim to have exhausted." This section plays with the notion that there is an overabundance in our discussions of race that can never be exhausted but that people attempt

to exhaust with the blanket claim that they are color-blind, though the world we live in points to the opposite.

10. Derrida, "The Truth that Wounds," 165. Derrida further explains the beginnings of an ethics or politics of reading whereby "one can inventory a multiplicity of meanings in a text, in a poem, in a word, but there will always be an excess that is not of the order of meaning, that is not just another meaning." This section then explores the idea of implicit bias that is not to be understood as just another meaning in relation to this ethics of reading.

11. Jeff Nesbitt, "America Has a Big Race Problem: When It Comes to Racial Bias, Nurture Trumped Nature Quite Some Time Ago," *U.S. News & World Report*, March 28, 2016, https://www.usnews.com/news/articles/2016-03-28/america-has-a-big-race-problem.

12. Derrida, "The Truth that Wounds," 166. Derrida adds a final clarification to this ethics or politics of reading by announcing, "I try therefore to make myself listen for something that I cannot hear or understand, attentive to marking the limits of my reading in my reading." This section considers the need to listen beyond the limits of my own reading and understand that what America is experiencing with the rise of Trump is simply a continuation of a history of race and racism.

13. Albert Samaha, Mike Hayes, and Talal Ansari, "The Kids Are Alt-Right: Kids Are Quoting Trump to Bully Their Classmates and Teachers Don't Know What to Do About It," *BuzzFeed News*, June 6, 2017, https://www.buzzfeed.com/albertsamaha/kids-are-quoting-trump-to-bully-their-classmates.

14. David R. Williams and Morgan M. Medlock, "Health Effects of Dramatic Societal Events—Ramifications of the Recent Presidential Election," *New England Journal of Medicine* 376 (2017): 2295–99, http://www.nejm.org/doi/full/10.1056/NEJMms1702111.

15. "On Views of Race and Inequality, Blacks and Whites Are Worlds Apart," Pew Research Center, June 27, 2016, http://www.pewsocialtrends.org/2016/06/27/on-views-of-race-and-inequality-blacks-and-whites-are-worlds-apart.

16. Derrida, "The Truth that Wounds," 166–67. Derrida then responds to Grossman's invocation of the wound: "Hence the duty of the reader-interpreter is to write while letting the other speak, or so as to let the other speak. It is this that I also call, as I was saying a moment ago, counter-signing." This section considers the idea of letting the other speak in one's own writing and reflections on what is occurring in the classroom.

17. Derrida, "The Truth that Wounds," 167. Following up on the wound, Derrida answers, "One speaks, trying to listen to the other. One should speak while leaving to the other the chance to speak, while giving the floor to the other. It is a question of rhythm, of time: not to speak too much, thereby imposing silence on the other, and not to remain too silent." This section considers the way in which students question and answered Chopin's text as well as the students' silences and the silences to be heard in Chopin's text if we refuse to suture the wound and adopt an ethical reading along the lines Derrida suggests.

18. Kate Chopin, "Désirée's Baby," *Kate Chopin International Society*, originally published 1893, last modified June 15, 2017, https://www.katechopin.org/pdfs/desirees-baby.pdf, 3.

19. Chopin, "Désirée's Baby," 4.

20. Derrida, "The Truth that Wounds," 167. In addressing the violence of interpretation in this ethical mode of reading, Derrida responds, "One can also take the risk, and it is sometimes an interesting risk, of writing about a poem something of which the signatory was, at the bottom, unaware, did not mean, did not master—in any case, would have been surprised to hear said of his own poem." This section considers possibilities in Hurston's text that outside what is both a standard reading and might be surprising.

21. Zora Neale Hurston, "Sweat," in *Literature: A Pocket Anthology*, 2nd ed., ed. R. S. Gwynn (New York: Pearson Education, 2005), 170.

22. Hurston, "Sweat," 171.

23. Hurston, "Sweat," 160–61.

24. Hurston, "Sweat," 162.

25. Hurston, "Sweat," 161.

26. Hurston, "Sweat," 162.

27. Derrida, "The Truth that Wounds," 167. Derrida further explains the wound by declaring, "If I do something, it must be something that apprises or surprises, teaches something to the reader but also to the I who signs the text." This last section speaks of an ethics of reading that apprises and surprises, attempting to pull together all the threads from Derrida, my own classroom experience, and the presentation of race in literature.

28. Toni Morrison, "Recitatif," in *The Oxford Book of Women's Writing in the United States*, ed. Linda Wagner-Martin and Cathy N. Davidson (Oxford: Oxford University Press, 1999), 160.

29. Toni Morrison, *Playing in the Dark: Whiteness and the Literary Imagination* (Cambridge, MA: Harvard University Press, 1992), xi.

30. Morrison, "Recitatif," 162–63.

31. Morrison, "Recitatif," 160.

32. Morrison, "Recitatif," 164.

33. Morrison, "Recitatif," 168.

34. Morrison, "Recitatif," 169.

BIBLIOGRAPHY

Chopin, Kate. "Désirée's Baby." *Kate Chopin International Society*. Originally published 1893. Last modified June 15, 2017. https://www.katechopin.org/pdfs/desirees-baby.pdf.

Derrida, Jacques. "But Beyond (Open Letter to Anne McClintock and Rob Nixon)." *Critical Inquiry* 13 (Autumn 1986): 155–70.

———. "The Truth that Wounds." In *Sovereignties in Question: The Politics of Paul Celan*, translated by Thomas Dutoit, 164–72. New York: Fordham University Press, 2005.

Frey, William H. "Census Shows Modest Declines in Black-White Segregation." Brookings Institution, December 8, 2015. https://www.brookings.edu/blog/the-avenue/2015/12/08/census-shows-modest-declines-in-black-white-segregation.

Hurston, Zora Neale. "Sweat." In *Literature: A Pocket Anthology*, 2nd ed., edited by R. S. Gwynn, 160–71. New York: Pearson Education, 2005.

Morrison, Toni. *Playing in the Dark: Whiteness and the Literary Imagination*. Cambridge, MA: Harvard University Press, 1992.

———. "Recitatif." In *The Oxford Book of Women's Writing in the United States*, edited by Linda Wagner-Martin and Cathy N. Davidson, 159–75. Oxford: Oxford University Press, 1999.

Nesbitt, Jeff. "America Has a Big Race Problem: When It Comes to Racial Bias, Nurture Trumped Nature Quite Some Time Ago." *U.S. News & World Report*, March 28, 2016. https://www.usnews.com/news/articles/2016-03-28/america-has-a-big-race-problem.

"On Views of Race and Inequality, Blacks and Whites Are Worlds Apart." Pew Research Center, June 27, 2016. http://www.pewsocialtrends.org/2016/06/27/on-views-of-race-and-inequality-blacks-and-whites-are-worlds-apart.

Samaha, Albert, Mike Hayes, and Talal Ansari. "The Kids Are Alt-Right: Kids Are Quoting Trump to Bully Their Classmates and Teachers Don't Know What to Do About It." *BuzzFeed News*, June 6, 2017. https://www.buzzfeed.com/albertsamaha/kids-are-quoting-trump-to-bully-their-classmates.

Williams, David R., and Morgan M. Medlock. "Health Effects of Dramatic Societal Events—Ramifications of the Recent Presidential Election." *New England Journal of Medicine* 376 (2017): 2295–99. http://www.nejm.org/doi/full/10.1056/NEJMms1702111.

PART II

SCHOLAR-ACTIVISM

Teaching for Social Justice

CHAPTER 5

TECHNOLOGIES OF DISCRIMINATION

Structural Racism beyond Campus

JASON E. COHEN

What we are now witnessing is not some new and complicated expression of white racism—rather, it's the dying embers of the same old racism that once rendered the best pickings of America the exclusive province of unblackness.

—Ta-Nehisi Coates, *We Were Eight Years in Power: An American Tragedy*

But community must not mean a shedding of our differences, nor the pathetic pretense that these differences do not exist.

—Audre Lorde, "The Master's Tools Will Never Dismantle the Master's House"

INTRODUCTION

I have developed a skeptical view of social media's potential to shape public discourse, a view based on events this essay investigates, but one also rooted in a reevaluation on a smaller scale of my own thinking on the relationship between identity politics and institutional politics that emerged from my first interactions with a student I will call Maurice (pronouns: they/them).[1] On the opening day of Freshman Composition in late August 2017, Maurice asserted that all institutions of higher learning and all professors working within them were "white supremacist, capitalist, patriarchal" holdouts. Maurice was self-consciously drawing on language propagated on social media by activists involved earlier that month in the civic actions in Charlottesville, Virginia. In so doing, Maurice rightly echoed social media calls for the persons and institutions harboring such beliefs to be held accountable, and as Emerald Christopher-Byrd's chapter also notes, that echo conveyed a focused rage. Maurice was consuming social media voraciously in the weeks after Charlottesville, but they were also digesting book pages just as voraciously: they were clearly invoking bell hooks's published words on institutional racism.[2] The freshness of those events and the raw power of their words brought me to confront in the classroom my own past words on Twitter, words that I will further address in a moment. Was my own classroom, Maurice's comment forced me to ask, tacitly invoking the language of white supremacist, capitalist patriarchy? For the first time, I had to recognize that they were right to be skeptical about the ways in which institutions distribute their messages about race and diversity, and that I, too, should be skeptical about how institutions like my own disseminate their educational missions through the language of race. Institutional uses of language about race run the risk of engaging white supremacist mechanisms because of the default position those institutions hold with regard to racialized power. In the classroom, it became my duty to own that problem and, even more urgently, to teach it critically. In the realm of social media, Maurice's reflection on hooks's words, echoed in Charlottesville, made me ask how we may more effectively bring light to the structurally interwoven strands and asymmetries of power not only within the classroom but also in its incarnations in social and digital media.

I want to ask the following question: What are the implications that our technologies hold for understanding the ways in which race functions today in institutions of higher education? This essay presents a long-lived attempt to think through questions about how racism functions in its technological instantiations in our institutional cultures, whether on a screen or otherwise mediated by our highly automated and information-rich culture. The stakes are high and the perils immediate when we consider how to teach our institutions to engage with racial discourse: if we shirk these duties, boards of trustees and media crises will shape moments that reveal racial dynamics, rather than the faculty, student, and staff voices that should be prominently and inclusively charged to address them. I want, then, to begin by considering the technological forms of discriminations in terms established by what the art historian W. J. T. Mitchell recently called the "medium" of race.[3] For Mitchell, thinking of race as a "medium" related to visual or textual production means that it functions "as an intervening substance that both enables and obstructs social relations" and is thus a formation "subject to social change."[4] By considering the functions of race in terms of representation, historical meaning, and relations in lived experience, and through broader institutional operations, Mitchell aims in the first place to wrest the imbricated concepts of race and racism back from the assertion of a post-racial contemporary society.[5] Mitchell's claim that race forms a medium rather than a single discourse allows his book to engage in a subtle examination of the multiple and interdependent representational forms at work when the languages of race and racism are deployed.

The present essay takes up the conception of race as "medium" that Mitchell describes in the new domain of technological and digital communications. In particular, I am interested in examining how each technological medium of discrimination simultaneously structures and is structured by the institutions of higher education. To those ends, in the remainder of this section, I examine the institutional ecologies of higher education within which the discourses of race and racism arise, and I offer a definition of the term I have been using to describe those ecologies, *technologies of discrimination*, according to its structural implications for academic institutional life and policy. In the second section, I study the historical background within which the term may be more deeply understood to operate in relationship to long-standing concerns in the academy for freedom of expression. The third section pursues an argument that reveals how academic freedoms incorporate and extend racial discourses within higher education. I turn in the fourth section to scrutinize how the discourses of race and racism affect social media as a specifically technological locus of discrimination, and finally, in the last section, the essay prescribes a set of institutional principles that recommend approaches to handling such apparently inevitable moments of crisis through a better approach to intervention and resolution.

My engagement with the social and institutional problems created by these technologies of discrimination also reveals a second, more personal source, one that I want to acknowledge in these early moments. In late

2011, I tweeted a student's name in a frustrated rant, and it produced far worse effects on my communities—professional, local, familial, and ultimately, national—than I could ever have anticipated. My words were at worst racist, and at best, terribly calibrated; I own that. Students called for my immediate termination on the floor of an emergency faculty meeting; Facebook shut down several pages threaded together by thousands of comments on the topic because of hate speech from outside commenters. I received explicit threats, and I was also told by white nationalist militants that protection was available, if I wanted it. I am bound moreover by a contract I signed as a part of my institutional judicial process at Berea College not to repeat the words I published on Twitter. In addition, the "original" digital artifacts have since been scrubbed from the Twitter and Facebook platforms because subsequent responses to my original tweet violated both corporations' user conduct policies on hate speech. In an ironic twist to claims for the ubiquity of web-driven information, I cannot point you to the immediate sources for those words. Echoes remain on the archive of Gawker and other sites that quoted the material, but they no longer trace the whole incident.

The institution responded officially by censuring me, placing me on probation, mandating a series of remediations, and extending my tenure clock; in addition, several years of institution-wide reform was initiated, including lasting changes such as creating a vice president of diversity and hiring an African American chaplain, among others. The institution's range of responses highlights the ripple effect of my tweet through the institution. The consequences have been palpable for me: after censure and a gauntlet at tenure, I had been terrified, both personally and professionally, to talk about that incident publicly in the years since then; now, nine years later, I understand my silence as an impediment. In a volume dedicated to teaching race in perilous times, this chapter maintains that in order to teach race and related forms of discrimination, it is at times necessary to reorient both ourselves and our institutions toward the medium of structural racism embedded in the technological matters our work now demands.

Let me say this as straightforwardly as possible: my words were unkind, and they used a student's name in a failed attempt at acerbic humor. Though I recognized them as biting and churlish, I did not consider my words racist. Still, the verbal act was rightly perceived as driven by racist dynamics, including hierarchies that prioritize the authority of a professor over a student, man over woman, white over black. My words leveraged institutional power in ways that, ultimately, proved racist. Of course, in shaming a student publicly, I also compromised my ethics. To pursue Marshall McLuhan's dictum in its digital moment: the (social) medium is ever more determinately the (social) message. Regardless of my intention, the message cannot be divorced from the racial effects it propagated, effects that now motivate my restorative work.

One key distinction this chapter locates within the present volume, moreover, is the institutional weight that teachers bear outside the bounds of the classroom. Despite pervasive calls for what administrators and accrediting agencies, following Dee Fink's research, call "high-impact practices" that aim to extend learning beyond the duration of a course meeting, teaching is usually understood to stop with the end of each session. Learning outside of that duration, high impact or not, often falls under other categories such as mentoring or advising, student research, or cocurricular activities. As Daniel Delgado and Keja Valens's chapter in this volume suggests, the dynamics of race extend to the very principles of curriculum design and implementation. Similarly, as Sharon Raynor's chapter also powerfully demonstrates, our training too rarely encourages us to think about the reach of the learning environment beyond the walls of the classroom. This incident, however, revealed to me the ways in which the learning environment can itself come to reflect a deeply embedded anti-blackness even within institutions that think of themselves as deeply liberal. When Audre Lorde called for new "blueprints of expectations and response" in support of critical moments not only of political but also of environmental turmoil, I think we are obligated also to read her words as a call for our classrooms and institutions to uphold a similarly clear route to new points of educational origin and new educational directions for students as well as teachers, both within the classroom and beyond.[6]

As Sara Ahmed has argued powerfully, institutions function in multiple domains as "orienting devices" that shape how bodies inhabit space and motivate the directions in which bodies move. This organizing principle of bodies moving within institutions, Ahmed maintains, thus creates interactional sites where the politics of race occur through lived experience, rather than as a fixed or essential element of an individual's racial status.[7] Ahmed's critique of the ways in which race orients bodies complements the work of Tricia Rose regarding how institutional structures circumscribe racial identity. Rose's work highlights the multiple ways in which institutions shape the domains that subjects are authorized to inhabit within them.[8]

In light of the institutional and bodily aspects of racialized power, the consequences of my own words are undeniable: my tweet ultimately became the source of a complex social, academic, and political discord that reverberated across campus for several years. The event and its aftermath shaped not only my place on campus but the institution itself because the college became entangled publicly in adjudicating my conduct vis-à-vis my electronic communication. Moreover, the crisis of public scrutiny my tweet provoked itself stood as a shibboleth on campus for individuals' positions regarding the institution's treatment of crises in social media more broadly. This reciprocity between institutions and bodies thus also lodges in a digitally enabled authority, one that has unfolded ever more fully as tweets from President Donald Trump daily revel in the undeniably racial contours of social media.

The events that my tweet provoked reflect a local impact in an ongoing national debate crystallized by Trump's presidency. The institutional and professional crisis set loose by my words mirrors the deeply conflicted historical and ideological roots of a formation I am calling *technologies of discrimination*. By way of definition, I see technologies of discrimination as an event horizon as well as a condition of practices: it is defined, first, by acts of discrimination carried out in uniquely non-local ways via technological platforms, particularly social media, and second, by the automated forms of amplification, echo, and citation of those events across other platforms (whether to positive or negative ends) through social media algorithms.

I am not making a soft claim that the passive nature of technological platforms can be appropriated for racist ends, though that is clearly true. My defining claim for a coherence among technologies of discrimination, rather, is strong: the principles of what the linguistic historian Walter Ong, following Thorstein Veblen, called "technological determinism" must be revised specifically to account for the prominence and effects of social media as a mode of communication.[9] We should be critical of the reductive force of the determinist model; nevertheless, technological determinism describes human interactions with social media forcefully. In reading technological uses according to a determinist logic, technologies of social media too easily beget racism in unanticipated and often virulent forms: the relational modes of information management and control on which social media rely also implicitly endorse the propagation of racism through the built-in structures of regulation (e.g., liking, reposting, retweeting, and rebranding material across platforms) and dissemination (e.g., friend networks, subscribed pages, shared logins, filtered news and event feeds, promoted materials, all parts of the echo chamber of materials streamed automatically to users based on algorithmic correlations) on which those platforms rely.[10] Inasmuch as individuals continue to be mobilized by technology for activist ends, and inasmuch as those same technologies continue to hold substantial promise as a mechanism to destabilize what bell hooks has since the 1980s called "imperialist white supremacist capitalist patriarchy,"[11] we are nevertheless witnessing a retrenchment against decentralized and non-deterministic media outlets.[12] By the same token, the implications of increasingly centralized internet media suggest that (technological) treatments of race resist a democratic logic of post-racial universalism: the highly agnostic medium of race pulls its discriminatory logic in one direction while attempts in the other direction to pull against that very logic continue unabated. Thus, in my understanding, technological racism defines the implicit tensions of regulation and dissemination on which social media rely, and further, which collectively undercut the politically unalloyed neutrality and productivity that made for the revolution in new media. To those ends, in the next section I want to step back from the present moment to consider the technological arc of discrimination in its *longue durée* and, in so doing, to provide its conceptual trajectory.

THEORETICAL BACKGROUNDS TO THE CONCEPT OF TECHNOLOGIES OF DISCRIMINATION

In order to think about the strands of this discourse of contemporary technologically enabled discrimination, I want to offer a broader account of the racial discourses of identity that led up to the powerful waves of social media–driven identity politics that are washing over us today. I am interested in this section to examine how social media has shifted long-standing concerns for the durability and accessibility of a reliable cultural archive or repository. How does social media influence the narratives available to those who wish to rely on those forms of political dissemination? To step backward a generation, then, to the wake of the Second World War, calls to transcend race stood on the shoulders of a secular, cosmopolitan vision of international humanism that associated race with nation and racism with the ultra-nationalism of European anti-Semitic right-wing political parties.[13] Distinguishing themselves from those earlier interests in diminishing race in the name of emphasizing secular universalism, recent calls to dismiss the category of race have relied on data and methods drawn from genetics and ethnogeography to muddy the distinction between the natural and social construction of racial identity.[14] If elections since 2016 reveal anything (not only in the United States, but in a global sweep of pro-nationalist elections from Poland, Hungary, and Turkey, to Brazil and Venezuela, to the Philippines and Myanmar), it is that ultra-nationalism inhabits the very technologies of communication and decentralization that were hailed as indicators of its decline. These technologies enmesh racial identity as a fundamental element in a reimagined community of citizens who operate in a digital world that often reinscribe in a digital sphere notions of a naturalized, imperialist, and socially determined racism.[15]

I have suggested briefly that the structures of dissemination and regulation implicit in social media provide some of the inherent problems of racial discourse within our technological domains. In particular, as we have come to understand them widely in the years since this incident, our news feeds and friend networks propagate unanticipated racial discourse in concentrations and streams that were not intended by the engineers who designed the platforms. What I want to add to that discussion at this point is a way of thinking about the distortions of narrative and archive embedded in the very search process itself.

Technology enables the dynamics of race, including racism, to participate in what the digital media researcher Mark Carrigan calls "algorithmic authoritarianism" in an unanticipated mode. "Algorithmic authoritarianism," for Carrigan, has two key elements: first, it signals the power and legitimacy claimed by the inclusion of a search result in a list returned to a query. Second, and even more importantly, its authority also indicates the probability that a given set of search results will be transparent and relevant for a researcher's work, as well as for shaping one's professional presence online.[16] Thus, the algorithmic authoritarianism of a given set of search results lies in the combination of legitimacy and relevance that accrues to any set of answers returned to a query. Because of the saturation Google has achieved across digital platforms (in which Facebook and most websites accept its ubiquity by embedding Google search tools into their own sites), there are few realistic alternative search options; even "no track" search engines like Duck Duck Go are built on Google's technology, and only the naive user would believe their anonymity to be well-kept by that interdependent relationship. This dominance is, in itself, authoritarian in flavor. But by reading with Carrigan, we can see that the problem becomes still worse: the authoritarianism of that algorithm grants a technocratic sovereignty to the very algorithm itself. Carl Schmitt, the political theorist and among the chief jurists of Nazi Germany, created the touchstone formulation for modern political sovereignty: "Sovereign is he who decides on the exception."[17] But what if the sovereign is neither he, she, nor they? What if the sovereign in the digital domain is *that* which decides the exception? A depersonalized, inhuman decision-making process underlies search queries, and Carrigan's work shows how this algorithmic and sovereign force undercuts the political domains of democratic thought and action. In so doing, Carrigan's distinction helps us to recognize that the technological racism of search functions lies in the capacity to deform results according to inscrutable criteria, and further, to shape the access to and framing of archives related to race and racist materials (on either side of the debate).

Yet, in moving beyond the automatic functions of search and toward its deeply human implications, technological racism reveals how such dynamics of authority and artificial legitimation cut across institutional structures in several directions at once. I noted that I am bound by contract not to repeat my tweet. Although it was scrubbed from Facebook and Twitter, you may still google my name if you want to see echoes of the baldly ugly rant I wrote in under 140 characters. Because of "archeological" functions of durability and site-location built into those search results, moreover, a search for this topic would return comments on and citations of parts of my remarks and the ensuing conversation it sparked. Let me unpack that claim further in light of the algorithmic authoritarianism it implies. Like those citizens convicted of past crimes whose rights continued to be curtailed beyond "official" punishment by job and housing applications, voter limitations, and loan processes (among others) that discriminate according to past actions, the digital footprint of this event is not neutral. While my offense was not criminal, the analogy nevertheless demands some attention. At the same time that European "right to be forgotten" laws have failed to gain footing in the US, the dominant internet search algorithm—Google's PageRank—heavily favors sites meeting several criteria, including high inbound traffic, those that are more frequently linked by other sites, and those holding more durable "legacy" information (relative to the age of materials in the digital realm). Thus, while my remark has been buried by newer content, Google still excavates the scrubbed and dated content because of the durability of linked platforms like Gawker, as well as the comparably high attention that moment received when weighed against other digital breadcrumbs associated with my identity.[18] Similarly on the other side of this structural analogy, PageRank also maintains the status of racist histories and sites by promoting them according to those same fundamental criteria of traffic, linking, and durability. Neither can one escape race as a function of social media on the side of recrimination, nor can one escape it on the side of equity. Race is, in this particular way, a "medium" in the sense that W. J. T. Mitchell suggested through which search functions thus also filter the histories and narrative relations of materials promoted in social media.

These features of search results and page rankings clearly also participated in the distortion of social media in the runup to the 2016 US presidential election. Automated bots used to create traffic, volume, and attention ultimately shaped the national political conversation toward racist and divisive discourses even during moments when citizens and the media began moving toward different topics. Taken together, the combination of archival durability and narrative deformation characterizes the technological form of racism I have called to our more immediate attention. In fact, digital surrogates of this history are, I submit, another frontier for the analysis of racial motivations. Ariella Azoulay distinguishes between the "abstract archive" and the "material archive," wherein, she maintains, the abstract archive "shows no trace of the people who created it, nor of those who use it," and represents a paradoxical fantasy of an archive that both *preserves* objects and *cancels* efforts to document the very use of archival objects.[19] Perceiving the fragile status of digital archival objects is thus critical to our understanding of their use and misuse in social media: in the effort to preserve and make an object ubiquitous, we also may erase the institutional context where our materials circulate. They may, after all, be re-blogged, pirated, quoted, moved across platforms or exhibits, and so on, all with the ease of a few clicks. By contrast, the "material archive" in Azoulay's formulation demands that we consider the institutions within which records are housed, the history of their use and access, and the affiliations those institutions maintain with external researchers, funding agencies, and so on. None of that material context is obvious for an abstract archive. While the opacity behind digital hosting of abstract archives may be an effect of making materials more accessible or more widely used, that same effect of opacity also and at the same time strips material archives of their legitimating functions. In their opacity, abstract archives thus level the field of historical materials in ways that are simultaneously both democratic and, perversely, demagogic, and that, in the end, make it more difficult to render informed decisions not only about what we are seeing but also about what may be obscured by our digital horizons.

The rise of abstract archives occurs on several levels: first, formal digital archival objects like the Walt Whitman Archive are held singly, whereas in a second instance, Thomas Jefferson's papers cross at least seven different digital holdings, and in a third, holdings in the World Newspaper Archive remain entirely behind paywalls. I am interested, rather, in a fourth scenario, wherein websites and web archives stand as less formal traces of their own histories.[20] Although the Internet Archive may map much of the historical internet, the day-to-day archives of a website like Amazon or even Gawker relies almost exclusively on its own cloud backups, which may remain inaccessible to the public either intentionally or unintentionally. Moreover, because search processes actively determine what results can be found—because, as Lev Manovich and N. Katherine Hayles have suggested, databases have supplanted archives in our daily interactions[21]—the nuance that we depend on scholars to bring to our work often now entails the capacity to locate materials that may be systematically deprecated. Facebook's efforts to scrub politically biased material from its site may support greater integrity in public discourse, but it also hides from view the very data that would allow anyone outside of its corporate domain to conduct objective analyses of that same bias. Search companies and their sponsors have thus become at least partially culpable in the rise of an unanticipated, darker version of what the anthropologist Arjun Appadurai called "mediascapes" generated by feedback loops within closed communities and homogenous audiences.[22] In this way, the problem of database-driven social networks that I have outlined above acts as a break on claims for the liberating effects of "networked media" or the "rewriting" of postcolonial archives heralded in the work of scholars such as Yochai Benkler and V. Y. Mudimbe.[23]

This combination of amplification and dissemination distinguishes a specifically *technological* form of discrimination tied to abstract archives. Therefore, when my own words became tied to the practices, interactions, discourses, and events shaped by a deeply racist series of replies to and comments on my post, technological racism re-presented the content with which I am now associated. The racism made explicit by comments that responded to my tweet became closely tethered to the tweet itself. When you find my tweet, you always find the hateful material that derived energy from the feedback loops and selective elevation and deprecation of material that I have described above in relationship to the abstract archive. My one tweet became a micro-instance of an abstract archive in which the tweet and its replies chart a full network of racial relations and power dynamics. As a result, replies to my tweet associated me with an amplified, distorted racism which I could neither meaningfully respond to nor meaningfully control. In addition, that past association continues to this very day to obscure the work I have attempted to accomplish to remedy my own mistakes on campus, both in the classroom and beyond it. I have had scholarly work rejected expressly because of the direct association online of my name with that abstract archive: for several years, my tweet's echoes represented my professional products more than any other work I accomplished. I know these seem like quotidian effects of social media misuse extended beyond the academy, but more pointedly, they signal an important vulnerability in the institutional discourses of race and equity in which those words are embedded.

The rhetorical, legal, and political domains highlighted by my remarks serve as foundational discourses to a future-oriented response to technological racism, and it is my hope now to suggest how those same technologies may alternatively facilitate possible modes of justice in the face of these racial formations. Returning to social media, then, with an investment in its structural implications directed by its use-value and functions on campus, my recommendations flow from two clear grounding assumptions: First, social media in all of its varieties are tools, and they should be thought of instrumentally not only by their users but also by the institutions whose faculty and staff implement these tools both within classrooms and outside of them. Pursuing a view of social media directed by its tool-functions would lead institutions, and perhaps teachers as well, to ask what ends are being invoked in various uses; and further, to ask what consequences, whether intended or not, should be considered in that light. Second, social media should not be considered an unvarnished good, nor should it be called a necessary component of academic work today. This view strongly contrasts recent calls for a ubiquitous scholarly or teacherly presence online, as well as for the unamalgamated good that social media presence may represent for an institution through the official purposes its faculty project in their research and teaching outlets. In other words, if race serves as a medium, then these technologies cannot continue to be thought of as transparent and value-neutral. When I used the instruments made available to me by social media via Twitter, I misread the pedagogical implications of that work because I was thinking narrowly about my scholarly community in a form outstripped by the reach of its digital instances. I might have groused to a colleague in person without this tool and identity misrecognition, but in the digital medium of race, no such separation was available. Thus, scholars should weigh their value against other contributions to the university as they are put to uses across our institutions: while it would be difficult for a grant, publication, or experiment to be leveled with the charge of racism, the same is not true for blogs and social media posts. I do not simply mean to issue a *caveat auctor*—the intellectual freedom and integrity of the student and faculty scholar alike demand vigilance when questions of race come to the surface.

I have outlined in this section how social media technologies both constrain and amplify the effects of racism in discourse online, giving rise to a distinct form that I am calling technologies of discrimination, whose hallmarks, while similar in kind, remain distinguished by their effects and scope. Those effects, I have suggested, derive from tensions inherent to social media and grounded on the one hand by a drive toward an integrity of discourse online and, on the other hand, by the drive to mitigate distortion as well as censorship. In the remainder of this essay, I move forward from my initial purpose of shedding light on institutional and structural forces that bear on an analysis of the recent and burgeoning technologies of discrimination across institutions of higher education. In the second half, the essay aims to provide a framework to shape the development of institutional policies regarding social media crises, particularly those focused on faculty and student actions.

HOW TECHNOLOGIES OF DISCRIMINATION WORK, AND WHY ACADEMIC FREEDOM REMAINS AT RISK

The notion that specific *technologies* of discrimination are bound together requires further examination in its academic context, both inside and outside of classrooms. I have demonstrated already that scholars of race from across multiple disciplines including sociology, law, literature, history, and African American studies programs suggest that racial language and discrimination must be studied through the lens of structural racism; further, I have suggested that those structural forms link the ways in which we consider our classrooms and students in their relationships to our larger institutional contexts. In addition to offering a close attention to individual instances as exemplars of specific cases, a structural approach includes an examination of the larger dynamics within which such cases operate.[24] In this way, the role of technology in defining a new mode of structural racism also extends the argument made convincingly by Etienne Balibar that a "neo-racism" emerged in the late twentieth century which took as its basis cultural and institutional differences rather than biological or geographic criteria for defining racially coded ideologies.[25] Since then, scholars including Michael Eric Dyson and Lewis R. Gordon have responded to Balibar by noting how shifting the national context correspondingly affects the forms of Balibar's distinctly French inflection of "neo-racism."[26] However, it is not only the relationship of technological media to institutional powers that must be addressed in the study of technological racism, because, as I suggest, the technologies themselves, above and beyond academic institutions, often embed racially charged criteria in their use and application. I focus my analysis on academic institutions in this section, therefore, first because of the tight allegiance that higher education institutions have traditionally nurtured with free speech in the form of cultural criticism on topics including racism and discrimination, and in addition, because of the particularly fraught context that historical allegiance has generated in light of social media use and conflicts across campuses.

At the level of that traditional allegiance between academic institutions and cultural criticism of race, scholarly attention to the racialized language of images began with modern film color matching and rapid processing in the 1960s. Since that time, art and social critics have grappled with the problematic relationship of image to skin tone. That fundamental issue has reemerged in the context of social and digital media: from the recent emergence of practices like "digital blackface," in which non-black people appropriate images of black culture in memes,[27] to the bias against dark complexion in facial recognition technology as well as in machine learning algorithms,[28] to the hidden racial bias in Airbnb and other sharing-economy rental and use patterns,[29] it is clear that whiteness, or rather what Christina Sharpe (echoing Frantz Fanon) calls "antiblackness," remains the default state of pathology for digital identity.[30] I adopt that distinction between a positive whiteness and a negative anti-blackness from Sharpe's recent examination of racial ecologies, *In the Wake*: "Weather is the totality of our environments; the weather is the total climate; and that climate is antiblack."[31] Moreover, in social and networked media platforms, pervasive African American images are not linked directly to local control over those images or their use. That failure of reciprocity reveals a Janus-faced relationship between technological controls and the reception of content that, as I demonstrate in the final section of this essay, should be countenanced directly. To present that dichotomy in brief, the same concerns with propriety and proportion that are relevant to questions about who controls an image or message, conversely, can lead institutions to react to complex moments of identity using reductive policies that reinforce Manichaean distinctions between intention and reception, authenticity and authority, and ultimately, with judgments about the guilt or innocence, the anti-black or pro-black climate, of social media and its users.

ACADEMIC FREEDOM AND RACIAL DISCRIMINATION

Institutional responses to social media crises in recent American higher education reveal that such crises extend beyond incidents driven narrowly by racially charged language. A brief survey of institutional responses to recent media crises across campuses nationwide will provide the context within which I hope to situate my comments on the matter and treatment of technological racism. A key question framing my remarks is: How should we understand the role technology plays specifically in the tense institutional domain of racial language and how can understanding that role help to distinguish between free speech and its distortion within a campus context?

The fear of suffering a major blow to a university's brand, coupled with a retrenchment against the risks of a volatile social media landscape, has led to a reconsideration of the strong relationship such institutions have traditionally maintained with academic freedom.[32] At the same time, as recently as 2016, the University of Chicago's dean of students, John Ellison, upheld an expansive view of academic freedom in a letter to incoming freshmen. Ellison's letter noted the importance of free academic expression to supporting an environment in which students and faculty together "are encouraged to speak, write, listen, challenge and learn without fear of censorship."[33] Professor Ellison's letter was written in response to the rise of "safe spaces" and "trigger warnings" on campuses nationwide, a trend that the letter expressly resists, suggesting rather that such developments signal a weakened commitment to the "free exchange of ideas."

The once clear principles of free speech have been destabilized by the paired phenomena of pervasive racist language online and decentralized media content, consumption, and audiences. While free speech was, in the era before digital media, understood to incorporate print publication and public speech, the limits of free speech and academic freedom have become less coherently articulated by institutions as the platforms and modes of speech have continued to proliferate. This parallel shift from print to digital and from more to less protected speech attends to the conditions underlying media production and consumption. The movement away from coherence and clarity in policy as well as conduct serves as a reminder of how the apparently noble principles represented in the University of Chicago's letter and endorsed widely by universities across the nation cannot operate in a vacuum. Indeed, Chicago's principles can now be read as a reaction, leaning in neither a recognizably liberal nor conservative direction, indirectly linked to the rise of identity politics on campus. Just as administrations have had to respond to decentralized media, campus unrest has also taken on a different tenor and pace as a result of those same decentralized effects of social media. At colleges and universities with activist traditions, such as Oberlin, Evergreen, Middlebury, and Reed Colleges, as well as at larger university campuses ranging from Drexel University to the University of California, Davis, and the University of Missouri, the sudden rise of student demonstrations for reasons that can have unique sparks, or that may cluster around larger and more galvanizing movements, calls attention to the significance of the rapid propagation and dissemination of information using the distributed platforms of social media.

At the same time that instant solidarity and virtually unlimited geographic reach become available to campus activists through electronic means, institutional authorities can leverage those same tools to shape the message and visible impacts of campus events. Examples such as the firings of Melissa Click from the University of Missouri and Steven Salaita from the University of Illinois at Urbana-Champaign, or the alt-right-driven resignation of Drexel University's George Ciccariello-Maher following his incendiary tweets, reveal that social media pressures and amplification can also lead to compromises in due process, academic freedom, and the breakdown of campus policies related to free speech at a time when the reputation and brand of institutions are under increasingly heavy and frequent scrutiny. Regardless of the understanding of the instances I have cited above, those events centered on racially charged language or events. Indeed some, like the video of Melissa Click calling for "muscle" to protect a student journalist, were read as racist or aggressive precisely because they were stripped of proper context. On closer inspection, Click's actions bear little immediate relationship to her involvements in racial dynamics on campus except insofar as she was trying (albeit clumsily) to protect student protesters who happened to be predominantly black and who were, as students, protesting campus policies on race. And yet her actions and her person were read according to racially motivated interpretations that linked her image to racial and political violence alongside an agenda retrospectively ascribed to her prior academic publications. The disruptive forces of activist social media seem to have been used to justify similarly blunt institutional responses across the powerful hierarchies implicit in institutions of higher learning, including those implicated in adjudicating issues of racial justice on campus. Again, the response to social media crises shows how in academia, the climate, as Afro-pessimist views including those of Christina Sharpe have it, is anti-black. By identifying the intersection of the body, institution, classroom, and larger academic environment as a part of the climate of social media at the same time as it shapes learning, I have aimed in this section to suggest how not only our conduct but also our institutional ideologies, as well as the daily practices that enact those codes of conduct, must account for tensions at work in the oscillation between the poles of academic freedom and of the deeply embedded powers of discrimination and coercion that have too often historically governed our institutions.

SOCIAL MEDIA ISSUES AND CRISES ON CAMPUS TODAY

Because of the far-reaching implications of the similarities I have described in the section above, the national reach of academic institutional responses to such crises calls for a brief census. Rather than responding to single incidents as case studies, part of my intention is to suggest a framework or series of criteria with which individual moments might be compared. A 2014 statement from the American Association of University Professors (AAUP) titled "Academic Freedom and Electronic Communications" represents the most comprehensive policy approach to these issues.[34] It notes the breakdown of "intramural and extramural speech" alongside the expanded "boundaries of the classroom," finding nevertheless that "most colleges and universities have yet to formulate policies regarding social-media usage by faculty members."[35] AAUP calls for institutions to develop policies through faculty consensus, remarking that the boundary between private and public speech should not be as centrally at issue as differentiating individual speech from speech intended to represent the institution more broadly and distinguishing free speech from forms of legally indefensible speech including defamation, hate speech, violations of professional ethics, or demonstrations of incompetence.[36]

In the absence of real institutional engagement with voices from the faculty and community, institutions tend to use social media policies, where they exist, to protect brand and image. Rather than working to protect the intellectual and interactional spaces of social media from market-driven distortions or the pressures of conforming with external views, institutions like those mentioned above—Drexel University, the University of Illinois at Urbana-Champaign, and the University of California, Davis—default to positions of risk management. Although Drexel University's social media policies, for instance, span three separate domains on their website, they can be summed up in one single provision: "Understand Your Responsibility and Know You Are Liable."[37] The University of California, Davis, is similarly conservative, with a policy that refuses to draw a distinction between the professional and private spheres of social media;[38] in addition, it expressly forbids "personal opinions," comments on "developing crisis situations," and remarks on "controversial topics" from its employees across social media platforms.[39] The University of Illinois offers the double-edged assurance "situations will often be evaluated on a case-by-case basis," and specifies particularly that their ad hoc terms for situational evaluation include social media crises.[40]

Across these institutions, the focus remains on risk management rather than the preservation of academic freedom or the enfranchisement of socially engaged voices from the faculty, staff, and students. On social media, institutions are proving perhaps even more conservative than they would be in local media relations for faculty as well as students. Increasingly, institutional language endorsing student empowerment and civic engagement, again, whether directed at students or at the faculty who sponsor clubs and support meetings, is hedged by the language of risk and brand management. To return to Sharpe, institutions work at every turn to resist the possibilities of change or new directions for movement represented in recognizing the "anagrammatical" shifts that differently identified bodies can and should bring to the institutional environments, whether in the classroom, office, or related administrative organs, by which academia and its assembled constituents are defined.[41]

As I turn in the following section to articulate what some key contours of such shifts might involve, I want to call our attention to the specific landscapes of our institutions and classrooms. I have been discussing large, research-oriented institutions of higher learning, whereas my own context is in is a small, liberal arts college with an undergraduate population and a focus on teaching over research. The scale of the institution is not a factor to overlook: a reduced size may diminish national visibility or, by contrast, increase local attention because of the relative significance of the college to its region and its social environment. Whatever the anagrammatical reconfigurations one might imagine to shift an institution toward a better equilibrium, they will not be universally applicable; rather, they will remain sensitive to the social ecologies of a place and the bodies that inhabit it. As Judith Butler noted in *Giving an Account of Oneself*, "It also turns out that self-questioning of this sort involves putting oneself at risk, imperiling the very possibility of being recognized by others, since to question the norms of recognition that govern what I might be, to ask what they leave out, . . . [is] to risk unrecognizability as a subject."[42] What I understand as central to Butler's insight here is her understanding that at the same time that we might call for critique, or self-critique, it has to be accomplished in a mode that can be recognized by our institutions. This chapter, like that of Delgado and Valens in their context of general education reform, is nothing less than a chance to give that very kind of account, and to do so in a way that is sensitive to the students, colleagues, and institutional structures that might otherwise militate against such an account. Given the prismatic effects our institutions have on the messages we deliver in and beyond our classes, refractions that ultimately discriminate among the frequencies and colors of a single source of light depending on the different angles or assumptions held across the parts of an institution, the problems of recognition that Butler identifies are no less pressing than those that attend the forms of critique in which this chapter has been engaging. It is because of such perpetual tension that I wish to turn in this final section to articulate a series of principles that could be generative sources for the emergence of new dispositions toward campus views on race, as well as new forms of intervention that such dispositions would call for.

INSTITUTIONAL PRINCIPLES AS INTERVENTION: ANTI-RACIST DISPOSITIONS ON CAMPUS

I have attempted in the previous two sections first to characterize the effects of social media on the campus discourses of race and subsequently to pull back from a tight examination on racism on campus in order to situate those features within the larger landscape of academic social media approaches, breakdowns, and horizons. This section returns specifically to address the question of how to address technological racism on campus through institutional principles and, to some extent, policy recommendations. I will suggest five areas for consideration to address issues of technological racism. Not all will be equally applicable in all settings or scenarios, but each of them merits consideration from our institutions and faculties as we move forward to ever greater degrees of technological mediation in academia.

As I noted earlier, I cannot directly print the terms of the contract I signed because of the related nondisclosure agreement I signed. In effect, that sealed status points to a major issue in the handling of my own case that provides a structural analogy to a multitude of situations nationwide: namely, my case was handled ad hoc by a dean and academic vice president, rather than by a standing judicial body, one with faculty and administrative representation, who might follow a clear procedure in reference to ready policy. I mention this not to judge that individual dean—his decisions were constrained by my prior action as well as competing demands; rather, my claim is that the institutional ecology, or *cultural disposition*, within which he made his decision was itself hostile because the sparsely described procedures available to him remained too inchoate to supply clear lines of oversight and review. Ultimately, we settled under the terms of a sealed contract because there were no other terms ready-to-hand to employ in a moment of crisis.

Consequently, my first principle on these matters of technological discrimination is in keeping with the suggestions the AAUP has championed: develop and pursue regular, open judicial procedures that (1) include clear faculty voices and (2) are not bound by nondisclosure agreements in processes created to handle social media crises. The two distinctions I would draw from the AAUP's recommendations are this: first, behavior, not technology, should be the object of the regulation; and second, faculty involvement needs to be integrated with executive procedures or roles and not subordinated or separated from them. In other words, faculty need to be seated at the table alongside staff and executive administration to set and implement those policies. On some campuses, student participation would also be likely, and in those cases both faculty and student roles as well as those of administrators should be well established prior to the beginning of a judicial process. Moreover, civically engaged campus culture is also more likely to create such procedures more conscientiously and to refine them accordingly over time.

As a counterexample, let us consider institutional judicial decisions that have excluded faculty, staff, and student voices from regular procedures. When, in late 2014, a student accused Oberlin theater professor Roger Copeland of creating "a hostile and unsafe learning environment," the dean of arts and sciences dismissed mitigating student testimony and asked Copeland to sign a confidential admission of the complaint. After retaining legal counsel, Copeland opted for a hearing over the matter from the Oberlin Professional Conduct Review Committee; the dean retracted his demand and closed the case without action.[43] The exceptional measures recommended by Oberlin's dean apparently would not have held up to reasonable doubt, and the request for process itself seems to have acted as a corrective lens in this case, both on campus and in social and traditional media. In the more recent case of Avital Ronell's interactions with a graduate student, Nimrod Reitman, New York University had already dismissed Reitman's claims of sexual assault when a combination of traditional and social media pressures forced the institution to reconsider his assertion of Ronell's professional misconduct. While the process here was more convoluted because it took Reitman's publication of an accusation in the *New York Times*, a prominent traditional media outlet, to revive an initially abbreviated judicial hearing, the outcome remains noteworthy for its shift in approach. In the retrial, faculty were seated on a judicial review board that had previously been the express domain of administrators. If, as critic Marjorie Perloff lamented about the Ronell case, "the real victim here . . . is not just NYU but the university at large," then perhaps one remediation should include regular adjudication by a larger audience, including faculty and perhaps also students, in social media–driven cases among other forms of adjudication for misconduct.[44]

As faculty, we need to advocate for the development of sensible social media policy through campus-based conversations with a variety of interested groups, and we need to develop formal policy recommendations on the scope of appropriate activities online, the boundaries and obligations of such material, and the procedures and policies related to professional failures of conduct or ethics on social media platforms. In addition, such policies need clear referral mechanisms, so that in a moment of crisis there are criteria to help determine whether actions should be referred to a campus conduct board, faculty appeals council, or other organs of administration, and at the same time, handled to avoid "double jeopardy" for any particular event. To return to my opening invocation in this essay of Mitchell's insight that race is a *medium* rather than a subject, this recommendation for policy development must be seen to bear widely across that medium and to shape the historical (and future potential) ways that we understand the medium of race to operate across a range of related and dynamic tensions on campus today.

My second principle grows from this concern for juridical processes: any framework for the administration of crises should be driven by the goal of restoration rather than retribution. A complementary way of thinking about this principle follows from the classic legal criteria of proportionality, which must be brought to bear on such matters within the bounds of academia. Kant recognized the principle of proportional justice as an ideal and potentially unattainable condition of humane punishment. For Kant, proportionality was defined by the treatment of the person as an end unto oneself, rather than as an object to be punished or made to suffer.[45] What that treatment implies, therefore, is that the punishment should directly contribute to the human being punished and address that person's wrong as something that could be set right. Punishment is not only for the community in Kant's vision: punishment conducted according to the principle of proportionality helps set a person back on the right path. As Kant recognized, proportion in punishment is difficult to achieve in a single case and perhaps impossible to transmit across instances. This scenario is further complicated by the highly mediated situation of digital communications. The syntax of proportion has to parse vague terms, such as who is harmed, how harm is conveyed, and how one might assess the degree or duration of an injury or impediment. In light of these complications to any policy of social media conduct, the principle of proportionality should be tied not to specific punishments or forms of retribution but to restoration as a framework for the administration of such crises.[46] It may not, I recognize, be possible to use a restorative framework in all cases, and at moments when clear breaches of ethics or professional conduct have been determined through a considered judicial process, then such decisions should be made only for individual cases during the punitive phase of any hearing for conduct.

Proportion, therefore, must accompany restoration. With this third principle recommendation, I am suggesting, in effect, that we need to find ways to nurture an environment that is not anti-black, and further, that treats transgressions against that cultural evolution not only as shortcomings but also as possible sites of intervention. Four decades ago, Orlando Patterson initiated a discipline-wide reorientation toward the study of how

Afro-pessimism shapes the social relations as well as the psychological and ontological dispositions of subjugated bodies.[47] A generation of scholars, including those on whose work I have relied throughout this essay, such as Sara Ahmed, Christina Sharpe, Tricia Rose, Lewis Gordon, and Fred Moten, has produced a corpus of responses to Patterson's recognition that an ontologically pessimistic attitude to the immediate lived environment pervades the inequitable social relations that define the "social death" inherent in slavery. The present call for restoration stands on the shoulders of their work. Such restoration could take many shapes, but one of them should include open forums or working groups on campus. Whether focused on research, teaching, social interactions, or some combination of those approaches, the participatory model of forums or working groups gives voice to a restorative logic that should be used to combat a pessimistic disposition of institutions toward racialized bodies, and in addition, of ourselves and our colleagues as members of those institutions.

Fourth, and most urgently, after proportional justice in conduct and restorative acts, the challenge remains to ensure propriety in the domain of social media. "Propriety" is usually defined, following John Locke, as the legitimate right to address, own, or influence something; thus, it represents a convention of impartial access tied, ultimately, to individual liberty.[48] In its social media flavor, propriety must therefore be understood to balance the competing rights of access, liberty, and normative convention. However, returning to Sara Ahmed's phenomenological notion that institutions orient bodies in space, a productive condition of propriety would then focus on the publics with which social media engages and to which it gives shape. When social media uses an institutional language to hail an individual, it organizes those bodies in space and thus bridges the institution from a private sphere into a political or, to use the language of Foucault, a "biopolitical" domain that control bodies through the political functions of institutional constraint.[49] By making the functions of social media propriety explicit in institutional policy—that is, by describing the functions of access, liberty, and conventional use expressly—the biopolitical function of social media policies may make clear their goals, including areas where discriminatory exclusions or imbalances may be silently operating.[50] Social media makes such logics all too easy to entertain, both for positive and negative ends. The very least that our institutions should do is to make clear how to approach those moments with an aim to let the medium of race thrive, perhaps in unsuspected ways, by supporting the propriety of those discourses on campus directly.

My fifth and last principle recommendation stands clearly in the shadow of faculty responsibilities within academic institutions: in order to understand blackness and address the many concerns it raises more empathetically and incisively, we need to see the teaching and research of blackness as being tied intimately on the one hand to a new and critical engagement with whiteness and, on the other hand, to the persistent problem of colorblindness, including the broad refusal to see race as a subject of legitimate study.[51] Ignoring or disparaging race will not make it go away as one of the central questions for our time. Sharon Raynor's chapter suggests, I would argue in this context, that race and gender suffuse institutional decisions in ways that often remain opaque to the institutions themselves because of the lack of perspicacity our institutions maintain toward their treatments of their faculty, its expertise, and the implications of teaching within highly siloed, highly constrained fields of study. Race bridges those fields and the individuals that shape them, sometimes for the better, sometimes not; it is incumbent upon us to use the classroom context as the spur for broader reformations within the classroom as well as across our institutions.

As we see in the work featured across this volume, we thus have to set our sights on the future, on the next decade. I would propose a consideration for you, reader: together, let us use 2030 as a landmark by which to measure subsequent progress toward establishing the fields of race studies with a stronger foundation through a wide spectrum of social issues, a broader social framework, a larger academic audience, and deeper public engagement. It is important to begin this work by recognizing the significant contributions to the field made in the present book and in the work of scholars I have cited here, as well as those working on topics that far exceed the scope of the current work. That horizon remains before us as the work yet to be done.

I have tried to suggest in this essay that the controlling images we see being propagated via social media are at once more complex and more threatening than academic institutions have traditionally recognized.[52] That perception may be changing, but not fast enough.[53] The institutional emplacements of control have moved to the new domains of digital and social media, and in addition, the parallel rise of the domains of resistance and activism online have thrown institutional systems of inquiry and judgment into disarray. I have written this piece because, after seven years of living in an environment of fear, I found silence a limitation rather than a protection. The digitally enabled, socially nimble, and ethically mutable powers that exert themselves over our campuses today demand, rather, that we begin to speak back differently than before.

NOTES

1. I have changed the name of the student to protect anonymity. I use the student's own pronouns, they/them/their, for Maurice, a trans male. Personal Interview, September 3, 2017.

2. See bell hooks, "Postmodern Blackness," in *Yearning: Race, Gender and Cultural Politics* (Boston: South End Press, 1990), 23–33.

3. W. J. T. Mitchell, *Seeing Through Race* (Cambridge, MA: Harvard University Press, 2012), 4 and 26–28.

4. Mitchell, *Seeing Through Race*, 4.

5. Mitchell, *Seeing Through Race*, 11 and 20–22 passim.

6. See Audre Lorde, "Age, Race, Class, and Sex: Women Redefining Difference," in *Sister Outsider: Essays and Speeches* (Berkeley, CA: Crossing Press, 1984), 123.

7. Sara Ahmed, "The Phenomenology of Whiteness," *Feminist Theory* 8, no. 2 (2007): 150.

8. See, for example, Rose's argument regarding how institutions shape how emotional intimacy can offer the possibility of an interpersonal justice within unjust systems. Tricia Rose, "Hansberry's *A Raisin in the Sun* and the 'Illegible' Politics of (Inter)Personal Justice," *Kalfou* 1, no. 1 (2014): 27–60.

9. See Walter J. Ong, *Orality and Literacy: The Technologizing of the Word* (New York: Methuen, 1982), 77–94.

10. See Safiya Noble's recent treatment of algorithms as vehicles for oppression: Safiya Noble, *Algorithms of Oppression: How Search Engines Reinforce Racism* (New York: NYU Press, 2018).

11. For a recent use of this term, see bell hooks, "Feminist Democratic Process," bell hooks Institute, blog, March 17, 2016, http://www.bellhooksinstitute.com/blog/2016/3/17/feminist-democratic-process. And see hooks, "Postmodern Blackness."

12. Thus, as Safiya Noble notes, the internet is becoming more centralized and more susceptible to monopolistic effects. See Noble, *Algorithms*, 23–26 and 38.

13. This argument has found a new voice in the work of Paul Gilroy's reinvigoration of the claims for a cosmopolitan and utopian form of liberated culture beyond race. See Paul Gilroy, *Against Race: Imagining Political Culture beyond the Color Line* (Cambridge, MA: Harvard University Press, 2000). For a critique of Fanon's use of Hegel, see Lewis R. Gordon, "Fanon, Philosophy, Racism," in *Racism and Philosophy*, ed. Susan E. Babbitt and Sue Campbell (Ithaca, NY: Cornell University Press, 1999), 32–49. As Fanon notes, "the moment of

'being for others' . . . is made unattainable in a colonialized and civilized society." See Frantz Fanon, *Black Skin, White Masks*, trans. Richard Philcox (New York: Grove, 2008), 109.

14. On the ethnic argument for transcending race as a category, see Steve Fenton, *Ethnicity* (Cambridge: Cambridge University Press, 2003). For a recent survey of the biological basis and shortcomings of genetic racial categories, see Heather Edgar and Keith Hunley, "Race Reconciled? How Biological Anthropologists View Human Variation," *Physical Anthropology* 139, no. 1 (2009): 1–4. For the most trenchant critique of the distinction between naturalized conceptions of race and its opposition to racial constructivism, see Anthony Appiah, "Race, Culture, Identity: Misunderstood Connections," in *Color Conscious*, ed. Anthony Appiah and Amy Gutmann (Princeton, NJ: Princeton University Press, 1996), 30–105.

15. These effects defy the work of Benedict Anderson to distinguish "imagined communities" through print dissemination beyond geographic borders. See Benedict Anderson, *Imagined Communities: Reflection on the Origins and Spread of Nationalism* (London: Verso, 1983), 129–30.

16. For a sociologically inflected discussion of ranking algorithms and how those structures affect academic social media, see Mark Carrigan, *Social Media for Academics* (Heidelberg: Springer, 2016), 153–54. For a deeper treatment, see also Mark Carrigan, "The Bureaucratic Origins of Algorithmic Authoritarianism," blog, November 14, 2016, https://markcarrigan.net/2016/11/14/the-bureaucratic-origins-of-algorithmic-authoritarianism. Carrigan also characterizes a "fragile" modernity as a counterpoint to a utopian vision of total social visibility. See Carrigan, "The Fragile Movements of Late Modernity," in *Morphogenesis and the Crisis of Normativity*, ed. Margaret S. Archer (Heidelberg: Springer, 2016), 191–215.

17. Carl Schmitt, *Political Theology: Four Chapters on the Concept of Sovereignty*, trans. George Schwab (Chicago: University of Chicago Press, 1985), 5.

18. Any substantive discussion of PageRank search results leads to a discussion of the composition and properties of the networked websites that are listed in the results. For a non-technical introduction to network theory, see Albert-László Barabási, *Linked: How Everything Is Connected to Everything Else and What It Means for Business, Science, and Everyday Life* (New York: Perseus, 2002), 219–27. For a mathematically robust discussion, see M. E. J. Newman, "Network Search," in *Networks: An Introduction* (New York: Oxford University Press, 2010), 705–26.

19. Ariella Azoulay, "Archive," Political Concepts: A Critical Lexicon, 2012, http://www.politicalconcepts.org/archive-ariella-azoulay.

20. See, for the digital Whitman archives, https://whitmanarchive.org; for references to the multiple Jefferson archives, https://guides.lib.virginia.edu/c.php?g=514930&p=3520130; and for the Internet Archive's remarkable crawler, https://archive.org/web.

21. See Lev Manovich, "The Database," in *The Language of New Media* (Cambridge, MA: MIT Press, 2001), 218–43. N. Katherine Hayles adopts the

narrative-database distinction from Manovich in *How We Think: Digital Media and Contemporary Technogenesis* (Chicago: University of Chicago Press, 2013), 175–99. See also the recent debate in *PMLA* over archival databases: Ed Folsom, Jonathan Freedman, N. Katherine Hayles, Jerome McGann, Meredith L. McGill, and Peter Stallybrass, "Responses to Ed Folsom's Database as Genre: The Epic Transformation of Archives," *PMLA* 122, no. 5 (2007): 1580–1613.

22. Arjun Appadurai, "Disjuncture and Difference in the Global Cultural Economy," *Public Culture* 2, no. 2 (1990): 9.

23. See, for instance, Yochai Benkler, *The Wealth of Networks: How Social Production Transforms Markets and Freedom* (New Haven, CT: Yale University Press, 2006); and Valentin Y. Mudimbe, "Discourse of Power and Knowledge of Otherness," in *The Invention of Africa: Gnosis, Philosophy and the Order of Knowledge* (Bloomington: Indiana University Press, 1988).

24. Tricia Rose Brown, "Public Tales Wag the Dog: Telling Stories about Structural Racism in the Post–Civil Rights Era," *Du Bois Review* 10, no. 2 (Fall 2013): 447–69, offers remarks that respond to the initial calls of Patricia Hill Collins, particularly *Black Feminist Thought: Knowledge, Consciousness and the Politics of Empowerment* (New York: Routledge, 2000), 25 passim.

25. Etienne Balibar and Immanuel Wallerstein, "Is There a 'Neo-Racism'?," in *Race, Nation, Class: Ambiguous Identities* (London: Verso, 1993), 17–28.

26. Michael Eric Dyson, "Race and Racism: A Symposium," *Social Text* 52 (Spring 1995): 13–14; and see Lewis R. Gordon, *Disciplinary Decadence: Living Thought in Trying Times* (New York: Routledge, 2006), 13–35.

27. A compelling case has been made in the pages, perhaps surprisingly, of *Teen Vogue*; see Lauren Michele Jackson, "We Need to Talk about Digital Blackface Reaction GIFs," *Teen Vogue*, August 2, 2017, https://www.teenvogue.com/story/digital-blackface-reaction-gifs.

28. Among recent reports of bias in skin tone, see Steve Lohr, "Facial Recognition Is Accurate, if You're a White Guy," *New York Times*, February 9, 2018, https://www.nytimes.com/2018/02/09/technology/facial-recognition-race-artificial-intelligence.html. The most comprehensive recent discussion of the biased forms of facial recognition focused on the taxonomy that built the ImageNet facial expression and human classifications training set, which underlies a host of artificial intelligence systems. The original project, ImageNet Roulette, has been pulled for reasons of privacy. Its replacement, https://www.excavating.ai, discusses the project as well as the ethics of these training sets for creating and detecting bias in machine learning systems.

29. See the coverage on National Public Radio: Maggie Penman, Shankar Vedantam, and Max Nesterak, "#AirBnBWhileBlack: How Hidden Bias Shapes the Sharing Economy," National Public Radio, April 26, 2016, https://www.npr.org/2016/04/26/475623339/-airbnbwhileblack-how-hidden-bias-shapes-the-sharing-economy.

30. Sharpe's echo of Fanon's work derives from his famous discussion of the "Fact of Blackness" in *Black Skin, White Masks*, trans. Charles L. Markman (New York: Grove, 1967). See also Lewis R. Gordon, *Existentia Africana: Understanding Africana Existential Thought* (New York: Routledge, 2000), chapter 4; and in addition, Lewis R. Gordon, *Bad Faith and Antiblack Racism* (Amherst, NY: Humanity, 1995). Fred Moten has recently offered an afro-optimist riposte to Fanon in Moten, "The Case of Blackness," *Criticism* 50, no. 2 (2008): 177–218.

31. Christina Sharpe, *In the Wake: On Blackness and Being* (Durham, NC: Duke University Press, 2016), 104.

32. Erwin Chemerinsky and Howard Gillman's book *Free Speech on Campus* (New Haven, CT: Yale University Press, 2017) offers the most robust account. For a review of other recent publications on this topic, see Henry Reichman, "Academic Freedom and the Common Good: A Review Essay," *Journal of Academic Freedom* 7 (2016): 1–19, https://www.aaup.org/JAF7/academic-freedom-and-common-goodreview-essay.

33. John Ellison, "Letter to Incoming Class of 2020 Students," via The Chicago Maroon (@ChicagoMaroon), "In a welcome letter to freshman, the College made clear that it does not condone safe spaces or trigger warnings," Twitter, August 24, 2016, https://twitter.com/ChicagoMaroon/status/768561465183862785.

34. The AAUP's definitive 1940 statement on academic freedom and its 1970 reinterpretation and elaboration, along with a variety of related policies, can be found in American Association of University Professors, *Policy Documents and Reports*, 11th ed. (Baltimore, MD: Johns Hopkins University Press, 2015). For analysis and critique, see especially Matthew W. Finkin and Robert C. Post, *For the Common Good: Principles of American Academic Freedom* (New Haven, CT: Yale University Press, 2009). Other major works concerning the academic freedom of college professors include Stanley Fish, *Versions of Academic Freedom: From Professionalism to Revolution* (Chicago: University of Chicago Press, 2014); Louis Menand, ed., *The Future of Academic Freedom* (Chicago: University of Chicago Press, 1996); William W. Van Alstyne, ed., *Freedom and Tenure in the Academy* (Durham, NC: Duke University Press, 1993); Joanna Williams, *Academic Freedom in an Age of Conformity* (London: Palgrave Macmillan, 2016); and John K. Wilson, *Patriotic Correctness: Academic Freedom and Its Enemies* (Boulder, CO: Paradigm, 2008).

35. American Association of University Professors, "Academic Freedom and Electronic Communications" (2014), https://www.aaup.org/report/academic-freedom-and-electronic-communications-2014.

36. This framework is further developed in Robert O'Neil et al., "Protecting an Independent Faculty Voice: Academic Freedom after *Garcetti v. Ceballos*," AAUP, November–December 2009: 67–88, https://www.aaup.org/file/Protecting-Independent-Voice.pdf. Further, Timothy Schiell discusses student academic freedom of speech in "The Case of the Student's Racist Facebook Message," *Journal*

of Academic Freedom 5 (2014), https://www.aaup.org/sites/default/files/Shiell.pdf.

37. Social media policy available online at http://drexel.edu/ucomm/about/policies/social-media, accessed January 3, 2018.

38. The discussion of "compelling circumstances" in the Electronic Communications Policy encompasses the evaluation of conduct in electronic communications in its broadest implications. See University of California Office of the President, Electronic Communications Policy, August 18, 2005, https://policy.ucop.edu/doc/7000470/ElectronicCommunications, appendix A, p. 18.

39. See University of California–Davis, "Social Media Best Practices," http://marketingtoolbox.ucdavis.edu/digital/social-media/best-practices.html.

40. The best practices for social media at the University of Illinois are here: http://publicaffairs.illinois.edu/resources/socialmediabestpractices.html.

41. For related issues on the liberal arts campus, see Nathan Heller, "The Big Uneasy: What's Roiling the Liberal Arts Campus?," *New Yorker*, May 30, 2016, https://www.newyorker.com/magazine/2016/05/30/the-new-activism-of-liberal-arts-colleges.

42. Judith Butler, *Giving an Account of Oneself* (New York: Fordham University Press, 2005), 23.

43. Heller, "The Big Uneasy."

44. Marjorie Perloff, "What the Avital Ronell Affair Says about the State of the Profession," *Los Angeles Review of Books* blog, August 29, 2018, https://blog.lareviewofbooks.org/essays/avital-ronell-affair-says-state-profession. Among key treatments of the Ronell affair, see also Masha Green, "An N.Y.U. Sexual-Harassment Case Has Spurred a Necessary Conversation about #MeToo," *New Yorker*, August 25, 2018, pp. 22–24; and Zoe Greenberg, "A Female Professor, Her Male Student and the Limits of #MeToo," *New York Times*, August 14, 2018, A1. It is telling that the courses Ronell has taught since returning to the classroom include a course on boundary crossing and a graduate course on grievances.

45. See Immanuel Kant, *Groundwork of the Metaphysics of Morals*, trans. Mary Gregor (New York: Cambridge University Press, 1991), 42. For a survey of theories of retribution in the philosophy of punishment, see Andrew von Hirsch, "Proportionality in the Philosophy of Punishment," *Crime and Justice* 16 (1992): 55–98.

46. The literature on restorative justice is vast. Two key texts are Desmond Tutu, *No Future without Forgiveness* (New York: Doubleday, 2009), and Thich Nhat Hahn, *Good Citizens: Creating Enlightened Society* (Berkeley, CA: Parallax, 2012). I thank Chad Berry first for encouraging me to develop this approach as a response to my actions, and further, for giving me the opportunity to see this work in action through his own response to those same actions.

47. For the foundational discussion of the conditions of slavery that gave rise to afro-pessimism, see Orlando Patterson, *Slavery and Social Death: A Comparative Study* (Cambridge, MA: Harvard University Press, 1982), 1–15.

48. John Locke, *An Essay Concerning Human Understanding* (Oxford: Clarendon Press, 1964), bk. II, §5, 219, p. 270. For a fuller discussion of the principle of propriety, see Duncan Kelly, *The Propriety of Liberty: Persons, Passions, and Judgment in Modern Political Thought* (Princeton, NJ: Princeton University Press, 2011), 175ff.

49. Michel Foucault, *Society Must Be Defended: Lectures at the College de France, 1974–1975*, trans. David Macey (New York: Picador, 2003). On "biopower," see Roberto Esposito, *Bíos: Biopolitics and Philosophy* (Minneapolis: University of Minnesota Press, 2008).

50. See Sara Ahmed, *On Being Included: Racism and Diversity in Institutional Life* (Durham, NC: Duke University Press, 2012), 176–79.

51. Key interventions in the study of seeing race and colorblindness as being tied to the status of whiteness include Ruth Frankenberg, *White Women, Race Matters: The Social Construction of Whiteness* (Minneapolis: University of Minnesota Press, 1993), 137–39; and Toni Morrison, *Playing in the Dark: Whiteness and the Literary Imagination* (Cambridge, MA: Harvard University Press, 1992), 17. On post-racial ideology in the wake, particularly, of Obama's 2008 election, see Ian Haney, "Is the Post in Post-Racial the Blind in Colorblind?" *Cardozo Law Review* 32, no. 3 (January 2011): 807–31; and Eduardo Bonilla-Silva and David Dietrich, "The Sweet Enchantment of Color-Blind Racism in Obamerica," *Annals of the American Academy of Political and Social Sciences* 634, no. 1 (2011): 190–206.

52. Patricia Hill Collins's discussion of "controlling images" of race and institution informs my conclusions here. See Patricia Hill Collins, "Mammies, Matriarchs, and Other Controlling Images," in *Black Feminist Thought*, 69–96.

53. The most piercing analysis to date of this difference is Ta-Nehisi Coates, *We Were Eight Years in Power: An American Tragedy* (New York: One World, 2017).

BIBLIOGRAPHY

Ahmed, Sara. *On Being Included: Racism and Diversity in Institutional Life*. Durham, NC: Duke University Press, 2012.

———. "The Phenomenology of Whiteness." *Feminist Theory* 8, no. 2 (2007): 149–68.

American Association of University Professors. "Academic Freedom and Electronic Communications." November 2013. https://www.aaup.org/report/academic-freedom-and-electronic-communications-2014.

———. *Policy Documents and Reports*. 11th ed. Baltimore, MD: Johns Hopkins University Press, 2015.

Anderson, Benedict. *Imagined Communities: Reflection on the Origins and Spread of Nationalism*. London: Verso, 1983.

Appadurai, Arjun. "Disjuncture and Difference in the Global Cultural Economy." *Public Culture* 2, no. 2 (1990): 9–28.

Appiah, Anthony. "Race, Culture, Identity: Misunderstood Connections." In *Color Conscious*, edited by Anthony Appiah and Amy Gutmann, 30–105. Princeton, NJ: Princeton University Press, 1996.

Azoulay, Ariella. "Archive." Political Concepts: A Critical Lexicon. 2012. http://www.politicalconcepts.org/archive-ariella-azoulay.

Balibar, Etienne, and Immanuel Wallerstein. *Race, Nation, Class: Ambiguous Identities*. London: Verso, 1993.

Barabási, Albert-László. *Linked: How Everything Is Connected to Everything Else and What It Means for Business, Science, and Everyday Life*. New York: Perseus, 2002.

Benkler, Yochai. *The Wealth of Networks: How Social Production Transforms Markets and Freedom*. New Haven, CT: Yale University Press, 2006.

Bonilla-Silva, Eduardo, and David Dietrich. "The Sweet Enchantment of Color-Blind Racism in Obamerica." *Annals of the American Academy of Political and Social Sciences* 634, no. 1 (2011): 190–206.

Brown, Tricia Rose. "Public Tales Wag the Dog: Telling Stories about Structural Racism in the Post–Civil Rights Era." *Du Bois Review* 10, no. 2 (Fall 2013): 447–69.

Butler, Judith. *Giving an Account of Oneself*. New York: Fordham University Press, 2005.

Carrigan, Mark. "The Fragile Movements of Late Modernity." In *Morphogenesis and the Crisis of Normativity*, edited by Margaret S. Archer, 191–215. Heidelberg: Springer, 2016.

———. *Social Media for Academics*. Heidelberg: Springer, 2016.

Chemerinsky, Erwin, and Howard Gillman. *Free Speech on Campus*. New Haven, CT: Yale University Press, 2017.

Coates, Ta-Nehisi. *We Were Eight Years in Power: An American Tragedy*. New York: One World, 2017.

Dyson, Michael Eric. "Race and Racism: A Symposium." *Social Text* 52 (Spring 1995): 1–52.

Edgar, Heather, and Keith Hunley. "Race Reconciled? How Biological Anthropologists View Human Variation." *Physical Anthropology* 139, no. 1 (2009): 1–4.

Esposito, Roberto. *Bíos: Biopolitics and Philosophy*. Minneapolis: University of Minnesota Press, 2008.

Fanon, Frantz. *Black Skin, White Masks*. Translated by Richard Philcox. New York: Grove, 2008.

Fenton, Steve. *Ethnicity*. Cambridge: Cambridge University Press, 2003.

Finkin, Matthew W., and Robert C. Post. *For the Common Good: Principles of American Academic Freedom*. New Haven, CT: Yale University Press, 2009.

Fish, Stanley. *Versions of Academic Freedom: From Professionalism to Revolution.* Chicago: University of Chicago Press, 2014.

Folsom, Ed, Jonathan Freedman, N. Katherine Hayles, Jerome McGann, Meredith L. McGill, and Peter Stallybrass. "Responses to Ed Folsom's Database as Genre: The Epic Transformation of Archives." *PMLA* 122, no. 5 (2007): 1580–1613.

Foucault, Michel. *Society Must Be Defended: Lectures at the College de France, 1974–1975.* Translated by David Macey. New York: Picador, 2003.

Frankenberg, Ruth. *White Women, Race Matters: The Social Construction of Whiteness.* Minneapolis: University of Minnesota Press, 1993.

Gilroy, Paul. *Against Race: Imagining Political Culture beyond the Color Line.* Cambridge, MA: Harvard University Press, 2000.

Gordon, Lewis R. *Bad Faith and Antiblack Racism.* Amherst, NY: Humanity, 1995.

———. *Disciplinary Decadence: Living Thought in Trying Times.* New York: Routledge, 2006.

———. *Existentia Africana: Understanding Africana Existential Thought.* New York: Routledge, 2000.

———. "Fanon, Philosophy, Racism." In *Racism and Philosophy*, edited by Susan E. Babbitt and Sue Campbell, 32–49. Ithaca, NY: Cornell University Press, 1999.

Green, Masha. "An N.Y.U. Sexual-Harassment Case Has Spurred a Necessary Conversation about #MeToo." *New Yorker*, August 25, 2018, pp. 22–24.

Greenberg, Zoe. "A Female Professor, Her Male Student and the Limits of #MeToo." *New York Times*, August 14, 2018.

Hahn, Thich Nhat. *Good Citizens: Creating Enlightened Society.* Berkeley, CA: Parallax, 2012.

Haney, Ian. "Is the Post in Post-Racial the Blind in Colorblind?" *Cardozo Law Review* 32, no. 3 (January 2011): 807–31.

Hayles, N. Katherine. *How We Think: Digital Media and Contemporary Technogenesis.* Chicago: University of Chicago Press, 2013.

Heller, Nathan. "The Big Uneasy: What's Roiling the Liberal Arts Campus?" *New Yorker*, May 30, 2016. https://www.newyorker.com/magazine/2016/05/30/the-new-activism-of-liberal-arts-colleges.

Hill Collins, Patricia. *Black Feminist Thought: Knowledge, Consciousness and the Politics of Empowerment.* New York: Routledge, 2000.

hooks, bell. *Yearning: Race, Gender and Cultural Politics.* Boston: South End Press, 1990.

Jackson, Lauren Michele. "We Need to Talk about Digital Blackface Reaction GIFs." *Teen Vogue*, August 2, 2017. https://www.teenvogue.com/story/digital-blackface-reaction-gifs.

Kant, Immanuel. *Groundwork of the Metaphysics of Morals.* Translated by Mary Gregor. New York: Cambridge University Press, 1991.

Kelly, Duncan. *The Propriety of Liberty: Persons, Passions, and Judgment in Modern Political Thought.* Princeton, NJ: Princeton University Press, 2011.

Locke, John. *An Essay Concerning Human Understanding*. Oxford: Clarendon Press, 1964.

Lohr, Steve. "Facial Recognition Is Accurate, if You're a White Guy." *New York Times*, February 9, 2018. https://www.nytimes.com/2018/02/09/technology/facial-recognition-race-artificial-intelligence.html.

Lorde, Audre. *Sister Outsider: Essays and Speeches*. Berkeley, CA: Crossing Press, 1984.

Manovich, Lev. *The Language of New Media*. Cambridge, MA: MIT Press, 2001.

Menand, Louis, ed. *The Future of Academic Freedom*. Chicago: University of Chicago Press, 1996.

Mitchell, W. J. T. *Seeing Through Race*. Cambridge, MA: Harvard University Press, 2012.

Morrison, Toni. *Playing in the Dark: Whiteness and the Literary Imagination*. Cambridge, MA: Harvard University Press, 1992.

Moten, Fred. "The Case of Blackness." *Criticism* 50, no. 2 (2008): 177–218.

Mudimbe, Valentin Y. "Discourse of Power and Knowledge of Otherness." In *The Invention of Africa: Gnosis, Philosophy and the Order of Knowledge*. Bloomington: Indiana University Press, 1988.

Newman, M. E. J. *Networks: An Introduction*. New York: Oxford University Press, 2010.

Noble, Safiya. *Algorithms of Oppression: How Search Engines Reinforce Racism*. New York: NYU Press, 2018.

O'Neil, Robert M., Judith C. Areen, Matthew W. Finkin, Larry G. Gerber, William W. Van Alstyne, and Cary Nelson. "Protecting an Independent Faculty Voice: Academic Freedom after *Garcetti v. Ceballos*." AAUP, November–December 2009: 67–88. https://www.aaup.org/file/Protecting-Independent-Voice.pdf.

Ong, Walter J. *Orality and Literacy: The Technologizing of the Word*. New York: Methuen, 1982.

Patterson, Orlando. *Slavery and Social Death: A Comparative Study*. Cambridge, MA: Harvard University Press, 1982.

Penman, Maggie, Shankar Vedantam, and Max Nesterak. "#AirBnBWhileBlack: How Hidden Bias Shapes the Sharing Economy." National Public Radio, April 26, 2016. https://www.npr.org/2016/04/26/475623339/-airbnbwhileblack-how-hidden-bias-shapes-the-sharing-economy.

Perloff, Marjorie. "What the Avital Ronell Affair Says about the State of the Profession." *Los Angeles Review of Books* blog, August 29, 2018. https://blog.lareviewofbooks.org/essays/avital-ronell-affair-says-state-profession.

Reichman, Henry. "Academic Freedom and the Common Good: A Review Essay." *Journal of Academic Freedom* 7 (2016): 1–19. https://www.aaup.org/JAF7/academic-freedom-and-common-goodreview-essay.

Rose, Tricia. "Hansberry's *A Raisin in the Sun* and the 'Illegible' Politics of (Inter) Personal Justice." *Kalfou* 1, no. 1 (2014): 27–60.

Schiell, Timothy. "The Case of the Student's Racist Facebook Message." *Journal of Academic Freedom* 5 (2014). https://www.aaup.org/sites/default/files/Shiell.pdf.

Schmitt, Carl. *Political Theology: Four Chapters on the Concept of Sovereignty.* Translated by George Schwab. Chicago: University of Chicago Press, 1985.

Sharpe, Christina. *In the Wake: On Blackness and Being.* Durham, NC: Duke University Press, 2016.

Tutu, Desmond. *No Future without Forgiveness.* New York: Doubleday, 2009.

Van Alstyne, William W., ed. *Freedom and Tenure in the Academy.* Durham, NC: Duke University Press, 1993.

von Hirsch, Andrew. "Proportionality in the Philosophy of Punishment." *Crime and Justice* 16 (1992): 55–98.

Williams, Joanna. *Academic Freedom in an Age of Conformity.* London: Palgrave Macmillan, 2016.

Wilson, John K. *Patriotic Correctness: Academic Freedom and Its Enemies.* Boulder, CO: Paradigm, 2008.

CHAPTER 6

TEACHING FROM THE TAP

Confronting Hegemony and Systemic Oppression through Reflection and Analysis

KERRI-ANN M. SMITH AND PAUL M. BUCKLEY

INTRODUCTION

Teaching in perilous, tenuous times can prove challenging, particularly when the tension comes about as a result of political turmoil. Consider what it must have been like, morally, for German educators during the Holocaust, for French educators during the Algerian war of independence, and for educators during other controversial times, including those teaching and living at the height of the civil rights movement in the United States. When we, as educators, are confronted with public opinions and current events that are opposed diametrically to our beliefs and commitments, we must find a pedagogical approach to promote critical thinking and advance a sense of fairness. The concern, however, is how we teach in an age of social and political unrest while remaining true to our own convictions—whatever they may be. The rise of sociopolitical tension in the 1960s gave birth to movements surrounding "multiculturalism, collaborative learning, learning communities, and service learning" in higher education.[1] Today's sociopolitical climate reflects arrant divisiveness and intractable racism, challenging educators to find new approaches in teaching toward justice.

Major historic events such as the September 11, 2001, tragedy, Hurricane Katrina, Hurricane Sandy, and the myriad school shootings have shaken the curriculum, forcing teachers and students to confront current affairs in more deliberate, meaningful ways. The same is true for the recent water crisis in Flint, Michigan, which began in 2014 and continues to cast a long shadow. In this chapter, we reflect on our approaches to teaching in two different courses at two institutional types, utilizing the crisis in Flint as our case study for confronting hegemony and systemic oppression. After a brief summary of that case, we present the design of our courses and offer reflections on our approaches to teaching using service learning, case study, reflection, and dialogue. Finally, we consider of our positionalities at two vastly different institutions of higher education that both present distinct opportunities for teaching and learning that advance principles of social justice for students and teachers alike.

It is dutiful for educators to engage, rather than ignore, social issues, thus helping our students provide analyses that connect these issues with their own experiences. The crisis in Flint is significant in that it amplifies existing inequities along race and class lines, as well as their devastating impacts. The focal point of the crisis began with the City of Flint's decision to switch the city's water supply from the Detroit Water and Sewerage Department, which sourced its water from Lake Huron, to the Karegnondi Water Authority, which sourced its water from the Flint River, on April 25, 2014. Subsequently, the pipes that pumped water to the city began to leach dangerous chemicals into the water. The water changed from the normal clear substance to a brown grime. Residents who used the polluted water reported symptoms such as dizziness and boils all over their bodies, among other deleterious effects. The children of Flint fared the worst, as there is no allowably safe level of lead for children's bodies. Any encounter with lead will, in fact, prove harmful to the brains of children and will have lasting, irreversible cognitive and other consequences.

People across the country became aware of Flint's water crisis as the national media picked up related stories in 2015, exposing early health impacts to Flint residents, including rashes and other illnesses. As news coverage increased, so did the progression of diseases and other health concerns as it became clear that lead poisoning from the water was also a major concern for Flint. The devastating and disturbing crisis confounds human understanding, particularly when we factor in the number of missed moments for seemingly obvious humane decision-making throughout the time line. How does a crisis of this proportion occur in the United States of America in the twenty-first century? What factors would allow the poisoning of a city to persist for over a year and a half, even while there was wide-scale public attention, prior to initiating any remediating actions?

We can pursue these critical questions and more in classrooms when we engage active learning strategies, including the use of case studies, service learning projects, experiments, discussions, and debates.[2] The Association of American Colleges and Universities (AACU) designates service learning as one of the eleven high-impact practices that have proven beneficial to students from diverse backgrounds. High-impact practices encourage student engagement and allow students to work directly with community partners to see the connection between the curriculum and the real world. Service learning has long been lauded as an effective tool in engaging students, particularly in writing courses, at community colleges.[3] In many cases, service learning has allowed students to improve their career skills, while focusing their attention on an issue of greater importance to the world and themselves. Service learning may also serve as a conduit for exposing social justice issues, thus allowing students to engage in transformative activism through service. In addition to teaching students how to identify and navigate systemic oppression, these projects help educators learn the diverse experiences of students and develop a larger worldview. In other words, we learn from our students and glean inspiration, as much as they learn from us and the projects we design. As bell hooks notes, "Professors who embrace the challenge of self-actualization will be better able to create pedagogical practices that engage students, providing them with ways of knowing that enhance their capacity to live fully and deeply,"[4] which affirms the work of liberal arts educators who prioritize teaching and learning partnerships with undergraduates through case studies and expository writing.

People—inside and outside the academy—may understand the concept of injustice when relating to their personal choices, their personal space, and their interactions with society. Consequently, they sometimes overlook other inequities and discrimination unless they can relate to the injustice directly or it affects someone in their immediate circles. Paulo Freire warns that "washing one's hands of the conflict between the powerful and the powerless means to side with the powerful, not to be neutral."[5] Freire teaches that it is the responsibility of educators to help students understand hegemony, by providing opportunities for them to confront issues, topics, and ideas that push against the status quo. In *Pedagogy of the Oppressed*, he declares, "Students, as they are increasingly posed with problems relating to themselves in the world . . . will feel increasingly challenged and obligated to rise to that challenge."[6] Service learning is the opportune vehicle through which students can learn concepts such as social justice and where students may also see how their involvement can foster a more equitable society. With a critical framing of the service needs, students can pursue social justice rather than self-satisfaction through volunteerism.

The breadth and scope of service learning projects have traditionally sought to focus on reflection. That is, students reflect on how their participation in a service learning project has influenced or changed their views on a topic. Students also reflect on how the skills they employed while doing the project are transferable to careers and academic subjects, as part of the mandate of service learning is to prepare more responsible citizens and leaders. Service learning can, however, be a crucial method to teach students how to be activists and advocates for themselves and others when it is approached from a social justice vantage point.

Critics of service learning and experiential learning note that such projects often set students apart from their partners, who often need the help or expertise of the students to complete important tasks. Consequently, students then see themselves as idealized outsiders looking in, or are so disconnected from the community[7] they are serving that they adopt a paternalistic approach to their projects, rather than see the ways in which their own existence may or may not contribute to the greater society in which they live. To allay these issues and in anticipation of avoiding this flaw of experiential learning, we asked our students to examine power dynamics and who these dynamics serve by asking Lee Anne Bell's critical questions: "In whose interests do systems operate? Who benefits and who pays?"[8] This line of inquiry updates for the classroom the classic legal question *Cui bono?*: Who stands to gain?

The state of exception in which we, as American educators, now find ourselves requires purposeful pedagogy, or *praxis* (to use the term from Freire), that engages students in critical consciousness and meaningful dialogue. This, then, is our central focus in the present chapter: we ask how we shall develop a teaching and learning praxis that meets the demands for a more incisive awareness about our moment and its contexts, for our students and ourselves. Pedagogy must encourage action, not just passive activism, and service learning or experiential learning can help buttress the movement toward action. These transformative projects help to foster justice-oriented citizenship with our students. This chapter outlines two such projects that focus specifically on the crisis in Flint, Michigan, where two instructors—one at an urban community college and the other at a liberal arts college—engage students in critical consciousness and meaningful dialogue on the subject.

SOCIAL JUSTICE EDUCATION

A key component of social justice education is the use of *praxis*. Educators who teach from a social justice perspective embrace action and reflection in their work and in that of their students.[9] Early scholars of service learning called for an emphasis on social justice, noting that experiential education can offer a "powerful tool on the journey toward justice."[10] Notably, bell hooks insists on a transformation in the academy, where educators deliberately seek to emphasize "action and reflection upon the world in order to change it."[11] Engaged pedagogy, hooks argues, helps professors and students achieve self-actualization, a key component that drives social justice activism. In order for students to situate injustice and unfairness in the world around them, they must first be able to position themselves and their lived experiences on the spectrum of power. For this purpose, educators must seek to design assignments that facilitate analyses of questions such as "whose interests are being served?," "who is being left out?," "who is responsible when systems fail?," and "how are they held responsible and at whose expense?" Such questions analyze the structures of power and oppression and the interstices between the two, all while ensuring that we do what Shane McCoy calls for in his chapter, engaging students in critical analysis by "scaffolding for justice."

According to the American Association of Community Colleges (AACC), 45 percent of all undergraduates attended community colleges in 2014. These students, often nontraditional, come with a wealth of experiences and ideas that pose challenges to the status quo of educational systems. Community college students also represent a part of the working class, since the average age of recent community college students is twenty-eight, with 49 percent ranging between the ages of twenty-two and thirty-nine. While 42 percent of all part-time community college students work full-time, 52 percent of all community college students receive some form of financial aid.[12]

The community college is an ideal space for service learning and community engagement. Oftentimes, students are residents of the area in which the school is located and can see the immediate benefits of working to enhance their own communities. Both Prentice and Taggart and Crisp discuss the various benefits of using service learning in community colleges, and they discuss why community college students are ideal for social justice projects. Further, Taggart and Crisp suggest that educators plan and enact deliberate strategies to engage social justice in service learning projects.[13]

Historically, small private residential liberal arts colleges have been composed of a less diverse population and have provided a less diverse range of academic and interpersonal experiences for students than larger public universities.[14] These experiences include courses, workshops, and other diversity initiatives, as well as interactions with people from backgrounds different than one's own. However, contemporary liberal arts colleges have developed the capacity for high exposure to purposeful diverse experiences for undergraduates and have demonstrated that their students are significantly more likely to engage these experiences than their counterparts at any other institutional type. While the full scope of the specific practices that inform these outcomes is still evolving, there is evidence of best educational practices among selective liberal arts colleges that produce positive student outcomes. These practices are centered on culturally responsive pedagogy,[15] which calls for and includes such features as frequent student-student interactions, frequent faculty-student interactions, strong faculty emphasis on diversity, frequent engagement of humanities and interdisciplinary courses, and a generous budget for student services.[16] This list suggests that the liberal arts college context is also an important site to engage impactful praxis toward social justice aims.

A culturally responsive model works for students in community college and liberal arts college classrooms, as they bring multivariate experiences to classroom discussions, making them rich and diverse in nature. The community college classroom often consists of students from marginalized backgrounds, who approach course materials with resonant and expansive perspectives on inequality and injustice, while liberal arts colleges pursue increasing opportunities for this level of expansiveness with significant socioeconomically privileged student populations. According to the AACC, women account for 52 percent of community college students; first-generation college students, 36 percent; veterans, 4 percent; second-career seekers, career upgraders, and students with disabilities together account for 12 percent; and adults over forty years old, 12 percent. Students come with perspectives that can help shape a curriculum committed to culturally relevant pedagogy[17] and social justice education.

One benefit of social justice education is that it allows room for us to apply theory to current affairs, while giving students the opportunity to situate themselves at the core of the issue, as opposed to merely stepping into a facility, providing assistance, using the tools they learned in class, and stepping back into their lives. When done well, learning assignments with a social justice approach can first change the individual from the inside out, empowering that individual to work toward changing their world through action. Community college students are ideal for enacting social justice assignments, as they already represent many groups that understand injustice or marginalization, as their identities intersect in many ways with groups that have encountered disadvantages. Students receiving a liberal arts education are also empowered to engage in social justice learning projects, as they are engaged in the depth and breadth of learning that prepares them to explore solutions to complex societal problems.

A social justice framework helps students at both community colleges and liberal arts colleges develop a "critical consciousness" with which they work with others to "question, analyze, and challenge oppressive conditions in the lives of others, rather than blame each other or fate," while doing service learning projects.[18] The consequence of being critically conscious is that students can see the intersections between occurrences in their own lives and their own society and the experiences of others, particularly those who reside in systems of oppression and marginalization.

Instructors may find that contemporary students are technologically savvy, but they may not be as connected to current affairs. This was the case in the remedial writing course, where students all reported some use of social media. Very few students in the courses watched or engaged with the news, but they were aware of current situations in popular culture. However, educators often mistake a lack of awareness for apathy, and consequently miss many teachable moments that could also double as stellar opportunities for experiential education projects. When used productively, students' lack of awareness can be channeled into activism once they learn more about a topic by situating themselves in the bigger picture.

The educator's process of encouraging student self-actualization is a key component to crafting and executing intentional projects that help students challenge oppressive practices within themselves and the communities of which they are a part.[19] Through service learning and ongoing reflection, students can expand their worldview and develop a critical lens that analyzes systemic oppression and its lasting effects. Students can take action, creating advances in society that would not otherwise be possible without their contribution.[20]

As we have already begun to suggest, the state of exception in which we now find ourselves requires purposeful pedagogy through a praxis that engages students in critical consciousness and meaningful dialogue. This critical consciousness connects the personal to the sociopolitical to understand both internal and external systems of oppression and the way people internalize them.[21] Pedagogy must encourage action, not just passive activism, and service learning/experiential learning can help bolster the shift toward action.

Bowen also highlights the pedagogical dimensions of social justice, claiming that pedagogy that engages social justice education is student-centered, experiential, collaborative, intellectual, analytical, multicultural, value-based, and activist. One may purport that this model could be more effective by including an additional dimension: intentionality. At the core of any activism is a direct intent that is related to the desired outcome. Civic action, when used in the academic context, requires intentionality that pushes students beyond mere learning into intentional activism. Bowen's model suggests that students be encouraged to act, but service learning allows for direct, intentional action that can influence immediate or long-term change in society.

TWO COURSE DESIGNS

The existing literature on service learning has long emphasized the positive impacts of service learning projects, particularly in writing courses.[22] Writing courses are unique in their malleability and the wide scope of materials that can be covered. This service learning project was designed for community college students in the lower level of a two-semester sequence of remedial writing. Students are eligible for the lower-level section of remedial writing if they have failed the entrance exam by more than 15 points (passing = 56 percent). Students in the lower-level writing course are often but not exclusively first-semester, first-year students who must pass remedial writing to take ENGL-101 and other writing-intensive courses.

The course objectives for the lower-level writing course focus on getting students prepared for college-level writing, and learning objectives include improving sentence structure, writing coherent arguments, forming cohesive paragraphs, and developing ideas in a logical sequence. Typically, students who pass this course advance to an upper-level course that ends in a standardized exit exam that moves them from remediation into the standard curriculum. Exceptional students are given the opportunity to test out of the upper-level course if they demonstrate readiness for ENGL-101. Students in this course are required to read texts that present analytical points on contemporary issues that can be analyzed by discussing a main idea, a significant idea, and a personal experience. These requirements are aligned with the those of the standardized test that students will take to exit remediation.

I aligned the service learning portion of the course with social justice by selecting reading materials focused on health, nutrition, social justice, and specifically the crisis in Flint, Michigan. Resources were selected from a course textbook, the *New York Times*, and other media sources. I also realigned the course objectives to include references to themes related to social justice. The listed project objectives state that at the end of the project, students should be able to identify the crisis in Flint; analyze the power brokers in the crisis; acknowledge the oppressed in the crisis; learn about the effects of lead poisoning on vulnerable populations; and create informational artifacts that would promote awareness on Earth Day.

In contrast, the second course we describe, People and the Environment, is a general studies course, designated GS100, that is utilized as a half-course-credit course for our matriculating first-year students in a summer bridge program at Colorado College. As a college matriculation course, it is offered as a pass/fail graded course within a two-week program focused on assisting students in acclimating to the intense academic experience and social culture of the college's block plan. The block plan requires daily classroom engagement for approximately three hours, at minimum. The course is co-taught, engaging an interdisciplinary learning opportunity for students to develop an understanding of race/racism and social justice, while also learning about the environment. The course focused on race and racism and is parallel to the earlier course in its similar emphasis on analyzing the 2014 water crisis manifested by the linked cycles of urban poverty, public neglect, and poor governmental management in Flint, Michigan.

PROJECT DESIGN AT THE COMMUNITY COLLEGE

Students in two sections of the lower-level course (Spring 2016) were asked to read and analyze an article by Charles M. Blow, "The Poisoning of Flint's Water," and to write an essay in which they analyzed the main idea, one significant idea, and a personal experience. The writing requirements were consistent with those on the remediation-exit examination. Students engaged in a Socratic discussion about the crisis in Flint, Michigan, where they included everything they knew beforehand about its contours. The discussion focused primarily on the points in the article, as students expressed a lack of awareness about the Flint water crisis.

For this course, I designed a service learning project around the crisis in Flint that would help students gather more information and use the tools they gain from research to inform their peers and to help directly those suffering in Flint. For this project, students would prepare a presentation for the college's Earth Day celebration and solicit donations for Flint. In this case, the community partner was the college, which included mostly their peers and professors. Students prepared poster boards and designed water bottle labels, ribbons, and stickers to help provide information on the water crisis. Students also created a social media profile and a hashtag to share information on the crisis. Students would provide information to their peers via their posters and then use donations from the products sold to contribute to solving the crisis in Flint.

The poster boards comprised research done by the students addressing three essential questions, designed using a social justice paradigm: Why is the crisis important? Who is the crisis affecting? What are the effects of the crisis on people's health? Students were divided into groups to conduct research to answer each question and design a social-justice-based informative poster board. Students in one section of the course selected the theme #FlintLivesMatter, a reflection of their understanding that the crisis is a social justice issue that is inextricably tied to other current social justice movements. Other students in a second section used the theme "Social Democracy and Justice for Flint" for their poster board.

Students opted to use water bottles as fundraisers, and they created four water bottle labels. Each label provided information on the dangers of lead poisoning, its effects on women and children, and information concerning the crisis in Flint. They also decided to use aqua blue ribbons as a symbol of support for Flint, similar to other campaigns such as those for breast cancer and heart disease. In addition, they designed five stickers with different images (e.g., a word cloud about Flint and pictures of dirty water) to help spread awareness by way of their Instagram page, which they also designed to curate their experiences at the Earth Day presentation and throughout class, as they developed the final project. One student, a talented artist, designed a backdrop for the Earth Day display constructed from cardboard, depicting a popular viewscape representing downtown Flint. On Earth Day, students from both sections used social media to extend their influence by creating an Instagram account (@students_4_Flint) to showcase their presentations using #QCC4Flint.

On their display table at Earth Day were also lead test kits, which they used as models to teach their peers how to test their water for lead. Students accepted donations at their table in exchange for the items they had created. They subsequently researched and selected two organizations and donated the funds to them. One organization focuses on literacy for young children suffering from the crisis; students connected with this organization since they were members of an academic literacy course. The other organization focuses on health education and advocates for clean water for pregnant women and children. Students opted to split the contributions 50/50 between the organizations, with hope that their small campaign will educate their peers and do something tangible for the citizens of Flint.

INTEGRATION OF COURSE OBJECTIVES

The CUNY Assessment Test in Writing (CATW) tests several domains in writing by way of a writing prompt and rubric measuring critical response, development, structure, and language use. The prompt states the following: "Read the passage above and write an essay responding to the ideas it presents. In your essay, be sure to summarize the passage in your own words, stating the author's most important ideas. Develop your essay by identifying one idea in the passage that you feel is especially significant, and explain its significance. Support your claims with evidence and examples drawn from what you've read, learned in school, and/or personally experienced." Students in the lower level of the two-class-sequence (BE-111 and BE-112) developmental writing course write four-paragraph essays similar to CATW essays to harness their writing skills and learn the importance of integrating examples and supporting details when constructing a well-developed essay. Students in the service learning sections of the course integrated the articles they read on the crisis in Flint into CATW essays about similar topics relating to food justice. In their responses, the students were able to make text-to-text references in the area of the essay that requires them to describe a personal experience. Students wrote pre-reflection essays. They also wrote summaries of articles relating to the Flint crisis. Using the resources in the Academic Literacy Learning Center's Computer Lab, students conducted research to answer three essential questions: 1) Why is the crisis important? 2) Who is the crisis affecting? 3) How does the crisis affect people's health?

PROJECT NOTES

The developmental writing classroom can sometimes be a site for enhancement, where students are led toward improving specific literacy skills and modes of communicating through writing. Particularly when promotion from developmental courses depends on students' performance on standardized tests, deviation from the standard curriculum can be difficult and, at times, risky. However, service learning research has shown small but important gains in students' academic performance in writing classes after participating in well-designed service learning activities.[23] Previous studies have not determined whether there is a direct connection between service learning and performance on standardized tests.

The service learning projects in the community college course described in this chapter began after the midterm examination was conducted. The midterm examination and the final examination follow the same format as the standardized exit exam that students must take to advance to credit-bearing English courses. The department allows exceptions for students to be considered for early testing if their test scores are 56 percent or above on both the departmental midterm and final exams. Students who test early and pass can skip the upper-level remedial writing course and subsequently enroll in ENGL-101 and other courses. The service learning project began right after the midterm exam was conducted. In the 8:00 a.m. class, seven students qualified for early testing, while in the 10:00 a.m. class, six students qualified. Of the thirteen students recommended, eleven were given a workshop and showed up for testing. All eleven passed the exit exam and registered for ENGL-101 in the following semester.

The camaraderie that the students shared was both inspiring and encouraging. Generally, in courses that do not integrate service learning projects, instructors have the onus of creating and fostering a unified classroom culture. However, an understated benefit of service learning, particularly in the context of social justice, is the ability to create a classroom climate of equity, justice, and productivity, as students see themselves as a team, working toward a noble cause.

In their reflections, in both classes, students reported that they applied academic course content during the service learning project (84 percent), that doing so helped them learn course material more effectively (79 percent), and that their project helped others (89 percent). Students also reported increased awareness of the greater issues facing society (84 percent) and the community need addressed by the service learning project (84 percent).

The students were given the opportunity to participate in the college's Teagle Foundation Grant project, which highlighted the Big Question: "How do we build our commitment to civic and moral responsibility for diverse, equitable, healthy, and sustainable communities?" Students engage the Big Question throughout the project and then write reflection papers that cover five domains: Statement of the Issues/Activities, Academic/Applied Learning, Change, Moral and Civic Engagement, and Commitment/Action. Each domain presents students with questions focusing on social justice. For example, one domain asks, "What elements of unfairness or injustice does the problem have? Do you think people should care more about the problem? Why or why not?" These questions help students think critically about their projects and serve as a guide for reflection on the true impact of their work. The Teagle Big Question inspired robust classroom discussions on injustice and influenced students to situate their ideas within the context of a "bigger picture." Students analyzed inequity as outsiders while considering their own agency.

The instructor also spent time in reflection and analysis,[24] while drawing inspiration from students as they developed the project. Students immersed themselves in the assignments and continued to discuss new ideas, even as they drew close to their deadline for Earth Day. They took ownership of the project and collaborated independently, formulating critical questions and using research to guide themselves toward a greater understanding of the subject. There is great joy in seeing students work together to create and to teach other students about social justice and equity.

Students even divided the tasks on their own for Earth Day, by drawing on each other's most notable skills. For example, the student who was most passionate about talking about the effects of lead poisoning was asked to field any questions about lead. It was inspiring to see the way students self-selected and delegated tasks to get the job done. Most inspiring, however, was the shift in the language they used in the classroom. Their language now included theoretical terms that describe injustice and ideas that question the way society works.

The transformation in their speech and in their writing was palpable. Students took the initiative to make posts on social media and share files and links to information about the crisis in Flint, Michigan. Even after the service learning project had ended, students continued to engage with issues surrounding social justice and equity. They challenged hierarchical systems and questioned hegemony.

I was impressed as I watched my students, who were unaware in the beginning, come alive with ideas and plans for how to make their world a better place. The inspiration lies in knowing that while we live in tenuous times and situations are not always kind, just, equitable, and palatable, there are a few young people who understand that they must stand in the interstices of cultural, sociopolitical, and religious dysfunction and take action to ensure that the world they build becomes one in which all citizens can work together and where governmental agencies perform the tasks they were elected to do. The students might not have done something impactful enough to end the crisis in Flint, which still persists today, but they learned the importance of civic engagement and now understand how to situate themselves and their ambitions on the spectrum of power and powerlessness. Teaching a course like this reassures me that when culturally responsive pedagogy is utilized in the classroom, students can transform and make informed decisions about effecting change in the world around them, despite the various forms of veiled discrimination and systemic oppression that exist in our world.

PROJECT DESIGN AT THE LIBERAL ARTS COLLEGE

The second course was designed as a collaborative interdisciplinary effort between two instructors who provided materials that offered common reporting of the crisis, as well as analyses of the case of the crisis in Flint. For the duration of the course, students were immersed in content that focused on both the crisis and theories surrounding social justice and inequity. Students used these materials as a basis for dialogue, reflection, and debate. In this transitional course during a bridge summer experience, each class session employed strong elements of meta-learning. Hence, not only were students engaged in dialogue and reflection assignments, but they were also prompted to think about and discuss the use of reflection and dialogue in their learning and the context of a liberal arts college classroom.

Grounding authentic reflection as a "practice of freedom," students were required to maintain a reflection log as the initial and ongoing assignment of the course. These logs allowed us to review the ways in which students were engaging the case content and making meaning of the crisis as an academic and personal experience. We provided prompts for the students' log writing and responded to each entry with reflective questions and additional prompts to clarify thoughts or nurture deeper critical consciousness on the topic. To exit the course, students were required to write two expository papers and make a group presentation. The goal of these assignments was to gauge the transformational process of students' critical thinking and the development of their desire to activate change. The logs and papers provided insight into how students were affected throughout the course. The information in these logs also helped us assess where gaps in learning occurred and determine how to modify future lessons to fill those gaps.

This instructor also engaged in reflection and deeper learning throughout the course by responding in conversation with the student logs. The goal in embracing a more fluid learning process was to nurture an inclusive classroom environment where students could freely challenge, support, and create new ideas. This environment permeated cocurricular and personal spaces as well, and it transposed office hours and out-of-classroom interactions into more empowering relationships. Teaching the course and sharing the responsibility of critical learning with students presented insightful information about the process of social justice education. For example, while students were interested in learning information and concepts, they also desired approval from the instructor; they wanted to be right. Detailed feedback helped not only to clarify the students' thinking but to confirm the goal of the course in developing consciousness, rather than performance.

At the heart of the case-study method is a storytelling process that invites participants to think of themselves and others in relationship to systems, institutions, and narratives. Specifically, students were invited to consider their own identities and positionality during the course. A lesson on intersectionality and exercises that promoted an examination of the multiple identities that individuals hold helped students consider the same for people involved in the Flint crisis—beyond the identity categories to their influence and molding of lived experiences. Each exercise was designed to foster personal, private reflection (i.e., written individual exercises), as well as broader critical engagements through pairing and class-wide dialogues.

Students were also able to see me as a raced and gendered (Black, male) person in the academy and to empathize with my teaching a course that is profoundly personal, in spite of the intellectual distancing and connecting required to teach the course. By demonstrating confidence and maturity in revealing how the Flint, Michigan, crisis affected me, I gave students room to discuss the case at a highly intellectual level that also honored the humanity of everyone in the class. That is, students engaged with the case with the awareness that Flint's problems were not a case study for academic spectacle but a situation in which cherished human beings were treated as devalued, disposable, and worthy of death. Learning about and confronting this profound reality promoted other analyses and connections with students' own lived experiences and challenged them to consider active resistance to injustices they observe in proximate situations.

CONCLUSION

Teaching conscientiously in any educational context requires educators to invest in the complex process of confronting social injustices and demonstrating their relevance to learners in the classroom. Utilizing high-impact practices that include reflection, service learning, storytelling, and making room for students to share their critical thinking on multiple platforms makes for meaningful praxis for personal and social transformation. While there are inherent risks for teachers to design critical opportunities for students to have an encounter with current events that reflect social inequities, the rewards for learning and conscientiousness are exponential. Beyond a deeper awareness of the case in Flint, Michigan, and other historical crises, students and educators can make other personal investments in support of the rights of their fellow citizens to obtain basic necessities such as clean water or control of their bodies and to demand democratic management of their city and the truth. Recognizing how these assumed privileges for all Americans are not equally provided is an education that equalizes the imperative for all people to work for a more just society.

NOTES

1. Adrianna Kezar and Robert A. Rhoads, "The Dynamic Tensions of Service Learning in Higher Education: A Philosophical Perspective," *Journal of Higher Education* 72, no. 2 (2001): 148–71.

2. S. Sandstrom, "Use of Case Studies to Teach Diabetes and Other Chronic Illnesses to Nursing Students," *Journal of Nursing Education* 5, no. 6 (2006): 229–32.

3. Mary Prentice, "Social Justice through Service Learning: Community Colleges as Ground Zero," *Equity and Excellence in Education* 40 (2007): 266–74.

4. bell hooks, *Teaching to Transgress* (New York: Routledge, 1994), 22.

5. Paulo Freire, *Pedagogy of the Oppressed*, 30th anniversary ed. (New York: Continuum, 2005), 35.

6. Freire, *Pedagogy*, 81.

7. Tasha Perkins, "School-Community Partnerships, Friend or Foe? The Doublespeak of Community with Educational Partnerships," *Educational Studies* 51, no. 4 (2015): 317–36.

8. Lee Anne Bell, "Theoretical Foundations for Social Justice Education," in *Teaching for Diversity and Social Justice*, 3rd ed., ed. Maurianne Adams and Lee Anne Bell (New York: Routledge, 2016), 3–26.

9. Maurianne Adams and Lee Anne Bell, eds., *Teaching for Diversity and Social Justice*, 3rd ed. (New York: Routledge, 2016).

10. Karen Warren, "Educating Students for Social Justice in Service Learning," *Journal of Experiential Education* 21, no. 3 (1998): 134–39.

11. hooks, *Teaching to Transgress*, 14.

12. Gloria Ladson-Billings, "Toward a Theory of Culturally Relevant Pedagogy," *American Educational Research Journal* 32, no. 3 (1995): 465–91.

13. Prentice, "Social Justice"; Amanda Taggart and Gloria Crisp, "Service Learning at Community Colleges: Synthesis, Critique, and Recommendations for Future Research," *Journal of College Reading and Learning* 42, no. 1 (2011): 24–44.

14. Paul D. Umbach and George D. Kuh, "Student Experiences with Diversity at Liberal Arts Colleges: Another Claim for Distinctiveness," *Journal of Higher Education* 77, no. 1 (2006): 169–92.

15. Zaretta Hammond, *Culturally Responsive Teaching and the Brain: Promoting Authentic Engagement and Rigor among Culturally and Linguistically Diverse Students* (Thousand Oaks, CA: Corwin, 2014).

16. Alexander W. Astin, "How the Liberal Arts College Affects Students," *Daedalus* 128, no. 1 (1999): 77–100; Ernest Pascarella, Ty Cruce, Gregory Wolniak, and Charles Blaich, "Do Liberal Arts Colleges Really Foster Good Practices in Undergraduate Education?," *Journal of College Student Development* 45, no. 1 (2004): 57–74.

17. Ladson-Billings, "Toward a Theory."

18. Bell, "Theoretical Foundations," 16.

19. Bell, "Theoretical Foundations," 16.

20. Glenn Bowen, "Promoting Social Change through Service Learning in the Curriculum," *Journal of Effective Teaching* 14, no. 1 (2014): 51–62.

21. Bell, "Theoretical Foundations."

22. Linda J. Sax and Alexander Astin, "The Benefits of Service: Evidence from Undergraduates," *Educational Record* 78, nos. 3–4 (1997): 25–32; Alexander

W. Astin, Lori J. Vogelgesang, Elaine K. Ikeda, and Jennifer A. Yee, "How Service Learning Affects Students," Higher Education Research Institute, January 2000, https://heri.ucla.edu/PDFs/HSLAS/HSLAS.PDF.

23. Sax and Asten, "Benefits of Service"; Robert Sigmon, *Linking Service with Learning* (Washington, DC: Council of Independent Colleges, 1994); Astin et al., "How Service Learning Affects Students."

24. Hibajene M. Shandomo, "The Role of Critical Reflection in Teacher Education," *School-University Partnerships* 4, no. 1 (2010): 101–13.

BIBLIOGRAPHY

Adams, Maurianne, and Lee Anne Bell, eds. *Teaching for Diversity and Social Justice.* 3rd ed. New York: Routledge, 2016.

American Association of Community Colleges. "Fast Facts 2018." https://www.aacc.nche.edu/wp-content/uploads/2018/04/2018-Fast-Facts.pdf.

Astin, Alexander W. "How the Liberal Arts College Affects Students." *Daedalus* 128, no. 1 (1999): 77–100.

Astin, Alexander W., Lori J. Vogelgesang, Elaine K. Ikeda, and Jennifer A. Yee. "How Service Learning Affects Students." Higher Education Research Institute, January 2000. https://heri.ucla.edu/PDFs/HSLAS/HSLAS.PDF.

Bell, Lee Anne. "Theoretical Foundations for Social Justice Education." In *Teaching for Diversity and Social Justice*, 3rd ed., edited by Maurianne Adams and Lee Anne Bell, 3–26. New York: Routledge, 2016.

Bowen, Glenn. "Promoting Social Change through Service Learning in the Curriculum." *Journal of Effective Teaching* 14, no. 1 (2014): 51–62.

Bringle, Robert, and Julie Hatcher. "Implementing Service Learning in Higher Education." *The Journal of Higher Education* 67, no. 2 (1996): 221–39.

Freire, Paulo. *Pedagogy of the Oppressed.* 30th anniversary ed. New York: Continuum, 2005.

———. *The Politics of Education: Culture, Power, and Liberation.* Westport, CT: Bergin and Garvey, 1985.

Hammond, Zaretta. *Culturally Responsive Teaching and the Brain: Promoting Authentic Engagement and Rigor among Culturally and Linguistically Diverse Students.* Thousand Oaks, CA: Corwin, 2014.

hooks, bell. *Teaching to Transgress.* New York: Routledge, 1994.

Kezar, Adrianna, and Robert A. Rhoads. "The Dynamic Tensions of Service Learning in Higher Education: A Philosophical Perspective." *Journal of Higher Education* 72, no. 2 (2001): 148–71.

Ladson-Billings, Gloria. "Toward a Theory of Culturally Relevant Pedagogy." *American Educational Research Journal* 32, no. 3 (1995): 465–91.

Pascarella, Ernest, Ty Cruce, Gregory Wolniak, and Charles Blaich. "Do Liberal Arts Colleges Really Foster Good Practices in Undergraduate Education?" *Journal of College Student Development* 45, no. 1 (2004): 57–74.

Perkins, Tasha. "School-Community Partnerships, Friend or Foe? The Doublespeak of Community with Educational Partnerships." *Educational Studies* 51, no. 4 (2015): 317–36.

Prentice, Mary. "Social Justice through Service Learning: Community Colleges as Ground Zero." *Equity and Excellence in Education* 40 (2007): 266–74.

Prentice, Mary, and Gail Robinson. "Improving Student Learning Outcomes with Service Learning." American Association of Community Colleges, 2010, https://files.eric.ed.gov/fulltext/ED535904.pdf.

Rice, Kathleen L., and Jane R. Brown. "Transforming Educational Curriculum and Service Learning." *Journal of Experiential Learning* 21, no. 3 (1998): 140–6.

Ringstad, Robin, Valerie Lester Leyva, John Garcia, and Kelvin Jaysek-Rysdahl. "Creating Space for Marginalized Voices: Refocusing Service Learning on Community Change and Social Justice." *Journal of Teaching in Social Work* 32 (2012): 269–83.

Sandstrom, S. "Use of Case Studies to Teach Diabetes and Other Chronic Illnesses to Nursing Students." *Journal of Nursing Education* 5, no. 6 (2006): 229–32.

Sax, Linda J., and Alexander Astin. "The Benefits of Service: Evidence from Undergraduates." *Educational Record* 78, nos. 3–4 (1997): 25–32.

Shandomo, Hibajene M. "The Role of Critical Reflection in Teacher Education." *School-University Partnerships* 4, no. 1 (2010): 101–13.

Sigmon, Robert. *Linking Service with Learning.* Washington, DC: Council of Independent Colleges, 1994.

Soria, Krista M., and Tania D. Mitchell, eds. *Civic Engagement and Community Service at Research Universities: Engaging Undergraduates for Social Justice Social Change and Responsible Citizenship.* Palgrave Studies in Global Citizenship Education and Democracy. London: Palgrave Macmillan, 2016.

Taggart, Amanda, and Gloria Crisp. "Service Learning at Community Colleges: Synthesis, Critique, and Recommendations for Future Research." *Journal of College Reading and Learning* 42, no. 1 (2011): 24–44.

Umbach, Paul D., and George D. Kuh. "Student Experiences with Diversity at Liberal Arts Colleges: Another Claim for Distinctiveness." *Journal of Higher Education* 77, no. 1 (2006): 169–92.

Warren, Karen. "Educating Students for Social Justice in Service Learning." *Journal of Experiential Education* 21, no. 3 (1998): 134–39.

Yerkes, Rita. "Service Learning Revisited." *Journal of Experiential Education* 21, no. 3 (1998): 117.

CHAPTER 7

"I NEVER TOUCH RACE"

Teaching Race in Online Spaces with Future Indiana School Leaders

RACHEL ROEGMAN AND SERENA J. SALLOUM

In October 2015, a female Black student was picked up from her seat, thrown to the ground, and arrested by a white school resource officer at a public South Carolina high school. One of her classmates captured the violence with her phone and, within days, the video went viral. Rachel, one of this chapter's authors, and one of her students were angry, frustrated, and scared by the increased violence of white authority figures on unarmed Black youth and talked about the video and potential actions that they could take at their institution broadly and in the educational leadership program specifically in response. At the time, Rachel was teaching a hybrid online/in-person course on school-community relationships for aspiring building-level administrators, and she thought this video presented an opportunity for her students to think about state violence against Black bodies and to imagine the role of the school principal in addressing this critical issue: How could a leader respond to this incident in ways that valued community perspectives and the racism that families and children experienced every day? She would not meet with her class in person until two months later and did not want to pass up an opportunity for her students to think deeply about this incident and its implications for school leadership, so she needed a way to address the topic during an asynchronous online session.

Rachel chose to give students an alternative assignment for the online discussion prompt for the week, in which students could respond to the violent incident, connect the weekly readings to ideas for a school-level response, and think about proactive measures schools could take to develop more authentic partnerships with school resource officers. They would post their responses on the course's online discussion board, and they were expected to read and respond to at least two peer responses. One of Rachel's students emailed her instead of posting to the class discussion board:

> I am really debating whether to jump into any conversation about that [incident] because of the way race conversations ALWAYS spiral in a negative direction. I fully believe that to resolve any issue, communication is vital. As a result, when racial issues come up, it is important to talk about it if you want to have a chance to resolve the situation.
>
> HOWEVER, there are three things I almost never touch when talking with people (in order): race, politics, and religion. The reason is, on these issues (especially race and politics), people have VERY deep and strongly held beliefs that no level of discussion will change.

For us, two junior faculty members, this is the exact reason that we need to be talking about race in leadership preparation, particularly in programs that utilize online instructional formats. If "communication is vital," then we need to make sure school principals are ready to lead these discussions. Racial incidents occur regularly, and K–12 students and teachers of color experience race and racism firsthand on a daily basis. Even when not discussed, race and racism permeate the experiences of Americans of all racial backgrounds.[1] If principals choose to "never touch" these conversations because they are afraid of the result, then oppression will persist and it will not be possible for schools to create equitable educational experiences for youth of color.

In this chapter, we discuss the importance and challenges of teaching race online in K–12 leadership preparation programs in Indiana from our standpoints as leadership preparation faculty in two different Indiana universities. Similar to Murrah-Mandril (this volume), we recognize the importance and complexity of facilitating discourse about race in virtual spaces. To support our coauthored approach, we drew on collaborative autoethnography as a way to explore and represent how we individually and collectively approached our topic.[2] As Delgado and Valens discuss in this volume, having a partner in the work of racial equity gives us inspiration, support, and critical, at times challenging, feedback. We are invested knowers in preparing equity-focused leaders for K–12 schools, and we are strongly committed to finding ways to engage future leaders in addressing issues of race in productive ways. We embed our specific experiences within the larger context of education in the United States, positing our practice as both personal and as situated.[3] We focus this chapter around a problem of practice from Serena's teaching that occurred several years before the writing of this chapter as a way to frame our collaborative discussion and analysis.

It is especially important to note the changing political climate across the United States in our work preparing future K–12 leaders. Since Trump's election to the presidency, Rogers and colleagues report that "the substance and tone of national political discourse" have become more contentious and divisive.[4] These changes have been apparent in many aspects of public life, including in K–12 schools, where school leaders, regardless of their beliefs, are expected to maintain an inclusive school climate for all students, whether they are undocumented, Muslim, transgender, or from any other group that is targeted by current or future proposed legislation. In addition to this charged rhetoric, there is empirical evidence that teachers perceive a negative impact on their students as a result of this new political environment.[5] In Indiana, where the majority of voters supported Trump (56.5 percent), there is still a sizable population who did not, meaning that it is likely that school leaders have students and parents from varied political perspectives, and they need to find a way to create a school culture for all students. While future elections will likely lead to different state and federal officials, the underlying issues related to race and racism will continue, as elections alone will not end racism, which is endemic to the United States.

In Indiana, preparing future leaders to face these challenges is moving rapidly into online spaces. All four major public universities offer entirely or partially online preparation and licensure programs, accounting for almost 600 new building- and district-level administrators annually.[6] Some of our students report working in districts that are experiencing growth in terms of racial, ethnic, and linguistic diversity and share their own experiences in talking about race in school contexts; the majority report coming from communities and districts with majority-white populations (some over 99 percent white), with limited experiences in participating in or facilitating conversations across racial difference or participating in or facilitating conversations about race in educational contexts. Faculty, including ourselves, who work with leadership candidates around issues of race therefore must do so primarily in online spaces with many white students who go their entire personal lives and professional careers interacting only with white students, teachers, and communities.

By online, we mean three different ways that our courses are structured, which impact the types of opportunities and challenges for addressing race.

Hybrid courses involve different combinations of online and in-person sessions.

Synchronous courses refer to courses (or sessions) in which all students and faculty participate in a session at the same time, generally through videoconferencing technology.

Asynchronous courses (or sessions) involve faculty postings readings, videos, and activities with deadlines that students complete at times of their choosing. Interactions may occur through discussion boards in which participants post at times of their choosing, often within a set period.

In the rest of this chapter, we introduce our teaching selves and our current teaching contexts. Next, we review the literature on teaching about race in K–12 teacher education and leadership preparation. We then present Serena's problem of practice that illustrates several of the challenges we have experienced. Finally, we analyze this problem of practice through the lens of culturally responsive school leadership and conclude with pedagogical implications for addressing race in online spaces.

OUR TEACHING SELVES AND CONTEXTS

Rachel is a queer white woman who taught English and social studies for nine years in the San Francisco Unified School District in both traditional and alternative schools. She is an assistant professor of educational leadership and policy studies at Purdue University.[7] Serena is a Middle Eastern woman. Prior to beginning her career in higher education, she taught for four years in urban schools, two years with Teach for America serving as a first-grade teacher in Los Angeles Unified Schools and then two years in a small charter school in Chicago. She is currently an associate professor of educational leadership at Ball State University. For both of us, our experiences in K–12 were foundational to our academic identities, which led us to enter academia in the field of educational leadership. Neither of us served as a formal school leader, though we took on various leadership roles in the schools where we taught.

We both prepare building- and district-level leaders in the state of Indiana. Purdue University is a land-grant university established in 1874 that has an enrollment of 40,000 students. Students can enroll in principal or superintendent licensure programs, earning an MS, EdS, or PhD. In all of the licensure programs, students' coursework is offered in a hybrid format, with the first and last class session held on campus and the remainder online. In the building-level program, all of the online sessions are asynchronous, while in the superintendent licensure program, about half of the online sessions are synchronous. All of the students are current school employees, teachers, administrators, or counselors; about 75 percent of the students are white and about 25 percent are Black. Students come to Purdue from across the state, from large and small districts, from rural and suburban areas.

Ball State University is a public university that originally served the state as a normal school (a university that focused on teacher preparation), with a student population of about 22,000. Consistent with the population of the state of Indiana, most of its students are white. The modal student in the school leadership program is interested in obtaining a master's (building-level) or doctorate (district-level) degree for career advancement and works full-time in a K–12 school or in a district's central office. The doctoral program serves students in an educational cohort, where the same group of students takes courses together. Coursework in the district-level program is blended; select sessions are conducted in person (about 25 percent) and the remainder of course delivery is online in asynchronous sessions.

TEACHING ABOUT RACE IN K–12 LEADERSHIP PREPARATION

Preparing future and current school leaders to address issues of race and interrupt racism, among other societal oppressions, has become a central aspect of several leadership preparation curricula and professional organizations across the United States.[8] The bulk of the research on addressing race within leadership preparation has focused on in-person programs and coursework, with an emphasis on specific assignments and experiences that leadership candidates complete. Several scholars have recently developed resources for in-service work in schools related to race and oppression,[9] and future scholarship can provide empirical evidence as to how these resources impact school communities. The current body of research has looked specifically at ways that preparation programs have supported candidates in developing racial awareness, self-awareness, and awareness of systemic societal inequities and how they impact students' educational experiences.[10]

Despite interest in social justice and race-related content in leadership preparation, the literature has shown that many programs "frequently neglect to provide their students with pedagogies that critically examine the multifaceted issues surrounding race and racism."[11] Rusch and Horsford argue that part of this neglect results from educational leadership faculty who themselves may be uncomfortable talking about race, and they suggest several strategies developed from critical race theory to address this.[12] These strategies include valuing voices of individuals of color and working to integrate multiple narratives, and the authors also call on white educators to relinquish their privilege and unlearn negative strategies that offer them a sense of protection, such as silence and false consciousness. Gooden and Dantley also suggest the use of critical theories such as critical Latinx theory or critical feminist theory as a grounding for working with leadership candidates around race.[13] They argue that critical theories demand a more sustained critique of institutional change, particularly focused on the ways in which educational leadership connects theory to the schooling realities that candidates and students face in their everyday experiences. Furthermore, Gooden and Dantley find that leadership preparation needs to focus specifically on race, and not merely on social justice. When programs focus on social justice, race often moves to the periphery.[14]

One important finding in this literature is that candidates of different racial backgrounds have different responses to race-focused curricula. Gooden and Dantley, for example, found that when white students wrote racial autobiographies, the concept of race became "more tangible," but students of color had difficulty completing the assignment because they were sharing experiences of pain.[15] Hernandez and Marshall's study of a course assignment in which students were asked to conduct an equity audit was based on a sample of students from one course that had nine white students and one student of color.[16] They focused on the student of color's different response to those of the white students. However, their research questions and sample size did not allow for a focus on how students' racial backgrounds served as a lens for the assignment or their learning from it, a compelling further line of inquiry. They conclude that course assignments have the greatest potential when they couple personal reflection and analyzing data to create action plans. This highlights Dantley and Gooden's recommendation of the need to couple theory and experience, and they suggested this was equally important for students of all racial backgrounds.[17]

TEACHING ABOUT RACE IN ONLINE K–12 SPACES

Research on teaching about race in online K–12 contexts focuses on preservice teacher preparation and notions of social justice. Teacher education is a field that has a long history of attempting different pedagogies to engage the primarily white, middle-class, female student population in understanding various issues of social justice, including race, in preparation for teaching students from different racial and ethnic backgrounds.[18] Recent work has highlighted specific pedagogical practices with potential to engage preservice teachers in analyzing their own identities and beliefs through developing online learning communities that create space for reflection and discourse.[19] In their online course, for example, Guthrie and McCracken had students complete a service learning project with a local organization as a way to bring experiential learning to the online classroom.[20] Students overall reported positive learning around the concept of social justice, and they reported that engaging in conversations with classmates about issues of social justice and reflecting in structured protocols supported their learning as well.

One key finding from this literature base is the importance of protocols and guidelines for critical conversations, echoing findings from online teaching more generally around the importance of structured guidelines and protocols in support preservice teacher learning.[21] Studies by Whipp, for example, found that when preservice teachers had specific guidelines about what to post, their posts demonstrated higher levels of reflection.[22] The instructor's presence in online discussions is another factor that led to more successful engagement around race in online courses.[23]

Some researchers report that online courses are often better suited for teaching about issues of race. For example, Merryfield, who taught both in-person and online multicultural education courses, found that students of color participated more, took greater risks, and expressed more vulnerability in online versions of the course.[24] Akintunde, who also taught in both formats, found that online conversations of race were more successful because students were less afraid of being confronted about their comments or beliefs.[25]

At the same time, these researchers have concerns about online courses addressing race. Researchers have reported the difficulty of building relationships between students and between student and instructor without any in-person sessions.[26] While the instructor presence is key to moderating online conversations, without such a presence, students may perpetuate deficit views related to race, in which individuals see race as a problem to be solved or overcome, instead of as an asset, and further, in which the dynamics of race are treated in a linear way as a moment in a progression, rather than as a topic that requires the student to address it iteratively. Holding deficit views is a problem on its own, and when these views are posted in online discussion boards, other students are negatively affected by reading their classmates' postings without a professor or classmate immediately challenging them.[27] Grant and Lee, in assessing several of their online course offerings related to issues of race, reflected on negative responses from their students around their identities as instructors—one is African American and one is Korean American.[28] They found some students had negative emotional responses to course content, which did not come out until semester-end evaluations. In online courses, faculty cannot read students' body language or facial expressions to assess their reactions to ideas, activities, or lectures.

Overall the literature is mixed, with online spaces offering potential and challenge, some of which is similar to talking about race in K–12 education in person, and some unique to online and hybrid courses. To illustrate potential dilemmas faculty members in educational leadership might face when teaching about race, we now discuss a problem of practice from a course that Serena taught.

SERENA'S PROBLEM OF PRACTICE

At the time of this case, Ball State's doctoral program did not have an explicit focus on issues of race, poverty, or social justice more broadly defined, and individual professors could choose to raise these topics, or not, in their courses. This is common across the United States, and efforts to implement required coursework in these areas is often met with resistance, as Delgado and Valens discuss elsewhere in this volume. In all of my courses, I (Serena) work to intertwine issues of race with course content. The problem of practice that I present occurred within my course on educational policy, which includes learning objectives related to policy impact on different demographic groups. I first provide a brief background of the class session from which the problem of practice arose and then share my problem of practice. Throughout, I draw upon verbatim quotes with pseudonyms for students and elucidate my thinking during this discussion.

In the middle of one of my courses on educational policy, during the first of our four in-person sessions, I engaged my students in conversation about *A Nation at Risk* (1983) and the *Manufactured Crisis* (1995), posing the question, Are American schools serving all children well today? There were twenty-two students in the class, three students of color and nineteen white students; eleven students were male and eleven female. In the ensuing conversation, several white male students resoundingly answered, "Yes," as illustrated by Ray, who said, "I don't think we are doing fine. I think we are doing spectacular." As the conversation continued, several students, all but one of whom were white, used generalizations and simplistic analogies that blamed poor students of color for their academic outcomes, while advancing the argument that schools in the United States were doing their job. Where schools are experiencing difficulties, this strand of the class suggested, it was because, as another student shared, "We don't get to discard the children that are flawed." Instead, the student argued, public schools have to teach all students, including those who come to school with severe challenges. The notion of a "flawed" student suggests the thinly veiled presence of language coded for race.

Honestly, I felt a bit stunned by these comments. I have spent my career to date focused on the inequities that plague the American school system, an understanding of policy that I had already shared with the class. I was perplexed that most of my students resolved that American schools were overall successful. These students' arguments suggested their lack of understanding of structural racism in determining students' access, opportunities, and outcomes. Instead, they drew on neoliberal arguments of individual determination and equal opportunity, ignoring the societal systems that have institutionalized white privilege.[29] The ease with which they drew on narratives that blamed parents, families, and children suggested implicit racism and deficit attitudes in their approach to working with families who do not conform to their beliefs or values. For the white students, it also suggests they may be experiencing "white fragility"—the destabilizing and uncomfortable reactions of guilt, defensiveness, or anger when race or racism is raised.[30] I was troubled by the conversation, but I was not sure how to interrupt the narratives. I asked different prompts to encourage students to consider alternate perspectives but left class disheartened. My discouragement was echoed in a student's email that I received the following day:

> Dear Serena,
>
> I wanted you to know that I purposely did not speak up at today's class. I was really struggling with some of the comments and belief systems of others in the class. The types of terms used to describe children, urban children, performance, expectations, parenting . . . were to me very biased and unfair. I did not feel comfortable pointing it all out. . . . I trust you "heard" what I heard. . . . I did not want you to think I was not participating. I was, internally, just struggling to figure out how to give my voice to the conversation without getting too passionate . . .
>
> Penny

Penny's email explicitly highlighted the issues of race and structural racism that were the subtext of our in-person session. Similar to Harris's elegant discussion (this volume) of teaching race and ethnicity, the receipt of Penny's email confirmed my failure. I had heard the implied racism within students' responses, the white fragility of white students, and the deficit thinking shared by white students and one student of color, and I knew I had to respond. If I were going to see all of the students in class the following week, I could have prepared a protocol for having difficult conversations around race, perhaps drawing on Singleton and Linton's foundational work on courageous conversations or a protocol such as the "5 Whys for Inquiry" protocol.[31] These protocols seemed ideal for an in-person class, but I did not see how they could work in an asynchronous session. I had three asynchronous class sessions scheduled for the next three weeks, during which students would be viewing videos, completing readings, and posting to the course discussion board on their own time. From Penny's response and my own reflections after class, it was clear I had not built sufficient community for all students to feel safe or to feel comfortable being vulnerable in course discussions, but I only had online sessions to follow up. I knew I would have to moderate any discussion board activity, but I also wanted to thoughtfully create reflective assignments that would support my students in unpacking what had happened.

In a nutshell: How could I authentically engage students in issues of race and racism expressed during this in-person session in an asynchronous online format in the following three weeks?

ASSESSING THE PROBLEM THROUGH CULTURALLY RESPONSIVE SCHOOL LEADERSHIP

Khalifa, Gooden, and Davis's framework for culturally responsive school leadership offers a powerful way to assess what happened in Serena's in-person class and provide suggestions for what she might cover in the ensuing sessions—which happened to be online in an asynchronous format.[32] The original plan had been for students to engage in readings and activities over the next three weeks and post about them in the class's online discussion room at times of their choosing. But before revising her lesson plans, Serena herself first needed to unpack what happened.

Building off Ladson-Billings's concept of culturally relevant teaching and Gay's concept of culturally responsive teaching,[33] culturally responsive school leadership is similarly predicated on the idea, shared by these scholars, that good teaching is not enough—teaching occurs within broader school contexts that perpetuate many of the actions that their approaches to teaching were meant to address. School leaders are responsible for ensuring that the entire school environment is more responsive to the needs of students who have traditionally been underserved by school systems in the United States.

In unpacking what happened, Serena recognized that she was not enacting culturally responsive school leadership as the formal leader in the classroom—the instructor who was meant to facilitate students' understanding of course objectives related to educational policy, race, and justice in the United States. Despite her commitments to educational equity, she struggled with how to respond to implied racism and ended up finishing the class without directly explaining how structural racism made equal opportunity a cultural myth; she knew she needed to interrupt the racist commentary and reframe the conversation but was unsure how. Culturally responsive school leadership requires leaders to engage in difficult conversations about race,[34] something that both school leaders and faculty working with school leaders continue to struggle with.[35] Even as committed anti-racist educators, we both experience the discomfort of white fragility that comes with addressing race directly and are working to see our discomfort as a sign for a need for dialogue—not as a sign to stop a conversation.

Additionally, as illustrated by Penny's email, some students were silenced in the discussion, marking evidence of a shortcoming in democratic discourse in the in-person classroom space.[36] Letting dominant views that perpetuated racist beliefs take over the classroom also unintentionally meant that the classroom had shifted away from providing a culturally responsive and inclusive learning environment. Instead, the classroom became a site of the production and reproduction of structural racism. Serena knew what happened was problematic, and we now look to Khalifa, Gooden, and Davis's framework to better understand the dominant voices in her classroom and what might be done to support those students' development as culturally responsive school leaders.[37]

One key aspect of culturally responsive school leadership that Khalifa, Gooden, and Davis identify is critical self-awareness, a useful tool for thinking about what happened in Serena's class.[38] Critical self-awareness refers to ways in which leaders are aware of their values, beliefs, and dispositions toward working with poor children of color. Also referred to as critical consciousness, critical self-awareness requires school leaders to "intently question their knowledge base and assumptions."[39] Gay and Kirkland, in discussing preservice teacher education, argue that educators need "deeper knowledge and consciousness about what is to be taught, how and to whom."[40] When Serena's students drew on individual experience as privileged members of society (most were white men, all were earning a middle-class or higher income, and all were well educated) and when they made generalizations about students who come to school lacking privilege, including students of color and poor students, they were demonstrating a shallow knowledge of K–12 educational systems and social structures in the United States that perpetuate racism, classism, and other forms of oppression. In fact, in addition to generalizing about the country at large, nearly half of her class argued that the schools they led as principals were equitable, and they denied the possibility that inequities existed along any lines in their own buildings.

Furthermore, instead of challenging whiteness as a source of privilege, the majority of students in Serena's class drew on deficit views of students of color and poor students to rationalize their academic performance; they implicitly argued that (wealthy, white) students who are successful succeed as a result of their own efforts, and not of systems that provide privilege. As Fergus argues, "A deficit ideology discounts the presence of systemic inequalities as the result of race-based process, practices, and policies. Most importantly, a deficit ideology blames the group for the conditions they find themselves as experiencing."[41] And, in schools, deficit thinking removes any blame from the school administration for what is going on. Where culturally responsive school leadership calls on school leaders to address and undermine racism, these students engaged in thinking that was more likely to perpetuate systems that provided inequitable experiences and outcomes to students based on their race and class.[42]

Critical whiteness studies offers another way to approach working with the predominantly white future leadership candidates. This line of research argues that white administrators are responsible for understanding how race impacts them and their leadership.[43] White administrators have difficulty talking about whiteness or understanding racism as systemic and, as Blackmore writes, "the whiteness of educational leaders is rarely questioned."[44] DiAngelo argues that because segregation continues to dominate US society, whites are insulated from racial discomfort; as a consequence, having explicit conversations about race makes them uncomfortable and they experience white fragility. She suggests that white Americans especially need to listen, get educated, and critically think about the roles we all play in maintaining racism, which we try to do in our online spaces.[45]

ADDRESSING THESE CONCERNS ONLINE

Online spaces offer unique possibilities for supporting students in developing the skills and dispositions needed to be culturally responsive school leaders and to explicitly raise and address issues related to race and racism in their school contexts. In an in-person course, with multiple students advancing a dominant perspective, students with minority perspectives may be less likely to contribute. Penny, for example, emailed Serena to make sure she knew that Penny was engaged but that she was not vocally participating because she "was, internally, just struggling to figure out how to give my voice to the conversation without getting too passionate."

This resonates with Merryfield's finding that students of color were more likely to express minority viewpoints in online discussions compared with in-person discussions.[46] Beyond creating space for non-dominant voices to participate in the conversation, we now consider other ways that online spaces can support developing critical self-awareness and addressing issues of race in leadership preparation courses.

Much work has already gone into the development of readings and activities that support the development of culturally responsive school leaders, such as Singleton and Linton's work on how to have conversations around difficult topics and Fergus's work on helping schools address issues of disproportionality by examining educators' belief systems.[47] Similarly, Lindsey, Nuri-Robins, and Terrell's manual for school leaders includes specific activities with guidelines for facilitators to help educators gain more comfort and confidence in talking about and addressing race and other societal oppressions.[48] For faculty interested in supporting students' development as culturally responsive school leaders, we offer these as suggestions for places to start that include detailed descriptions of underlying theory and rationale, as well as specific activities and protocols to follow. As faculty consider how to adapt these and other resources to online contexts, we contribute to this impressive body of literature by considering the unique challenges and possibilities for talking about race online.

Hybrid, synchronous, and asynchronous courses each offer different structures for curriculum and pedagogical practice. Hybrid courses may be particularly suited to supporting conversations around race because of the value of in-person sessions in developing group norms and trust.[49] When in-person sessions occur early in the semester, faculty can intentionally raise and address issues of race, noting that talking about race is difficult but necessary, and creating activities that allow students to practice constructive difficult conversations, drawing on the work of scholars such as Singleton and Linton.[50] Faculty can draw on many of the resources related to culturally responsive school leadership for case studies, readings, and activities that they can facilitate, such as Lindsey, Nuri-Robins, and Terrell's work on cultural proficiency or Fergus's work on addressing bias-based beliefs in school settings.[51]

Synchronous courses are similar in many ways to in-person sessions, with the faculty and students all meeting at the same time, providing faculty with the opportunity to lecture or engage the class in various activities and conversations. However, depending on the technology used, these sessions are often quite different structurally. For example, in some videoconferencing technology, participants can only see a few other participants—they cannot see everyone who is logged in at the same time (depending, of course, on class size). Not seeing everyone in general may not be important, but for individuals who may consider taking a risk in revealing a vulnerability or challenging a classmate's deficit-based comment, not seeing the entire class and their classmates' nonverbal responses would likely influence students' decisions to participate or not. Rachel experienced this in a synchronous online class in which several students lacked the technology to connect via video (or chose not to share their video); not being able to see students' facial expressions made it incredibly difficult to decide the types of follow-up questions to ask, when to pause for students to meet in breakout groups, or whether to modify the next week's assignment based on how the class was reacting. In future classes, Rachel will be explicit about expectations to connect video, if possible, and will include more in-the-moment check-ins to get a sense of the "room."

In addition, instead of a professor making notes on a chalkboard, a professor might use a shared word-processing software such as Google Docs or the videoconferencing software itself to take notes on a shared document that the students also have access to. For faculty who frequently use participation strategies such as "turn and talk," in which students talk to a classmate about a prompt, some videoconferencing allows for students to have private conversations, while in others, students may use chat features, talk on their phones, or text each other to discuss the prompt. Faculty may need to consider new participation strategies in these formats, such as students simultaneously completing a shared online document, that take advantage of technology and facilitate difficult conversations. The literature strongly suggests, however, that how instructors group students and the degree to which they moderate discussions matter. Without careful attention to how conversations are set up, students can just as easily be sharing deficit views and perpetuating problematic frameworks for race if they choose partners with similar views and if the instructor is not able to participate in the conversation. Without an instructor or peer actively challenging ideas, participation strategies that have promise may become another format that perpetuates the very things instructors hope to change.

Asynchronous courses create the most possibility for students to have time to reflect and respond, instead of getting caught up in majority viewpoints or feeling silenced. In leadership preparation, asynchronous sessions often use a discussion board format. In this format, faculty ask students to ask or answer questions related to course readings, and students are expected to respond to each other's posts. These conversations can take place over multiple days or weeks, depending on the instructor's deadline. In some cases, students may also complete an activity on their own and then reflect upon it within a discussion board format. Especially when addressing race, faculty need to monitor conversations and support students in developing constructive responses to deficit-based views as well as explicitly racist or oppressive comments.[52] Rachel experienced a serious microaggression/racist comment in which a white student referred to students of color as "colored students" on an online discussion board. If she had been skimming, it would have been easy to miss, or it could have been a week in which she did not read every response. In reflecting on how to respond (aside from a direct email to the student), Rachel had to think about how students of color in particular would feel if they read this comment and did not see any response by their professor. With no public response, she would have condoned this language; other students would read it and see no evidence that the professor had challenged it. This was also an opportunity—to show how Rachel could respond to this type of comment in a constructive way. Her initial instinct was to delete the post (and avoid discomfort), but reflection and conversation with colleagues led her to respond in the discussion board.

In both synchronous and asynchronous formats, technology is a critical tool to support online learning that faculty can harness to address and analyze race, especially as race manifests in conversations, through both discussion forums and in-person sessions. In Serena's case, for example, all in-person sessions are recorded, and students have access to past lectures and discussions from previous sessions. Having such records allows students to analyze discussion dynamics and reflect on their participation in class discussions. After a challenging conversation, such as the one Serena shared, faculty can ask students to analyze their role in the discussion by watching the discussion again, with the support of a guiding prompt or questions. For example, she might ask students to identify excerpts of the conversation that espoused a color-neutral mentality and use this as a jumping-off point to better understand what "color-neutral" means and how it affects their work as school leaders. If faculty are concerned that focusing on others might make students more reticent in future conversations, students can focus on their own contributions and silences. Faculty can also take excerpts from discussion forums conversations and have the class analyze them. In both instances, students will be role-playing the work they will need to do as school leaders to support their teachers in addressing bias-based beliefs such as color-blindness.[53]

Perhaps most importantly, faculty need support in developing the skills and knowledge to interrupt bias-based conversations, either in person or online. We both realize this is an area of growth for us, and the literature suggests that across the United States, university faculty in educational leadership, even those committed to racial justice, often lack the ability to transmit this explicitly to students throughout a course.[54] Asynchronous courses provide the time to consult colleagues and consider various responses before posting or deleting a thread; synchronous and hybrid courses give the opportunity to be flexible and make changes to syllabi as issues arise and an instructor realizes that racist narratives are dominating course discussions. Education leadership faculty need to commit themselves and their departments to be able to address these narratives in person as well. Engaging in this type of pedagogy will be most effective if it occurs across a leadership preparation program's coursework and is not isolated in one course or one assignment.[55] Faculty meetings or program area meetings of various groups could be used as spaces for faculty to talk about ways that race emerges implicitly and explicitly in their courses, both in person and online, and then faculty can also role-play how to address racist narratives when they arise.

SERENA'S RESPONSE

I took advantage of the time to reflect on my response, after reviewing the in-class discussion and consulting with several colleagues. I chose to record a video message for my students to watch before completing the next week's assignment. In my message, I pointed out a few themes I noticed when analyzing our conversation, including the fact that some students' voices dominated while some seemed to be silent, and that generalizations based on individual experiences abounded. I also used this message as an opportunity to review norms for class discussion that had been in the syllabus but never discussed. Then I suggested that students watch the video and analyze the discussion as well and be prepared to talk about it in our next in-person class. Doing so enabled all students to have time to think about what they wanted to say, and it also created opportunities for students to reflect on their own participation in the discussion.

When we gathered in person three weeks later, we had a class discussion about norms for participation and how we could talk about race in constructive ways that did not silence any class members. Penny shared her reflection that one perspective had dominated the prior discussion. As class continued, students were more careful to qualify their statements as their experience or opinion, and some began to refer to course readings as evidence of their claims. While the students did not become culturally responsive school leaders as a result of this one session, the experience has supported my own growth as a faculty member hoping to develop the values, skills, and knowledge of culturally responsive school leadership within my students. Were I to do this again, I would be more explicit about my process of critical self-awareness, making direct connections between how I am leading class and the type of leadership that I would like students to enact as future leaders. I would acknowledge the difficulties that I have in talking about race and in challenging others' views in constructive ways, and I would reflect on my own learning about teaching and leadership.

PEDAGOGICAL IMPLICATIONS FOR LEADERSHIP PREPARATION

We are both committed to achieving racial equity in K–12 schools, and at the same time, we both struggle with how to interrupt racist narratives within our own courses in ways that support all of our students—students of color, white students, students who espouse explicit or implicit racist beliefs, and students who identify as culturally responsive school leaders. What do we do when someone is blatantly or subtly racist in person or in an online discussion? How do we respond in ways that support students' development as future school leaders, keeping them engaged in the conversation and challenging them at the same time? To a degree, these questions are rhetorical, as each instance is context-specific in many ways; but in other ways, these are the questions that we as leaders and teachers of leaders must actively be working to answer ourselves, with our colleagues, and with our students. Instead of answering these questions definitively, we ask faculty and future leaders to grapple with them alongside us.

Supporting school leaders who are committed to equity and racial justice has been challenging for us, particularly when working in online spaces with mostly white students who often have had few interactions with people of color. The slice of instruction that Serena shared is not unlike conversations that have occurred in Rachel's classes, and is likely similar to conversations across the country, within and outside of leadership preparation. The question of how to confront implicit racist thinking in productive ways is critical, not only in educational leadership preparation, but in any context in which issues such as race are raised. In line with culturally responsive school leadership, faculty members need to know their students as members of a group as well as individuals and to understand the diverse contexts in which they teach. While the majority of our students are white and work in racially homogenous settings, we also teach students of color and white students who come to our classes committed to racial equity and culturally responsive school leadership. We need to ensure that course readings, activities, and conversations allow for growth for all students. A view of cultural responsiveness as a constantly moving target, as opposed to an end point, helps us do so.[56]

There are a variety of experiences represented in any given cohort of educational leaders, and understanding student experience is helpful in framing class discussion. This requires skill on the part of the faculty member to know not only how to connect theory and practice but also how to facilitate discussion in productive ways. Faculty members need to approach discussions with clear goals in mind and ensure that conversations remain coherent and on topic. Furthermore, faculty must model the discourse they would like to see used by their students as future leaders. For example, listening carefully, using generous language, drawing on text to make points, asking probing questions, effectively challenging students, building on students' ideas, and so on—these are among the strategies faculty members can employ. Faculty members also need to anticipate that deficit thinking will be exhibited in classroom discussions and that students may come to class unaware of the ways that structural racism impacts different groups of students; preparing for how to react in the moment or in an asynchronous environment will serve them well. In other words, faculty, including ourselves, will benefit from many of the readings and activities related to culturally responsive school leadership that we have discussed as we reflect on our own practice.

We live in a time where students' race as well as the racial makeup of individual school districts continue to be a predictor of educational experiences and outcomes, where racialized incidents make the headlines across the country, where Black and Brown children are systematically denied the education that equity and democracy demand. As faculty who work with future school leaders—the future principals and superintendents who will create the policies, practices, and school cultures that can support or hinder students of color—it is our ethical obligation to ensure that our teaching is informed by culturally responsive school leadership, whether our course is about management, finance, or relationships. It is incumbent upon us to ensure that our students enter the workforce with the ability to talk about hard topics such as race, if not with comfort, then at least with the knowledge, philosophy, and skills of how to do so in ways that can move our educational systems toward achieving racial justice.

NOTES

1. James C. Jupp, Theodorea Regina Berry, and Timothy J. Lensmire, "Second-Wave White Teacher Identity Studies: A Review of White Teacher Identity Literatures from 2004 through 2014," *Review of Educational Research* 86, no. 4 (2016): 1151–91; Gloria Ladson-Billings, "Just What Is Critical Race Theory and What's It Doing in a Nice Field Like Education?," *International Journal of Qualitative Studies in Education* 11, no. 1 (1998): 7–24.

2. Lesley Coia and Monica Taylor, "Co/autoethnography: Exploring Our Teaching Selves Collaboratively," in *Research Methods for the Self-Study of Practice*, ed. Deborah L. Tidwell, Melissa L. Heston, and Linda M. Fitzgerald (Heidelberg, Germany: Springer Netherlands, 2009), 3–16; Carolyn Ellis, *The Ethnographic I: A Methodological Novel about Autoethnography* (Walnut Creek, CA: Rowman Altamira, 2004).

3. Mary Lynn Hamilton, Laura Smith, and Kristen Worthington, "Fitting the Methodology with the Research: An Exploration of Narrative, Self-Study and Auto-Ethnography," *Studying Teacher Education* 4, no. 1 (2008): 17–28.

4. John Rogers et al., *Teaching and Learning in the Age of Trump: Increasing Stress and Hostility in America's High Schools* (Los Angeles, CA: UCLA's Institute for Democracy, Education, and Access, 2017), 3.

5. Rogers et al., *Teaching and Learning.*

6. Indiana Department of Education, "Annual Educator Licensing Summary Report and Recommendations for Educator Recruitment and Retention: July 1, 2015–June 30, 2016," 2017, https://iga.in.gov/legislative/2017/publications/agency/reports/idoe/#document-958e748a.

7. After this was written, Rachel accepted a position at the University of Illinois, Urbana-Champaign in the Department of Education Policy, Organization, and Leadership.

8. Jill Blackmore, "Leadership for Social Justice: A Transformational Dialogue," *Journal of Research on Leadership Education* 4, no. 1 (2009): 1–10; Willis Hawley and Rebecca James, "Diversity-Responsive School Leadership," *UCEA Review* 51, no. 3 (2010): 1–5; Gaetane Jean-Marie, Anthony H. Normore, and Jeffrey S. Brooks, "Leadership for Social Justice: Preparing 21st Century School Leaders for a New Social Order," *Journal of Research on Leadership Education* 4, no. 1 (2009): 1–31.

9. Edward Fergus, *Solving Disproportionality and Achieving Equity: A Leader's Guide to Using Data to Change Hearts and Minds* (Thousand Oaks, CA: Corwin, 2017); Randall B. Lindsey, Kikanza Nuri-Robins, and Raymond D. Terrell, *Cultural Proficiency: A Manual for School Leaders*, 3rd ed. (Thousand Oaks, CA: Corwin, 2009).

10. Mark A. Gooden and Ann O'Doherty, "Do You See What I See? Fostering Aspiring Leaders' Racial Awareness," *Urban Education* 50, no. 2 (2015): 225–55; Frank Hernandez and Joanne Marshall, "Auditing Inequity: Teaching Aspiring Administrators to Be Social Justice Leaders," *Education and Urban Society* 49, no. 2 (2017): 203–28; Muhammad A. Khalifa, Mark Anthony Gooden, and James Earl Davis, "Culturally Responsive School Leadership: A Synthesis of the Literature," *Review of Educational Research* 86, no. 4 (2016): 1272–1311; C. M. Miller and B. N. Martin, "Principal Preparedness for Leading in Demographically Changing Schools: Where Is the Social Training?," *Educational Management Administration & Leadership* 43, no. 1 (2015): 129–51.

11. Sarah Diem and Bradley W. Carpenter, "Turnaround, School Choice, and the Hidden Discourses of Race in Leadership Preparation," in *The Handbook of Urban Educational Leadership*, ed. M. Khalifa, C. Grant, and N. W. Arnold (Lanham, MD: Rowman and Littlefield Education, 2015): 401–11.

12. Edith A. Rusch and S. Douglass Horsford, "Changing Hearts and Minds: The Quest for Open Talk about Race in Educational Leadership," *International Journal of Educational Management* 23, no. 4 (2009): 302–13.

13. Mark A. Gooden and Michael Dantley, "Centering Race in a Framework for Leadership Preparation," *Journal of Research on Leadership Education* 7, no. 2 (2012): 237–53.

14. Gooden and Dantley, "Centering Race."

15. Gooden and Dantley, "Centering Race," 249.

16. Hernandez and Marshall, "Auditing Inequity."

17. Gooden and Dantley, "Centering Race."

18. Lauren Anderson and Jamy Stillman, "Student Teaching's Contribution to Preservice Teacher Development: A Review of Research Focused on the Preparation of Teachers for Urban and High-Needs Contexts," *Review of Educational Research* 83, no. 1 (2013): 3–69; James J. Mahan, "Native Americans as Teacher Trainers: Anatomy and Outcomes of a Cultural Immersion Project," *Journal of Educational Equity and Leadership* 2 (1982): 100–10; Patricia L. Marshall, "Toward Developmental Multicultural Education: Case Study of the Issues Exchange Activity," *Journal of Teacher Education* 49 (1998): 57–65; Christine E. Sleeter, "Chapter 6: Epistemological Diversity in Research on Preservice Teacher Preparation for Historically Underserved Children," *Review of Research in Education* 25, no. 1 (2000): 209–50.

19. Elizabeth Bondy et al., "Developing Critical Social Justice Literacy in an Online Seminar," *Equity & Excellence in Education* 48, no. 2 (2015): 227–48; Kristine S. Lewis Grant and Vera J. Lee, "Wrestling with Issues of Diversity in

Online Courses," *Qualitative Report* 19, no. 12 (2014): 1–25; Kathy L. Guthrie and Holly McCracken, "Teaching and Learning Social Justice through Online Service-Learning Course," *International Review of Research in Open and Distance Learning* 11, no. 3 (2010): 78–94; Omiunota Nelly Ukpokodu, "Teachers' Reflections on Pedagogies that Enhance Learning in an Online Course on Teaching for Equity and Social Justice," *Journal of Interactive Online Learning* 9, no. 3 (2010): 227–55.

20. Guthrie and McCracken, "Teaching and Learning."

21. Janet M. Zydney, Aimee deNoyelles, and Kay Kyeong-Ju Seo, "Creating a Community of Inquiry in Online Environments: An Exploratory Study on the Effect of a Protocol on Interactions within Asynchronous Discussions," *Computers & Education* 58, no. 1 (2012): 77–87.

22. Joan L. Whipp, "Scaffolding Critical Reflection in Online Discussions: Helping Prospective Teachers Think Deeply about Field Experiences in Urban Schools," *Journal of Teacher Education* 54, no. 4 (2003): 321–33.

23. Bondy et al., "Developing Critical Social Justice Literacy"; Zydney, deNoyelles, and Seo, "Creating a Community."

24. Merry M. Merryfield, "The Paradoxes of Teaching a Multicultural Education Course Online," *Journal of Teacher Education* 52, no. 4 (2001): 283–99.

25. Omowale Akintunde, "Diversity.com: Teaching an Online Course on White Racism and Multiculturalism," *Multicultural Perspectives* 8, no. 2 (2006): 35–45.

26. Bondy et al., "Developing Critical Social Justice Literacy"; Merryfield, "Paradoxes of Teaching."

27. Miguel M. Licona and Binod Gurung, "Asynchronous Discussions in Online Multicultural Education," *Multicultural Education* 19, no. 1 (2011): 2.

28. Grant and Lee, "Wrestling with Issues," 2.

29. Sabine E. Vaught and Angelina E. Castagno, " 'I Don't Think I'm a Racist': Critical Race Theory, Teacher Attitudes, and Structural Racism," *Race Ethnicity and Education* 11, no. 2 (2008): 95–113.

30. Robin DiAngelo, *White Fragility: Why It's So Hard for White People to Talk about Racism* (New York: Beacon, 2018).

31. Glenn E. Singleton and C. Linton, *Courageous Conversations about Race: A Field Guide for Achieving Equity in Schools* (Thousand Oaks, CA: Corwin, 2006); National School Reform Faculty, "The 5 Whys for Inquiry," accessed January 28, 2019, http://www.coloradoedinitiative.org/wp-content/uploads/2018/06/5-Whys-Protocol.pdf.

32. Khalifa, Gooden, and Davis, "Culturally Responsive School Leadership."

33. Ladson-Billings, "Critical Race Theory"; Geneva Gay, *Culturally Responsive Teaching: Theory, Research, and Practice* (New York: Teachers College Press, 2010).

34. Singleton and Linton, *Courageous Conversations*, ch. 6; Glenn E. Singleton, *More Courageous Conversations about Race* (Thousand Oaks, CA: Corwin, 2012), 14.

35. Bradley W. Carpenter and Sarah Diem, "Talking Race: Facilitating Critical Conversations in Educational Leadership Preparation Programs," *Journal of School Leadership* 23, no. 6 (2013): 902–31; Michelle D. Young and Julie Laible, "White Racism, Antiracism, and School Leadership Preparation," *Journal of School Leadership* 10, no. 5 (2000): 374–415.

36. Carolyn J. Riehl, "The Principal's Role in Creating Inclusive Schools for Diverse Students: A Review of Normative, Empirical, and Critical Literature on the Practice of Educational Administration," *Review of Educational Research* 70, no. 1 (2000): 55–81.

37. Khalifa, Gooden, and Davis, "Culturally Responsive School Leadership."

38. Khalifa, Gooden, and Davis, "Culturally Responsive School Leadership."

39. Khalifa, Gooden, and Davis, "Culturally Responsive School Leadership," 10.

40. Geneva Gay and Kipchoge Kirkland, "Developing Cultural Critical Consciousness and Self-Reflection in Preservice Teacher Education," *Theory Into Practice* 42, no. 3 (2003): 181–87.

41. Fergus, *Solving Disproportionality*, 38.

42. George Theoharis and Marcelle Haddix, "Undermining Racism and a Whiteness Ideology: White Principals Living a Commitment to Equitable and Excellent Schools," *Urban Education* 46, no. 6 (2011): 1332–51.

43. Zues Leonardo, "The Souls of White Folk: Critical Pedagogy, Whiteness Studies, and Globalization Discourse," *Race, Ethnicity and Education* 5, no. 1 (2002): 29–50.

44. Brenda McMahon, "Educational Administrators' Conceptions of Whiteness, Anti-Racism and Social Justice," *Journal of Educational Administration* 45, no. 6 (2007): 684–96; Jill Blackmore, " 'The Other Within': Race/Gender Disruptions to the Professional Learning of White Educational Leaders," *International Journal of Leadership in Education* 13, no. 1 (2010): 45.

45. DiAngelo, *White Fragility*.

46. Merryfield, "Paradoxes of Teaching."

47. Singleton and Linton, *Courageous Conversations*; Fergus, *Solving Disproportionality*.

48. Lindsey, Nuri-Robins, and Terrell, *Cultural Proficiency*.

49. Bondy et al., "Developing Critical Social Justice Literacy."

50. Singleton and Linton, *Courageous Conversations*.

51. Lindsey, Nuri-Robins, and Terrell, *Cultural Proficiency*; Fergus, *Solving Disproportionality*.

52. Bondy et al., "Developing Critical Social Justice Literacy"; Zydney, deNoyelles, and Seo, "Creating a Community."

53. Fergus, *Solving Disproportionality*.

54. Carpenter and Diem, "Talking Race."

55. Marilyn Cochran-Smith, Joan Barnatt, Audrey Friedman, and Gerald Pine, "Inquiry on Inquiry: Practitioner Research and Student Learning," *Action in Teacher Education* 31, no. 2 (2009): 17–32.

56. Khalifa, Gooden, and Davis, "Culturally Responsive School Leadership."

BIBLIOGRAPHY

Akintunde, Omowale. "Diversity.com: Teaching an Online Course on White Racism and Multiculturalism." *Multicultural Perspectives* 8, no. 2 (2006): 35–45.

Anderson, Lauren, and Jamy Stillman. "Student Teaching's Contribution to Preservice Teacher Development: A Review of Research Focused on the Preparation of Teachers for Urban and High-Needs Contexts." *Review of Educational Research* 83, no. 1 (2013): 3–69.

Blackmore, Jill. "Leadership for Social Justice: A Transformational Dialogue." *Journal of Research on Leadership Education* 4, no. 1 (2009): 1–10.

———. " 'The Other Within': Race/Gender Disruptions to the Professional Learning of White Educational Leaders." *International Journal of Leadership in Education* 13, no. 1 (2010): 45–61.

Bondy, Elizabeth, Elyse Hambacher, Amy Murphy, Rachel Wolkenhauer, and Desi Krell. "Developing Critical Social Justice Literacy in an Online Seminar." *Equity & Excellence in Education* 48, no. 2 (2015): 227–48.

Carpenter, Bradley W., and Sarah Diem. "Talking Race: Facilitating Critical Conversations in Educational Leadership Preparation Programs." *Journal of School Leadership* 23, no. 6 (2013): 902–31.

Cochran-Smith, Marilyn, Joan Barnatt, Audrey Friedman, and Gerald Pine. "Inquiry on Inquiry: Practitioner Research and Student Learning." *Action in Teacher Education* 31, no. 2 (2009): 17–32.

Coia, Lesley, and Monica Taylor. "Co/autoethnography: Exploring Our Teaching Selves Collaboratively." In *Research Methods for the Self-Study of Practice*, edited by Deborah L. Tidwell, Melissa L. Heston, and Linda M. Fitzgerald, 3–16. Heidelberg, Germany: Springer Netherlands, 2009.

DiAngelo, Robin. *White Fragility: Why It's So Hard for White People to Talk about Racism*. New York: Beacon, 2018.

Diem, Sarah, and Bradley W. Carpenter. "Turnaround, School Choice, and the Hidden Discourses of Race in Leadership Preparation." In *The Handbook of Urban Educational Leadership*, edited by M. Khalifa, C. Grant, and N. W. Arnold, 401–11. Lanham, MD: Rowman and Littlefield Education, 2015.

Ellis, Carolyn. *The Ethnographic I: A Methodological Novel about Autoethnography*. Walnut Creek, CA: Rowman Altamira, 2004.

Fergus, Edward. *Solving Disproportionality and Achieving Equity: A Leader's Guide to Using Data to Change Hearts and Minds*. Thousand Oaks, CA: Corwin Press, 2017.

Gay, Geneva. *Culturally Responsive Teaching: Theory, Research, and Practice*. New York: Teachers College Press, 2010.

Gay, Geneva, and Kipchoge Kirkland. "Developing Cultural Critical Consciousness and Self-Reflection in Preservice Teacher Education." *Theory Into Practice* 42, no. 3 (2003): 181–87.

Gooden, Mark A., and Michael Dantley. "Centering Race in a Framework for Leadership Preparation." *Journal of Research on Leadership Education* 7, no. 2 (2012): 237–53.

Gooden, Mark A., and Ann O'Doherty. "Do You See What I See? Fostering Aspiring Leaders' Racial Awareness." *Urban Education* 50, no. 2 (2015): 225–55.

Grant, Kristine S. Lewis, and Vera J. Lee. "Wrestling with Issues of Diversity in Online Courses." *Qualitative Report* 19, no. 12 (2014): 1–25.

Guthrie, Kathy L., and Holly McCracken. "Teaching and Learning Social Justice through Online Service-Learning Courses." *International Review of Research in Open and Distance Learning* 11, no. 3 (2010): 78–94.

Hamilton, Mary Lynn, Laura Smith, and Kristen Worthington. "Fitting the Methodology with the Research: An Exploration of Narrative, Self-Study and Auto-Ethnography." *Studying Teacher Education* 4, no. 1 (2008): 17–28.

Hawley, Willis, and Rebecca James. "Diversity-Responsive School Leadership." *UCEA Review* 51, no. 3 (2010): 1–5.

Hernandez, Frank, and Joanne Marshall. "Auditing Inequity: Teaching Aspiring Administrators to Be Social Justice Leaders." *Education and Urban Society* 49, no. 2 (2017): 203–28.

Indiana Department of Education. "Annual Educator Licensing Summary Report and Recommendations for Educator Recruitment and Retention: July 1, 2015–June 30, 2016." 2017. https://iga.in.gov/legislative/2017/publications/agency/reports/idoe/#document-958e748a.

Jean-Marie, Gaetane, Anthony H. Normore, and Jeffrey S. Brooks. "Leadership for Social Justice: Preparing 21st Century School Leaders for a New Social Order." *Journal of Research on Leadership Education* 4, no. 1 (2009): 1–31.

Jupp, James C., Theodorea Regina Berry, and Timothy J. Lensmire. "Second-Wave White Teacher Identity Studies: A Review of White Teacher Identity Literatures from 2004 through 2014." *Review of Educational Research* 86, no. 4 (2016): 1151–91.

Khalifa, Muhammad A., Mark Anthony Gooden, and James Earl Davis. "Culturally Responsive School Leadership: A Synthesis of the Literature." *Review of Educational Research* 86, no. 4 (2016): 1272–1311.

Ladson-Billings, Gloria. "Just What Is Critical Race Theory and What's It Doing in a Nice Field Like Education?" *International Journal of Qualitative Studies in Education* 11, no. 1 (1998): 7–24.

———. "Toward a Theory of Culturally Relevant Pedagogy." *American Educational Research Journal* 32, no. 3 (1995): 465–91.

Leonardo, Zeus. "The Souls of White Folk: Critical Pedagogy, Whiteness Studies, and Globalization Discourse." *Race, Ethnicity and Education* 5, no. 1 (2002): 29–50.

Licona, Miguel M., and Binod Gurung. "Asynchronous Discussions in Online Multicultural Education." *Multicultural Education* 19, no. 1 (2011): 2–8.

Lindsey, Randall B., Kikanza Nuri-Robins, and Raymond D. Terrell. *Cultural Proficiency: A Manual for School Leaders*. 3rd ed. Thousand Oaks, CA: Corwin, 2009.

Mahan, James J. "Native Americans as Teacher Trainers: Anatomy and Outcomes of a Cultural Immersion Project." *Journal of Educational Equity and Leadership* 2 (1982): 100–10.

Marshall, Patricia L. "Toward Developmental Multicultural Education: Case Study of the Issues Exchange Activity." *Journal of Teacher Education* 49 (1998): 57–65.

McMahon, Brenda. "Educational Administrators' Conceptions of Whiteness, Anti-Racism and Social Justice." *Journal of Educational Administration* 45, no. 6 (2007): 684–96.

Merryfield, Merry M. "The Paradoxes of Teaching a Multicultural Education Course Online." *Journal of Teacher Education* 52, no. 4 (2001): 283–99.

Miller, C. M., and B. N. Martin. "Principal Preparedness for Leading in Demographically Changing Schools: Where Is the Social Justice Training?" *Educational Management Administration & Leadership* 43, no. 1 (2015): 129–51.

National School Reform Faculty. "The 5 Whys for Inquiry." Accessed January 28, 2019. http://www.coloradoedinitiative.org/wp-content/uploads/2018/06/5-Whys-Protocol.pdf.

Riehl, Carolyn J. "The Principal's Role in Creating Inclusive Schools for Diverse Students: A Review of Normative, Empirical, and Critical Literature on the Practice of Educational Administration." *Review of Educational Research* 70, no. 1 (2000): 55–81.

Rocco, Sharn. "Making Reflection Public: Using Interactive Online Discussion Board to Enhance Student Learning." *Reflective Practice* 11, no. 3 (2010): 307–17.

Rogers, John, Megan Franke, Jung-Eun Ellie Yun, Michael Ishimoto, Claudia Diera, Rebecca C. Geller, Anthony Berryman, and Tizoc Brenes. *Teaching and Learning in the Age of Trump: Increasing Stress and Hostility in America's High Schools*. Los Angeles, CA: UCLA's Institute for Democracy, Education, and Access, 2017.

Rusch, Edith A., and S. Douglass Horsford. "Changing Hearts and Minds: The Quest for Open Talk about Race in Educational Leadership." *International Journal of Educational Management* 23, no. 4 (2009): 302–13.

Singleton, Glenn E. *More Courageous Conversations about Race*. Thousand Oaks, CA: Corwin, 2012.

Singleton, Glenn E., and C. Linton. *Courageous Conversations about Race: A Field Guide for Achieving Equity in Schools*. Thousand Oaks, CA: Corwin, 2006.

Sleeter, Christine E. "Chapter 6: Epistemological Diversity in Research on Preservice Teacher Preparation for Historically Underserved Children." *Review of Research in Education* 25, no. 1 (2000): 209–50.

Theoharis, George, and Marcelle Haddix. "Undermining Racism and a Whiteness Ideology: White Principals Living a Commitment to Equitable and Excellent Schools." *Urban Education* 46, no. 6 (2011): 1332–51.

Ukpokodu, Omiunota Nelly. "Teachers' Reflections on Pedagogies that Enhance Learning in an Online Course on Teaching for Equity and Social Justice." *Journal of Interactive Online Learning* 9, no. 3 (2010): 227–55.

Vaught, Sabine E., and Angelina E. Castagno. " 'I Don't Think I'm a Racist': Critical Race Theory, Teacher Attitudes, and Structural Racism." *Race Ethnicity and Education* 11, no. 2 (2008): 95–113.

Whipp, Joan L. "Scaffolding Critical Reflection in Online Discussions: Helping Prospective Teachers Think Deeply about Field Experiences in Urban Schools." *Journal of Teacher Education* 54, no. 4 (2003): 321–33.

Young, Michelle D., and Julie Laible. "White Racism, Antiracism, and School Leadership Preparation." *Journal of School Leadership* 10, no. 5 (2000): 374–415.

Zydney, Janet M., Aimee deNoyelles, and Kay Kyeong-Ju Seo. "Creating a Community of Inquiry in Online Environments: An Exploratory Study on the Effect of a Protocol on Interactions within Asynchronous Discussions." *Computers & Education* 58, no. 1 (2012): 77–87.

CHAPTER 8

SCAFFOLDING FOR JUSTICE

Deploying Intersectionality, Black Feminist Thought, and the "Outsider Within" in the Writing about Literature Classroom

SHANE A. McCOY

INTRODUCTION

The ever-changing landscape of teaching race and ethnicity in higher education coupled with resurgent white nationalism most recently affirmed in President Donald Trump's new world order are indeed critical pedagogical concerns in our current moment. In the wake of recent protest movements by Black Lives Matter and other social activists, designing and developing a social-justice-oriented curriculum is imperative for teaching students how to engage with contemporary sociocultural phenomena that disrupt the neoliberal ethos of meritocracy, color-blindness, and unquestioning allegiance to US nationalism and free-market ideology. While the theoretical depth and understanding offered by critical race theorists and Black feminist thinkers provides us with a sound intellectual and pedagogical framework for teaching about race and ethnicity in academia,[1] the place of the general education classroom and how to craft pragmatic solutions for teaching first- and second-year undergraduate students deserves much-needed attention in our present time of civil and campus unrest.

However, before we can teach for justice in general education courses populated with first- and second-year undergraduates, we need to *scaffold for justice* with critical reading and writing practices that enlist undergraduate students as knowledge producers in the classroom. I write this from the position of a graduate student with extensive pedagogical training in teaching writing about literature courses, which allows me the necessary experience and expertise to enter into the discussion about how we might teach the rising generation of students about race and ethnicity, and yet it situates me in a less secure position, one closer to my own students and to that of contingent faculty, as well as in greater proximity to other insecure job positions across our emergent "gig economy." Unlike previous scholars, my intervention in this chapter offers a more robust engagement with social justice pedagogies for designing and developing counter-curricula that train students in ethical reading and writing practices and cultivating students' awareness of social justice. With a primary course text—Chimamanda Ngozi Adichie's novel *Americanah* (2013)—alongside a selection of classroom exercises and assignment prompts, I demystify how I implement social justice pedagogies in my classroom and make the case for *how* and *why* these procedures are imperative for enabling students with the critical capacities for reading and writing *for justice*.

In this chapter, I argue for a reorientation to pedagogy in critical race and ethnic studies specifically through the ways in which we scaffold the curricula for teaching undergraduates about race and ethnicity. I focus on the minutiae of everyday classroom activities—the mundane aspects of the curricula—in order to examine the extent to which our scaffolding procedures affect students' learning. I synthesize intersectionality, Black feminist thought, and the concept of the "outsider within" for the purposes of crafting critical reading and writing practices that train undergraduate students to adopt a social-justice-oriented lens. I describe how scaffolding for justice, in general, and *reading for justice* and *writing for justice*, in particular, serve as catalysts for advancing social justice in the writing about literature classroom. Specifically, I foreground a set of values and commitments for "teaching for justice" vis-à-vis reading practices, writing practices, and critical pedagogy.[2] I present how to scaffold for justice in relation to texts and assignment sequences and make the case for how these aspects of the curriculum foster students' abilities to engage in such difficult topics that we find ourselves teaching in today's college classroom.

Finally, I contend that intersectionality, Black feminist thought, and the figure of the "outsider within" affect students emotionally and cognitively, for better or worse.[3] Specifically, I unpack how students' affective relationship to reading and engaging with intersectionality, Black feminist thought, and the figure of the "outsider within" conjures both positive and negative affect, which often manifests in the form of empowerment, resistance, and/or cognitive dissonance. As I illustrate throughout this chapter, we have the power to reshape students' affective relationship to intersectionality and Black feminism vis-à-vis the contents of our curricula and how we construct course content that advances social justice and reconditions students' affective relationship to such causes. The critical pedagogical stakes of my inquiry thus reflect the need to empower multicultural students and dismantle the "unacknowledged inheritance" of whiteness in predominantly white institutions (PWIs).[4] Only through an explicit engagement with the unearned privileges of whiteness do both white and non-white students become aware of their place in the university and the historical legacies of social injustices. To that end, I assess the efficacy of my pedagogical choices for advancing social justice in the general education classroom and the extent to which intersectionality, Black feminist thought, and the "outsider within" influences students' awareness of social justice for better or for worse.

SCAFFOLDING FOR JUSTICE: BACKGROUND AND CONTEXT

To effectively mobilize intersectionality and Black feminist thought in the writing about literature classroom, I construct what I call *scaffolding for justice*. Scaffolding for justice cultivates students' critically edged capacities for reading and intervening into social injustices. Scaffolding for justice offers general education instructors a pragmatic framework for "teaching for justice."[5] Often framed within the context of early childhood development and education, the idea of instructional scaffolding evolved from Jerome Bruner's readings of Russian psychologist Lev Vygotsky's *Mind in Society* (1930).[6] During the scaffolding process, a teacher strategizes components of the curriculum in order to meet the educational needs of novice learners.[7] This process includes the sequencing of reading and writing assignments that enable the instructor to develop tasks that are scaled in correspondence to the level of complexity and students' academic abilities.[8] As such, scaffolding impacts the development of the curriculum for better or for worse and informs my inquiry into why it is important to consider how we design and develop (or *scaffold*) our curriculum for teaching about race and ethnicity in academia. Without proper scaffolding protocols, the dissemination and acquisition of knowledge content remains largely ineffective for mobilizing social justice using the curriculum. Scaffolding therefore provides a crucial theoretical paradigm for implementing an intersectional feminist pedagogy in the writing about literature classroom.

With scaffolding as a conceptual framework, scaffolding for justice thus functions as a general rubric and set of ethics that crafts critical reading and writing exercises largely influenced by intersectionality, Black feminist thought, and employing what Patricia Hill Collins calls the "outsider within" perspective as a heuristic for designing and developing a social-justice-oriented curriculum. In "Learning from the Outsider Within: The Sociological Significance of Black Feminist Thought," Hill Collins argues that the "outsider within" position offers a lens for reading and interpreting history, culture, and society.[9] The "outsider within" also makes privy the position of the cultural outsider to cultural insiders. According to Hill Collins, "many Black female intellectuals have made creative use of their marginality—their 'outsider within' status—to produce Black feminist thought that reflects a special standpoint on self, family, and society." She contends that the "outsider within" perspective produces "distinctive analyses of race, class, and gender." Hill Collins's concept thus extends the discussion of the interlocking oppressions first articulated by the Combahee River Collective in 1977 and highlighted elsewhere in this collection by Emerald Christopher-Byrd. I find her framework of the "outsider within" and the "interlocking nature of oppressions" helpful for conceptualizing a critical intersectional feminist pedagogy that is attentive to how multiple sites of oppression shift and transform over time and across space. In the sections that follow, I describe how we might engage with the "outsider within" and Black feminist thought through both reading for justice and writing for justice in the writing about literature classroom.

READING FOR JUSTICE

The first aspect of scaffolding for justice is the importance of close-reading practices. Conceptualizing this as *reading for justice*, I emphasize how intellectual inquiry in the writing about literature classroom is historically bound; thus, for students to be attentive to the political, cultural, and historical stakes of a given text, the teacher must be attentive to how they situate these texts within a contextualized milieu. Reading for justice employs counter-canons and counter-curricula to teach students the importance of ethical close-reading practices.[10] Reading for justice also endorses what Ellen Carillo calls "mindful reading."[11] Hoad's paradigm for ethical close-reading practices wedded to Carillo's "mindful reading" paradigm frames my pedagogical approach to reading instruction, and I encourage students to read for justice.

One of the ways in which my curriculum trains students to read for justice is through open-ended guided questions. I consider open-ended guided questions essential tools that create entry points for students. As intellectual "training wheels," guided questions model for undergraduates how to intellectually discuss and engage with the texts under consideration and thoughtfully consider unfamiliar content. Earlier in my chapter, I introduced Chimamanda Ngozi Adichie's novel *Americanah* (2013), which models the kind of critical close-reading practices that reading for justice endorses. This novel features the perspective of a Nigerian international student named Ifemelu. As the protagonist, Ifemelu brings into focus the intersection of race, class, gender, sexuality, and immigration. *Americanah* challenges students to rethink their common assumptions about the African continent, in general, and African women writers in particular. Students may elect to use these questions as starting points for guiding their reading practices and, as I will later explain, their writing practices.

While discussing Adichie's *Americanah* in class, I developed several guiding questions to scaffold students' reading practices. These questions were as follows:

- In chapter 40, the beginning of the 2008 election is made much more salient for readers. Why would this chapter be important for the novel? Furthermore, what might the blog post at the end of chapter 40 have to do with this chapter?
- How does Ifemelu obtain US citizenship? What significance might this hold for a discussion on contemporary immigration and US citizenship? And how does this information conflict with your own knowledge of the citizenship process?
- Discuss the significance of the passport. What purpose might a passport serve? What class themes might it be related to? How and why?

These questions engage students' initial reactions to the literature as they participate in collaborative discussions with their peers. Through "bounded framing," students practice critical close-reading skills and consider the author's intent behind plot elements in the text and what significance these plot elements might hold for unlocking and decoding the meaning of the text. Students also consider how basic plot elements in *Americanah* speak to the central issues of race, class, gender, and immigration in a real-world context, the "expansive framing" of course content.[12]

As such, open-ended guided questions model what Paulo Freire calls a "co-intentional" pedagogical style, where students are trained to become knowledge producers.[13] The pedagogical function of open-ended guided questions through structured collaborative discussions thus allows undergraduates to consider what new knowledge about the texts they might be acquiring and how the texts they are reading shapes that new knowledge. In this way, reading for justice emphasizes collaboration and critical reflection, which allows students to make explicit connections between what they have learned about race, class, gender, and immigration vis-à-vis Adichie's *Americanah*.

WRITING FOR JUSTICE

The second aspect of scaffolding for justice is *writing for justice*. Writing for justice extends Shari Stenberg's understanding of the kinds of subversive research that can be performed in the neoliberal university regarding a "repurposing" of the composition classroom.[14] Stenberg's manifesto for subversive writing instruction situates how writing for justice aims to cultivate students' emotional and intellectual awareness through writing assignments.

First, writing for justice encourages students to participate in the process of annotation as practicing critical engagement with the text. Annotation, as a methodology, runs counter to a neoliberal logic of accounting and ranking competencies. Secondly, annotation activates a student's metacognitive awareness and higher-order thinking skills by allowing them to craft reflective writing assignments that assess the rhetorical effects of their writing choices and how one's writing choices affect potential audiences. As an example, in one short assignment, students were required to choose a passage from the novel *Americanah* that they find to be of interest and close-read the passage. Although this exercise might ask students to demonstrate an elementary skill such as rhetorical analysis and annotation, the assignment is particularly significant for gauging students' interest in the novel and the context in which it is being presented—race, racism, and unjust immigration laws and policies. The required practice of annotation functions as a method of inquiry development and enables students to track their reading processes and to use those ideas in writing assignments. Annotations also facilitate a continuous dialogue between the student and the text. I ask students to consider "what stood out to you as important or significant in this passage" and to "develop a claim on the purpose of this passage. How does the passage function in the novel? In other words, what might be the purpose (significance) of the passage?" Students must also "explain why you chose this particular passage. What did you find interesting? What in the passage appealed to you as a reader? Refer to your annotations to track your own thoughts about the passage." These rhetorical questions and directive statements are intended to spark students' ideas and motivate them to reflect on the extent to which they connected either cognitively or emotionally to the course material. Although the genre of the assignment might be generic in form, structure, and requirements, the primary course text (Adichie's *Americanah*) offers students an opportunity to work through their affective relationship to the course content by analyzing the novel through close-reading practices and to articulate *why* they chose the passage based on their personal interests.

Second, writing for justice engages undergraduates in the research and revision process by allowing them to author original texts and to make connections to real-world contexts. Instructing a writing course that emphasizes both research and revision allows me to scaffold for students how to employ library research to generate novel ideas and also to implement revision as a process of self-assessment and becoming more critical of one's own writing. Earlier, I explained how an "expansive framing" of course content motivates students to author original work and connect this work to prior learning experiences. When authoring knowledge, students "transfer-in" prior knowledge and understand how "authoring knowledge as a practice involves generating and adapting knowledge."[15] The student adapts the content from prior contexts to new situations and generalizes based upon prior knowledge experience. This process makes the student "accountable for continuing to share that content" and "when faced with a new problem that prior knowledge cannot directly answer, the student adapts his/her knowledge rather than say 'Don't know' or giving up."[16] This intricate process of creating original work and making relevant the course content increases the possibility that the student will transfer knowledge and "recontextualize" it from one context to the next.[17]

During this process, two features are important for writing for justice and its impact on my curriculum design and development: first, how I encourage students to "connect settings"; and second, how I encourage students to experience "authorship" of original work. I create opportunities for students to find voice in authoring original work as modeled in the academic essay. Creating opportunities for students to author original work through the academic essay are important because this pedagogical approach positions "students as authors through the use of expansive framing [which] may . . . promote accountability in ways that lead to transfer. If a student shares particular content knowledge, that student can be framed as the author of that content and be publicly recognized as such. The student then becomes expected to be able to use that content during transfer opportunities."[18] Students embody the role of "author" and orient their reading practices toward reflecting on the potential sociopolitical implications of various sources presented in the class. For instance, in another writing assignment prompt, I pose rhetorical questions to spark students' ideas: "Why do these texts matter for intersectional feminist inquiries? Furthermore, how does genre mediate feminist political commitments?" I also remind students in the "content" section of the prompt that they should discuss what their topic has to do with the broader picture. "Why does it matter that we should notice this issue?" This writing genre allows students to explore multiple perspectives and ideas on a given topic in the course. While my classes provide students with a range of options in secondary research, students are always required to incorporate research from outside of the course into their essays, as I believe that only through secondary research do students discover their own set of commitments and values as writers and thinkers.

In this way, writing for justice activates students' metacognitive awareness and engages them in fundamental research and revision processes that are imperative for academic success. Moreover, through "expansive framing," students are encouraged to find relevance for what they are learning beyond my classroom—the "intercontextuality" of successful transfer situations.[19] Thus, writing for justice complements reading for justice, as both are essential for teaching about race and ethnicity in higher education. While I imagine all literature courses use both reading and writing extensively, framing these aspects of the curriculum as vehicles for social justice might enable students to make new and unexpected connections, ones that reinforce the relevance of course content and motivate students to orient their worldviews toward advancing social justice.

HOW SCAFFOLDING FOR JUSTICE AFFECTS STUDENTS

In this section, I assess the efficacy of scaffolding for justice and the extent to which my scaffolding protocols affect students. To that end, I present evidence drawn from anonymous course evaluations and students' final in-class reflection essays (with pseudonyms) in order to illustrate for readers how both white students and students of color were affected by the "outsider within" perspective and the extent to which they report being changed by an intersectional feminist pedagogy, for better or for worse. While I aim to expose students to outsider perspectives that are often marginalized in the university, I also seek to empower underrepresented students and encourage them to acknowledge their experiences of disenfranchisement as sources of knowledge. Therefore, because of the ethnic and racial demographics of my courses, I initially believed that a racially and ethnically diverse group of students would connect with Hill Collins's concept of the "outsider within" and, perhaps, even learn to view themselves as empowered agents. As Hill Collins explains, "a variety of individuals can learn from Black women's experiences as outsiders within: Black men, working-class individuals, white women, other people of color, religious and sexual minorities, and all individuals who, while from social strata that provided them with the benefits of white male insiderism, have never felt comfortable with its taken-for-granted assumptions."[20] Indeed, I hoped that Hill Collins's essay would engender cross-racial solidarity between white students and students of color, as well as cross-gender solidarity between female students and male students.

However, what was revealed in the ubiquitous teaching evaluations of one course populated by mostly white female students was an altogether different story—that the people who were most upset by taking a course on Black feminist thought may not be white men (as one might readily assume) but, in fact, *white women*. As one student anonymously wrote, "The topic of oppression in regards to black feminism was not at all what I had planned on studying when getting into this class. I was severely disappointed in how this was handled." By engaging with Black feminist thought, white female students were made to divest themselves from their sense of white privilege despite their gender. Rather than learning how to use their positions as "outsiders within" at the university and learn from other "outsiders within," many of them expressed anger, discontent, silence, and altogether contrary emotions. As multicultural education scholar Robin

DiAngelo argues in *White Fragility: Why It's So Hard for White People to Talk about Racism*, white female students' negative emotional reactions to Black feminist thought within a predominantly white institution should come as no surprise. Like fellow contributor Douglas Julien's chapter earlier in this volume, we might consider white female students' negative emotional reactions as symptomatic of color-blind racism and implicit bias, featured most recently in Donald Trump's rise to power.[21]

If given the opportunity to teach this novel again, I will be mindful of situating the novel within a broader historical context. Similar to Brooms and Brice's chapter in part 4 of this volume, I will strive to include a historical approach to scaffolding *Americanah* better in order to allow students greater insight into the historical, social, political, and cultural particularities of white supremacy in the United States. Allowing students to contemplate these historical aspects of white supremacy and the extent to which they influence social, cultural, and political realities might have allowed the lesson plan to be better understood both emotionally and intellectually by such resistant students.[22]

Despite some negative reactions to the material, several students across race and gender categories reported in their final in-class reflection essays that they found the course to be both culturally relevant and culturally responsive to the current moment due to its focus on racial justice.[23] For instance, Wendy, a white female student, reported that in addition to learning valuable lessons in critical writing, she also "learned important lessons and values from the primary sources that we read [and watched]. I learned about the outsider within status and who is affected. I was challenged intellectually because I was forced to compare many different texts and ideas into a 'bigger picture' topic."[24] Like Wendy, Mark, a white male student, reported in his reflection essay that prior to the class, he "had never really thought about the importance of reading the marginalized viewpoint and the unique perspective that might bring of a societal 'outsider' looking in at the working[s] of society while also being a part of [it]." Now, after the course and reflecting on his prior experiences with texts such as *One Flew Over the Cuckoo's Nest* and *Frankenstein*, both of which he argued feature "outsiders within" of some sort, Mark reports that the course enabled him to understand "that the big and powerful must not be looked to as the only source of truth."[25]

While some could understand the relevance of the course and what Hill Collins calls the "sociological significance" of the "outsider within" viewpoint, other students reported in their final reflection essays that they were able to envision themselves as stakeholders in the course. For example, Whitney, a black female student, reported that she initially expected to not learn as much as she did because she was already familiar with Patricia Hill Collins and Black feminism. However, she discovered that she "learned a numerous amount of [new] information and . . . was given a countless amount of additional papers to read and feed my growing interest. As a black woman, this content I feel has taught me a lot about myself, through the types of assignments we were given and the aspect of connecting our arguments with the texts."[26] These students' responses illustrate that both white students and students of color experienced a *pedagogy of empowerment* by envisioning themselves as stakeholders in the issues brought to bear in the classroom, and several of my pupils cultivated the power to use their own experiences as a source of knowledge and as catalysts for critical thinking and engaged intellectual pursuit.

Although Wendy, Mark, and Whitney reported positive experiences with learning from the "outsider within" perspective, we might also take note of *how* and *why* negative emotions arise in undergraduates, especially in overrepresented white, able-bodied, middle-class, heterosexual students who stand to lose power and privilege and who often find conversations about social justice disempowering for them. These students wrongfully assume that "everyone who supports cultural diversity wants to replace one dictatorship of knowing with another, changing one set way of thinking for another. This is perhaps the gravest misconception of cultural diversity."[27] Indeed, much like my co-contributors, including Julien's contribution on color-blindness and white fragility and Emerald Christopher-Byrd's chapter on the uses of rage and passion, I found that white students' psychical investment in maintaining positions of power and privilege typically manifests itself in the form of resistance to intersectional feminist pedagogy. Such responses complicate our attempts to encourage civic debate and dialogue in general education courses. Such occurrences underscore how intersectionality, Black feminist thought, and the "outsider within" affect a *pedagogy of discomfort* for overrepresented white students who hold unacknowledged emotional and psychical investment in white privilege and white supremacy.[28] Their reactions might be considered when recalibrating our curricula and learning how to teach students who embody resistant attitudes and worldviews that conflict with intersectional feminist pedagogies.

TEACHING IN THIS MOMENT: REFLECTION AS CONCLUSION

Throughout this chapter, I have argued for a reorientation to critical pedagogy in race and ethnic studies. Specifically, I have illustrated how scaffolding for justice with critical reading and writing practices functions as a pragmatic framework for enlisting students as knowledge producers in the social justice classroom. With the "outsider within" perspective as a heuristic for designing and developing the curriculum, I advanced an intersectional feminist pedagogy that frames critical reading and writing assignments as vehicles for social justice pedagogy. To conclude, I wish to reflect on my experiences teaching about race and ethnicity as a graduate student and offer several recommendations for teacher-scholars in critical race and ethnic studies and the future training of graduate students in our field.

First, while some graduate seminars at my institution may engage with pedagogy, the attention given to the teaching of critical race studies vis-à-vis critical pedagogy is largely absent from my preprofessional training. As a trained composition teacher, I have received extensive training in writing pedagogy. In fact, my preprofessional training has been almost exclusively limited to writing instruction and teaching undergraduates how to produce coherent documents that adhere to professional standards.[29] This does not include any formal engagement with critical race pedagogy or how to respond to students who react in negative ways to the study of race and ethnicity. Although English departments have made significant improvements to the content of the curriculum, beginning in the 1980s and 1990s with the re-envisioning of the canon,[30] the pedagogical training of graduate students on how to engage undergraduates in the study of race and ethnicity in general education courses has changed very little.

Second, if we wish to enact radical social change, teaching about race and ethnicity in higher education must become a vehicle for advancing the commitments and ideals that lead to a more just society, one that functions based upon the responsibility of educators whose aim is to "examine society and try to change it . . . no matter what risk."[31] As part of the ever-increasing pool of contingent academic labor, teaching about race and ethnicity in the shadow of Donald Trump's presidency continues to be a topic that carries with it heightened tension and tremendous risk for all faculty. However, because graduate students and other contingent faculty lack the protection that tenure grants, we are forced to adopt a *pedagogy of risk*. Indeed, we are too often placed in precarious situations, and this new normal compounded by students' claims to "free speech" leaves us very few options when teaching about race and ethnicity today.

Third, given the increasingly explicit ideological rifts evident in contemporary culture, many graduate studies programs have begun to hold training sessions that seek to address race and ethnicity and how students react emotionally to such issues in the classroom. These workshops have been initiated to help instructors navigate tense post-election situations in the classroom and allow opportunities to have important conversations about how to proceed with discussing such events.[32] Before Trump's election, such events were absent from the university campus. But hostility toward instructors who teach about race and ethnicity is nothing new, as the authors in this volume can easily attest to with our experiences in the classroom. While I appreciate such gestures by my graduate institution and others like it, these post-election events and workshops are largely reactionary and often lack a focus on pragmatic solutions to teaching about race and ethnicity from a structural perspective. Sociologist Eduardo Bonilla-Silva reminds us that to think from a structural perspective requires us to acknowledge the possibility that "racism is only part of a larger racial system."[33] More proactive measures and "rethinking racism" as symptomatic of a larger structural social system are both needed in order to radically change the institutions in which we labor.

And, finally, as a graduate student at a public research institution, I find that the pedagogical dimensions of race and ethnic studies are too often marginalized. Many graduate students such as myself seek professional guidance and leadership from those who have the power to make structural changes to the curriculum in graduate studies departments and enable future teacher-scholars to cultivate a critical pedagogical tool kit for teaching about race and ethnicity. The marginalization of pedagogy in race and ethnic studies programs will continue to have a detrimental effect on the rising generation of scholars who lack the necessary experience and mentorship needed to navigate an uneven and hostile educational terrain.

This deficiency in preprofessional training extends beyond graduate students, as undergraduates will also be adversely affected by such neglect. Paulo Freire contends that education should aim to condition students to understand how "a culture of domination" has produced a historically contingent class of "professional women and men" to which many undergraduate students belong by virtue of pursuing university education. But many of these students are "afraid" of disrupting the status quo and "reluctant to engage in humanizing action" that intervenes in systemic inequalities.[34] To disrupt the reproduction of systemic inequalities in higher education, undergraduates should be "*reclaimed by the revolution*" brought about by insurgent education, in general, and critical pedagogues, in particular.[35] If we wish to harness Freire's call to action to intervene in the sociocultural conditioning of students by educational institutions that perpetuate the status quo and produce pupils for the managerial class of "professional women and men of any specialty," then we will need to consider how we teach undergraduates to adopt a social-justice-oriented lens for reading, writing, and intervening into hegemonic cultural formations of systemic inequalities. Put another way, we might think critically about *how* we scaffold a curriculum that is oriented toward social justice while also training undergraduate students in critical reading and writing practices.

Because of this insufficiency in my preprofessional training, I encourage faculty in critical race and ethnic studies programs to create alliances with graduate students and undergraduates. My own experiences with faculty mentors have had a phenomenal impact on my research and scholarship, but these experiences (as I have already noted) do not engage with the pedagogical discussions under examination in this volume. In fact, pedagogy does not seem to be an urgent topic among many in race and ethnic studies. To fill this gap, I suggest a more collective effort undertaken by all stakeholders, especially those who wield the power and privilege to make significant changes to how graduate students are pedagogically trained to teach undergraduates. Many graduate students share my dissatisfaction with our pedagogical training. Although we may have the skills necessary to address how race and ethnicity function as intellectual concerns, we often lack a coherent protocol for addressing how race and ethnicity function as *pedagogical* concerns. Critical race scholars might consider the ways in which our institutions enact proactive measures that seek to address hostile learning environments. Rather than continue to develop responses to the crisis of now, we need to learn how to craft responses to the crisis of the future. This continued gap in the training of graduate students deserves attention, especially when so many future scholars lack the necessary skills to teach undergraduates how to both critically write *and* critically read about race and ethnicity. My hope is that this collection on the pedagogical decisions that shape our learning environments will become the impetus for future teacher-scholars who wish to improve upon both their knowledge of and teaching on race and ethnicity in academia.

NOTES

1. See Kimberlé Crenshaw, "Mapping the Margins: Intersectionality, Identity Politics, and Violence against Women of Color," *Stanford Law Review* 43, no. 6 (1991): 1241–99, https://doi.org/10.2307/1229039; Patricia Hill Collins, "Learning from the Outsider Within: The Sociological Significance of Black Feminist Thought," *Social Problems* 33, no. 6 (1986): S14–S32, https://doi.org/10.2307/800672; Patricia Hill Collins, *Black Feminist Thought: Knowledge, Consciousness, and the Politics of Empowerment* (New York: Routledge, 1991); bell hooks, "Toward a Revolutionary Feminist Pedagogy," in *Talking Back: Thinking Feminist, Thinking Black* (Boston, MA: South End Press, 1989), 49–54; bell hooks, *Teaching to Transgress: Education as the Practice of Freedom* (New York: Routledge, 1994).

2. M. Jacqui Alexander, *Pedagogies of Crossing: Meditations on Feminism, Sexual Politics, Memory, and the Sacred* (Durham, NC: Duke University Press, 2005).

3. Hill Collins, "Learning from the Outsider Within," S14

4. Greg A. Wiggan, *Power, Privilege, and Education: Pedagogy, Curriculum, and Student Outcomes* (New York: Nova Science, 2011).

5. Alexander, *Pedagogies of Crossing.*

6. For more on scaffolding within early childhood development and education, see Laura Berk and Adam Winsley, *Scaffolding Children's Learning: Vygotsky and Early Childhood Education* (Washington, DC: National Association for the Education of Young Children, 1995); Nicola Yelland, *Promoting Meaningful Learning: Innovations in Educating Early Childhood Professionals* (Washington, DC: National Association for the Education of Young Children, 2000); Anne Keil Soderman, Kara M. Gregory, and Louise T. McCarty, *Scaffolding Emergent Literacy: A Child-Centered Approach for Preschool through Grade 5* (Boston, MA: Pearson/ Allyn and Bacon, 2005); Sandra Smidt, ed., *Key Issues in Early Years Education: A Guide for Students and Practitioners* (London: Routledge, 2010); Jefj Van Kuyk, "Scaffolding: How to Increase Development?," *European Early Childhood Education Research Journal* 19, no. 1 (2011): 133–46; and Ashley Pinkhams, Yanya Kaefer, and Susan Neuman, *Knowledge Development in Early Childhood: Sources of Learning and Classroom Implications* (New York: Guilford, 2012).

7. The idea of instructional scaffolding evolved from Jerome Bruner's readings of Russian psychologist Lev Vygotsky's 1930 *Mind in Society: The Development of Higher Psychological Processes*, trans. Michael Cole (Cambridge, MA: Harvard University Press, 1978). See Jerome Bruner, David Wood, and Gail Ross, "The Role of Tutoring in Problem Solving," *Journal of Child Psychology and Psychiatry* 17, no. 2 (1976): 90.

8. Defining "complexity" has been debated in composition studies, in particular. For more on sequencing in relation to complexity and its impact on students' cognitive development in writing courses, see Elizabeth Rankin, "From

Simple to Complex: Ideas of Order in Assignment Sequences," *Journal of Advanced Composition* 10, no. 1 (1990): 126–35.

9. Hill Collins, "Learning from the Outsider Within," S15.

10. Neville Hoad, *African Intimacies: Race, Homosexuality, and Globalization* (Minneapolis: University of Minnesota Press, 2007).

11. Ellen C. Carillo, *Securing a Place for Reading in Composition: The Importance of Teaching for Transfer* (Logan: Utah State University Press, 2015).

12. In "How Does Expansive Framing Promote Transfer?," Randi A. Engle, Diane P. Lam, Xenia S. Meyer, and Sarah E. Nix argue that "expansive framing" enables teachers to frame the content of the course within "big picture" ideas that exceed the boundary of the classroom walls. "How Does Expansive Framing Promote Transfer? Several Proposed Explanations and a Research Agenda for Investigating Them," *Educational Psychologist* 47, no. 3 (2012): 215–31, https://doi.org/10.1080/00461520.2012.695678.

13. Paulo Freire, *Pedagogy of the Oppressed*, 30th anniversary ed. (New York: Continuum, 2000).

14. Shari J. Stenberg, *Repurposing Composition: Feminist Interventions for a Neoliberal Age* (Boulder, CO: Paradigm, 2015).

15. Engle et al., "Expansive Framing," 220.

16. Engle et al., "Expansive Framing," 221.

17. Rebecca S. Nowacek, *Agents of Integration: Understanding Transfer as a Rhetorical Act* (Carbondale: Southern Illinois University Press, 2011).

18. Engle et al., "Expansive Framing," 224–25.

19. Engle et al., "Expansive Framing," 224.

20. Hill Collins, "Learning from the Outsider Within," S29.

21. As many journalists have already documented, Donald Trump earned 53 percent of white female voters in the 2016 general election. For more, see Susan Chira, "'You Focus on the Good': Women Who Voted for Trump, In Their Own Words," *NY Times*, January 14, 2017, https://www.nytimes.com/2017/01/14/us/women-voters-trump.html; and Phoebe Lett, "White Women Voted Trump. Now What?," *NY Times*, November 10, 2016, https://www.nytimes.com/2016/11/10/opinion/white-women-voted-trump-now-what.html.

22. Many thanks to the anonymous reviewer of this chapter who encouraged me to contemplate this situation more deeply.

23. In *Culturally Responsive Pedagogy: Theory, Research, and Practice*, multicultural education scholar Geneva Gay proposes "culturally responsive pedagogy" and "culturally responsive curriculum" as influential aspects of educating students, specifically multicultural students (2nd ed., New York: Teachers College, 2010).

24. Wendy, "Reflecting on ENGL 111 Fall 2015," unpublished paper, December 6, 2015.

25. Mark, "Reflecting on ENGL 111 Fall 2015," unpublished paper, December 5, 2015.

26. Whitney, "Reflecting on ENGL 111 Fall 2015," unpublished paper, December 6, 2015.

27. hooks, *Teaching to Transgress*, 32–33.

28. Robin DiAngelo, *White Fragility: Why It's So Hard for White People to Talk about Racism* (New York: Beacon, 2018).

29. Sharon Crowley, *Composition in the University* (Pittsburgh: University of Pittsburgh Press, 1998).

30. Gerald Graff, *Beyond the Culture Wars: How Teaching the Conflicts Can Revitalize American Education*, 1st ed. (New York: W. W. Norton, 1992); Jodi Melamed, *Represent and Destroy: Rationalizing Violence in the New Racial Capitalism* (Minneapolis: University of Minnesota Press, 2011).

31. James Baldwin, "A Talk to Teachers," *Yearbook of the National Society for the Study of Education* 107, no. 2 (2008): 18.

32. Janie Worm, "Conflict in Classrooms," Department of English, University of Washington, April 27, 2017, https://english.washington.edu/news/2017/04/27/conflict-classrooms; and Brian Reed, "English Department Statement, January 2017," Department of English, University of Washington, January 31, 2017, https://english.washington.edu/news/2017/01/31/english-department-statement-january-2017.

33. Eduardo Bonilla-Silva, "Rethinking Racism: Toward a Structural Interpretation," *American Sociological Review* 62, no. 3 (1997): 467, https://doi.org/10.2307/2657316.

34. Freire, *Pedagogy*, 158.

35. Freire, *Pedagogy*, 158; emphases added.

BIBLIOGRAPHY

Ahmed, Sara. *The Cultural Politics of Emotion*. New York: Routledge, 2004.

Alexander, M. Jacqui. *Pedagogies of Crossing: Meditations on Feminism, Sexual Politics, Memory, and the Sacred*. Durham, NC: Duke University Press, 2005.

Armstrong, Patricia. "Bloom's Taxonomy." Vanderbilt University Center for Teaching. Accessed April 1, 2017. https://cft.vanderbilt.edu/guides-sub-pages/blooms-taxonomy.

Baldwin, James. "A Talk to Teachers." *Yearbook of the National Society for the Study of Education* 107, no. 2 (2008): 15–20.

Bilge, Sirma, and Patricia Hill Collins. *Intersectionality*. Malden, MA: Polity, 2016.

Bloom, Benjamin S., and David R. Krathwohl. *Taxonomy of Educational Objectives: The Classification of Educational Goals*. New York: Longmans, 1956.

Bonilla-Silva, Eduardo. "Rethinking Racism: Toward a Structural Interpretation." *American Sociological Review* 62, no. 3 (1997): 465–80. https://doi.org/10.2307/2657316.

Bracher, Mark. *Literature and Social Justice: Protest Novels, Cognitive Politics, and Schema Criticism*. Austin: University of Texas Press, 2014.

Bransford, John, and D. Schwartz. "Rethinking Transfer: A Simple Proposal with Multiple Implications." *Review of Research in Education* 24 (1999): 61–100. https://doi.org/10.2307/1167267.

Bruner, Jerome, David Wood, and Gail Ross. "The Role of Tutoring in Problem Solving." *Journal of Child Psychology and Psychiatry* 17, no. 2 (1976): 89–100.

Carillo, Ellen C. *Securing a Place for Reading in Composition: The Importance of Teaching for Transfer*. Logan: Utah State University Press, 2015.

Chowdhury, Kanishka. "Teaching the Postcolonial Text: Strategies and Interventions." *College Literature* 19/20, nos. 3/1 (1992–93): 191–94.

Colorado State University. "Sequencing Writing Assignments." WAC Clearinghouse. Last modified April 2006. Accessed March 20, 2017. http://wac.colostate.edu/teaching/tipsheets/sequencingSB.doc.

Crenshaw, Kimberlé. "Mapping the Margins: Intersectionality, Identity Politics, and Violence Against Women of Color." *Stanford Law Review* 43 (1991): 1241–99. https://doi.org/10.2307/1229039.

Crowley, Sharon. *Composition in the University*. Pittsburgh: University of Pittsburgh Press, 1998.

DiAngelo, Robin. *White Fragility: Why It's So Hard for White People to Talk about Racism*. New York: Beacon, 2018.

Dua, Ena, and Alissa Trotz. "Transnational Pedagogy: Doing Political Work in Women's Studies." *Atlantis* 26, no. 2 (2002): 66–77.

Engle, Randi A., Diane P. Lam, Xenia S. Meyer, and Sarah E. Nix. "How Does Expansive Framing Promote Transfer? Several Proposed Explanations and a Research Agenda for Investigating Them." *Educational Psychologist* 47, no. 3 (2012): 215–31. https://doi.org/10.1080/00461520.2012.695678.

Felski, Rita. *Uses of Literature*. Malden, MA: Blackwell, 2008.

Flynn, Elizabeth. "Strategic, Counter-Strategic, and Reactive Resistance in the Feminist Classroom." In *Insurrections: Approaches to Resistance in Composition Studies*, edited by Andrea Greenbaum, 17–34. Albany: SUNY Press, 2001.

Freire, Paulo. *Pedagogy of the Oppressed*. 30th anniversary ed. New York: Continuum, 2000.

Gay, Geneva. *Culturally Responsive Teaching: Theory, Research, and Practice*. 2nd ed. New York: Teachers College, 2010.

Giroux, Henry. "Academic Freedom Under Fire: The Case for Critical Pedagogy." *College Literature* 33, no. 4 (2006): 1–42.

———. "Insurgent Multiculturalism and the Promise of Pedagogy." In *Multiculturalism: A Critical Reader*, edited by David Theo Goldberg, 325–43. Cambridge, MA: Blackwell, 1994.

Graff, Gerald. *Beyond the Culture Wars: How Teaching the Conflicts Can Revitalize American Education*. 1st ed. New York: W. W. Norton, 1992.

Hill Collins, Patricia. *Black Feminist Thought: Knowledge, Consciousness, and the Politics of Empowerment*. New York: Routledge, 1991.

———. "Learning from the Outsider Within: The Sociological Significance of Black Feminist Thought." *Social Problems* 33, no. 6 (1986): S14–S32. https://doi.org/10.2307/800672.

Hoad, Neville. *African Intimacies: Race, Homosexuality, and Globalization*. Minneapolis: University of Minnesota Press, 2007.

Hong, Grace Kyungwon. *Ruptures of American Capital: Women of Color Feminism and the Culture of Immigrant Labor*. Minneapolis: University of Minnesota Press, 2006.

hooks, bell. *Teaching to Transgress: Education as the Practice of Freedom*. New York: Routledge, 1994.

———. "Toward a Revolutionary Feminist Pedagogy." In *Talking Back: Thinking Feminist, Thinking Black*, 49–54. Boston, MA: South End Press, 1989.

Landry, Donna, and Gerald MacLean. "Introduction: Reading Spivak." In *The Spivak Reader*, 1–14. New York: Routledge, 1996.

McCoy, Shane. "Short Assignment 1." Teaching artifact, September 29, 2015.

———. "Major Paper 2." Teaching artifact, November 2, 2015.

McLaren, Peter. "White Terror and Oppositional Agency: Towards a Critical Multiculturalism." In *Multiculturalism: A Critical Reader*, edited by David Theo Goldberg, 45–74. Cambridge, MA: Blackwell, 1994.

Melamed, Jodi. *Represent and Destroy: Rationalizing Violence in the New Racial Capitalism*. Minneapolis: University of Minnesota Press, 2011.

Mohanty, Chandra Talpade. "Race, Multiculturalism, and Pedagogies of Dissent." In *Feminism without Borders: Decolonizing Theory, Practicing Solidarity*, 190–220. Durham, NC: Duke University Press, 2003.

Nowacek, Rebecca S. *Agents of Integration: Understanding Transfer as a Rhetorical Act*. Carbondale: Southern Illinois University Press, 2011.

Perkins, D., and Gavriel Salomon. "Knowledge to Go: A Motivational and Dispositional View of Transfer." *Educational Psychologist* 47, no. 3 (2012): 248–58. https://doi.org/10.1080/00461520.2012.693354.

———. "Teaching for Transfer." *Educational Leadership* 46, no. 1 (1988): 22–32.

Rankin, Elizabeth. "From Simple to Complex: Ideas of Order in Assignment Sequences." *Journal of Advanced Composition*, 10, no. 1 (1990): 126–35.

Shaull, Richard. "Foreword." *Pedagogy of the Oppressed*, by Paulo Freire, 29–34. 30th anniversary ed. New York: Continuum, 2000.

Sheth, Falguni A. "Why Our Best Students Are Totally Oblivious." *Salon.com*, September 13, 2013. http://www.salon.com/2013/09/13/why_our_best_students_are_totally_oblivious.

Shor, Ira. "What Is Critical Literacy?" *Journal of Pedagogy, Pluralism, and Practice* 1, no. 4 (1999). http://www.lesley.edu/journal-pedagogy-pluralism-practice/ira-shor/critical-literacy.

Stenberg, Shari J. *Repurposing Composition: Feminist Interventions for a Neoliberal Age*. Boulder, CO: Paradigm, 2012.

University of Michigan. "Sequencing and Scaffolding Assignments." Gayle Morris Sweetland Center for Writing. https://lsa.umich.edu/sweetland/instructors/teaching-resources/sequencing-and-scaffolding-assignments.html.

Vygotsky, Lev. *Mind in Society: The Development of Higher Psychological Processes*. Translated by Michael Cole. Cambridge, MA: Harvard University Press, 1978.

Walqui, Aida, and Kathryn Strom. "Scaffolding." New York City Department of Education. Accessed March 20, 2017. http://schools.nyc.gov/NR/rdonlyres/A7CBC9AC-6BD7-4886-998C-788A65ABBCB6/0/ScaffoldingWalquiandStromBrief_73015.pdf.

Wiggan, Greg A. *Power, Privilege, and Education: Pedagogy, Curriculum, and Student Outcomes*. New York: Nova Science, 2011.

Yancey, Kathleen Blake. *Teaching Literature as Reflective Practice*. Urbana, IL: National Council of Teachers of English, 2004.

PART III

PRECARIOUS INSTITUTIONS, PRECARIOUS APPOINTMENTS

CHAPTER 9

INSTITUTIONALIZING (IN)EQUALITY

The Double-Edged Sword of Diversity Requirements

DANIEL J. DELGADO AND KEJA VALENS

The turn of the twenty-first century has been marked by US institutions of all types moving to implement an array of "diversity-aware" practices and policies, targeting everything from bathroom access to universal design. In 2012, the Black Lives Matter movement refocused attention and energy across the United States, and across US universities, on the persistence of racism and on the power dynamics and social injustice that both feed and result from it. An increase in pro-diversity rhetoric, we were reminded, does not suffice to address institutionalized racism and inequity. At many colleges and universities, students have been the ones demanding, vocally and visibly, that classrooms and curricula must address diversity, power dynamics, and social justice in substantive ways from the micro-level of interpersonal interactions to the macro-level of examining structural inequalities and ways to dismantle them.[1] An increasing number of colleges and universities have responded by adding courses and requirements focused on the study of "diversity."[2]

Post–Ferguson protests, post–hashtag campaigns, and post–student protests, as we enter the third decade of the twenty-first century, a significant amount of racist discourse persists, arguably becoming—or remaining—the norm for many college and university campuses. Black and Latinx students are regularly harassed, attacked, and subjected to violence at and by their institutions of higher learning. Throughout the decade, students of color have experienced high-profile incidents of racism and violence at schools including Yale University and Harvard University, as well as Texas A&M University, University of California, Los Angeles, and University of Wisconsin. We know this violence is not new, nor are the ways that it manifests for students of color in self-doubt, feelings of inadequacy, and imposter syndrome. Indeed, in his autobiography, W. E. B. Du Bois describes how "I was desperately afraid of intruding where I was not wanted; appearing without invitation; of showing a desire for the company of those who had no desire for me. I should in fact have been pleased if most of my fellow students had wanted to associate with me; if I had been popular or envied. But the absence of this made me neither unhappy nor morose. I had my 'island within' and it was a fair country."[3] None of these institutions were meant to be spaces for people of color but rather were intended for the maintenance of an elite class consisting of mainly whites.

Du Bois's "island within" was his way of coping with this violence, and his autobiographical account speaks to the larger issue of fear faced by students of color on university campuses. That the fear of rebuke, violence, and attack are common in our present where students fail to see an institution that reflects their own experiences and subjectivities reminds us (as Douglas Julien in "Can the White Boy Speak?" points out) that racial violence, overt and covert, externalized and internalized, is not "over there" in the past, that Du Bois is important not only as a chronicler of the history of racism in US institutions but remains "in here." Du Bois is sustained as an important reflection of what we see and feel in the present day. In an attempt to make inside changes, changes inside the structures of the institutions that do hear and respond to the calls of Du Bois that resound in the calls of students today, many colleges and universities have institutionalized "diversity" departments, programs, and policies and have included changes to the curriculum itself as a form of practice for "diversity" implementation. That these are far from the first set of institutional changes that faculty, administrators, students, and staff have called for and implemented reminds us that, as Felicia L. Harris notes in "Multiple Pedagogies Required," "oftentimes individuals with hopes of liberation subconsciously emulate the oppressive conditions that have structured their thinking." Thus, even as we celebrate this institutional change, we must interrogate it. We argue that the presence of these "diversity" policies represents a double-edged sword, as they can become a source of respite, relief, and safety for students of color but can also become a site for denial, violence, and curtailment. Despite providing aid, "diversity" policy can reside in an institution as the only means for alleviating institutional issues and can ultimately limit student growth as a result of academic siloing.

Students at Salem State University protested university policies, forming a race-based student organization that they named Black, Brown, and Proud. They were able to leverage a seat at the table with the university administration. Through a series of conversations they made several requests to address issues of racism and inequality. Student experiences with the alienation and exclusion described by Du Bois were not uncommon at Salem State University, and the diversity requirement was one piece directed at alleviating this experience of oppression. Yet, unlike Du Bois, SSU students had a history of Black and Latinx protest histories to rely on to guide their actions.

One particular request was the implementation of a change in the university curriculum that addressed the realities of the student body and reflected a race-conscious interpretation of their education. Of particular interest is that prior to the student-led protests and requests for change, the university was working, albeit slowly, on the implementation of a "diversity" requirement. Although many of the student actions were met with a combination of resistance and pandering by executive administration, they were successful in bringing about significant changes in the university, including tipping the tides toward a successful and rapid adoption of the general education "diversity" requirement.

We keep putting "diversity" in scare quotes, however, because what exactly that term means, how it can be taught well, and how its study can be required effectively continue to be of concern to us. We are scholars and teachers whose areas of focus are "diverse"—Daniel works in sociology on Latinx, anticolonial thought, racialization, and intersectionality, Keja works in English on Caribbean, Black, and Latinx diaspora, multicultural American literatures, and queer theory. The academic study of diversity thus presents a primary place for our work that attempts to understand across this spectrum of methods and materials what diversity is, how it works, and how it impacts us and our students in our classrooms, our university, and each of our various communities. In our roles as scholars and teachers, we question how the term "diversity" is constructed, how it functions as a catchphrase and in a context of political correctness, what differences it conveys, and what norms it reifies. We agree with Chandra Mohanty that "one of the fundamental challenges of 'diversity' after all is to understand our collective differences in terms of historical agency and responsibility so that we can understand others and build solidarities across divisive boundaries."[4] At the same time, as a result of our scholarly and pedagogical commitments and also of our institutional roles—Daniel as the Faculty Fellow for Latino Student Success and Keja as a member of both the President's Advisory Committee on Diversity and the General Education Committee—we led the institutional effort to add a "Diversity, Power Dynamics, and Social Justice (DPDS)" requirement to the general education curriculum at Salem State University.

Taking our professional involvement in the creation of an institutional response to the need for curriculum-level diversity as a case study, in this chapter we draw on our experience developing and implementing the DPDS requirement at Salem State to consider how diversity requirements, particularly in general education curricula, function as part of scholarly, pedagogical, and institutional commitments to, in the words of bell hooks, "confront the biases that have shaped teaching practices [and] ways of knowing," as well as the information, values, and beliefs that have shaped curricula, especially in majority-white, middle-tier institutions.[5] But we also explore our concerns, following Audre Lorde, that "the master's tools will never dismantle the master's house"—that diversity requirements, like the academic feminisms Lorde critiqued, "may allow us to temporarily beat [the master] at his own game, but they will never enable us to bring about genuine change."[6] Can the tools of institutional requirements, we ask, work like the "social practice" in which, as Jason Springs argues, "appropriating and reconfiguring the 'master's tools' turns out to be a condition for the possibility of systematic critique and resistant action that might disassemble and genuinely transform 'the master's house' "?[7] The academy itself has long been a place of instruction in mastery of and through dominant ideology and also of questioning, critiquing, and challenging hegemonic beliefs and practices.[8] It may be the training ground for those entering the master's house, but it may also be the training ground for those set to dismantle and remodel the master's house. Our central question is: Will a diversity requirement enable the diversity goals of an institution of higher education rooted in academia?[9] We believe diversity initiatives are double-edged: on the one hand, they can facilitate equity while, on the other hand, they may simultaneously reinscribe existing inequalities. To be clear, then, we argue that the production of equality in social institutions, such as academia, often requires compromise with past ideologies and discourse that carry significant possibilities for retrenchment and the consequent reproduction of inequality.

The success of our work to establish the DPDS requirement at Salem State has heightened both our hopes and our concerns for making the study of diversity a requirement. The hopes: That as students encounter classrooms that center on diversity, they learn to critically examine the ideological and institutional structures that maintain, and challenge, hegemonic power, and they emerge able and ready to demand and to work for diversity, equity, and inclusion throughout the university and their lives. That as all students are required to have this opportunity, we become a university community increasingly able to engage in constructive civil discourse and academic, professional, and civic engagement on and beyond campus, aimed at achieving social justice, in the context of the complex, diverse local and global communities that we inhabit. That in addition to the already documented effects of diversity in the curriculum to reduce prejudice and improve campus climate, critical thinking, cognitive development, civic engagement, and moral development, our diversity requirement makes space for and even fosters what hooks calls "radical pedagogy," "learning at its most powerful" that can "indeed liberate."[10] The concerns: that these institutional requirements, even—or rather especially—for the study of diversity, may be at best unrelated to and at worst incompatible with our commitment to what hooks calls "education as a practice of freedom," which relies on "teaching that enables transgressions—a movement against and beyond boundaries";[11] that they serve an academic commodification of diversity;[12] that students acquire a surface-level set of terms and tools that allow them to appear "politically correct" or "empowered" but that do not transform them, or worse, that they come to view the requirement as something to "get through" and become further isolated and polarized, angry at an institution that, depending on their perspective, forces them to sit through liberal orthodoxies or fails to provide emancipatory education. We are concerned that, as Bonilla-Silva argues, we are providing students with the tools to be color-blind rather than teaching them to fully see race.[13] We teach them to understand the language of diversity but don't provide the proper tools for dismantling the master's house. We believe that diversity initiatives can challenge, alleviate, and reproduce inequality. In what follows, we address this *double-edged sword of diversity requirements* through a discussion of practices undertaken at Salem State University.

ADOPTING A DIVERSITY REQUIREMENT AT A PUBLIC REGIONAL INSTITUTION: SALEM STATE UNIVERSITY

Salem State is part of the Massachusetts public university system and serves the area north of Boston. In 2017, about 50 percent of the student body was first generation to college, about 50 percent of undergraduates received federal Pell Grants, and about 36 percent of the student body registered as racially and ethnically "diverse." This represents the most diverse student body at a state university in Massachusetts.[14] The importance of this diversity at Salem State was clear to the institution as it was an early adopter of a general education diversity requirement in the 1990s.[15] In 2012–13, Salem State completed a much-needed overhaul of the general education program that resulted in a new general education curriculum with no diversity requirement. The argument that carried this decision, though certainly contested, was that diversity had become a "guiding principle" of the university, infused throughout our curriculum. This argument was reproduced with the implementation of the DPDS requirement and we believe it to be a source for the reproduction of inequality, as we note below.

A significant minority of faculty, students, staff, and administrators, however, were not satisfied with either the symbolic institutional commitment to curricular diversity and the academic study of power dynamics and social justice or the degree to which diversity was actually infused throughout the curriculum. Our own anecdotal experience suggested that the understanding of diversity was diffuse and incredibly varied across the faculty. Only the few faculty whose own area of academic study was directly focused on diversity had clear ideas about ways to integrate materials and pedagogies to study diversity in our fields and to critically examine power dynamics and social justice in our disciplines, classrooms, and institutions. At the same time, many of those courses that focused on diversity, which had easily filled when they satisfied the old diversity requirement but which no longer fulfilled any general education requirements, were being cancelled due to under-enrollment.

In 2014–2015, a curriculum subcommittee of the President's Advisory Committee on Diversity (PAC-D) compared Salem State's general education curriculum to that of peer and aspirational institutions and determined that our lack of diversity requirement should be corrected and, along with the faculty fellows for diversity and Latinx student success, began working to reintroduce a diversity requirement into our general education curriculum. We submitted an initial proposal for a new general education diversity requirement in May 2015 but withdrew it in September 2015 due to a lack of support across campus. Much of the resistance came in the form of faculty who believed that diversity was indeed already infused across our curriculum, or at least across specific departments, and that it would be unnecessarily "cumbersome" to add another requirement to the general education curriculum. Our argument about the importance of diversity in the curriculum, in other words, was received with widespread agreement and at the same time had little effect in moving the faculty or the administration to accept the recommendation to add a DPDS general education requirement. Many of our colleagues believed that we were already doing enough, that we should certainly consider supporting minors or concentrations or certificates that foster and recognize the focused study of diversity, but that our general institutional commitment and the experience of our students in their general education program was already sufficiently engaged with diversity. Similar positions had blocked diversity requirements, and led to bitter and divisive battles on other campuses, perhaps most drawn out and documented at UCLA.[16]

It was around this time that the Black, Brown, and Proud student movement mobilized on campus and presented demands to the university that included "Require Diversity courses into general education, General Education Requirement." We recognized both the increased urgency for the requirement in the independent corroboration by students and the increased potential for a bitter division, in which we feared that the institutional forces of heterogeneity and privilege would combine with the likes of the academic feminism in which Lorde finds "a tragic repetition of racist patriarchal thought."[17] And so those of us working for the diversity, power dynamics, and social justice requirement focused efforts on trying to convince rather than to fight our colleagues.

In fall 2016, the Diversity, Power Dynamics, and Social Justice General Education Requirement was unanimously approved by Salem State's University Curriculum Committee, Academic Policies Committee, All-College Committee, academic provost and vice president, president, and board of trustees:

> The Diversity, Power Dynamics, and Social Justice requirement stands as an institutional commitment to develop and teach different ways of thinking which have been drawn from and

address the multiple histories and cultural heritages that shape the United States. It recognizes that individuals develop their identities in response to particular cultural and social experiences. At the same time, individuals are located within sociocultural historical contexts that include oppression, inequality, and differences in power and privilege within society. Course material will engage in a cross cultural analysis of historical and contemporary inequities such as those associated with race, ethnicity, sex and gender, sexual orientation, nationality, ability, religion, age, or socio-economic status. Its goal is to replace stereotyping with informed reasoning, understanding, and judgment skills and to facilitate and enhance students' ability to consider ethical and social decisions from multiple perspectives. No one orthodoxy or perspective encompasses the examination of diversity, power dynamics, and social justice; this may include perspectives from any political and social vantage point.

- This category functions as an overlay and does not require the addition of any credits to the general education curriculum.
- DPDS courses can be used to satisfy both the DPDS category and another General Education category at the same time.
- DPDS courses can be used to satisfy both the DPDS category and a requirement in the student's major at the same time.

Courses approved for this category will address the following criteria:

Criterion 1: Examine the people, structures, systems, and ideologies that sustain discrimination, asymmetries of power, and resource inequities in society (e.g., social, political, economic, environmental, or cultural) and how unequal power impacts the individual and the community.

Criterion 2: Examine the experiences and the contributions of individuals and communities with social identities rendered other or alien, or generally oppressed by asymmetrical power structures within the United States, including but not limited to for reasons associated with race, ethnicity, sex and gender, sexual orientation, nationality, ability, religion, age, or socio-economic status.

Criterion 3: Engage students to explore their own social locations, social identities, privileges, and experiences of inequity to better understand their own place in existing social structures, communities, and power structures.

Criterion 4: Foster students' ability to act in a manner that recognizes the feelings, lives, and perspectives of diverse others by imploring them to face how people, systems, and social structures function to maintain inequality and deny integrated diversity.

Learning Outcomes:

Intercultural knowledge and competence

Critical Thinking

Associated LEAP VALUE RUBRICS: INTERCULTURAL KNOWLEDGE AND COMPETENCY; CRITICAL THINKING.[18]

We do believe in the importance of symbolic action and representation: that words matter, that the way we tell stories, including institutional stories, of who we are and what we teach shapes our experiences and reality. Insisting on the title "diversity, power dynamics, and social justice," we recognize that courses fulfilling this requirement will address the underlying and systemic causes and consequences of inequity as much as they would look at individuals, groups, and categories treated as "different" or "diverse." These will not be courses in which, as hooks writes, knowledge, even knowledge about diversity, is "about information only"; these courses will engage students in practices of freedom that, as for hooks, open them "to be changed by ideas," "where it was assumed that the knowledge offered students would empower them to be better scholars, to live more fully in the world beyond academe."[19] The transformations, of students, classrooms, and institutions, wrought by this diversity requirement increase our freedom to acquire mastery and to take ownership of our academic institutions in which the diversity and power dynamics would be shifted. For we do believe that critical inquiry—examining deeply and from multiple perspectives the causes and results of differential treatment based on diverse social identities and locations—is a practice of freedom. These practices are explicitly independent of any particular political ideology or program and pointed toward purposefully undetermined shifts in power dynamics and increases in social justice tied to greater equity across diverse social identities and locations. And yet neither do they let "anything go," nor do they allow the status quo to persist.

Mohanty argues that "resistance lies in self-conscious engagement with dominant, normative discourses and representations and in the active creation of oppositional analytic and cultural spaces."[20] And Foucault, while cautioning that more knowledge is not a neat path to more power and certainly not a neat path to more liberation, does lay out ways that knowledge, especially about the discursive and ideological conditions in which it is authorized, is part of "the mobile and transitory points of resistance" to hegemonic power that may not produce "radical ruptures" in dominant power structures. But "just as the network of power relations ends by forming a dense web that passes through apparatuses and institutions, without being exactly localized in them, so too the swarm of points of resistance traverses social stratifications and individual unities" to the point that "the strategic codification of these points of resistance . . . makes a revolution possible."[21] Rather than faltering in the distance between the classroom as "the most radical space of possibility in the academy"[22] and the institutional structures that maintain the status quo, we hope that our general education diversity requirement can be part of education as a practice of freedom. Education as a practice here is not only about the instantiation of theory or habitual repetition but also about processes of preparing. The reiteration of trying on and trying for freedom are the ends and the means of the diversity requirement as a practice of freedom. For freedom itself involves not only liberation from domination or force but also liberty to participate fully in the privileges, rights, duties, and requirements of the institution, the state, the nation.

THE CUTTING EDGES OF DPDS IMPLEMENTATION: AN ANALYSIS

Questions of whom our institution serves intertwine with questions of what and whom a diversity requirement "is for." A set of courses designed for the general education curriculum at a white-majority university seems necessarily addressed in some significant ways to a white-majority audience. It will certainly be delivered by a white-majority faculty for the foreseeable future. But if we conceive of the diversity requirement as "for" the white students, we end up with what Lorde calls "an old and primary tool of all oppressors to keep the oppressed occupied with the master's concerns."[23] Eve Sedgwick in her writing on queer pedagogy, hooks in her articulation of racially radical pedagogy, and Harris in this volume all speak to the importance of centering Black and queer students in the classroom, not only as a way to ensure that their concerns matter but also as a way to engage all students in considering the privileges and oppressions involved in assuming you are or are not the ideal audience of a course, a degree, or a university. It is a key and delicate project to make the "we" of a classroom and the "we" of an institution not only have room on the margins for a few "others" but have space at the center for "we" to be non-white, non-straight, differently abled, multigenerational, and more. Only when that happens do our classrooms and our institutions offer more than just "information about" diversity and transform their own power dynamics.

The issues of who delivers and who is the ideal recipient of a diversity requirement came up explicitly in our discussions during the extended proposal process. Faculty spoke alternately of the need to attend to the demands of Black, Brown, and Proud and other affiliated student groups for a diversity requirement and of concerns about potential backlash from white students who would feel that the requirement was not "for them," was a distraction from their real concerns, or was forcing them to spend time on things not deeply relevant to their careers and lives. At the same time, a campus art gallery show[24] and classroom experiences during a #BlackLivesMatter Teach-In brought to the fore concerns of students of color that faculty and administrators were inadequately prepared to address diverse topics and to teach diverse groups students in the classroom and in the co-curriculum. The difficulty of these conversations underlines not only the importance of faculty development for the implementation of a diversity requirement but also that the work on creating and passing the requirement is the beginning of that faculty development, just as crafting the requirement is a first step in ensuring that it addresses and serves both white and non-white students and faculty.

And writing this feels like a reification of the very ideology and structures that we want to challenge, a kind of worst version of identity politics that identifies and classifies a population by race and ethnicity and uses that information to make generalizations about who needs what, that divides "needs" by racial identity groups, that acts as if racial identity groups were simple and solid, let alone given ("real"). The question at the heart of this essay reemerges: How do we engage from within a system whose very construction we want to challenge?

In what we hope is a practice of collaborative process that might be at the heart of radical pedagogy in the institution as well as in the classroom, before we re-introduced the proposal for our diversity, power dynamics, and social justice general education requirement, we invited the full campus community to participate in revising it, using an online survey, public forums, private conversations to share our data and our reasoning but also to invite revision to the wording and other details of the proposal.[25] At the same time, in what we understand as participation in an institutional reliance on quantitative assessment that depends on hierarchical categorization and is rife with high-stakes consequences that curtail freedom, we also turned to an inventory of course catalog descriptions. Only 33 percent of general education sections that we offered in spring 2016 specifically included diversity, power dynamics, and social justice in the course description. The numbers showed that while any number of general education courses *might* address diversity, power dynamics, and social justice, because those are not explicitly incorporated into the course description and the inclusion of such material is not further ensured by any certification or classification, most of our general education courses do not *necessarily* include the study of diversity, power dynamics, and social justice; and any assessment of whether specific sections of any course actually do so would not be generalizable to the course as whole and would not ensure that any future iteration of the course did so in the future.

One of the primary arguments for the DPDS category in our general education curriculum is indeed to ensure that the teaching of "diversity" occurs in a regular, sustained, and assessable manner. We are on the side, in other words, of the "layers of institutional structures [that] will always ensure that accountability for what happens in the classroom rests with the teacher" in a way that is necessarily in tension with a radical pedagogy like that of hooks, which destabilizes the power of the teacher and the institution.[26] Furthermore, one of the anti-radical institutional structures, according to hooks, is that of accountability measured in skills. And indeed, as a public institution we assess general education courses in ways that relate to accountability not only to the students and the university but also to the state. A general education category lays out "measurable" criteria that any course in the category must meet and ties them to the American

Association of Colleges and Universities' Liberal Education and America's Promise Essential Learning Outcomes that have been adopted by the Massachusetts Department of Higher Education.[27] A series of committees elected through the shared governance process certifies courses for the requirement by focusing on how the (measurable) objectives or learning outcomes of the course match the (measurable) criteria of the category.

The principles guiding diversity work in the academy regularly require significant negotiation, compromise, and challenge. In our work on the DPDS, we hosted numerous info sessions and forums for discussion. Our colleagues provided feedback in a university-wide survey, and we had a disciplinarily diverse body of faculty that constituted the DPDS committee. This amounted to the futility of herding cats rather than the institutionalization of equality and equity. To be clear, we rarely experienced consensus on many of our discussions. However, we often found a basic and agreed-upon belief only when we reproduced problematic language, concepts, and ideologies. This meant that the new diversity policy requires the reproduction of past racist, sexist, or homophobic ideologies, practices, and frameworks in conjunction with the reproduction of progressive policy.

In these instances of both regressive and progressive policy and language we found the discursive institutional lubricant to facilitate the creation of the DPDS requirement. Because we recognized that what hooks called the trappings of "white supremacist patriarchal anti-queer capitalism"[28] often force us all into a binary position regarding how institutions function—racist or not racist, homophobic or not homophobic—we found that the institutionalization of diversity policy and curriculum wasn't binary. It was a juxtaposition of varying forms of progressive equality and varying forms of regressive reproductions of inequality. Ultimately, we realized these regressive reproductions were required to facilitate progressive productions of equality and equity.

As noted above, the Salem State curriculum previously had a diversity requirement, but this was often used to pass over many courses that dealt with social justice or power dynamics for courses that focused on diversity in its broad interpretation as variation. This meant, as one faculty member noted to Daniel, that courses such as Feminist Theory offered in political science were interpreted as too narrow to constitute diversity since they focused primarily on feminism, not varieties of theoretical or social frameworks. While, of course, feminist theory fits well with many diversity requirements at many institutions, it wasn't conceptualized to be broad enough for Salem State's diversity requirements. The production of patriarchy was clear in this instance as gender was considered too narrow. Failing to acknowledge the lack of feminist theory, pedagogy, and literature in the overall curriculum, instead, in an effort to exclude feminist theory, some clamored for broader inclusion of all theory. Just as the chants of "All Lives Matter" are attempts to drown out cries that "Black Lives Matter," SSU decided that rather than focus on how feminism matters, they would argue that "all theories matter" more.

Similarly, the inclusion of our DPDS requirement encountered claims of narrowness, as several colleagues noted they disagreed with the institutionalization of a specific requirement. Their argument was that this didn't facilitate a totality of diversity, power dynamics, and social justice into the curriculum of the university as a whole. They instead suggested that no policy should be instituted and a liberal approach be utilized, with each department moving to institute such requirements in their own respective curriculum. Their resistance was not about the content of the DPDS requirement but rather that this requirement wasn't comprehensive in addressing structural inequality. It's important to note that we didn't disagree, yet in an effort to ensure the implementation of equity, we believed policy was required. These colleagues were making a "good faith" argument when we already had direct experience of the ways that, because many disciplines and individuals have varying interpretations of what constitutes DPDS in the curriculum, leaving its inclusion to "good faith" not only allows the reproduction of the status quo, but it also curtails the campus-wide discussions that, difficult as they may be, can engage us in institutional as well as individual transformation.

This left the faculty fellows leading the campus discussion, us, as the bridge between the current and future technologies of diversity. We were the physical presence that connected problematic past institutional practice with the current progressive practice. Sara Ahmed notes this in her critique of diversity practice and language: "diversity officers work to align their own units, and even their own bodies, with the values that are embedded within academic culture, and the management of the universities."[29] Her analysis illustrates how diversity workers in universities are often caught between numerous competing and challenging narratives of what constitutes diversity and ultimately how these varying interpretations should be implemented.

The various narratives and technologies for implementation of diversity congealed in the creation of the above descriptions of the DPDS requirement for the university, yet this required a narrow interpretation of diversity. Specifically, we made a claim for diversity interpreted through power dynamics and social justice in an attempt to move diversity toward, as Deem and Ozga describe, the issues of distributive justice and equalizing power dynamics.[30] This ultimately shaped a diversity requirement that was simultaneously focused on addressing oppression and, at times, rife with language that reproduced these oppressions. Ahmed clarifies how this happens: "For it seems clear that if 'diversity' does not have any necessary meaning, or if diversity is 'cut off' from a specific referent, then it does not necessarily work only to conceal inequalities. We might not know what diversity does in practice in advance of its circulation within organizations."[31]

Such an example was pointed out in the use of the language "minorities" in the DPDS proposal. In a university-wide forum one faculty member pointed out that this was an "old" term and now many groups use different language. This instance was a prime example of the strange unities of diversity implementation, as this faculty implicitly recognized the term was meant to address particular groups (i.e., distributive justice) yet realized it would reproduce racism, sexism, and homophobic interpretations of oppressed groups. Like the word "diversity," "minority" was interpreted as a problem especially because it, as Ahmed described, is "removed from its referent" or an interpretive context. This illustrates the importance of a shared interpretive context for the creation of the DPDS requirement. As the cyborg technologies of old and new combined, we created new interpretive contexts for each and revealed a new understanding of a diversity requirement that addressed distributive justice, inequality, and social power.

CONCLUSION

The creation of the DPDS requirement often required physical and emotional labor on the part of both authors. We were pulled in numerous directions all asking us to fulfill particular interpretations and iterations of what diversity should look like. Yet we worked with our colleagues and created the documents that enabled the adoption of the DPDS requirement into the curriculum, which led to us serving as the faculty fellows responsible for its implementation. These initiatives, as this chapter's title indicates, have felt like a double-edged sword. We are what Ahmed describes as the "diversity champions," and the institutional constraints of that role often require our own positionalities and interpretations of diversity issues to be framed in a larger institutional context.

For Daniel this institutional context often required the subordination of anticolonial and critical race positions/interpretations to reproductions of white supremacy and oppression. I recognized that to create opportunities for complex distributive justice I was often required to allow particular manifestations of racism and white supremacy to be connected to the DPDS initiative. While I agree with the initiative's premise, I found it to be too broad to capture the realities of how racism is experienced by people of color. I grappled with feelings that recognized the function of a DPDS that served white faculty and white students, and not students of color. Rather than explicitly note a whiteness studies component, we had to choose the language of "race" and "inequality" to address such issues, which left the door open for less critical interpretations of how racism functions in the United States. Had we been able to include an explicit requirement to examine how racism functions, the diversity requirement would be more comprehensive and ultimately would have provided a clearer route for distributive justice for students of color. I reconciled these concerns with a realization that there was opportunity for the work to be an initial step toward a larger institutional practice of equality for students, faculty, and staff.

For Keja the work involved encountering at every turn my ambivalence about how to use institutionalized practices (such as general education requirements) and terms (such as "diversity") to transform power dynamics and achieve social justice, as well as my deep ambivalence about academia and the parts of academia to which I want to devote my energy. At Salem State, faculty teach a 4-4 load. For the work preparing the DPDS requirement, I had no release. As the faculty fellows for implementing DPDS, Daniel and I share just over one course release per semester.[32] The work is physically and emotionally consuming, necessarily cutting into the time and energy that I have to work in my community supporting, for example, public bilingual and bicultural K–8 programs, or to prepare my courses. Rereading hooks and Freire for this chapter, I am reminded of the incredible power and reach of public K–12 education and of the deep need to work for emancipatory education in that system. And talking about the delivery of the DPDS requirement, I keep coming back to the profound importance at any grade or level of examining what actually happens in the classroom. In the classroom, I can see and feel shifts in power and understanding; I can modify my practice when I recognize that it is reproducing rather than challenging inequity or hegemony. But of course in my own classes I can only work with about 100 students per semester, and I cannot influence whether my courses are the exception or the rule in their academic experience. The indirectness of working on structural components such as the DPDS requirement is part of the challenge, but so is the nagging sense that I'm devoting time and energy not to working with students to improve our lives but to working with an administrative structure to improve its standing. So I feel like I am spending all of this energy so that Salem State can have a symbolic academic commitment to diversity at the very same time that I worry about the university's ability to do the deep self-examination and restructuring work that might actually transform our own power dynamics. Self-examination, which for me in this case appears through ambivalence, is emotional and intellectual work that rarely gets acknowledgment. The ability to have a partner in this work with whom to share the experience of ambivalence as well as the effort of the work—the ways that Daniel and I shared the conversations that led to this chapter, the ways that we could exit a meeting where we just agreed to, or even argued for, deeply problematic language, and simply share that we feel ambivalent about this—has been of the utmost importance to me. Similarly, the idea and then the practice of writing this chapter, of having a space to acknowledge, reflect on, and share the ambivalence, renders the work of creating the DPDS a practice, an effort, a trying, and also shows how being ambivalent is work, is part of the academic work and the social justice work that we are doing.

Our next challenge was, and continues to be, developing institutional structures to support faculty who develop and teach the courses that are part of the DPDS general education requirement. As we noted at the outset, and as the authors throughout this volume detail, teaching DPDS courses in a transformative manner involves not only imparting knowledge about "diverse groups" but also practicing hooksian pedagogies that work to do such things as "affirming Black humanity" (Brooms and Brice, in this volume) and make "conversations about race a productive experience of rupture" (Westmoreland, in this volume). We must remain dedicated to academic freedom as itself one of the ways that faculty can experiment and be protected from institutional racism and also deeply attentive to the testimonies of students who bear the pain that results when "individuals with hopes of liberation subconsciously emulate the oppressive conditions that have structured their thinking," as Harris details in the present volume. The present volume offers invaluable lessons and tools for instructors ready to and in the midst of engaging those pedagogies, but we are concerned that without institutional recognition and support, when we encourage faculty to heed what Julien terms "a call to struggle" requiring that "I myself remain vulnerable," we render ever more precarious those same faculty's positions and ever more strained their emotional and physical resources. Yet of course institutional support and recognition also involves institutional control and the kinds of compromises that seem to be inimical to anything radical.

We do not believe our institution to be an anomaly. We share with many colleagues at other universities the plight of Ahmed's "diversity champions," caught in institutional structures that require the reproduction of inequalities as we implement social-justice- and equality-framed policies and initiatives. With inadequate compensation and little individual outlet or release for our own emotional strain, not to mention the "feeling of hostility aimed at instructors and institutions who critique the master narrative" that Scott Manning Stevens explores in "On Native American Erasure in the Classroom," the cost of doing diversity work is significant for the "champions" who are called upon time and again to do this work. While different institutions have different initiatives and practices in place, few have adequately addressed race, class, gender, ability, and sexuality, and many require the combination of both regressive and progressive policy to merely start programs. Institutions of higher education, already notoriously slow to change, are often even slower to accommodate growing diverse populations not only of students but also of faculty, staff, and, hopefully, administrators.

A clear example, and final note, are Salem State University's plans to become a Hispanic-serving institution (HSI), the only one granting four-year degrees in Massachusetts. While this is in many ways an important move, its initial undertaking appears to involve looking to a growing student population with very little attention to the groundwork necessary to create a university environment that would facilitate the significant change from a historically white-serving university to a campus that will be over 30 percent Latinx. The institutional desires for change are present in the form of many in the executive administration who would like to move forward on an HSI designation but without, as yet, the dedication of any real resources to such things as the implementation of Latinx faculty, staff, and administrative hiring. A significant opportunity to move in this direction was recently lost when a Latina was considered (with 71 percent faculty support for her hiring) for the presidency, but she was ultimately passed over for an internal candidate who is a white man. This illustrates the all-too-common structural, cultural, and systemic context wherein a desire for change supported by little knowledge of how to implement such change leads to reliance upon tradition. Tradition of course easily reproduces racial structures and practices and so Salem State hired another white New Englander as university president to lead an aspirant HSI.

NOTES

1. At the end of 2015, the website www.thedemands.org collected recent student demands regarding racial justice from fifty-one US campuses (https://www.thedemands.org). Similar demands continue to be made at other institutions, for example at Salem State in 2016 and at the University of Chicago in 2017 (Luke Mikelionis, "U of Chicago Students Demand Race-Specific Housing and Requiring 'Diversity and Inclusion' to Graduate," *Heatstreet*, May 23, 2017, https://heatst.com/culture-wars/u-chicago-students-demand-race-specific-housing-and-requiring-diversity-and-inclusion-to-graduate).

2. For discussions of new diversity requirements in 2010–16, see Karl Badger, "Peer Institution St. Olaf College Amends Diversity Requirement," *Luther College Chips*, April 15, 2016, http://www.lutherchips.com/1716/news/peer-institution-st-olaf-college-amends-diversity-requirement; California State University East Bay, "Cal State East Bay Adding New Diversity, Social Justice and Sustainability Requirements," April 28, 2016, http://www.csueastbay.edu/news/2016/04/04282016.html; Jeff Charis-Carlson, "UI Sets New Diversity Requirement for 2017," *Iowa City Press-Citizen*, December 21, 2015, http://www.press-citizen.com/story/news/education/university-of-iowa/2015/12/21/ui-sets-new-diversity-requirement-2017/77694850; Michael Coyne, "Panel Discusses Diversity Requirement for Incoming Class," *Georgetown Voice*, April 28, 2016, http://georgetownvoice.com/2016/04/28/panel-discusses-diversity-requirement-for-incoming-class; Department of American Studies, University of Notre Dame, "Department Endorses Diversity Requirement," *University of Notre Dame*, February 13, 2015, http://americanstudies.nd.edu/news/55874-department-endorses-u-s-diversity-requirement; Editorial Board, "Diversity Makes Sense as a Gen Ed Requirement," *Cavalier Daily*, June 11, 2016, http://www.cavalierdaily.com/article/2016/04/diversity-makes-sense-gen-ed; Colleen Flaherty, "Majoring in Diversity," *Inside Higher Ed*, July 26, 2010, https://www.insidehighered.com/news/2016/07/26/hamilton-colleges-new-department-specific-diversity-requirement-sparks-debate; Emilia Otte, "A New Diversity Requirement at Bryn Mawr?," *Bi-College News*, February 27, 2016, http://www.biconews.com/2016/02/27/diversity-conversation; Josh Jaschik, "UCLA Faculty Approves Diversity Requirement," *Inside Higher Ed*, April 13, 2015, https://www.inside

highered.com/news/2015/04/13/ucla-faculty-approves-diversity-requirement; Kyle Plantz, "Univ. of Michigan Adds Required Diversity Courses to Business School Curriculum," *Campusreform.org*, November 19, 2015, http://www.campusreform.org/?ID=7014; Lornet Tumbell, "University of Washington Diversity Course Now Required for Graduation," *Huffington Post*, August 10, 2013, http://www.huffingtonpost.com/2013/06/10/university-of-washington-diversity-course-now-required-for-graduation_n_3413770.html; Alexandra Vollman, "Wheaton College Adopts Diversity Requirement after Months of Controversy," *Insight into Diversity*, 2016, http://www.insightintodiversity.com/wheaton-college-adopts-diversity-requirement-after-months-of-controversy; Jordan Yount, "A&S Faculty Approve Diversity Requirement," University of Missouri College of Arts and Sciences, March 26, 2016. https://coas.missouri.edu/news/faculty-approve-diversity-course-requirement.

3. W. E. B. Du Bois, *The Autobiography of W.E.B. Du Bois: A Soliloquy on Viewing My Life from the Last Decade of Its First Century* (New York: International Publishers, 2007), 139.

4. Chandra Talpade Mohanty, "Race, Multiculturalism, and Pedagogies of Dissent," *Feminism without Borders* (Durham, NC: Duke University Press, 2003), 194. Mohanty further specifies, "Difference seen as benign variation (diversity), for instance, rather than as conflict, struggle, or the threat of disruption, bypasses power as well as history to suggest a harmonious, empty pluralism. On the other hand, difference defined as asymmetrical and incommensurate cultural spheres situated within hierarchies of domination and resistance cannot be accommodated within a discourse of 'harmony in diversity.' A strategic critique of the contemporary language of difference, diversity, and power thus would be crucial to a feminist project concerned with revolutionary social change" (193).

5. bell hooks, *Teaching to Transgress* (New York: Routledge, 1994), 12.

6. Audre Lorde, *Sister Outsider: Essays and Speeches* (Berkeley, CA: Crossing Press, 1984), 112.

7. Jason A. Springs, " 'Dismantling the Master's House': Freedom as Ethical Practice in Brandom and Foucault," *Journal of Religious Ethics* 37, no. 3 (2009): 421, JSTOR, www.jstor.org/stable/40378114.

8. Althusser lays out this dual role as inherent in all levels of education in "Ideology and Ideological State Apparatuses." Louis Althusser, *On the Reproduction of Capitalism: Ideology and Ideological State Apparatuses* (New York: Verso, 2014). It is apparent as early as Plato's dialogues on the academy in *The Republic*, throughout the Enlightenment—as well as critiques and defenses of the Enlightenment (Jonathan Israel, "Enlightenment! Which Enlightenment?," *Journal of the History of Ideas* 67, no. 3 (2006): 523–45, JSTOR, www.jstor.org/stable/30141040)—and reaches a moment of particular salience in debates about the Humboldtian model, which is in many ways foundational for the contemporary American university (Peter Uwe Hohendahl, "Humboldt Revisited: Liberal Education, University Reform, and the Opposition to the Neoliberal University," *New German Critique*, no. 113

(2011): 159–96, JSTOR, www.jstor.org/stable/41288137). Mohanty summarizes the contemporary engagement with this dual role of the university as that argument "that education represents both a struggle for meaning and a struggle over power relations" ("Pedagogies of Dissent," 194).

9. Springs speaks of "expressive freedom" that "affords an orientation by which to gauge [Foucault's] practices of freedom, namely, in the direction of expanded and more encompassing forms of expressive freedom. These will be marked by the increased capacities and opportunities of those who have been dominated—or been denied candidacy as agents for whom expressive freedom was even possible—to participate in the dismantling of that domination, refashioning and transforming oppressive conditions." Furthermore, "the resistant and transformative potentials of expressive freedom do not present one horn of the old revolution/reform dilemma. Rather, they aid the kind of analysis that might mediate this dilemma" ("Dismantling the Master's House," 444).

10. hooks, *Teaching to Transgress*, 4. On campus climate, see Mitchell Chang, "The Impact of an Undergraduate Diversity Course Requirement on Students' Racial Views and Attitudes," *Journal of General Education* 51, no. 1 (2002): 21–42; Sarah Brown, "Diversity Courses Are in High Demand. Can They Make a Difference?" *Chronicle of Higher Education*, January 7, 2016, http://chronicle.com/article/Diversity-Courses-Are-in-High/234828. On critical thinking, Darnell Cole and Ji Zhou, "Diversity and Collegiate Experiences Affecting Gains in Self-Perceived Critical Thinking: Which Works, and Who Benefits?" *Journal of General Education* 61, no. 1 (November 2014). On cognitive development, Ernest Pascarella et al., "Effects of Diversity Experiences on Critical Thinking Skills Over 4 Years of College." *Journal of College Student Development* 551, no. 1 (January 2014): 15–34. On civic engagement, Michelle Castellanos and Darnell Cole, "Disentangling the Impact of Diversity Courses: Examining the Influence of Diversity Course Content on Students' Civic Engagement," *Journal of College Student Development* 58, no. 8 (2015): 794–811. On moral development, Eugene Parker, Cassie Barnhardt, Ernest Pascarella, and Jarvis McCowen, "The Impact of Diversity on College Students' Moral Development," *Journal of College Student Development* 57, no. 4 (May 2016): 395–410.

11. hooks, *Teaching to Transgress*, 12.

12. For a detailed discussion of the commodification of "diversity" in the academy, see Mohanty, "Pedagogies of Dissent."

13. Eduardo Bonilla-Silva, *Racism without Racists: Color-Blind Racism and the Persistence of Racial Inequality in America* (Lanham, MD: Rowman and Littlefield, 2013).

14. The exact numbers vary depending on the source. This data was distributed to faculty in 2016–17. Salem State University's Diversity and Inclusion statement says, "Salem State University is the most diverse public university in the Commonwealth with over 29 percent of the student population from

underrepresented backgrounds" (https://www.salemstate.edu/salem-state-difference/mission-vision-and-strategic-plan/diversity-and-inclusion, accessed May 9, 2017). Niche.com in its "Most Diverse Colleges and Universities in Massachusetts" ranks Salem State as the most diverse state university in Massachusetts (and the 56th most diverse of all Massachusetts colleges and universities) with a "53% student racial diversity index," although it does not explain the index (https://www.niche.com/colleges/rankings/most-diverse-colleges/s/massachusetts, accessed May 9, 2017).

15. In 2000, an American Association of Colleges and Universities survey found that about 54 percent of US colleges and universities had general education diversity requirements, while in 1990 about 12 percent of US colleges and universities had general education diversity requirements. Debra Humphreys, "National Survey Finds Diversity Requirements Common around the Country," *Diversity Digest*, Fall 2000, http://www.diversityweb.org/digest/F00/survey.html.

16. Jaschik, "UCLA Faculty."

17. Lorde, *Sister Outsider*, 113.

18. Taken from the "Diversity, Power Dynamics, and Social Justice Form," part of the General Education Category Certification Forms of the Salem State University Curriculum Committee. It is located on the "Curriculum Committee Channel" of the employee-facing internal web.

19. hooks, *Teaching to Transgress*, 3, 6.

20. Mohanty, "Pedagogies of Dissent," 196.

21. Michel Foucault, *The History of Sexuality*, vol. 1, *An Introduction* (1978; repr., New York: Vintage, 1990), 96.

22. hooks, *Teaching to Transgress*, 12.

23. Lorde, *Sister Outsider*, 113.

24. Salem State's "State of the Union" art show's manner of including a painting depicting the KKK, student reaction to the show, and the university's response were reported on in the *Boston Globe* (Olivia Quintana, "Salem State Art Exhibit Temporarily Suspended after Student Complaints," *Boston Globe*, November 22, 2016, https://www.bostonglobe.com/metro/2016/11/22/salem-state-art-exhibit-temporarily-suspended-for-controversial-painting/TnH1rMgdq4fNYqB9bErR8I/story.html) and *Inside Higher Ed* (Josh Jaschik, "When Art Offends (and Isn't Understood)," *Inside Higher Ed*, November 28, 2016, https://www.insidehighered.com/news/2016/11/28/salem-state-university-facing-criticism-minority-students-shutters-art-exhibit).

25. In doing this, we still wonder, were we practicing the kind of collaborative and truly shared governance that might be at the heart of radical pedagogy not only in the classroom but also in the institution? Or did we allow our already compromising practice of drawing up a proposal that would fit the form of a general education category, and that could be applied by any faculty member in any discipline, and that could be evaluated by curriculum and general education committees, to be further compromised by the heterogeneity that comes with asking the institution to construct its own reform?

26. hooks, *Teaching to Transgress*, 8.

27. The Massachusetts Department of Higher Education proposal to join the AAC&U's LEAP State Initiative was accepted in 2011. For more details, see Massachusetts Department of Higher Education, "The Vision Project: A Public Agenda for Higher Education in Massachusetts," accessed June 12, 2017, http://www.mass.edu/visionproject/sl-leapstate.asp.

28. hooks, *Teaching to Transgress*.

29. Ahmed, "Language of Diversity," 249.

30. Rosemary Deem and Jenny Ozga, "Women Managing Diversity in a Postmodern World," in *Feminist Critical Policy Analysis II*, ed. Catherine Marshall (London: Falmer, 1997), 25–40.

31. Ahmed, "Language of Diversity," 237.

32. In an important show of the sustained institutional support for not only implementing but actually supporting the DPDS requirement, in 2019 Salem State increased the course releases for the two Faculty Fellows for Diversity, Power Dynamics, and Social Justice to one course release per semester per faculty fellow.

BIBLIOGRAPHY

Ahmed, Sara. "The Language of Diversity." *Ethnic and Racial Studies* 30, no. 2 (March 2007): 235–56.

Althusser, Louis. *On the Reproduction of Capitalism: Ideology and Ideological State Apparatuses*. New York: Verso, 2014.

Bonilla-Silva, Eduardo. *Racism without Racists: Color-Blind Racism and the Persistence of Racial Inequality in America*. Lanham, MD: Rowman and Littlefield, 2013.

Brown, Sarah. "Diversity Courses Are in High Demand. Can They Make a Difference?" *Chronicle of Higher Education*, January 7, 2016. http://chronicle.com/article/Diversity-Courses-Are-in-High/234828.

Cagni, Caitriona. "The Final Push: An Ongoing Struggle for an Academic Diversity Requirement." *Georgetown Voice*, March 19, 2015. http://georgetownvoice.com/2015/03/19/the-final-push-an-ongoing-struggle-for-an-academic-diversity-requirement.

Castellanos, Michelle, and Darnell Cole. "Disentangling the Impact of Diversity Courses: Examining the Influence of Diversity Course Content on Students' Civic Engagement." *Journal of College Student Development* 58, no. 8 (November 2015): 794–811.

Chang, Mitchell. "The Impact of an Undergraduate Diversity Course Requirement on Students' Racial Views and Attitudes." *Journal of General Education* 51, no. 1 (2002): 21–42.

Cole, Darnell, and Ji Zhou. "Diversity and Collegiate Experiences Affecting Gains in Self-Perceived Critical Thinking: Which Works, and Who Benefits?" *Journal of General Education* 61, no. 1 (November 2014): 15–34.

Deem, Rosemary, and Jenny Ozga. "Women Managing Diversity in a Postmodern World." In *Feminist Critical Policy Analysis II*, edited by Catherine Marshall, 25–40. London: Falmer, 1997.

Du Bois, W. E. B. *The Autobiography of W. E. B. Du Bois: A Soliloquy on Viewing My Life from the Last Decade of Its First Century.* New York: International Publishers, 2007.

Foucault, Michel. *The History of Sexuality*. Vol. 1, *An Introduction*. 1978. Reprint, New York: Vintage, 1990.

Hansen, Allison. "USC Students Pass Resolution Demanding $100 Million-Plus Be Devoted to 'Diversity' Endeavors." *College Fix*, November 11, 2015. https://www.thecollegefix.com/post/25014.

Hohendahl, Peter Uwe. "Humboldt Revisited: Liberal Education, University Reform, and the Opposition to the Neoliberal University." *New German Critique*, no. 113 (2011): 159–96. JSTOR, www.jstor.org/stable/41288137.

hooks, bell. *Teaching to Transgress*. New York: Routledge, 1994.

Humphreys, Debra. "National Survey Finds Diversity Requirements Common around the Country." *Diversity Digest* 5, no. 1 2000: 1–2.

Israel, Jonathan. "Enlightenment! Which Enlightenment?" *Journal of the History of Ideas* 67, no. 3 (2006): 523–45. JSTOR, www.jstor.org/stable/30141040.

Jaschik, Josh. "UCLA Faculty Approves Diversity Requirement." *Inside Higher Ed*, April 13, 2015. https://www.insidehighered.com/news/2015/04/13/ucla-faculty-approves-diversity-requirement.

———. "When Art Offends (and Isn't Understood)." *Inside Higher Ed*, November 28, 2016. https://www.insidehighered.com/news/2016/11/28/salem-state-university-facing-criticism-minority-students-shutters-art-exhibit.

Lorde, Audre. *Sister Outsider: Essays and Speeches.* Berkeley, CA: Crossing Press, 1984.

Massachusetts Department of Higher Education. "The Vision Project: A Public Agenda for Higher Education in Massachusetts." Accessed June 12, 2017. http://www.mass.edu/visionproject/sl-leapstate.asp.

Mikelionis, Luke. "U of Chicago Students Demand Race-Specific Housing and Requiring 'Diversity and Inclusion' to Graduate." *Heatstreet*, May 23, 2017. https://heatst.com/culture-wars/u-chicago-students-demand-race-specific-housing-and-requiring-diversity-and-inclusion-to-graduate.

Mohanty, Chandra Talpade. "Race, Multiculturalism, and Pedagogies of Dissent." In *Feminism without Borders*, 190–217. Durham, NC: Duke University Press, 2003.

Parker, Eugene, Cassie Barnhardt, Ernest Pascarella, and Jarvis McCowen. "The Impact of Diversity on College Students' Moral Development." *Journal of College Student Development* 57, no. 4 (May 2016): 395–410.

Pascarella, Ernest, Georgianna Martin, Jana Hanson, Teniell Trolian, Benjamin Gillig, and Charles Blaich. "Effects of Diversity Experiences on Critical Thinking Skills over 4 Years of College." *Journal of College Student Development* 551, no. 1 (January 2014): 86–92.

Quintana, Olivia. "Salem State Art Exhibit Temporarily Suspended after Student Complaints." *Boston Globe*, November 22, 2016. https://www.bostonglobe.com/metro/2016/11/22/salem-state-art-exhibit-temporarily-suspended-for-controversial-painting/TnH1rMgdq4fNYqB9bErR8I/story.html.

Springs, Jason A. " 'Dismantling the Master's House': Freedom as Ethical Practice in Brandom and Foucault." *Journal of Religious Ethic* 37, no. 3 (2009): 419–48. JSTOR, www.jstor.org/stable/40378114.

CHAPTER 10

"SURVIVAL IS NOT AN ACADEMIC SKILL"

Life behind the Mask

SHARON D. RAYNOR

We wear the mask that grins and lies,
It hides our cheeks and shades our eyes,—
This debt we pay to human guile;
With torn and bleeding hearts we smile
And mouth with myriad subtleties.

Why should the world be over-wise,
In counting all our tears and sighs?
Nay, let them only see us, while
    We wear the mask.

We smile, but, O great Christ, our cries
To thee from tortured souls arise.
We sing, but oh the clay is vile
Beneath our feet, and long the mile,
But let the world dream otherwise,
    We wear the mask!

—Paul Laurence Dunbar, "We Wear the Mask"

In 1913, Paul Laurence's Dunbar's usage of the metaphorical mask in his poem "We Wear the Mask" suggested that blacks were commodities and marginal citizens as far as their rights as human beings were concerned. His approach was to assist white America in acknowledging the trials and tribulations blacks faced on a daily basis, from blacks having to silence or "mask" their voices to be accepted by white America to having to "mask" the pain, anguish, and suffering at the hands of others. So what is the motivation behind wearing a mask or masking? And why is the racial sentiment of Dunbar's era during the nineteenth century still prevalent for blacks today in higher education well into the twenty-first century? Is it that blacks are ultimately seeking acceptance in white America? Do blacks need to find a voice and be heard amid the racial injustices that plagued them? Or is wearing a mask a part of the American experience, and when blacks wear it, it contradicts our longing for a representative reality? Perhaps the masking metaphor is a means to extract one's voice from white representations in order to combat the negative stereotyping that plagues blacks. It is a racial manifestation that epitomizes the angst blacks found and still find ourselves experiencing while attempting to construct an identity amid the preexisting racial hierarchy.[1] Masking, however, is filled with dualities. In literary and language conventions, it is considered both a rhetoric of deception and a cultural tradition that distinguishes one group of people from other. Masking can also be considered "masks in motion," which act as facades for messages communicated that are central to the black experience in America.[2] By the turn of the twentieth century, W. E. B. Du Bois coined the term "double-consciousness," describing a world which yields the black American no true self-consciousness but only lets him see himself through the revelation of the other world. It is a peculiar sensation, this double-consciousness, this sense of always looking at oneself through the eyes of others.[3] These ideologies are important to understanding just a notion of the black experience in higher education. Audre Lorde contends,

> For those of us who stand outside the circle of this society's definition of acceptable know that survival is not an academic skill. It is learning how to stand alone, unpopular and sometimes reviled, and how to make common cause with those others identified as outside the structures in order to define and seek a world in which we can all flourish. It is learning how to take our differences and make them strengths. For the master's tools will never dismantle the master's house. They may

> allow us temporarily to beat him at his own game, but they will never enable us to bring about genuine change.[4]

So therein lies the ultimate question that informs my narrative: But why not genuine change? This question, however, led to many more questions: How do we treat the members of our own profession? How do we respond to professional and political cunning, to the raw and ruthless ambition, to the plight of those considered the Other—the outsiders? What are we personally willing to give up for the "public good"? What personal gestures or reparations are we willing to make? What risky research are we willing to undertake or what unfashionable conversations are we willing to have?[5] If survival, according to Lorde, is not an academic skill, then how have I survived for more than two decades? Was I masking? Was I completely aware of my own double-consciousness? What were the advantages of being the Other and how did I use them to my benefit? What are we ultimately teaching about race and how are "we" responsible for "teaching race" not only to our students but also to each other? And within these teachings, how can we bring about effective change in the academy? In my attempt to answer some of the aforementioned questions, I want to focus this essay on the conversations and interactions that happen between and among academics when others are not around to witness the gestures or hear the language being used to separate, judge, silence, and create vulnerabilities within those deemed the Other. My story, like other narratives of survival, as Michal Ginsburg discusses, is typical in design. It is linear and straightforward, not recursive nor governed by a goal where survival is merely a taken-for-granted precondition for higher pursuits or a transparent means to an end with a punctual overcoming of obstacles. It is, however, a narrative about progress—forward movement—the shaping of cultural notions of what makes a life worth living.[6] During my tenure in the academy, I have been keenly aware that others believed that I was masking just to be a part of the academy, but the deception of the mask is rooted in my understanding of Frantz Fanon's concept of how one's black skin will always contradict the mask, W. E. B. Du Bois's ideology of double-consciousness, Toni Morrison's updated interpretation of "Othering," and Audre Lorde's and bell hooks's notions of survival. The life behind one's preconceived mask is often not what others thought and can be devastating to those who believed they created it. Let's take a peek, shall we?

WEARING THE MASK . . . BECOMING THE OTHER

Frantz Fanon, in *Black Skin, White Masks*, discusses the attempt to overcome feelings of inferiority felt by the colonized black people by identifying with the white colonizers—to metaphorically wear a mask that identifies them with the white colonizer. However, this strategy is doomed to fail because blacks cannot escape their feelings of inferiority, so they will never fully identify with the white colonizer. While the behavior may impersonate that of the white person, it will never identify. For blacks even to attempt to fully identify—to wear the white mask—they have to ascribe to both features and behaviors which are influenced and controlled by the white colonizers, whose views dehumanize and belittle blacks. The dilemma of wearing the white mask *is* the black skin, which leads directly back to subjection and alienation. This happens because the colonizer not only controls the features of the mask but also classifies and defines those very features to belittle the colonized. Once an independent assertion of black identity emerges, the colonizer, who may feel a loss of control, ascribes a new set of features to the mask, but even those new features are still inferior. Once black people identify as such and define what it means to be independent of the expectations of white colonizers, they can take control of the mask without subjection and alienation of being forced to live up to those expectations.[7] As Fanon continues in *The Wretched of the Earth*, colonization has dehumanizing effects on the individual and the nation, but decolonization is a violent process without exception.[8] To this end, let us update this thinking a bit and move beyond the terms *colonizer* and *colonized* to Morrison's updated interpretation from Edmund Husserl and Michel Foucault of the Other and Othering and how that informs my narrative and my lived experiences as a black academician. The mask is what others created for me to wear. For example, they assumed that I should get a particular degree or teach a particular subject; that I should look or even behave in a specific way; that my students would react to me in a certain manner; that I would not be successful in publishing, writing grants, or acquiring research fellowships; that I do not deserve to achieve tenure or promotion; or that I should never be in any leadership position within the academy. They never chose to peek behind the very mask that they supposedly created for me to wear. Instead, they participated in the process of Othering.

Some scholars, such as Edward Said, argue that Western identity and culture are fundamentally forged by an Othering logic, one that dehumanizes or devalues other people. An essential feature of Othering is denying the Other their own voice, denying them the opportunity to speak for themselves and instead attributing qualities, opinions, and views that refer to one's own identity and culture. Whether one can speak on behalf of another whose voice has been silenced or whether it is possible to transcend Othering and establish a genuine understanding with the Other through the use of reason or empathy is debatable. Perhaps the Other should be recognized as a diverse and complex entity—an object of love and desire, a potential enemy and victim, a model for emulation and identification, an object of care and hospitality, a subject of one's own destiny. We may still come to recognize that the Other, like the Self, has many faces.[9] Toni Morrison updates this line of thinking and contends, in *The Origin of Others*, that every group on earth, with or without power, enforces their beliefs by constructing an Other. One purpose of scientific racism is to identify an outsider in order to define one's self. Another possibility is to maintain (even enjoy) one's own difference from the Othered. Humans as an advanced species tend to separate and judge those not in our clan as the enemy, as the vulnerable. What is the nature of Othering's comfort, its allure, its power (social, psychological, or economical)? Is it the thrill of belonging—which implies being part of something bigger than one's solo self and therefore stronger? It almost becomes essential to figure out the benefits in creating and sustaining the Other—identifying the stranger—which often creates an exaggerated fear. Does the dominant culture most fear that the stranger will disturb, betray, or prove that we are not like them? So what do they do with us? Why should they want to know a stranger when it is easier to estrange us? Why should they want to close the distance when they can close the door, forbidding entrance into what is perceived to be the dominant culture? Since the stranger is not foreign, they are random; not alien but remembered; and it is the randomness of the encounter with the already known—although unacknowledged—selves that summons a ripple of alarm, that makes them reject the figure and the emotions it provokes, especially when their emotions are profound. It is also what makes them want to own, govern, and administer the Other. In either case, whether out of alarm or false reverence, they deny the Other personhood, the specific individuality we insist upon for ourselves.[10]

TEACHABLE AND QUESTIONABLE MOMENTS

Let me drop the mask for a moment. I want to suggest how Othering informs the need for masking, and to do so, I want to step backward in time. Starting as an undergraduate, I attended a predominantly white institution (PWI) for each degree, and throughout my tenure as faculty in higher education, I have had the privilege to teach in Historically Black Colleges and Universities (HBCUs), PWIs, and private and public, small and large, liberal arts and research institutions. A series of conversations and interactions reminded me of how I have been perceived as the Other by my colleagues, supervisors, and even students. During my doctoral studies, I was questioned by the coordinator of the graduate programs, a white female professor, about why I chose to focus my dissertation project on trauma and silence in the testimonies of black Vietnam veterans instead of on a black female writer and why I was trying to matriculate through the program quicker than the seven-year time frame. She also changed the scheduled time for the comprehensive exams to better accommodate the white students without telling the only two black students in the program. I shared these disturbing interactions with my dissertation advisor, and he made a conscious decision to support me, to voice his concerns and do what was fair. He confronted her about her line of questioning and the sudden change in the exam schedule. Because of his authority and seniority within the program, she retreated. Although she never acknowledged or apologized for her bad behaviors, she neither presented any obstacles nor offered any support during my doctoral studies. She was more confused and perplexed by the relationship I had established with my dissertation advisor and even more surprised by his willingness to confront her. These exchanges taught me how important mentorship is to one's survival in the academy. This notion will be revisited later in my narrative.

At the start of my teaching career, I was a non-tenure-track lecturer in the Department of English at a PWI doctoral research institution. I had experiences teaching courses such as First-Year Composition, Studies in World Literature, Black Literature in America, Women in Literature, and Introduction to Women's Studies, in which I was focused on introducing diverse texts and topics to my students. It was during this time that a Cherokee female professor, who was "passing" for white, asked me if I taught my classes from the position of a woman or a black woman. An interesting conversation ensued about racial identity, class, gender, and her true sense of self and belonging. Koa Beck proposes that the definition of passing has not narrowed but grown for those individuals who decide to pass, and she suggests that their experience has proved to illuminate the overwhelming power of privilege, even if it creates marginalization.[11] I asked this professor why she felt comfortable passing. What were the benefits and advantages for her? What did she gain from denying her rightful identity to take on the veil of another? Perhaps it's no surprise that she continued to pass for white to avoid what she anticipated would happen to her within this department as a woman of color. This confirmed, as Lorde contends, that

> white women ignore their built-in privilege of whiteness and define woman in terms of their own experience alone, then women of Color, become "other." The outsider whose experience and tradition are too "alien" to comprehend . . . , however, they face the pitfall of being seduced into joining the oppressor under the pretense of sharing power. This possibility does not exist in the same way for women of Color. The tokenism that is extended to us is not an invitation to join power; our racial "otherness" is a visible reality that makes that quite clear. For white women there is a wider range of pretended choices and rewards for identifying with patriarchal power and its tools.[12]

Because she was passing, she absolutely recognized the prejudices and biases that existed within this institution but chose, instead, to pretend to be one of them—to not only pass but to also mask—in order to fit in. However, her facade would soon fade, as all masks do, when she married an Italian colleague and became pregnant. They decided to relocate to another university before the baby was born in case the baby's skin tone would reveal her secret and ultimately work in contradiction to the mask. Her narrative of racial passing taught me that, for some, race was a social construct that, if performed appropriately, allowed for privilege and advancement.

At this institution, I never experienced many racial issues with students, but early in my career, I had a few involving both students and colleagues that shifted my thought process a bit about being a African American professor and a representative of the "Other." A white female student who was also a cheerleader accused me of "giving" her a grade of D simply because I did not like her. I did not know this student personally because she was one of the forty-nine students in a Studies in World Literature course. When she first questioned me about the grade, she screamed and yelled, but I quickly diffused the situation by asking her to calm down and explain why she was upset. She chose not to continue to talk to me. Eventually her parents called my department chair to inform him of their daughter's accusations and complaints about her professor. The chair asked me to reconsider her grade so perhaps she could remain on the cheerleading squad. He told me to keep in mind that he could overturn my decision and change her grade himself. I was very curious about his interest and investment in this particular student such that he would demand such a drastic resolution to this situation. I stood my ground and refused to adjust her grade since she had not done anything to warrant receiving a higher grade other than complain to her parents and my supervisor. I also informed him that if he decided to change her grade, then I would change the grades of all the other forty-eight students in the course so everyone would receive an A, whether they deserved it or not. My resistance and reaction were to illustrate how irrational his actions would be to simply accommodate a student who rarely attended class or submitted work. The student's behavior was not acceptable, but perhaps her perceived privilege in this situation allowed her, her parents, and the department chair to question the authority of the classroom instructor. While he did not respect my teaching values about fairness, he decided not to change her grade. She received the D she earned. From his position of power, his language and actions were familiar to me. He would not soon forget what he perceived as an act of defiance on my part and my unwillingness to openly reject his treatment of me. However, his begrudging behavior and attitude would later systemically allow him to exact his revenge.

While at this same university, I attended a meeting in which this same department chair informed all the non-tenure instructors that if we were interested in keeping our jobs, then we should consider pursuing a terminal degree. A few of us, mostly women, decided that this would be the perfect time to return to school in hopes of securing employment and perhaps advancement. I worked on my PhD while still teaching four courses with at least 125 students per semester. Upon completion of my degree, I decided to meet with the department chair to inform him of my accomplishment and to inquire about the possibility of advancement within the department. My news and inquiry were met with an abrasive and condescending tone. He informed me that he would neither consider me for promotion to assistant professor nor would be even change my title from lecturer to visiting assistant professor because there was not an open tenure-track position in African American literature. I politely reminded him that my PhD was in literature and criticism with a unique focus on oral history, trauma literature, war narratives, and narrative discourse and *not* African American literature. Out of 103 full-time professors in the English department, I was the only full-time black woman and there was only one full-time tenure-track black man. Although no professors were teaching or researching in the specific areas of my doctoral specialization, the department chair still refused the consideration. I decided to continue this conversation with the dean of the college. He supported the department chair, so I moved the discussion a bit further to the EEOC (Equal Employment Opportunity Commission) office. The director, a black woman, as I learned throughout this discussion process, was only there to appease complainants, not to resolve blatant and intentional acts of racial and gender discrimination. She worked for the university, not for the greater good of equality and fairness. She was not only masking but also participating in the Othering process. Marybeth Gasman discusses how faculty will bend rules, knock down walls, and build bridges to hire the people they really want, which are often white colleagues.[13] However, when having to hire faculty of color, everyone has to "play by the rules" and they get angry when any exceptions are made. After I decided to leave this university for a tenure-track position, that department chair and dean were soon asked to resign their positions because of their continuous racist and sexist practices. The university could not continue to ignore multiple complaints that were similar to my own.

As I advanced in my career and took on administrative roles as department chair and program director at an HBCU, my racialized existence was also coupled with gender issues. During my first semester, I taught a general education liberal studies course entitled Identity: African American and Other Cultural Traditions, a first-year course required for graduation. I had an interesting encounter with one student who was both Asian American and African American but who identified only as African American. One day in class, I simply asked her, "Why do you only identify with one race/culture?" Her initial response was a simple, "I don't know." I then asked her if she was willing to explore the question further and she said yes. Like so many other students in this course, she identified with the race and culture of the dominant parent in the household. While attending college for me was based on my family's socioeconomic situation, here, at this HBCU, I grasped a deeper understanding of how race definitely shaped the decision of where some students decided to attend school in an environment where they would be seen, heard, and not considered the Other. These students at that time were willing to pay at least $25,000 per year for the black college experience that celebrated and embraced their racial and cultural heritage. They recognized, despite the costs and perhaps the expectation to mask their true feelings and emotions, the true importance of attending an HBCU.

In 2017, Betsy DeVos, the secretary of education, in a statement she released after a meeting with HBCU administrators at the White House stating that HBCUs were founded as a solution to America's problem of equal access to education in which African American students would have a choice of where to attend school in a system that was not working and in the absence of opportunity.[14] Her statement garnered immediate backlash and criticism: "HBCUs arose in response to racist Jim Crow laws in the American South that enforced segregation, shutting out black students from traditionally white schools with a few exceptions." "The system [she's] describing isn't 'choice.' It's Jim Crow and segregation." Representative Barbara Lee said the statement was " 'tone-deaf' and 'uninformed,' noting that for many years, HBCUs weren't additional options but the 'only option.' "[15] DeVos did not fully understand the significant role of HBCUs in African American communities, but she also puts a face to the dominant oppressive cultural views that sometimes exist at these very schools.

The animosity toward me heightened, whether it was from black men or both white women and men who had an issue with being supervised by a black woman. It would surface and sometimes change forms, from confrontational behavior or condescending and disrespectful emails and comments to intentionally creating uncomfortable and often hostile work environments. They felt very comfortable demonstrating their displeasure of my leadership position. I was told and often shown that I was not wanted there because at some point, they had decided that I didn't belong there. Even black and white women, during annual evaluation meetings, would talk only to the dean of faculty, an older white gay man. Even though I was in charge of the meeting as the department chair, they would never make eye contact with me or directly answer my questions. Some would direct their attention, their answers to my questions, and their own comments toward him, while others would even cry. This dean would, on a regular basis, send me rude emails quite early every morning and initiate verbal face-to-face confrontations. He would give me zeros in categories on my annual evaluations because he felt that is what I deserved. One year, he omitted documentation from my evaluation portfolio while giving another female professor credit for the work I had completed. She did not see an issue with this. After numerous complaints, human resources suggested that perhaps we had a personality conflict and we should seek meditation. My definition of workplace harassment and creating a hostile work environment, one supported by federal regulation, was their definition of a personality conflict that needed mediating. As bell hooks contends, many white gay people are unable to bridge the gap with people of color because they remain unable to look at the way in which whiteness and white power give them access to privilege in the role of dominator. They cannot see the ways in which discrimination can impact on our consciousness differently even though the forms it takes are the same. Often gay white people look down on black people because they perceive us to be more homophobic or less sexually progressive. These stereotyped assumptions are rooted in white supremacist thinking in which whites are always more sophisticated and complex than people of color. Even if they consider themselves anti-racist, they may often resort to these behaviors to prove that they are intellectually superior or even afraid of us.[16] In fall 2013, of all faculty at degree-granting postsecondary institutions, including those employed on a part-time, limited-term, or adjunct basis, 43% were white males, 35% were white females, 3% were black males, 3% were black females, 2% were Hispanic males, 2% were Hispanic females, 6% were Asian/Pacific Islander males, and 4% were Asian/Pacific Islander females. Making up less than 1% each were full-time faculty who were American Indian/Alaska Native and of two or more races. Among full-time permanent faculty, 58% were white males, 26% were white females, 2% were black males, 1% were black females, 2% were Hispanic males, 1% were Hispanic females, 7% were Asian/Pacific Islander males, and 2% were Asian/Pacific Islander females. Making up less than 1% each were professors who were American Indian/Alaska Native and of two or more races.[17] These statistics reveal more than just the underrepresentation of women of color in the academy among all part-time and full-time faculty nationwide; further, it speaks directly to how frequently some faculty of color are already situated and silenced within the academy as the Other.

While still at this teaching institution, it was also important for me to also take advantage of visiting professorships and faculty fellowships at research universities, which were often prestigious white schools, particularly because it helped strengthen my research pedagogy, expanded my network, and provided me the opportunity and platform to engage with students who otherwise may never have a black woman professor. At the start of one of my visiting professorships, a white female colleague boldly shared that since I was black I would probably experience quite a few issues with the wealthy, privileged, and entitled white students that I would teach there. She also asked if I had the opportunity to stay at the university at the end of my visiting professorship, since our department had a reputation of not keeping black faculty. During my time there, I taught a diverse body of students who were open and engaging, and since I did not anticipate this behavior she spoke about, I also did not experience it. At the end of my professorship, that same colleague, who had obviously talked to and questioned my students, shared, "Your students really love you, and they said that they enjoyed being in your class." She sounded both surprised and disappointed. While her prediction for my time there did not come true, she, perhaps, struggled with her own inability to comprehend my seamless transition into a very traditional department at this prestigious, conservative institution. How could we both be a "good fit" for this university? While she was willing to acknowledge that these institutional practices of racism existed, she was not willing to confront or fight against these practices. Were her conversations with me based on her own ignorance or fear or her belief in the myth of white privilege? Her silence was just as demeaning and perhaps participatory because she chose not to acknowledge or confront these racist practices. Perhaps it was easier to make me the Other, so she did not have to participate in any reconciliation or progress.

While still at my HBCU, there was a white male colleague who I spent a significant amount of time with, since we started working at this institution at the same time. When it was time for both of us to go up for promotion to full professor, his behaviors and actions toward me began to change. He pressed me with questions about the process and even acted as if it was a competition. By this time, I had spoken with the dean, who was also a white man, about submitting my application for promotion to full professor. He informed me, via email, that upper administration probably would not promote two professors in the same department at the same time. The dean made it perfectly clear that since my colleague had already spoken to him first, he planned to support his application over mine. While this came as no surprise to me, he was careless enough to put this decision, not supported by any university policy, in writing. But even more clearly, both the dean and the department chair had started the Othering process long before the opportunity for promotion came about. While they were aware of my innovative teaching, publications, and grants, they had started denying me opportunities for merit and bonus pay, refusing to support any applications for university research and travel and making me teach only freshmen- or sophomore-level classes. "The system of patriarchy ensures that the individual black females who excel, both in the past and in the present day, are rarely accorded the respect and attention that their male colleagues receive," hooks suggests.[18] At a certain point, they both even stopped speaking to me altogether.

In my last few years at this university, I taught an online sophomore-level literature course, The American Horror Story. Now that course is being taught in a face-to-face format by my former department chair. The course has an accompanying online module in which professors are encouraged to share an introductory audio, a video, or a welcome letter to the students. In his letter to students, he posts a disclosure in which he makes students (and others) sound like loaded weapons rather than students who have complex life stories. His disclosure included the following statement:

> Nevertheless, there is something all of you should know before this class begins. One of the key elements of horror is encountering "the other." This Other is somehow monstrous, uncanny, and/or threatening. Within the American context, we tend to divide out the Other by race. This means that some of our readings will include racist images and language. The appearance of this material should not be seen as an endorsement of the racist viewpoints being espoused in these texts. If you do not think you can engage with the topic or racism within an academic context (for whatever reason), you should consider whether or not this course is for you.

Reading this material in a course I had initially developed, what struck me immediately was the stark contrast of his view on "horror as the other," which evokes "racist" images and languages, standing in opposition to how I approached the topic in my open letter to the students, in which I focused on how horror evokes various responses to terror, suspense, the unknown, and the supernatural while sometimes emphasizing race, gender, terror, and fantasy. His insinuation and suggestion to the students is that race is not only "horrific" but signifies the "horrific Other." The only recourse offered to the students in his *welcome* letter was to reconsider taking this class if they were not prepared to handle this engagement about racism.

Toni Morrison asks very profound questions that connect the notions of race and Othering: "What is race (other than genetic imagination) and why does it matter? Once its parameters are known, defined (if at all possible), what behavior does it demand/encourage? . . . What would we be or do or become as a society if there were no ranking or theory of blackness? Once blackness is accepted as socially, politically, and medically defined, how does that definition affect black people? . . . Race is the classification of a species, and we are the human race, period."[19] "Morrison continues, "In what public discourse does the reference to black people not exist? It exists in every one of this nation's mightiest struggles."[20] While I was a bit surprised by this professor's approach to the course, I was not surprised by his behaviors and how they manifested in his teachings and interactions with those he deemed the Other—his students. What is his true motivation for using race/racism as the underlying premise for teaching this course? Maybe the professor believes that "it is the horror of one drop of the mystical 'black' blood, or signs of innate white superiority, or of deranged and excessive sexual power [that frames his] meaning of color" within his own lived experiences.[21] Does the professor's welcome letter enforce his own beliefs by constructing the Other arbitrarily based on race/racism and the horror it entails? For the students in his class, has their race already been deemed as the unknown or the Other—monstrous, uncanny, and/or threatening? How does this Othering give him both power and control? Toni Morrison states, "Race has become metaphorical—a way of referring to and disguising forces, events, classes, and expressions of social decay and economic division far more threatening to the body politic than biological 'race' ever was. It seems that it has a utility far beyond economy, beyond the sequestering of classes from one another, and has assumed a metaphorical life so completely embedded in daily discourse that it is perhaps more necessary and more on display than ever before."[22] "Morrison references Bruce Baum's book, *The Rise and Fall of the Caucasian Race*, when she states, "Race, in short, is an effect of power."[23] As Carole Boyce Davies contends, "Race has been a constant arbiter of difference, as have wealth, class, and gender—each of which is about power and the necessity of control."[24] Perhaps in the wake of the Black Lives Matter movement and teaching in the post-Obama Trump era at an HBCU, the professor decided to use this peculiar class to discuss race/racism. While unsuspecting students signed up for a class to perhaps engage classic American horror stories, they are now confronted with what he purposes as the main element of horror, or rather the main element of his class: defining race as the horrific as well as separating the Other based on race. From his personal interactions with me to his willingness to marginalize his students, based on a course that I originally created, his need for power and control were obvious. But this need for power and control also manifests in various capacities within the academy.

While I was serving as the chair of a search committee, a senior-level white staffer attempted to influence the selection of a candidate by secretly talking to other white committee members. Those members shared their concerns with me and how they felt about her racialized intentions to influence the candidate selection. These behaviors also manifested themselves in more aggressive forms, including the actual rationalization against hiring a person of color, the debate that ensues when the candidates are the same race, and their willingness to select the least qualified candidate, who is often not the best fit for the university. These moments reminded me of my own experiences during the interviewing process, in which someone on the committee indicated that I was not who they really wanted, whether through their line of questioning, their disinterest in my answers to their questions, or blatant rude and condescending remarks in hopes of unraveling my demeanor. How I responded was crucial and significant not only in maintaining the integrity of the hiring process but also in how to confront racism in the workplace via policy and procedure. As I saw these similar situations continue to manifest during the hiring process, I grew concerned that the university was not doing enough to make sure that the committees comprised a group of diverse faculty and staff with no ulterior motives for hiring a particular candidate. In a similar context, Marybeth Gasman discusses how the word *quality* is used to dismiss people of color who are otherwise competitive for faculty positions. Even members on the search committee who seem pro-equality and dedicated to access will reference the word *quality* or lack thereof to not recommend hiring a person of color. This could be an indicator that "quality" means that the person did not attend an elite institution for their doctoral degree or was not mentored by a well-known scholar in their field, forgetting that attending an elite institution is directly connected to social capital, which systemic racism ensures that people of color have less of. Search committees are typically not trained in recruitment or diversity issues, perhaps are not even diverse in their own makeup. They are more interested in hiring more people just like them rather than diversifying their department. Even when they receive a diverse application pool, they typically decide that some of those candidates are not "the right fit" for the institution, while thinking unconsciously that the "right fit" is someone just like them.[25] These hiring practices speak directly to the statistics cited earlier that keep specific people, especially women of color, in the lowest percentage categories in the academy. Lorde contends that "when the tools of a racist patriarchy are used to examine the fruits of that same patriarchy, the most narrow perimeters of change are possible and allowable."[26] In another incident, three white members of a search committee reported me to human resources for following the instructions of the hiring manager by ensuring that the candidates we interviewed were diverse in race, gender, ethnicity, and so forth. The complaints against me and the discontent with the idea of diversity came in the form of emails and telephone conversations. Their ulterior motive was to guarantee a particular hire—someone they knew who looked like them. They grew even more enraged when both human resources and senior administration verified the need to diversify the faculty and dismissed their baseless complaints. Because the university was made aware of such tendencies within these search committees, this HBCU mandated, for all employees, an equal employment opportunity and diversity fundamental training that includes seven online modules that take three hours to complete, a final assessment, and a full-day instructor-led classroom training session. In order to combat racist practices, we must be willing to confront those injustices to initiate change, regardless of how narrow the perimeter, and be willing to participate in those changes.

LIFE BEHIND THE MASK

Given the many conversations, interactions, and possible teachable (and questionable) moments I shared, and the many ways in which I was Othered, what has contributed to my survival in the academy for over twenty years? From my freshmen year in college, I was thoroughly introduced to the metaphor of masking by my black English professor. This knowledge was only reaffirmed by the other black professors I had while attending a PWI for my undergraduate studies. Did my previous knowledge about how others would perceive me help me survive in this profession? A significant part of my survival was to establish a few non-negotiables, such as having a basic understanding of how others may perceive me based on a myth of privilege; acknowledging that survival is not an academic skill and that the master's tool will never dismantle the master's house; respecting the positions of authority but not allowing them to abuse or disrespect me from their power positions; prioritizing the importance of building relationships with diverse mentors; and holding true to my own convictions about fairness and justice and never apologizing for standing up for something or someone.

Quenton Baker discusses how certain realities are the result of a shared existence of people bound by the mask-as-survival-tool. In the first line of Dunbar's poem, the mask is grinning, lying. Though the faces may be laughing, the mask is there to mislead, to pacify those who are watching. The mask can then act as a mitigating agent, as the best defense against the constant threat of violence and destruction. Presenting a non-threatening facade and fitting exactly into the subservient, non-threatening roles that white supremacy designates are the critical functions of the mask. Dunbar intimates the necessity of survival, that the mask is not accommodationism; it is the wisdom of endurance. Though it is a skill—the evasion, the misdirection, the guile—Dunbar continues to inform that every concealment, no matter how necessary, is injurious to the individuals and/or groups that carry out the illusion. The "torn and bleeding hearts" are created in the violent environment of racial hatred, and they remain damaged because they aren't allowed to be fully, openly human. Dunbar anticipates W. E. B. Du Bois's double-consciousness ideology, the inherent and necessary duality of the black person's self-awareness: the ability to see one's own self clearly and to see how that same self will be reflected in the distorted mirror of white supremacy. We are aware of how the world sees them and how to go about keeping that dream and hope untroubled by reality.[27] Du Bois's double-consciousness ideology is also coupled with the issues of gender because black women have on one hand always been highly visible and yet, on the other hand, have been rendered invisible through the depersonalization of racism. Black women, or women of color, exist as multiple performances of gender and race and sexuality based on the particular cultural, historical, geopolitical, and class communities in which black woman exist. All African American women share the common experience of being black women in a society that denigrates women of African descent.[28] Katie Cannon observes, "Throughout the history of the United States, the interrelationship of white supremacy and male superiority has characterized the Black woman's reality as a situation of struggle—a struggle to survive in two contradictory worlds simultaneously, one white, privileged and oppressive, the other black, exploited, and oppressed."[29] For to survive, as Audre Lorde contends, "we have had to learn this first and most vital lesson—that we were never meant survive. And that the visibility which makes us most vulnerable is that which also is the source of our greatest strength."[30]

A university typically operates as a machine, although covertly, on systemic and institutionalized practices of gender bias, racist ideologies, and class prejudices. For me, they could quickly become a "site of resistance," a place in which I could no longer "learn to love or respect myself in the culture of white supremacy," that seem to say "danger," "you do not belong here," "you are not safe." It was important for me to feel at home in the "midst of oppression and domination."[31] So how could I continue to resist these oppressive views and actions instituted by the dominant culture? Peter Hitchcock in *Dialogics of the Oppressed* defines the oppressed as "those who are socially, economically or culturally marginalized, subordinated or subjugated in a myriad of ways, but whose singular mark lies not in the oppression itself but in their capacity to end it."[32] How do we ensure our colleagues are not being made to ever feel this way? We cannot participate in conversations or behaviors that contribute to these feelings of marginalization. Those who are in positions of authority are sometimes caught off guard when they are faced with those they cannot control—those who do not wear the mask well—and then they may possibly become offensive. They also cannot reconcile why they harbor such offensive feelings or thoughts. When leaders cannot control the narrative, they often want to change the story. They may assume that I am their competition as opposed to someone who can help expand their vision.

Early in my career, my mentors, who were mostly older white men with years of experience navigating these academic spaces designed primarily for them, shared a bit of wisdom that helped determine my next steps. Growing up poor on a farm affected how I related to people, perhaps. Our livelihood on the farm was based on survival, not race. In my hometown, all poor people lived among each other, regardless of race, so I was probably drawn to these men who offered their support and advice. They never acted in a patronizing manner or as if they understood my experiences; they, instead, were willing to engage in critical conversations about the state of the academy. Some of their advice echoed the words of my mother, who told her children that we had to be twice as good as whites to succeed in this world. These older white men shared that I needed to concentrate on self-preservation and building a strong work ethic by, first and foremost, establishing myself as a unique scholar in this profession through teaching, publishing, grantsmanship, and service to my students and the communities in which I lived and worked. They helped me see possibilities and opportunities in otherwise desolate situations and to concentrate on the larger, conceptual picture of myself within the academy. I was told to avoid working never-ending hours for any university that could ultimately contradict my own values in an attempt to diminish my self-worth and create vulnerabilities; to use my scholarship to build a platform that could shed light on pressing issues that continuously surface for professors and students of color within the academy; to continue to resist the oppressive views of others. I agree with bell hooks when she discusses that when people of color embrace the reality that white people who choose to do so can be anti-racist and do so genuinely and sincerely, so then we are drawn to them. This does not mean that they may never enact racial domination or race privilege or make other mistakes on an unconscious level, but they are willing to admit those mistakes and work diligently toward repairing those relationships.[33] Over time, I was able to build relationships with a diverse group of mentors who offer advice and continuously help me survive the academy. I have now learned that every institution presents its own unique set of challenges, but I have several mentors to help guide me through these often predictable and uncomfortable situations. We must remember to surround ourselves with others who are willing to help us reach our destiny because they are not intimidated by our positions and have achieved a certain level of success themselves.

However, when I dare to be powerful, as Audre Lorde puts it, "to use my knowledge and skills in service of my students and vision, then it becomes less and less important whether I am afraid when I am confronted with these issues at work."[34] Black academics can no longer be fearful of speaking their own individual and collective truths about their experiences in institutions of higher education. Within this country, racial difference creates a constant, if unspoken, distortion of vision. As Lorde contends that each of us "must recognize our responsibility to seek those words out, to read them and share them and examine them in their pertinence to our lives. That we not hide behind the mockeries of separation that have been imposed upon us and which so often we accept as our own."[35] So in reality, the mask does not hide much at all. If it did, none of the interactions and conversations I shared earlier would have even been necessary. If the mask is designed as Dunbar describes, to hide our bleeding hearts so the world can think all is well, then the dominant culture failed at their attempt at docility, silencing, and Othering. Sometimes, survival is simple. As they participated in the process of Othering and while they believed that I was masking, I was simply surviving the game by allowing them to see what they wanted—what they perceived about me—the mask they thought they gave me to wear. I was grateful that everyone did not participate in this process, which I witnessed marginalize and alienate so many other women of color. I know the reasons why so many leave the academy and walk away from their dream. Our stories are the same; however, we did not all survive because we were not all equipped to survive. In either scenario, survival or not, the mask still failed. The black skin, as Fanon predicted, always contradicted the white mask. Our true feelings and convictions about who we are always prevail and shatter the mask's facade. My dream to be a teacher when I was just a child scribbling on my chalkboard, teaching to my imaginary students, far outweighed anybody else's intentions for my existence in the academy. My survival, above all else, was innate and instinctual.

NOTES

1. Willie Harrell Jr., *We Wear the Mask: Paul Laurence Dunbar and the Representation of Black Identity (Paul Laurence Dunbar Collection)* (Kent, OH: Kent State University Press, 2010), x–xi.

2. Lena Ampadu, "The Poetry of Paul Laurence Dunbar and the Influence of African Aesthetics: Dunbar's Poems and the Tradition of Masking," in Harrell, *We Wear the Mask*, 4.

3. W. E. B. DuBois, *Souls of Black Folk* (Boston: Bedford, 1997), 38.

4. Audre Lorde, *Sister Outsider: Essays and Speeches* (Berkeley, CA: Crossing Press, 1984), 112.

5. Toni Morrison, *What Moves at the Margin* (Jackson: University Press of Mississippi, 2008), 196.

6. Michal Peled Ginsburg, "Narratives of Survival," *Novel: A Forum of Fiction* 42, no. 3 (2009): 410.

7. Frantz Fanon, *Black Skin, White Masks* (New York: Grove, 1952), 18–19, 21–23.

8. Frantz Fanon, *Wretched of the Earth* (New York: Grove, 1961), 35–37.

9. Yiannis Gabriel, "The Other and Othering: A Short Introduction," blog, September 10, 2012, http://www.yiannisgabriel.com/2012/09/the-other-and-othering-short.html.

10. Toni Morrison, *The Origin of Others* (Cambridge, MA: Harvard University Press, 2017), 5–39.

11. Koa Beck, "The Trouble with 'Passing' for Another Race/Sexuality/Religion," *Guardian*, January 2, 2014, https://www.theguardian.com/commentisfree/2014/jan/02/trouble-with-passing-race-sexuality-religion.

12. Lorde, *Sister Outsider*, 117, 118, 119.

13. Maybeth Gasman, "An Ivy League Professor on Why Colleges Don't Hire More Faculty of Color: 'We Don't Want Them,'" *Washington Post*, September 26, 2009, https://www.washingtonpost.com/news/grade-point/wp/2016/09/26/an-ivy-league-professor-on-why-colleges-dont-hire-more-faculty-of-color-we-dont-want-them.

14. US Department of Education, "Statement from Secretary of Education Betsy DeVos Following Listening Session with Historically Black College and University Leaders," Department of Education, February 28, 2017, https://www.ed.gov/news/press-release/statement-secretary-education-betsy-devos-following-listening-session-historically-black-college-and-university-leaders.

15. Emmanuella Grinberg, "DeVos Under Fire for Calling HBCUs 'Pioneers' of School Choice," *CNN*, February 28, 2017, http://www.cnn.com/2017/02/28/politics/betsy-devos-hbcu-school-choice/index.html.

16. bell hooks, *Teaching Community: A Pedagogy of Hope* (New York: Routledge, 2003), 62.

17. US Department of Education, National Center for Education Statistics, *The Condition of Education 2016* (NCES 2016–144), https://nces.ed.gov/programs/coe/indicator_csc.asp.

18. bell hooks, *Teaching Critical Thinking: Practical Wisdom* (New York: Routledge, 2003), 15.

19. Morrison, *Origin of Others*, 58.

20. Toni Morrison, *Playing in the Dark: Whiteness and the Literary Imagination* (New York: Random House, 1992), 65.

21. Morrison, *Origin of Others*, 41.

22. Morrison, *Playing in the Dark*, 63.

23. Morrison, *Origin of Others*, 25.

24. Carole Boyce Davies, *Black Women, Writing and Identity: Migrations of the Subject* (London: Routledge, 1994), 3–8.

25. Maybeth Gasman, "An Ivy League Professor on Why Colleges Don't Hire More Faculty of Color: 'We Don't Want Them,'" *Washington Post*, September 26, 2009, https://www.washingtonpost.com/news/grade-point/wp/2016/09/26/an-ivy-league-professor-on-why-colleges-dont-hire-more-faculty-of-color-we-dont-want-them.

26. Lorde, *Sister Outsider*, 110–11.

27. Quenton Baker, "The Message of the Mask," *Parlour: A Journal of Literary Criticism and Analysis*, January 11, 2016, https://www.ohio.edu/cas/parlour/news/growlery/archive/message-mask.

28. Davies, *Black Women, Writing and Identity*, 8–9.

29. Katie Geneva Cannon, "The Emergence of Black Feminist Consciousness," in *Feminist Interpretation of the Bible*, ed. Letty M. Russell (Philadelphia: Westminster Press, 1985), 30.

30. Lorde, *Sister Outsider*, 42.

31. bell hooks, "Homeplace (A Site of Resistance)," in *Yearning: Race, Gender, and Cultural Politics* (Boston: South End Press, 1990), 384–88.

32. Peter Hitchcock, *Dialogics of the Oppressed* (Minneapolis: University of Minnesota Press, 1993), 207n7.

33. hooks, "Homeplace," 384–88.

34. Lorde, *Sister Outsider*, 110–11.

35. Lorde, *Sister Outsider*, 43.

BIBLIOGRAPHY

Ampadu, Lena. "The Poetry of Paul Laurence Dunbar and the Influence of African Aesthetics: Dunbar's Poems and the Tradition of Masking." In *We Wear the Mask: Paul Laurence Dunbar and the Representation of Black Identity (Paul Laurence Dunbar Collection)*, edited by Willie Harrell Jr., 3–16. Kent, OH: Kent State University Press, 2010.

Baker, Quenton. "The Message of the Mask." *Parlour: A Journal of Literary Criticism and Analysis*, January 11, 2016. https://www.ohio.edu/cas/parlour/news/growlery/archive/message-mask.

Beck, Koa. "The Trouble with 'Passing' for Another Race/Sexuality/Religion." *Guardian*, January 2, 2014. https://www.theguardian.com/commentisfree/2014/jan/02/trouble-withpassing-race-sexuality-religion.

Cannon, Katie Geneva. "The Emergence of Black Feminist Consciousness." In *Feminist Interpretation of the Bible*, edited by Letty M. Russell, 30–40. Philadelphia: Westminster Press, 1985.

Davies, Carole Boyce. *Black Women, Writing and Identity: Migrations of the Subject*. London: Routledge, 1994.

Du Bois, W. E. B. *Souls of Black Folk*. Boston: Bedford, 1997.

Fanon, Frantz. *Black Skin, White Masks*. New York: Grove, 1952.

———. *Wretched of the Earth*. New York: Grove, 1961.

Gabriel, Yiannis. "The Other and Othering: A Short Introduction." Blog, September 10, 2012. http://www.yiannisgabriel.com/2012/09/the-other-and-othering-short.html.

Gasman, Marybeth. "An Ivy League Professor on Why Colleges Don't Hire More Faculty of Color: 'We Don't Want Them.'" *Washington Post*, September 26, 2009. https://www.washingtonpost.com/news/grade-point/wp/2016/09/26/an-ivy-league-professor-on-why-colleges-dont-hire-more-faculty-of-color-we-dont-want-them.

Ginsburg, Michal Peled. "Narratives of Survival." *Novel: A Forum of Fiction* 42, no. 3 (2009): 410–16.

Harrell, Willie Jr. *We Wear the Mask: Paul Laurence Dunbar and the Representation of Black Identity (Paul Laurence Dunbar Collection)*. Kent, OH: Kent State University Press, 2010, x-xi.

Hitchcock, Peter. *Dialogics of the Oppressed*. Minneapolis: University of Minnesota Press, 1993.

hooks, bell. "Homeplace (A Site of Resistance)." In *Yearning: Race, Gender, and Cultural Politics*, 384–88. Boston: South End Press, 1990.

———. *Teaching Community: A Pedagogy of Hope*. New York: Routledge, 2003.

———. *Teaching Critical Thinking: Practical Wisdom*. New York: Routledge, 2003.

Lorde, Audre. *Sister Outsider: Essays and Speeches*. Berkeley, CA: Crossing Press, 1984.

Morrison, Toni. *The Origin of Others*. Cambridge, MA: Harvard University Press, 2017.

———. *Playing in the Dark: Whiteness and the Literary Imagination*. New York: Random House, 1992.

———. *What Moves at the Margin*. Jackson: University Press of Mississippi, 2008.

US Department of Education, National Center for Education Statistics. *The Condition of Education 2016* (NCES 2016–144). https://nces.ed.gov/programs/coe/indicator_csc.asp.

CHAPTER 11

REFLECTIONS FROM A PRECARIOUSLY EMPLOYED CARPETBAGGER

A Canadian's Experience Teaching in the South

STEPHEN W. SHEPS

In the summer of 2015, I moved from Toronto, Canada, to teach sociology at the University of Tennessee at Chattanooga. Barely one year removed from defending my PhD, I found myself in an unexpected position: precariously employed, living far from home, and coming up against the real, lived experiences of race and racialization in the South. As an outsider in terms of both nationality (Canadian) and religion (Judaism), I became the embodiment of a "carpetbagger"—a Northern white intellectual brought to the South, hired because of my international research experience to "educate students who probably have never even left East Tennessee, let alone the South," as one colleague told me. I was very much an outsider in every sense of the word, and these are my reflections.

"Dr. Sheps, how is it that a white Jewish kid from Canada barely out of grad school gets the racial thing better than professors who've been here twenty years?" This seemingly innocent question came from two African American students in a third-year sociology course at a medium-sized state university in Tennessee in late 2015. The question, while innocuous on the surface, acts as a frame around my experience of teaching race and ethnicity and perhaps my entire, albeit limited, professional teaching career.

As I was hired on a one-year contract with the promise of a tenure-track conversion, I was faced with challenges from above, including very little support at the departmental level, and from below, with challenges like knowledge and skill-set gaps, primarily from racialized, first-generation, and working-class students. Before I found out I was not being considered for the permanent position, I followed my colleagues' "don't drop your standards but maybe lower your expectations" rhetoric and worked to build resources that the entire department could use to help teach foundational knowledge.

Upon being passed over, I took greater risks with content, delivery, and my approach to teaching, and refused to lower my standards while reaching the students in different ways than I ever had before. Instead of letting potential teachable moments slip away, I engaged directly with overtly political subjects as well as social movements like Black Lives Matter in the US, Idle No More in Canada, and other movements around the world. I worked to encourage a culture of student activism and pushed the boundaries of my students' sociological imaginations both inside the classroom and in their daily lives away from campus.

In this chapter I will not be telling a wholly new story; there is nothing uniquely innovative in my teaching practices or even in my experience as a visiting assistant professor. Indeed, this is not a singular scenario—recently granted a doctorate, the limited-term teacher uproots life for a one-year contract and moves to a new city, state, region, or country with the promise, potential and precarious, of its future conversion. The recent grad is then profoundly shocked by the working conditions and students' lack of knowledge and tries to avoid being a "carpetbagger," "white savior," or any other clichéd trope that can be associated with young, white educators, particularly those coming from the North to the South. This is the reality of academia today—contract faculty members take personal risks in order to advance professionally, while institutions see those faculty members as necessary evils in the face of shrinking budgets, rising enrollment, and education policies that undermine public education with alarming frequency.

In this chapter I explore the link between precarious academic employment and shifting teaching practices as a result of this precariousness, and I continue to develop the concept of classrooms as dilemmatic spaces. I began developing this work in a previous project, and I want to define this notion briefly to draw on some continuities as well as differences with that project.

Dilemmatic spaces result from structural conditions and everyday practices. As teachers negotiate the different values and perspectives held by their students and the complexity of teaching in a perpetual conflict zone, dilemmas often occur as a result, placing teachers in emotionally vulnerable and often-precarious professional spaces.[1] Methodologically informed by *performative autoethnography*,[2] this project explores the ways that I approach teaching about race, settler-colonialism, and social inequality as an outsider to a student body that was 35 percent African American, and contrast the differences in my approach to both content and classroom management before and after I was passed over for a tenure-track position, hopefully without throwing my colleagues under the bus. My own experience will be the case study, in which I tried to avoid being the "white savior" educator[3] and balance the needs of a diverse and nontraditional student body with my own desire to remain employed in the field.

In teaching for my job, I took fewer risks with content while trying to establish my own value to the department; when I taught with nothing to lose, it opened up my teaching practice to possibilities and risks I never imagined I would take. My precarity informed my teaching practice, but ultimately it did not stop me from teaching about race and settler-colonialism to students that grew up in a racially charged environment yet rarely had been provided opportunities to think critically about these matters.

METHODOLOGY

Autoethnography allows researchers to situate themselves within the research and provide a unique and built-in way of overcoming bias. In a sense, the researcher can be reframed as the subject. This particular technique allows the opportunity to reflect on the personal intersecting with the social, using my own experiences as a product of the system I am studying to have a voice, primarily in how it "illuminates the culture under the study."[4] Personal narrative does matter, particularly in projects like the one I am attempting to complete. Laurel Richardson questions the notion of truth, or at least that of a single truth.[5] This is why some ethnographic writers tend to frame their work as fiction, or poetic representation, to avoid the cliché of simply presenting information or social facts as the only form of social scientific writing. As Carolyn Ellis suggests:

> Auto-ethnography is an autobiographical genre of writing and research that displays multiple layers of consciousness, connecting the personal to the cultural. Back and forth auto-ethnographers gaze, first through an ethnographic wide-angle lens, focusing outward on social and cultural aspects of their personal experience; then, they look inward, exposing a vulnerable self that is moved by and may move through, refract, and resist cultural interpretations. Usually written in first person voice, auto-ethnographic texts appear in a variety of forms—short stories, poetry, fiction, novels, photographic essays, personal essays, fragmented, layered writing, and social science prose.[6]

This methodological choice is particularly effective when examining the role of race and racialization in the classroom, from a pedagogical perspective as well as from an experiential one.

J. L. Pennington asserts that using autoethnography as both a method of inquiry and a teaching practice allows students and teachers the opportunity to reexamine and reposition their own subjectivities, making space for counternarratives to our own stories and experiences.[7] As educators, understanding our own subject positions in the classroom as well as how those subject positions might be perceived by students, colleagues, and administrators will influence our pedagogies and performances. In this case, Laurel Richardson's notion of writing as its own method of inquiry provides the space to tell a specific story, placing the author's own biases and subjectivities out in the open, while ensuring that the story is both adequately theorized and contextualized. As the researcher-teacher, I use this method to provide a critical-reflexive account of my own experiences, one that deals with my disconnection to space and place, the precarity of my employment, and the ways I negotiated balancing the demands of the job with the ethical responsibility I had to my students.

DILEMMATIC SPACES

Dilemmatic spaces, according to Fransson and Grannäs,[8] are the result of structural conditions and are relational in nature—ever present in the ways in which we engage with space and often contingent upon the reactions of others to the choice that we make. This is amplified in educational settings, as any given teacher is responsible to their students, their colleagues, and their superiors. As such, educators often find themselves inside of dilemmatic spaces almost as a matter of course. As Fransson and Grannäs state, "In their daily work, teachers sometimes find themselves in situations characterized as dilemmatic in relation to various kinds of factors, such as the expectations of others, competing goals in the curricula or issues concerning who should control what in education."[9] My previous research focused on how both Jewish and Palestinian teachers in Israel approach teaching about race, ethnicity, and citizenship using a curriculum that focuses on a single national narrative. In this work, I focused on the idea of the classroom as a dilemmatic space created by the unique demands of teaching in an ongoing ethno-national conflict.[10]

While teaching in the American South is far from the sort of classroom-as-battleground that my interview subjects found themselves in, I found myself experiencing some of the same issues that the Israeli teachers described to me five years ago, including coded language from colleagues about what to expect from my students, as well as feeling my own otherness as soon as I set foot in the classroom. It still appeared as though I had the wrong idea about whether the classroom is an inherently political space. In my case, the competing goals and expectations of others clashed with my own goals and expectations, while internally it seemed my own goals were also at cross-purposes. How was I to maintain a degree of integrity in the classroom and do right by my students while also knowing that I was under intense scrutiny from the moment I arrived? Because the new hiring committee was made up of my peers, it felt like every time I interacted with any faculty member aside from the chair, anything I said could be used against me when it came time to short-list candidates. In essence, each element of my experience—from neoliberal models of surveillance and control, to content and curricular challenges, to the daily struggle of fitting in as an outsider in the eyes of both my students and the institution itself—acts as a part of a larger, structural dilemmatic space.

THE NEOLIBERAL INSTITUTION

When discussing the role of neoliberalism in higher education, there is a tendency to focus on a rather amorphous sort of instrumental-rationality approach to the term, cloaking the impact that neoliberal policies have had on public institutions, or as Rowlands and Rawolle suggest, we perpetuate it as the dominant discourse rather than disrupt it.[11] While scholars like Henry Giroux poignantly describe the erosion of higher education as part of the broader death of the public sphere, there is a tendency for faculty members to collectively shrug as we "slip into a disciplinary apparatus that views the university not as a place to think but as a place to prepare students to be competitive in the global marketplace" without resistance.[12] Scholars are expected to produce in order to justify a department's existence, and early-career academics tend to take on more and more teaching to remain employed.

Of course it is something of a zero-sum game, as the more one teaches, the less one has time to perform new research to "find their niche" in the hyper-competitive and ever-scarce tenure-track job market.[13] Young scholars are never not "on the market," looking for anything at all in order to stay in the field. As stories of adjuncts on food stamps and welfare become the norm rather than the exception, it is easy to see why one might jump on the chance to go anywhere.[14] It seemed too good to be true—either a one-year contract in a place I had never visited or the potential to put down roots and start my career.

While there is disagreement on whether or not the "precariat" is a new class formation, there is little doubt that precariousness has become a weapon used to both "exploit adjuncts, part-time workers and temporary laborers and to suppress dissent by keeping them in a state of fear over losing their jobs."[15] The latter of course was my life for the first part of my appointment. Beyond not knowing if I was staying and applying for other positions alongside reapplying for "my own," feeling under surveillance was the most emotionally draining aspect, knowing that any potential misstep could be used to justify not retaining me. That fear carried into the classroom, as I deliberately chose safer texts and safer teaching practices.

Often understudied are the emotional consequences of this precarious, uncertain work-life balance[16]—never feeling stable or secure, feeling constantly under surveillance from colleagues, trying to find ways to ensure that you will in fact be retained longer than the terms of your contract. Every choice I made at the start of my appointment was carefully considered. I even took on additional unpaid labor, thinking that the extra effort would help to strengthen my place within the department. This included a full week of guest lectures in an upper-division research methods course to help fill in the course instructor's own knowledge gaps—a tenure-track instructor who already had a lighter teaching load than I did and was also on the hiring committee. In essence, I was trying to be the model neoliberal subject, focused more on managing risk and ensuring my own survival than really considering the needs of my students, running counter to my own values and historical approach to teaching and learning.[17]

TEACHING OR SURVIVING?

When I began my appointment, one of the first things I was "warned" about by my colleagues was their belief that, coming from Canada, I would need to adjust and manage my expectations about my students' abilities. They firmly believed that while I should not have to change my approach to teaching, I would find myself surprised and frustrated by a lack of foundational knowledge.

Essentially from the moment I arrived, it felt as though my peers framed me as a sort of "carpetbagger." The term's historical meaning speaks to the complexity of the competing narratives of the South, tied to Civil War Reconstruction and the resentment that Southerners have about Northerners coming down to rebuild, reeducate, and re-socialize. It also made me somewhat uneasy about what my role would actually be, given the constraints and conditions being placed upon me by my peers and despite my own belief that education transcends borders.[18] The idea of being a carpetbagger in the classroom is nothing new. Humpal describes his experience of being a Northerner in a Southern, mostly White classroom and the mental health challenges he experienced from being disconnected from his own space, place, and cultural community—a set of experiences and emotions that resonated deeply with me: "As a White male educator in a predominantly White rural high school community, introducing curriculum that focuses on race, ethnicity, class, gender, and mental ability, can be risky. It was not that I felt I was the next 'great White hope.' I actually felt like a White, Northern carpetbagger having difficulty selling his goods in a predominantly White, rural southern community."[19] Similarly, the curricular risks that Humpal describes taking were high on my own priority list, especially given that I was teaching introductory classes as well as a course on social inequalities in the US my first semester. Such themes (race, ethnicity, class, gender) are entirely necessary topics in any critical sociology course, yet I felt compelled to play it safe at first, especially to avoid falling into the trap of touting the Northern superiority about Southern racial politics that has become so common. Much like Humpal's experience, I also had a difficult time "selling my goods," but for different reasons. By playing it safe, I mostly taught to the text, relying upon the theoretical frameworks used in the books to inform my own lectures, rather than using the textbooks and readers as a guide and providing more in-depth analysis, counterpoints, and alternative theoretical positions. It seemed best to toe the company line and stay inside the institution's established comfort zone as long as I was teaching for my job. As Kevin Birmingham states, "junior faculty play it safe—conceptually, politically and formally."[20]

The rationale for the duality of my pedagogical approach is admittedly somewhat problematic; because I was under review, I spent far too much time worrying that if I went too far down an unconventional or politicized path, students would resist and complain, which would damage my chances of remaining. However, if I did not engage in my own best teaching practices, there was the potential for doing a disservice to my students anyway. In many ways, it was an impossible scenario, reinforcing an increasingly commonly held belief among contract faculty that precarious employment restricts the potential for academic freedom.[21]

At first, students were entirely unsure what to do with me, particularly freshmen. Coming out of Tennessee's public high schools, many of the students grew up under the No Child Left Behind (NCLB) and Common Core systems. Rote learning and teaching to the test were the only types of teaching practices my students were familiar with, the sort of structures Ernst and Vallack refer to as "idiot-proof" teaching.[22] Several students reached out at the beginning of the semester asking to have more regular evaluations and were extremely intimidated by the idea of writing as both a method of inquiry and a method of assessment. Of course, this speaks to the structural dismantling and devaluing of public education in the United States much more than it says anything at all about my students' abilities and desires to learn. It did mean, however, that much more foundation building was necessary than I was expecting, which required a shift in my curriculum to meet my students where they were.

One of the more frustrating moments I had in this regard was during a teaching practices workshop I was asked to lead for my colleagues, in what was intended to be the first of a monthly workshop in the department. In a conversation about foundational knowledge, I suggested revising the first-year curriculum and developing a set of foundational goals that each instructor teaching the course could include. The concepts were very basic critical thinking skills as well as reading comprehension and writing fundamentals, the sorts of skills that would benefit students throughout their degrees, and with particular benefit to the majors and minors. The idea was summarily rejected by almost all of the faculty members. Many continued to assert that my expectations of the students were too high, specifically because of my Canadian teaching experience, and that I should not expect students at my institution to need or want this knowledge outside of a few gifted students who already possessed it.

The response from my colleagues felt akin to a defeat at the hands of neoliberal education processes—market forces prevailed and good students would choose to go elsewhere, so why bother teaching up the predominantly weak students we have? The end result of these discussions was that nothing would change, that any effort to try to elevate the students' foundational knowledge was not worth the time or the potential fight over teachers' individual course autonomy and academic freedom. It seemed obvious that this rejected plan was at the expense of students whose own skills and worth were deemed as less than by my colleagues. As several of my students had never been exposed to close-reading a text, let alone how to write a thesis or properly take notes in class, I developed and implemented the resources for my own classes that I still use today.

NOTHING LEFT TO LOSE: ON IMPLEMENTING A RADICALLY DEMOCRATIC PEDAGOGY

It was an entirely different experience teaching my students before and after being passed over for a permanent position in my department. No matter what, I tried to put my students first, but the way I approached teaching changed dramatically, particularly between the first and second semesters. Once I knew I was not returning, I was relieved that I was no longer under surveillance; but more than relief, there was the sense that I could finally teach the kinds of courses I always wanted to. The smaller class sizes of my upper-level courses provided the flexibility to have more dialogue-based classes, seminars, and roundtable discussions, as well as student-chosen topics based on current sociopolitical events and affairs. Indeed, I began to align my approach to teaching much more closely with my idealized classroom, one that is democratic, critical, and unabashedly activist-oriented.

One of these moments was in early November 2015, days after discovering I would not be interviewed for the tenure-track position. Spurred by the actions of the university's football team, a protest at the University of Missouri resulted in the eventual resignation of the university's president for his failure to address the growing racism on campus, a topic that Felicia Harris's chapter discusses in a different register. Rather than carrying on with the planned lecture for my social inequalities class, I had the students sit in a circle to talk about the significance of the protest, the football team's decision to go on strike, and the potential reactions and responses on our own campus. The African American students spoke and the White students mostly listened, occasionally trying to express empathy, but it was a remarkably difficult class. I simply moderated the conversation and used references to course content to keep the discussion focused. Two African American students came up to me afterward and asked the question I opened this chapter with. It broke my heart.

Lynn Davies describes interruptive democratic education as "the process by which people are enabled to break into practices which continue injustice" and notes that it contains five distinct elements: a basis in rights; the handling of identity and fear; the need for deliberation and dialogue; the need for creativity, play, and humor; and the impetus for a defiant agency.[23] In my own way, I made a commitment to ensure that my courses would have the potential to incorporate all five elements throughout the semester, particularly in terms of identity and fear, deliberation and dialogue, and defiant agency. I sought to create a culture where there was safety to disagree, to engage with troubling elements in our own communities and connect those issues to the broader social world. In essence, I was attempting to actually make my classes into applied sociological spaces rather than purely theoretical—scaffolding social justice approaches not just into content and assessment but also into the conversations held in the space.

Davies implies that critical, dialogue-based education allows for a more deliberative democratic practice in the classroom, one that I felt I could not effectively use at first but gradually became more comfortable with once I knew I would not return. Indeed, it was almost freeing in a sense to know that I was no longer under consideration, and with the permission of my department chair, I designed a deliberately challenging set of courses and readings. I felt as though I was finally able to teach what I always wanted to teach, and the way I always hoped I could—politically challenging, dialogue and participation-heavy, and using examples of movements and moments from the real world to help work through complex theoretical texts.

For example, in an upper-division course on globalization and social change, I introduced students to a set of complex social and political discourses as well as social movements that aimed to disrupt the established order, beginning with Michel Foucault's "The Unities of Discourse," in order to establish what discourse is and why it matters, in the context of both our classroom and the broader social world.[24] Many students were unfamiliar with most of these ideas, and almost all were uncomfortable with challenging the status quo, even as an academic exercise.

One of the first assignments was a response paper in which students needed to apply a theoretical position of their choice to an object in the world. These objects could be broad, such as a Marxist critique of globalization, or as narrow as an intersectional feminist perspective on paid parental leave. No outside sources were required and no previous knowledge on the subject was necessary—in essence, I wanted to know that the class had (a) read the course materials and (b) understood what the materials were about. Predictably, the students had never been asked to do that sort of work before, and most of the submissions had completely missed the point. Instead I received what amounted to op-eds, response papers without any engagement with course content and critiques that relied solely upon the students' unsubstantiated personal opinions on the objects they chose rather than an analysis of a specific issue through a specific theoretical lens.

As both Lynn Davies and, a generation earlier, Paulo Freire suggest, dialogue is about emergence: unmasking new ideas, new concepts, and alternative ways of both seeing and thinking about the world. However, dialogue requires the right conditions to be an effective teaching practice.[25] The globalization class provided those conditions in ways I did not expect, creating space for an activist culture to emerge organically from the course content. As students learned to recognize structural inequalities and engage with political and social issues from a variety of perspectives, the course started to become more of a community than a classroom. What began as an exercise in developing the students' abilities to be more critically minded and flexible learners actually proved to flow in both directions. In many ways, that course became closer to something in between Freire's model of dialogue-based learning—where students become teachers and teachers become students, depending on the day, the topic, and where the community felt it needed to go[26]—and a classroom that utilized Indigenous pedagogical practices. Lesson planning began to shift away from merely summarizing and analyzing the readings to more seminar-style discussions, including a roundtable on current events in the region every second Friday. The Indigenous pedagogical practices I adopted included the model of Teaching and Sharing Circles to develop techniques that allowed students to focus on personal reflection and change and to "apply their learning to real world situations."[27] As Leanne Simpson describes, "Teaching Circles can be used to ensure students have the chance to participate in class discussions, while Sharing Circles can assist students in working through emotional aspects of the curriculum. All of these components promote Indigenous Knowledge as a process and support the essence of Indigenous education philosophies."[28] In those sessions, we began to connect social movements happening in the world to events and movements happening locally, developing an understanding that Black Lives Matter, while unique to the current sociopolitical and historical conditions in the US in 2016, was also connected to Idle No More in Canada, the Zapatistas in Mexico, Palestinian resistance movements, and the problem of settler-colonialism. This nexus, a combination we also see in essays in this volume by Christopher-Byrd and Brooms and Brice, motivated our immediate response.

Student reaction to these ideas was complex to say the least. I had begun a process of using the classroom as a way to "unsettle," to destabilize the sorts of histories and politics that many of my students had always known. It was certainly not an easy process; it reminded me of the challenges the Israeli and Palestinian educators I worked with had experienced in their own classrooms.[29] While at no point was there the outright, vocalized racism that some of the Israeli teachers described, I too felt the need to take on unpopular perspectives with the hope that students would "be enabled to discuss exclusionary identities, not just overlapping or cooperative ones."[30]

Connecting BLM and other social movements resisting anti-Black violence and institutional racism to settler-colonialism and the process of decolonization was one of the more difficult and controversial areas that we engaged as a class. Such an intervention allowed students with no prior knowledge of the history of decolonization and the work of scholars like Frantz Fanon to think more about their place within these struggles, subconsciously drawing upon C. Wright Mills's "Sociological Imagination" framework.[31] Of course this was met with resistance at times from some of the White students, and at one point during a seminar, there was a heated discussion of the "Black Lives Matter versus All Lives Matter" debate.

Strangely enough, students commented that despite my Whiteness, my outsider status, not being from the South or immersed in Southern culture or holding typically American-centric individualistic-focused political values, helped to create a classroom culture that allowed for politically ultra-sensitive debates. We created almost a self-contained activist-oriented community for ourselves, one that focused on respecting differences and making space for marginalized voices. There were many seminars where I would facilitate but the students would lead, steering conversation toward local issues like homelessness, food insecurity, or accessibility on campus. One culminated in an extra-credit assignment that involved attending a local protest against proposed restrictions on accessibility for Trans students. Nearly 75 percent of the students in the class attended the protest, and some even brought their children. I was astonished by the way the students shifted from the start of the term to the end—barely able to tell the difference between opinion and fact at the start to critically engaging with local sociopolitical issues and in some cases actually joining local social movements by the end. This shift was exactly the sort of emergence that Davies, Freire, and Simpson each described as outcomes of this kind of pedagogical practice.[32] In a sense, these results validated my choice to disregard the repeated warnings of my colleagues that the students were not necessarily strong enough to learn what I was trying to teach.

CONCLUSIONS

As difficult as my time in Tennessee was, once I started to take more risks, the classroom became much more rewarding for my students and for myself. Yet the experience left me wondering just how many other young faculty members endure the same sorts of structural and institutional barriers I faced. Is the resistance to critical thinking from students endemic to higher education in the United States and Canada? How many other young scholars have been blocked by their own colleagues and set up to fail in the same way I felt I was? I know my story is not unique; there are hundreds, perhaps thousands, of passionate and dedicated academics and educators looking for an opportunity to do right by their students while still having the ability to build stable lives for themselves, to not feel constantly under surveillance or concerned that any potential misstep could prevent their contracts from being renewed or extended.

The less-than-ideal working conditions certainly impacted my approach to teaching almost as much as the culture shock.

Precariousness and uncertainty have a definite impact on teaching practices, particularly upon those educators who desire to teach complex sociopolitical matters like race. It is difficult to engage with such issues when precarious faculty members are more concerned with where they might be in six months or how they are going to manage their debts and put food on the table. Yet as I learned, playing it safe did not necessarily guarantee the desired outcome for either myself or my students; playing by the rules and adhering to the logic of neoliberal universities meant accepting my subject position as merely another in the rising ranks of the academic precariat, which was not a choice I was willing to make.

NOTES

1. Göran Fransson and Jan Grannäs, "Dilemmatic Spaces in Educational Contexts—Towards a Conceptual Framework for Dilemmas in Teachers Work," *Teachers and Teaching: Theory and Practice* 19, no. 1 (2013): 4–17; cited in Stephen W. Sheps, "History and Civics Education in Israel: Reflections from Israeli Teachers," *Critical Studies in Education* 60, no. 3 (2019): 361.

2. See Carolyn Ellis, *Revision: Autoethnographic Reflections on Life and Work* (Walnut Creek, CA: Left Coast Press, 2009); Tami Spry, "Performative Autoethnography: Critical Embodiments and Possibilities," in *Collecting and Interpreting Qualitative Materials*, 4th ed., ed. Norman K. Denzin and Yvonna S. Lincoln (London: Sage, 2013), 213–44.

3. Julie L. Pennington, "Silence in the Classroom/Whispers in the Halls: Autoethnography as Pedagogy in White Pre-Service Teacher Education," *Race Ethnicity and Education* 10, no. 1 (2007): 93–113, https://doi.org/10.1080/13613320601100393.

4. Ellis, *Revision*, 211.

5. Laurel Richardson and Elizabeth Adams St. Pierre, "Writing: A Method of Inquiry," in *The Sage Handbook of Qualitative Research*, 3rd ed., ed. Norman K. Denzin and Yvonna S. Lincoln (Thousand Oaks, CA: Sage, 2005), 959–78.

6. Ellis, *Revision*, 209.

7. Pennington, "Silence in the Classroom," 100.

8. Fransson and Grannäs, "Dilemmatic Spaces."

9. Fransson and Grannäs, "Dilemmatic Spaces," 5.

10. Sheps, "History and Civics."

11. Julie Rowlands and Shaun Rawolle, "Neoliberalism Is Not a Theory of Everything: A Bourdieuian Analysis of *Illusio* in Educational Research," *Critical Studies in Education* 54, no. 3 (2013): 260–72.

12. Henry A. Giroux, *Neoliberalism's War on Higher Education* (Toronto, ON: Between the Lines, 2014), 17.

13. Catherine Hartung et al., "Beyond the Academic Precariat: A Collective Biography of Poetic Subjectivities in the Neoliberal University," *Sport, Education and Society* 22, no. 1 (2016): 40–57.

14. See Jordan Weissmann, "Someone Calculated How Many Adjunct Professors Are on Public Assistance, and the Number Is Startling," *Slate*, April 13, 2015, http://www.slate.com/blogs/moneybox/2015/04/13/adjunct_pay_a_quarter_of_part_time_college_faculty_receive_public_assistance.html; Laura McKenna, "The Cost of an Adjunct," *Atlantic*, May 25, 2015, https://www.theatlantic.com/education/archive/2015/05/the-cost-of-an-adjunct/394091; Kevin Birmingham, "The Great Shame of Our Time," *Chronicle of Higher Education*, February 12, 2017, http://www.chronicle.com/article/The-Great-Shame-of-Our/239148.

15. Giroux, *Neoliberalism's War*, 55.

16. See Ruth Barcan, *Academic Life and Labour in the New University: Hope and Other Choices* (London: Taylor and Francis, 2016); Hartung et al., "Beyond the Academic Precariat."

17. Henry A. Giroux, "Neoliberalism and the Death of the Social State: Remembering Walter Benjamin's Angel of History," *Social Identities* 17, no. 4 (2011): 587–601; Giroux, *Neoliberalism's War*.

18. Henry A. Giroux, *Border Crossings: Cultural Workers and the Politics of Education* (New York: Routledge, 1992).

19. David L. Humpal, "The Lost Carpetbagger: Complicating Geographical and Psychological 'Place' in the South for a Northern-Born White Teacher," *SAGE Open* 3, no. 3 (2013): 1–8, https://doi.org/10.1177/2158244013502493.

20. Birmingham, "The Great Shame of Our Time."

21. Giroux, *Neoliberalism's War*; Meagan Gillmore, "OPSEU Ramping Up Efforts to Organize Contract College Instructors," *Rabble.ca*, July 4, 2017, http://rabble.ca/news/2017/07/opseu-ramping-efforts-organize-contract-college-instructors.

22. Ruth Ernst and Jolene Vallack, "Storm Surge: An Autoethnography about Teaching in the Australian Outback," *Qualitative Inquiry* 21, no. 2 (2015): 157.

23. Lynn Davies, "Interruptive Democracy in Education," in *Comparative and Global Pedagogies: Equity, Access and Democracy in Education*, ed. Joseph Zajda, Suzanne Majhanovich, and Lynn Davies (Heidelberg, Germany: Springer Netherlands, 2008), 19.

24. Michel Foucault, "The Unities of Discourse," in *Archaeology of Knowledge and the Discourse on Language* (New York: Pantheon, 1972), 21–30.

25. See Davies, "Interruptive Democracy"; and Paulo Freire, *Pedagogy of the Oppressed* (New York: Continuum, 1970).

26. Freire, *Pedagogy of the Oppressed*.

27. Leanne Simpson, "Indigenous Environmental Education for Cultural Survival," *Canadian Journal of Environmental Education* 7, no. 1 (2002): 13–25.

28. Simpson, "Indigenous Environmental Education."

29. Sheps, "History and Civics."

30. Ayman K. Agbaria, Muhamad Mustafa, and Yousef T. Jabareen, " 'In Your Face' Democracy: Education for Belonging and Its Challenges in Israel," *British Educational Research Journal* 41, no. 1 (June 2014): 143–75.

31. C. Wright Mills, *The Sociological Imagination* (New York: Oxford University Press, 1959).

32. See Davies, "Interruptive Democracy"; Freire, *Pedagogy of the Oppressed*; Simpson, "Indigenous Environmental Education."

BIBLIOGRAPHY

Agbaria, Ayman K., Muhamad Mustafa, and Yousef T. Jabareen. " 'In Your Face' Democracy: Education for Belonging and Its Challenges in Israel." *British Educational Research Journal* 41, no. 1 (June 2014): 143–75. https://doi.org/10.1002/berj.3133.

Barcan, Ruth. *Academic Life and Labour in the New University: Hope and Other Choices*. London: Taylor and Francis, 2016.

Birmingham, Kevin. "The Great Shame of Our Time." *Chronicle of Higher Education*, February 12, 2017. http://www.chronicle.com/article/The-Great-Shame-of-Our/239148.

Davies, Lynn. "Interruptive Democracy in Education." In *Comparative and Global Pedagogies: Equity, Access and Democracy in Education*, edited by Joseph Zajda, Suzanne Majhanovich, and Lynn Davies, 15–31. Heidelberg, Germany: Springer Netherlands, 2008.

Ellis, Carolyn. "Autoethnography, Personal Narrative, Reflexivity: Researcher as Subject." In *Collecting and Interpreting Qualitative Materials*, 2nd ed., edited by Norman K. Denzin and Yvonna S. Lincoln, 199–258. Thousand Oaks, CA: Sage, 2003.

———. *Revision: Autoethnographic Reflections on Life and Work*. Walnut Creek, CA: Left Coast Press, 2009.

Ernst, Ruth, and Jolene Vallack. "Storm Surge: An Autoethnography about Teaching in the Australian Outback." *Qualitative Inquiry* 21, no. 2 (2015): 153–60.

Foucault, Michel. "The Unities of Discourse." In *Archeology of Knowledge and the Discourse on Language*, 21–30. New York: Pantheon, 1972.

Fransson, Göran, and Jan Grannäs. "Dilemmatic Spaces in Educational Contexts—Towards a Conceptual Framework for Dilemmas in Teachers Work." *Teachers and Teaching: Theory and Practice* 19, no. 1 (2013): 4–17.

Freire, Paulo. *Pedagogy of the Oppressed*. New York: Continuum, 1970.

Gillmore, Meagan. "OPSEU Ramping Up Efforts to Organize Contract College Instructors." *Rabble.ca*, July 4, 2017. http://rabble.ca/news/2017/07/opseu-ramping-efforts-organize-contract-college-instructors.

Giroux, Henry A. *Border Crossings: Cultural Workers and the Politics of Education*. New York: Routledge, 1992.

———. "Neoliberalism and the Death of the Social State: Remembering Walter Benjamin's Angel of History." *Social Identities* 17, no. 4 (2011): 587–601. https://doi.org/10.1080/13504630.2011.587310.

———. *Neoliberalism's War on Higher Education*. Toronto, ON: Between the Lines, 2014.

Hartung, Catherine, Nicoli Barnes, Rosie Welch, Gabrielle O'Flynn, Jonnell Uptin, and Samantha McMahon. "Beyond the Academic Precariat: A Collective Biography of Poetic Subjectivities in the Neoliberal University." *Sport, Education and Society* 22, no. 1 (2016): 40–57. https://doi.org/10.1080/13573322.2016.1202227.

Humpal, David L. "The Lost Carpetbagger: Complicating Geographical and Psychological 'Place' in the South for a Northern-Born White Teacher." *SAGE Open* 3, no. 3 (2013): 1–8. https://doi.org/10.1177/2158244013502493.

McKenna, Laura. "The Cost of an Adjunct." *Atlantic*, May 25, 2015. https://www.theatlantic.com/education/archive/2015/05/the-cost-of-an-adjunct/394091.

Mills, C. Wright. *The Sociological Imagination*. New York: Oxford University Press, 1959.

Pennington, Julie L. "Silence in the Classroom/Whispers in the Halls: Autoethnography as Pedagogy in White Pre-Service Teacher Education." *Race Ethnicity and Education* 10, no. 1 (2007): 93–113. https://doi.org/10.1080/13613320601100393.

Richardson, Laurel, and Elizabeth Adams St. Pierre. "Writing: A Method of Inquiry." In *The Sage Handbook of Qualitative Research*, 3rd ed., edited by Norman K. Denzin and Yvonna S. Lincoln, 959–78. Thousand Oaks, CA: Sage, 2005.

Rowlands, Julie, and Shaun Rawolle. "Neoliberalism Is Not a Theory of Everything: A Bourdieuian Analysis of *Illusion* in Educational Research." *Critical Studies in Education* 54, no. 3 (2013): 260–72. https://doi.org/10.1080/17508487.2013.830631.

Sheps, Stephen W. "History and Civics Education in Israel: Reflections from Israeli Teachers." *Critical Studies in Education* 60, no. 3 (2019): 358–74. https://doi.org/10.1080/17508487.2016.1263966.

Simpson, Leanne. "Indigenous Environmental Education for Cultural Survival." *Canadian Journal of Environmental Education* 7, no. 1 (2002): 13–25.

Spry, Tami. "Performative Autoethnography: Critical Embodiments and Possibilities." In *Collecting and Interpreting Qualitative Materials*, 4th ed., edited by Norman K. Denzin and Yvonna S. Lincoln, 213–44. London: Sage, 2013.

Standing, Guy. *The Precariat: The New Dangerous Class*. London: Bloomsbury Academic, 2011.

Weissmann, Jordan. "Someone Calculated How Many Adjunct Professors Are on Public Assistance, and the Number Is Startling." *Slate*, April 13, 2015. http://www.slate.com/blogs/moneybox/2015/04/13/adjunct_pay_a_quarter_of_part_time_college_faculty_receive_public_assistance.html.

CHAPTER 12

UNDOCUMENTED LEARNING OUTCOMES AND CYBER COYOTES

Teaching Ethnic Studies in the Online Classroom

ERIN MURRAH-MANDRIL

> Those involved in the articulation of minority discourses of all kinds act like coyotes, smuggling across national, disciplinary, and methodological boundaries (for a price) agents who already challenge the significance of those boundaries. While there will be those who seek to enact laws that counter this alien movement, already the aliens serve us, already the aliens move among us. Indeed, already, always, we are the aliens. The aliens are us.
>
> —Rafael Pérez-Torres, "Chicano Culture Reclaiming Our America: Coyotes at the Border"

In common usage, a coyote is someone who smuggles undocumented immigrants across Mexico's northern border into the United States. Coyotes (the animals) also appear as trickster figures in Chicana/o literature and folklore, acting as symbols of "resistance to Anglo American cultural paradigms."[1] I draw on Rafael Pérez-Torres's conceptual use of "coyote" to highlight the way that ethnic studies teachers incorporate unstated, or "undocumented," learning outcomes in their pedagogy to promote empathy, ethnic pride, self-awareness, or other intentions that do not fit neatly into assessment-based models of learning. In particular, I am interested in the possibility of bringing these "undocumented" learning outcomes into an online ethnic studies course. Coyotes (the border smugglers) rely on performativity in their smuggling endeavors; they participate in an extralegal economy; and they inhabit a double position within border culture as both subversive hero and exploitative parasite. Coyotes traffic in the fluidity of racial and national identity, often instructing immigrants on how to change from rural Mexican dress to urban Chicana/o style in order to pass as "American." Teachers of ethnic studies—Mexican American studies in my case—also communicate knowledge within and beneath the authorized discourse, which, for contemporary college educators, is the discourse of learning objectives and assessment. The goal of ethnic studies is not to teach students to "pass" as "American" but rather to give them the tools to understand, explore, and self-consciously engage in identity construction. The importance of navigating official pedagogical discourse in an ethnic studies class takes on new urgency when the classroom is a virtual one. In fall 2016, I created an online Introduction to Mexican American Studies class for my university. The process was structured through student learning objectives to produce a course that could be taught by any instructor in a distance or asynchronous learning environment. After designing the course, I had the unique opportunity to run it concurrently with a face-to-face class that covered the same material. While I had taught and designed several English classes online and had taught Mexican American studies and literature courses face-to-face for years, bringing those two sets of knowledge together was a new challenge. The comparison helped me articulate some of the learning outcomes in ethnic studies which do not, and often cannot, appear on a syllabus, but which, nonetheless, might be smuggled into an online class.

The timing of the course helped highlight a major disjuncture in online and face-to-face pedagogy, particularly as it relates to minority discourse. I designed the online class in spring 2015, before Donald Trump was elected US president, and ran it for the first time during the fall 2016 elections. Having undergone an extensive (and beneficial) process of review and editing in collaboration with my institution's distance education office, I could not easily change the online course structure or content. I had been under contract to create it. It passed review and got its papers, so to speak. My face-to-face class had an impromptu discussion the day after Trump's election. Students expressed their reaction to the nation's embrace of a man that characterized Mexican immigrants as drug dealers, criminals, and rapists in his infamous June 16, 2015, speech; claimed that US District Judge Gonzalo Curiel was unfit to rule on a lawsuit against Trump University because of his Mexican heritage; and led campaign rallies with the chant "build the wall" as he promised to make Mexico pay for a massive border wall.[2] Almost every student in the face-to-face class had Latina/o heritage; many of them were Mexican immigrants or children of immigrants. The conversation was cathartic and productive as students expressed differing and sometimes very personal views about the election in a safe space. By contrast, the online class continued with nary an announcement. Students had just completed a unit on the Chicano Movement and Chicana feminism and were about to start studying contemporary issues concerning education and immigration. I wondered, would the online content I created be enduring and adaptable in the new reality? Had lessons about the Chicano Movement inspired and empowered students to face the barrage of alternative facts, anti-immigrant propaganda, misogyny, and racism that was still yet to come? The computer seemed more like a barrier than a portal at that moment—like a border wall. Despite all the weekly learning outcomes and alignment of activities to course objectives that I had worked on, there was no way to measure the one outcome I cared most about: Did my students feel enriched and empowered by the class?

I teach Mexican American studies and American literature at a Hispanic-serving institution in a conservative state historically known for its discrimination against Latinas/os—from its nineteenth-century Mexican American land dispossession to its twentieth-century lynching and segregation of Mexican Americans and its twenty-first-century anti-immigrant laws. The majority of students in my classes identify as Mexican, Mexican American, or Latina/o.[3] Many are first-generation college students, often with full-time jobs and families to care for. I am a white woman on the tenure track from a poor, working-class background, having spent most of my life in another state with a large Latina/o population but with a very different cultural and political climate. One of my goals as a teacher is to create a space where Latina/o students feel comfortable expressing ethnic pride in a formal, intellectual (not just social) environment. I also bring to class an ingrained sense of Chicanas/os as native inhabitants of the Southwest, which runs counter to discourses of immigration that dominate the region where I teach. This information does not generally appear in writing, certainly not on my CV, syllabus, or class handouts. These are ideas that I express in person, sometimes unconsciously, during the semi-spontaneous unfolding of class discussions and lectures—a comment here, a gesture there, a salient pause before responding, each expression as dependent on students' nonverbal cues as they are on my own intellectual persona. Yet, as Roegman and Salloum note in their contribution to this volume, that nuance and spontaneity disappeared as I tried to design an online course that could be taught by any instructor to students I would never see. How do teachers share their attitudes and beliefs when physical bodies recede into the cyberspace of learning management systems (LMS) and when learning objectives structure every typed or spoken word in the online class?

Online education aims, in part, to remove teachers' attitudes and beliefs from the classroom. Initially, online education was hailed as a democratic space where everyone's voice could be heard and the absence of visual cues for race and gender would remove bias.[4] Likewise, liberated from their physical identity, students would be free to represent themselves on their own terms. Yet, as Frank Valk noted in 2008, "there is mounting evidence that a surprising number of social norms are replicated, and in some cases even accentuated, in virtual environments."[5] Beyond the problematic idealization of a raceless environment, contemporary concerns about cyber bullying and the rise of the alt-right have undermined utopic projections of an egalitarian internet. Some online courses avoid the negative potential of disembodied communication by prescribing social norms for online discourse. My university's guidelines for "netiquette" (online etiquette) asks students to convey "a non-threatening tone," refrain from sarcasm, and respect others' opinions. However, I believe these recommendations discourage students from discussing controversial topics online, where responses to classmates' work are often friendly, banal statements of agreement. Upon reflection, I realized that netiquette runs counter to the communication norms of my face-to-face classes. Humor and sarcasm can be tools for disrupting structural racism. Likewise, the very concept of "respect" can enforce social norms when students do not feel comfortable challenging dominant racist conventions. Within the limited period of a face-to-face class, students and teachers do not give equal weight to every idea but, instead, convey a non-threatening tone through their actual tone of voice and body language. Though writing about a face-to-face class, Peter Kerry Powers highlights the problems of teaching ethnic studies without significant faculty involvement: "The assumption seems to be that relations of power and oppression are institutionally embodied in the figure of the teacher, or, perhaps more broadly, in the curriculum and other features of the educational institution. But power and oppression function 'democratically' as well, in dispersed forms of discourse and daily practice."[6] Online classes help students acquire knowledge and skills, but their disembodied, highly regulated structure is less suited to ethnic studies' emphasis on encouraging new attitudes, questioning social norms, and modeling critical engagement. Outside of the classroom, internet culture creates niche communities where users may, in fact, be discouraged from meaningfully engaging and critiquing social norms. Building these practices into an online class does, at times, feel like a subversive act of smuggling.

UNDOCUMENTED OUTCOMES: TEACHING THE VALUES OF ETHNIC STUDIES

Many university courses are structured through learning objectives, a concept intertwined with the industrial revolution and its development of a modern workforce.[7] Classes are "reverse engineered," student learning is measurable, and classroom activities are carefully aligned with objectives. This format makes the learning process more transparent to students and external observers of the education system. But within the lived, embodied experience of a physical classroom, there are always slippages, excesses that do not fit neatly into stated objectives. It is in this excess that we teach undocumented outcomes through the intentional, unconscious, or barely conscious beliefs we hold about what and who we teach. Undocumented outcomes rely on the subtle nuances of body language, ancillary comments, and the flow of classroom discussions.

Whether intentional or unintentional, the key feature of undocumented outcomes is that they remain unwritten in the official apparatus of instruction—i.e., they are not listed on syllabi, in handbooks, or on department websites. For example, professors of literature may know that reading fiction increases empathy, and may be aware of studies which measure that increase, but the learning objective "students will increase empathy" is not likely to appear in their course descriptions.[8] Administrators who perform the program assessments that drive learning objectives do not see empathy as a measurable or valuable goal within the twenty-first-century politics that (de)fund US education. Guidelines for learning objectives, in fact, advise instructors to avoid the words "understand" and "appreciate" because they are not measurable.[9] Psychologists who study fiction's effect on empathy measure *understanding* and *appreciation* of diverse viewpoints in order to quantify empathy, but their methods are used exclusively in research, not as measures of academic achievement. Nonetheless, professors of literature direct empathy toward particular types of people (characters) through their text selection and deepen or trouble that empathy through their pedagogical performance. For example, when teaching Luis Valdez's play *Zoot Suit* in my Latino Literature course, I once asked the class, "What do you think about El Pachuco?" A lone student offered, "I like his style." I smiled, some students laughed, and I wrote the word "style" on the board. This exchange opened into a lesson on the historical signification of zoot suit fashion and culture followed by a discussion of the Brechtian features of the play's form, but it also subtly authorized the anger and disaffection El Pachuco displays in the play, even as we unpacked his troubling effect on the protagonist, Henry Reyna. Students still needed to explain the historical context and the genre features of the play on their final exam, but their possible empathy with El Pachuco was a subjective, unwritten outcome of the class.

Embodiment is often at the center of ethnic studies pedagogy. In the example above, multiple bodies converge to make meaning—the bodies of the play's actors and those of the students and professor. Amanda Wray explains, "The teacher's body functions as an intersection of power where cultural norms and idealized notions of authenticity are mapped out and, perhaps, challenged."[10] The racialized bodies of students and teachers come together to form a key context of learning to such an extent that pedagogical articles about ethnic studies almost always discuss the race of the instructor and the class makeup. Jennifer Ho describes the "authority/authenticity paradox that many instructors of color face when teaching multiethnic literature" to white students. She writes, "For [students] my intellectual authority was subverted by my authenticity as a woman of color teaching multiethnic literature, even though they consistently depended on me to answer their questions about the cultural and ethnic signifiers that they did not fully understand in these texts."[11] On the other hand, when teaching multiethnic literature, Rebecca Meachem wonders if her whiteness makes her "students question [her] 'cultural authority,'" adding, "At the same time, I also wonder when they don't."[12] Norma Cantú describes the pitfalls of assuming that shared race and economic background between teacher and students denote a shared identity. Returning to south Texas in the 1980s, Cantú describes being "met with awe and hostility" when she used the term *Chicano* and encouraged students to "be themselves in the classroom as they were in the bilingual/bicultural community where they lived"; she explains, "I had become an outsider."[13] In my own context, I often consider the strangeness of a white teacher encouraging Chicana/o ethnic pride and cultural belonging, but I hope that my presence leads students to expect white people not only to respect Latina/o history and culture but to seek out, support, and learn from Latinidad as a core (rather than peripheral) aspect of US identity.

In an ethnic studies classroom, signifying bodies are both the subject of study and the conduits through which we navigate that subject—performing, modeling, embracing, distancing, and subverting particular identities to communicate not only skills and knowledge but also new epistemologies that do not easily fit on a college syllabus. LMS like Blackboard and Canvas (which dominate the higher education market) promote disembodied learning and rigid structures for organizing information and designing assignments. Teachers using alternate platforms, like open-source LMS or teacher-generated web pages, are already subverting the system by smuggling unofficial interfaces into the online classroom. Faculty who develop a "master course" that their institution can assign to other instructors are usually required to use the contracted LMS and participate in a process of "course alignment," where each activity is matched to a specific learning outcome in order to eliminate any excess or unruly educational content.

Disciplines within the liberal arts have made headway in developing assessments that measure some of the complex and nuanced values that our fields impart to students. In particular, writing programs have driven outcomes assessments to measure revision, reflection, and attention to social context through appropriate use of genre and audience. Yet high-quality assessments in the liberal arts are time-consuming to develop and implement, which places an extra burden on academic fields already struggling to maintain funding and defend their value in a climate that has privileged STEM fields for decades. Instructors who do not have the time or resources to develop programmatic outcomes for the social and intellectual qualities our students learn are left smuggling undocumented outcomes into their classroom. These are often the forms of growth and education to which humanities scholars are most deeply committed, the conscious and unconscious desires that shape our performance as teachers every time we enter a class. The fact that they remain undocumented perpetuates a system in which many of the most important contributions of humanities scholars and teachers (like empathy) remain invisible.[14]

At the same time, leaving certain learning outcomes undocumented may be a strategy for survival—a way of going underground. If we are discouraged from asking students to understand and appreciate other people, how can we design classes meant to help them better understand themselves? One of the key benefits of ethnic studies courses is the effect they have on students of color. In a research review for the National Education Association, Christine Sleeter explains that "studies using different research methodologies, investigating students at middle school through university levels, in different regions of the U.S., consistently find a relationship between academic achievement, . . . and positive identification with one's own racial group."[15] Again, while "positive identification with one's own racial group" (which sounds strikingly similar to ethnic pride) is measurable to social scientists, that educational outcome is not likely to appear on a college syllabus in the near future—not because of its measurability but because of its politics. A syllabus may be a contract between students and instructors, but it can also be a tool of surveillance. In Texas, for example, HB 2504, implemented in fall 2010, mandates that all faculty at state-funded colleges and universities make their syllabi publicly available online, and they must:

1. satisfy any standard adopted by the institution,
2. provide a brief description of each major course requirement, including each major assignment and examination,
3. list any required or recommended reading,
4. provide a general description of the subject matter for each lecture or discussion.[16]

The online public space of Texas syllabi places them in a decontextualized, possibly hostile setting where promoting ethnic pride may not feel like a safe possibility for untenured or contingent faculty.

Humanities fields, and especially ethnic studies, are inherently political in a way that STEM fields purport not to be. Under the presidency of Donald Trump, the political climate for the arts and humanities has shifted from neglect to open hostility. Two years after Texas implemented HB 2504, the Texas GOP, which controls the state's executive and legislative branches, published a platform that stated, "We oppose the teaching of Higher Order Thinking Skills (HOTS) (values clarification), critical thinking skills and similar programs that . . . have the purpose of challenging the student's fixed beliefs and undermining parental authority."[17]

While parental authority legally ends before college, the GOP's platform clearly privileges conservative values contrary to ethnic studies' interest in questioning social norms. At the time, news and entertainment writers lampooned the seemingly ridiculous tenet, but in 2017 Trump's plan to eliminate the National Endowment for the Arts (NEA) and the National Endowment for the Humanities (NEH) represented the potential large-scale enactment of such a platform. Humanities and social science's critical thinking skills—like self-reflection, interrogating power structures, and empathizing with others—are the very tools that can combat authoritarian power. As such, in some of their more specific iterations they are threatening to dominant ideologies and power structures.

Ethnic studies in particular has become a target that right-wing conservatives vilify, ironically, by deploying the neoliberal rhetoric of colorblindness as a conservative appropriation of anti-racist discourse, transforming any discussion of race into a categorical form of racism itself and citing reverse racism as a red herring to reject material correctives to structural racism. For example, in 2010, Arizona HB 2281 attempted to block Mexican American studies in public schools by implying that the program "promote[d] resentment of a race or class of people" and "promote[d] the overthrow of the U.S. government."[18] HB 2281 was specifically used to dismantle Mexican American studies at the high school level in Tucson Independent School District, leaving other ethnic studies programs across the state intact. Cabrera, Maez, and Rodriguez argue that HB 2281's description "relies on a racist framing of Latinas and Latinos as foreign 'others' worthy of increased scrutiny and suspicion [and] . . . plays to the popular racist view that Latinas and Latinos are not fully American, that their national loyalty is in question."[19] Yet the law's exaggerated mischaracterization also belies a well-founded conservative fear that ethnic studies education works to fundamentally transform (one might even say overthrow) the social systems of racism upon which HB 2281's authors depend for their political power. In January 2017 Arizona Representative Bob Thorp introduced HB 2120, which sought to extend the ban on ethnic studies to state universities. In response to HB 2281, Tony Diaz began a movement of *librotraficantes*, or book smugglers, who have organized the distribution of books banned in Arizona public schools to locations throughout the Southwest and especially in Tucson. HB 2281 is a lesson in the way politics can pose a divisive and debilitating threat to ethnic studies, but it is also a lesson in the survival of knowledge production and distribution through unofficial channels. Leaving some learning outcomes undocumented, particularly in the semi-public space of the internet, may allow them to pass unnoticed within systems of state surveillance that threaten academic freedom.

Learning outcomes and corresponding assessments are supposed to make education more accessible to students who may not be familiar with the cultural norms of university classrooms. But, Sleeter notes, increased emphasis on assessment correlates with a de-emphasis on ethnic studies at the K–12 level: "Ironically, what counts as program evaluation data shifted toward experimental research using test scores at the same time that education policy made it more difficult to develop and sustain K–12 ethnic studies curricula. The standards-based reform movement, although ostensibly designed to address the racial achievement gap, has pressed schools that serve students of color and students from high-poverty communities toward standardized, often scripted, test-prep curricula . . . a shift that careful perusal of NAEP test scores from the 1970s onward, desegregated by race, should cause us to question."[20] College-level assessment may be more nuanced than that of K–12 curriculum, but its drive for standardization can still lead to mechanistic homogeneity that ignores the needs and interests of minority students. Ethnic studies programs teach students decolonial epistemologies and the importance of culturally situated knowledge production, but they are then required to assess student learning through Western methodologies like exams, essays, and presentations. The tension between ethnic studies content and assessment arises, in part, from the history of ethnic studies programs, which were often founded by students' and community members' demanding culturally relevant education. As Hu-DeHart puts it, ethnic studies "were insurgent programs with a subversive agenda from the outset. Hence they were suspect and illegitimate even as they were grudgingly allowed into the academy."[21] Assessment is thus part of a broader negotiation within ethnic studies fields between claiming institutional legitimacy and focusing on student and community needs. The values students learn in ethnic studies, such as "positive identification with one's own racial group," often help them overcome, rather than overturn, the structural racism of standardized education, while ethnic studies departments and scholars are themselves still struggling to navigate Eurocentric knowledge and power structures.

The US education system is designed with a presumption of students' white identity. Multicultural courses and anti-racist pedagogies are no exception. Many focus on introducing white students to the writing and experiences of people of color, raising their awareness of racism, and promoting social justice. Whiteness studies forms a key influence in the pedagogy, if not the content, of such classes. As Douglas Eli Julien's essay in this collection also reflects, while Whiteness studies does the critical work of making white culture visible—attempting to decenter whiteness as a universalized identity in the US and thus expose white privilege—it nonetheless continues to orient conversations about race on white behaviors and attitudes. Deanna Blackwell writes of her experience as a graduate student of color in an anti-racist classroom: "The preoccupation with bringing white students into race awareness and coalition building renders students of color invisible in classrooms that employ critical white pedagogy, and otherwise positions communities of color in mentorship roles to white students."[22] Blackwell goes on to describe three common roles for students of color: cultural experts; teachers' aids who help describe and verify racism; and witnesses of white students' coming to racial consciousness, so that their education becomes "participant observation in the field of whiteness," rather than a development of their own intellectual trajectory.[23] Indeed, lessons that ostensibly center on people of color, what Nida Denson classifies as "diversity activities" in the college classroom, impact white students more substantially because of their insulation from discussions of race outside of the classroom.[24] This pedagogy reveals another way that, as Sharon Raynor writes in her chapter, "a university typically operates as a machine, although covertly, on systemic and institutionalized practices of gender bias, racist ideologies and class prejudices." The benefit of ethnic studies for white students has been a selling point among programs vying for scarce resources in the academy that must justify their benefit to majority student populations and speak to predominantly white administrations. To remain non-threatening, ethnic studies programs are often forced to address a white audience, ironically catering to the very white fragility it seeks to abolish. Unlike multicultural education and anti-racist pedagogy, however, ethnic studies is grounded in its historical establishment by students of color for students of color. Students' ethnically inflected subjectivity and racial identity are at the core of ethnic studies' ability to subvert learning objectives and smuggle undocumented outcomes into the classroom.

SMUGGLING UNDOCUMENTED OUTCOMES INTO THE ONLINE CLASS

Ethnic studies focuses on people of color as not only the object of study but as the subject of education; studying one's own culture is fundamental to its ability to undermine systemic racism. Institutionalized education, as the standard-bearer of ideology, is heavily invested in producing subjectivity through an Althusserian process of hailing. Outcomes and assessment are dominated by the process and the product of a learning outcome, but the first word, "students" (Students will . . . identify, analyze, describe, discuss, apply, write, produce, explain, compare, solve, define, or compose something), brings into being a subject that is directed to process and (re) produce information. Rick Voithofer implores online teachers to be aware of the modes of address that determine "how power gets articulated to knowledge by the ways an online pedagogy offers particular social and cultural positions to students."[25] Through modes of address, "the content becomes inscribed by the delivery medium and vice versa . . . In other words, the discourse of the content—its tone, language, structure, visual representation, and icons—all possess interpretive structures (literacies) that have implications for the way a course 'hails' the learner."[26] Learning management systems and learning outcomes prescribe dominant modes of address by using Standard English, structuring material linearly and hierarchically, and limiting students' self-expression. Online curricular modes of address repeat the fallacy of a universalized white male subjectivity as the default subject position in their very attempt at objectivity. When I designed my online class, I tried to counter the ideology of universal white subjectivity by purposefully designing the course for Latina/o students. Again, while I teach predominantly Latina/o students in my face-to-face classes, I had not critically reflected on the way that impacts my course design until I was faced with imagining a student I would likely never meet.

Imagining a specifically racial or ethnic subjectivity for online students runs the risk of essentialism, but failing to do so runs the risk of reproducing the privilege afforded to an imagined universal—i.e., white—student identity. Faculty seeking to develop strategies for Latina/o students to express and reflect upon their collective and individual identities in an online environment must think critically about their own beliefs and perceptions of Latina/o students. In the physical classroom, I tend to steer discussion toward the heterogeneity of Mexican Americans in the US in terms of diverse class, racial, linguistic, national, and gender identity. Mexican American identity is always already multiple in its orientation toward *mestizaje*, a hybrid Spanish and Indigenous heritage, to which students can add gendered, national, and other racial and ethnic hybridities. While the content of the online course retains that complexity, its formal structure is designed to support the knowledge, values, and skills that Latina/o students often bring to class, including a decentered view of the United States' position within the American hemisphere; an openness to the Spanish language with various degrees of fluency; and a proclivity to complicate racial binaries such as Black/white or white/non-white. Students who come to the class with these attributes are better able to navigate the readings and assignments. Honoring students' cultural fluency is the foundation for importing undocumented outcomes into my online ethnic studies course because it aligns knowledge and power with Latina/o students' ethnic identity.

Another benefit of ascribing a particular racial/ethnic identity to the student/subject is that, done well, it re-introduces the excesses of meaning that occur in a face-to-face course. Latina/o identity is not unified, as you can see in my textual shifting between Mexican American, Chicana/o, and Latina/o. Students reflect upon this multiple subjectivity in the first week by writing definitions for Latina/o, Mexican American, and Chicana/o in an online journal. They then read "Toward an Operational Definition of the Mexican American" by Fernando Peñalosa and write a follow-up post about how their definitions were affected by the article.[27] I mention different orthographic ways of expressing Chicana/o, Chican@, Chicanx, Xicana/o, and corresponding versions of Latina/o in the assignment instructions and invite them to use any form they choose throughout the class. The lesson also includes two optional readings: a blog by pop icon Cheech Marin about the meaning of "Chicano" and a *Univision News* article about the term "Latinx." Formal features of the assignment hail students as Latina/o by asking them to reflect on identity through their own knowledge and experience before engaging with the required text, which is a foundational journal article from the early days of Chicano studies that models intellectual discourse and authorizes discussion of Mexican American identity as a scholarly field of inquiry.

The optional readings act as supplements from popular discourse to highlight the way ethnic identity is constantly in flux as part of a dynamic social system. The fact that they are optional positions them in the excess space of the course, that which cannot be contained in the assignment or the assessment. Yet their presence signals that culturally inflected popular discourse is a valid space of knowledge production. The *Univision News* article contains hyperlinks to a number of other important articles about Latinx identity, offering a tailored and non-linear or non-sequential learning experience, where students in the online classroom blur the boundaries of official education. Other weekly lessons introduce students to contemporary and historical Latina/o online spaces like the Librotraficante website, the Onda Latina Archive of Mexican American radio programs, and the Bracero History Archive, all spaces that invite students to follow a path of individualized intellectual engagement. The web of hyperlinks helps reproduce the excess and slippages of unscripted classroom encounters while fulfilling some of the criteria Kathy Davidson envisions as "the future of learning" by promoting self-learning through "horizontal structures" to decenter the authority of the instructor and instead place students in a network of interconnected meaning-making.[28] These skills are especially important for Latina/o students who may not find culturally relevant information in traditional print or broadcast media. Yet even when hyperlinked sources are part of the core, rather than the optional, content for a lesson, it is difficult to quantify the outcome of non-linear, individualized learning through uniform assessment of knowledge and skills.

One of the more successful assignments invites students to become co-creators of knowledge as they engage with news media. Students are asked to find three news articles that describe and discuss a single current event related to immigration and to analyze its causes and ramifications. While I update the lecture notes and reading material annually to address immigration policy changes, this assignment adapts to the rapid and dramatic shifts in immigration policy and, again, honors students' own knowledge and experience. For this discussion forum, more than others, students in the online class enacted key features of a methodology known as *plática*. González and Portillos describe pláticas as "intimate conversations" that are "critical intellectual dialogs," based on traditional Latina/o social practices.[29] Plática has become an important part of Chicana/o studies pedagogy as well as a research methodology. Pláticas validate Mexican American experience and provide a space for healing when they "flow from past stories of pain and trauma, current negotiations, and future hopes," according to Fierros and Bernal.[30] A number of students chose to discuss Trump's attempt to repeal DACA during the semester and related personal stories of family and friends who feared deportation in their analysis of the executive order. Student responses to each other were more reflective and substantive in this discussion than they had been in previous assignments. Though González and Portillos describe pláticas between teacher and student, students can participate in pláticas among themselves as well. Despite the distance and the disembodied nature of online education, students were able to engage personally and critically with material by incorporating their own testimony. Indeed, Roegman and Salloum's chapter points to research that "found that students of color participated more, took greater risks, and expressed more vulnerability in online versions of [a] course." This was an organic moment in the course, but I plan to formally incorporate it by describing plática as a methodology of inquiry and referring to discussion posts as pláticas in the course.

Online communication may be disembodied, but it is nevertheless highly performative. In fact, students perform multiple online identities on social media through their discourse styles, screen names, media sharing, avatars, or profile pictures. These personae draw on but are not limited to students' physical embodiment or experience. The restrictions LMS place on students' self-constructed persona pose a major barrier to online learning and community building. While I encourage students to upload a profile picture or icon, their pictures appear as a very small display, barely larger than the text of their names. Likewise, their screen names are automatically generated and replicate their legal name. In this way, the educational platform enforces officially constructed identities (their legal name) with homogenous, nearly faceless, dehumanizing visual representations. It seems counterproductive to ask students to reflect upon their identity and then block them from expressing that identity in name and image. I am still working to overcome this hurdle. One possibility is to encourage students to create an external blog on a free platform like WordPress, or a video blog (a "vlog") they can post in lieu of the Blackboard blog. These ideas are certainly not new or innovative. LMS are so notoriously clunky that it has become commonplace for instructors to circumvent them by incorporating alternate online platforms (like blog-building websites) into their courses. Doing so is itself an act of smuggling that pushes the limits of authorized content, complicates grading and assessment, and sometimes butts up against university regulations.

Despite the barriers to self-representation, online education does lend itself to imaginative performance even within a restrictive LMS. Throughout the semester students put themselves in Latina/o subject positions that encourage empathy and identification across time, class, and gender. The first of these assignments draws on Antonia Castañeda's article "Engendering the History of Alta California 1769–1848," about the experiences of women in various racial and class categories.[31] Students write a journal entry from the perspective of a widow in New Spain or Mexico. They may select a race and class position of their choosing, and then they have to describe the social options available to them, choose whether they would remarry, and explain how they might negotiate that choice and what the consequences might be. The assignment forces students to align themselves with Latina subjectivity at the same time that it emphasizes the wide range of possibilities for race and class within that identity dating back over 200 years.[32] Scholars like Voithofer, Dare, and Valk have mused about the pedagogical possibilities for students to perform racial and gender identities other than their own in online spaces. I am wary of the potential for a kind of cyber blackface, but a structured assignment grounded in historical detail with a high level of self-reflexivity can promote identification either across ethnic groups or within an imagined heritage, depending on the student. Another activity, adopted from the Bracero History Archive, asks students to trace the route of Juan Loza, a migrant Bracero farmworker, by creating a Google map.[33] In the online pilot class, both performative assignments seemed to produce a deeper sense of historical awareness and identification than occurred in my face-to-face class, where students read the same texts but did not do the imaginative assignments.

It is worth noting that in the above assignment, Juan Loza's interview is available to students in both Spanish and English. Navigating language and the different kinds of fluency that students may possess is an important part of the course's mode of address, offering "particular social and cultural positions to students," to invoke Voithofer again.[34] In addition to Loza's narrative, a few other texts like *corridos*, or border ballads, appear in both Spanish and English. Additionally, texts that incorporate code switching are left untranslated so that monolingual English speakers must do the work of trying to understand some Spanish. This move, drawing from borderland theorist Gloria Anzaldúa, helps decenter English as the only language available for discourse and forces the English speaker to inhabit a space of difference and opacity for a moment.[35] Beyond these instances, the online and face-to-face classes take place in English despite the fact that a number of students are native Spanish speakers, and the majority of the people we study in the course wrote in and spoke Spanish. Linguistic features of Latina/o subjectivity were easier to traverse in the face-to-face class, where code switching occurred more naturally among students, than in the written format of the online class. One small group in the face-to-face class conducted most of their discussions in Spanish and, as a non-native speaker, I made no bones about my heavily accented, awkward Spanish in a pedagogical performance of vulnerability and openness. Online students did not have as many options to express a variety of linguistic identities, and the fact that I wrote and spoke only in English reinforced its place as the official language of communication. One group assignment encouraged/allowed students to write newspaper headlines in Spanish if their group agreed to do so. Again, it was easier for students to observe and perform other people's Latina/o subjectivities in the online course than it was for them to perform their own uniquely inflected identity within the constraints of the class.

In contrast, I was able to perform a pedagogical persona and insert my values and desires into the course more easily than students. I created videos during the semester to comment holistically on student work and discuss course material with the kind of asides and seemingly unscripted discourse I use in class. I specifically situated the videos in a transient time and space that could not be replicated in future courses. For example, I filmed one video in a garden on a fall-break trip to my hometown, effectively inviting students into a space outside the classroom that holds personal, cultural meaning for me. Other visual choices in the online course are less obviously personal but nonetheless constitute a pedagogical performance. Images and documentary videos further the opportunity for excess, unofficial meaning. Taken together, the images throughout the course perform a diverse Mexican American aesthetic. Students are asked to conduct visual analyses of a handful of images, including a unit on Chicana/o art of the 1980s and '90s. Other images appear in the lecture notes and assignment prompts, where I do not explicitly direct students to study them. Like the optional readings, they invite, rather than require, students to reflect. Some, like the black-and-white photographs of zoot suit riots or the Chicano Moratorium, bear witness to history. But they also hold the potential for what Roland Barthes calls the *punctum*, a metonymic function of the unplanned details in a photo that trigger intensely personal responses from the viewer.[36] The course is emptied of embodied discourse, but the visual space of the classroom is at least peopled with both powerful and vulnerable images of Brown bodies who have marched, worked, collaborated, and created Mexican American history. Images of art in the course cross genres and historical periods to include highbrow, pop culture, and folk art of many styles to set a tone that can be serious, playful, subdued, defiant, and emotional in a number of ways.

Students in an online course do not necessarily recognize the art and historical photographs as part of a pedagogical performance. Their instructor is in the video commenting about student work, behind the emails and the assignment feedback. In fact, students often do not know who has generated what aspect of the content when a course is designed and taught by multiple people. Donna Haraway writes in her cyborg manifesto, "the relation between organism and machine has been a border war," and Chela Sándoval builds on that by outlining a "Cyber Consciousness" through "oppositional technologies of power."[37] Both feminist scholars describe a mobile, responsive merging of human and technology that uses the tools at hand to disrupt oppressive power structures. The cyber coyote is one such agent, smuggling empathy and ethnic pride across the borderlands of mechanistic, online classrooms. Despite the problems of disembodied communication in an online ethnic studies course, it also allows bodies that cannot be in a physical classroom to learn the lessons of Mexican American studies. On the other side of the computer screen is a student completing assignments on a company computer during work breaks, writing late at night after a long day of serving other people at work and home, typing with a baby on their lap, or sitting in a hospital room where they help care for an ailing grandparent.[38] The dubious position of a coyote is not lost on me. Coyotes can be celebrated for their ability to subvert oppressive US power structures and evade *la migra*, but they are also capable of exploiting and abusing those who look to them for guidance. Professors produce and consume education as part of a larger colonial or neocolonial system of knowledge and power, and it is important to keep the structural inequality between students and instructors as well as the university's own internal hierarchy at the forefront of pedagogical self-reflection. In this system, online courses are a source of revenue as well as a way of reaching students who might not otherwise have access to higher education. They can be designed by (relatively) well-paid faculty and then taught by adjunct instructors for poverty-level wages. Missing from this essay is the subjectivity of adjunct teachers or graduate students who may be assigned to teach the course in the future. As I built the online course, I tried to remain cognizant of their time and labor constraints as well, the way their subjectivity will enter into the course, and the undocumented outcomes that they will surely smuggle across cyberspace.

NOTES

1. Paul Allatson, "Coyote," in *Key Terms in Latino/a Cultural and Literary Studies* (Cambridge, MA: Blackwell, 2007), 80–81.

2. Nina Totenberg, "Trump Presses Case that 'Mexican' Judge Curiel Is Biased Against Him," NPR, June 4, 2016, https://www.npr.org/2016/06/04/480714972/trump-presses-case-that-mexican-judge-curiel-is-biased-against-him.

3. Other identity markers include Chicana/o, Hispanic, and Latinx, but these are not used as frequently by my specific students when they enter a class.

4. See Tisha Bender, *Discussion-Based Online Teaching to Enhance Student Learning: Theory, Practice, and Assessment* (Sterling, VA: Stylus, 2012); Cathie English, "Finding a Voice in a Threaded Discussion Group: Talking about Literature Online," *English Journal* 97, no. 1 (2007): 56–61; and counter arguments in Frank Vander Valk, "Identity, Power, and Representation in Virtual Environments," *Journal of Online Learning and Teaching* 4, no. 2 (2008): 205–11; and Alexa Dare, "(Dis)Embodied Difference in the Online Class: Vulnerability, Visibility, and Social Justice," *Journal of Online Learning and Teaching* 7, no. 2 (2011): 279–87.

5. Valk, "Identity, Power, and Representation," 206.

6. Peter Kerry Powers, "The Ghost in the Collaborative Machine: The White Male Teacher in the Multicultural Classroom," in *Race in the College Classroom: Pedagogy and Politics*, ed. Bonnie TuSmith and Maureen T. Reddy (New Brunswick, NJ: Rutgers University Press, 2002), 31–32.

7. Objectives oriented education likely began with John Franklin Bobbit's 1918 *The Curriculum* (Chicago: Houghton Mifflin, 1918). Bloom's Taxonomy, one of the dominant structures for organizing learning outcomes, was first published in 1956 in Benjamin Bloom, *The Taxonomy of Educational Objectives* (New York: Longman, 1956).

8. Keith Oatley, "Fiction: Simulation of Social Worlds," *Trends in Cognitive Science* 20, no. 8 (August 2016): 618–28; Maja Djikic, Keith Oatley, and Mihnea C. Moldoveanu, "Reading Other Minds: Effects of Literature on Empathy," *Scientific Study of Literature* 3 (2013): 28–47; and David Comer Kidd and Emanuele Castano, "Reading Literary Fiction Improves Theory of Mind," *Science* 18 (2013): 377–80.

9. See, for example, the Carnegie Mellon Eberly Center for Teaching Excellence and Educational Innovation, "Design and Teach a Course," accessed January 25, 2019, https://www.cmu.edu/teaching/designteach/design/learningobjectives.html; and University of Illinois at Urbana-Champaign Library, Information Literacy Portal, "Tips on Writing Learning Outcomes," accessed January 25, 2019, http://www.library.illinois.edu/infolit/learningoutcomes.html.

10. Amanda Wray, "Race, Region, and Ethos," *Pedagogy: Critical Approaches to Teaching Literature, Language, Composition, and Culture* 17, no. 1 (2017): 59–76.

11. Jennifer Ho, "When the Political Is Personal: Life on the Multiethnic Margins," in TuSmith and Reddy, *Race in the College Classroom*, 67.

12. Rebecca Meacham, "The Entanglements of Teaching *Nappy Hair*," in TuSmith and Reddy, *Race in the College Classroom*, 73.

13. Norma E. Cantú, "Centering the Margins: A Chicana in the English Classroom," in TuSmith and Reddy, *Race in the College Classroom*, 235.

14. Women and faculty of color already perform invisible labor by mentoring more students, sitting on more committees, and taking on more service projects than white male colleagues, and the labor of documenting outcomes, or teaching additional outcomes that remain undocumented, is another layer of this

important yet uncompensated work. See Audrey Williams June, "The Invisible Labor of Minority Professors," *Chronicle of Higher Education*, November 8, 2015; or Social Sciences Feminist Network Research Interest Group, "The Burden of Invisible Work in Academia: Social Inequalities and Time Use in Five University Departments," *Humboldt Journal of Social Relations* 39 (2017): 228–45.

15. Christine E. Sleeter, *The Academic and Social Value of Ethnic Studies: A Research Review* (Washington, DC: National Education Association, 2011), www.nea.org/assets/docs/NBI-2010-3-value-of-ethnic-studies.pdf, p. 8. The phrase "positive identification with one's own racial group" already signals the inability of educators to promote or discuss ethnic pride as a legitimate learning objective.

16. Texas HB No. 2504.

17. The 2012 Texas GOP platform, quoted in Valerie Strauss, "Texas GOP Rejects 'Critical Thinking' Skills. Really," *Washington Post*, July 9, 2012, https://www.washingtonpost.com/blogs/answer-sheet/post/texas-gop-rejects-critical-thinking-skills-really/2012/07/08/gJQAHNpFXW_blog.html.

18. Liquor Omnibus, Arizona H.B. 2281, 54th Leg., 1st Regular (2019).

19. Nolan L. Cabrera, Elisa L. Meza, and Roberto Dr. Cintli Rodriguez, "The Fight for Mexican American Studies in Tucson," North American Congress on Latin America (NACLA), December 8, 2011, https://nacla.org/article/fight-mexican-american-studies-tucson.

20. Sleeter, *Academic and Social Value*, 7.

21. Evelyn Hu-DeHart, "Ethnic Studies in U.S. Higher Education: History Development and Goals," in *Handbook of Research on Multicultural Education*, 2nd ed., ed. James A. Banks and Cherry A. McGee Banks (San Francisco: Jossey-Bass, 2004), 874.

22. Deanna M. Blackwell, "Sidelines and Separate Spaces: Making Education Anti-Racist for Students of Color," *Race Ethnicity and Education* 13, no. 4 (2010): 478, 484.

23. Blackwell, "Sidelines and Separate Spaces," 487.

24. See Nida Denson, "Do Curricular and Co-curricular Activities Influence Racial Bias? A Meta-Analysis," *Review of Educational Resources* 79, no. 2 (2009): 824.

25. Rick Voithofer, "Nomadic Epistemologies and Performative Pedagogies in Online Education," *Educational Theory* 52, no. 4 (2002): 486.

26. Voithofer, "Nomadic Epistemologies," 487.

27. Fernando Peñalosa, "Toward an Operational Definition of the Mexican American," *Aztlán: A Journal of Chicano Studies* 1, no. 1 (1970): 1–12.

28. Kathy Davidson and David Theo Goldberg, *The Future of Learning: Institutions in a Digital Age*, John D and Katherine T McArthur Foundation Reports on Digital Media and Learning (Cambridge, MA: MIT Press, 2009), https://clalliance.org/wp-content/uploads/files/Future_of_Learning.pdf, pp. 26–27.

29. Juan Carlos González and Edwardo L. Portillos, "Teaching from a Critical Perspective: Enseñado de una Perspectiva Crítica: Conceptualization, Reflection,

and Application of Chicana/o Pedagogy," *International Journal of Critical Pedagogy* 4, no. 1 (2012): 19.

30. Cindy O. Fierros and Dolores Delgado Bernal, "Vamos a Pláticar: The Contours of Platicas as Chicana/Latina Feminist Methodology," *Chicana/Latina Studies: The Journal of Mujeres Activas en Letras y Cambia Social* 15, no. 2 (2016): 98–121.

31. Antonia I. Castañeda, "Engendering the History of Alta California 1769–1848: Gender, Sexuality, and the Family," *California History* 76, nos. 2/3 (1997): 230–59.

32. Students are also prepared for the assignment by a previous lesson about the casta system and the way racial constructions in New Spain differ from historical and contemporary constructions of race in the US.

33. "Activity-Tracing the Route of a Bracero," *Bracero History Archive*, Center for History and New Media, 2017, http://braceroarchive.org/items/show/3009.

34. Voithofer, "Nomadic Epistemologies," 486.

35. Gloria Anzaldúa, "Preface to the First Edition," *Borderland/La Frontera: The New Mestiza*, 3rd ed. (San Francisco: Aunt Lute, 2007), 20.

36. Roland Barthes, *Camera Lucida: Reflections on Photography*, trans. Richard Howard (New York: Hill and Wang, 1982).

37. Donna Haraway, "A Cyborg Manifesto: Science, Technology and Socialist Feminism in the Late Twentieth Century," in *Simians, Cyborgs, and Women: The Reinvention of Nature* (New York: Routledge, 1991), 292; Chela Sándoval, "New Sciences: Cyborg Feminism and the Methodology of the Oppressed," in *The Cyber Cultures Reader*, ed. David Bell and Barbara M. Kennedy (New York: Routledge, 2000), 376.

38. These are all actual places that my students have worked.

BIBLIOGRAPHY

Allatson, Paul. "Coyote." In *Key Terms in Latino/a Cultural and Literary Studies*, 80–81. Cambridge, MA: Blackwell, 2007.

Anzaldúa, Gloria. *Borderland/La Frontera: The New Mestiza*. 3rd ed. San Francisco: Aunt Lute, 2007.

Barthes, Roland. *Camera Lucida: Reflections on Photography*. Translated by Richard Howard. New York: Hill and Wang, 1982.

Bender, Tisha. *Discussion-Based Online Teaching to Enhance Student Learning: Theory, Practice, and Assessment.* Sterling, VA: Stylus, 2012.

Blackwell, Deanna M. "Sidelines and Separate Spaces: Making Education Anti-Racist for Students of Color." *Race Ethnicity and Education* 13, no. 4 (2010): 473–94.

Bloom, Benjamin. *The Taxonomy of Educational Objectives*. New York: Longman, 1956.

Bobbit, John Franklin. *The Curriculum*. Chicago: Houghton Mifflin, 1918.

Cabrera, Nolan L., Elisa L. Meza, and Roberto Dr. Cintli Rodriguez. "The Fight for Mexican American Studies in Tucson." North American Congress on Latin America (NACLA), December 8, 2011. https://nacla.org/article/fight-mexican-american-studies-tucson.

Cantú, Norma E. "Centering the Margins: A Chicana in the English Classroom." In *Race in the College Classroom: Pedagogy and Politics*, edited by Bonnie TuSmith and Maureen T. Reddy, 226–38. New Brunswick, NJ: Rutgers University Press, 2002.

Castañeda, Antonia I. "Engendering the History of Alta California 1769–1848: Gender, Sexuality, and the Family." *California History* 76, nos. 2/3 (1997): 230–59.

Center for History and New Media. "Activity-Tracing the Route of a Bracero." *Bracero History Archive*. Accessed January 25, 2019. http://braceroarchive.org/items/show/3009.

Dare, Alexa. "(Dis)Embodied Difference in the Online Class: Vulnerability, Visibility, and Social Justice." *Journal of Online Learning and Teaching* 7, no. 2 (2011): 279–87.

Davidson, Kathy, and David Theo Goldberg. *The Future of Learning: Institutions in a Digital Age*. John D and Katherine T. McArthur Foundation Reports on Digital Media and Learning. Cambridge, MA: MIT Press, 2009. https://clalliance.org/wp-content/uploads/files/Future_of_Learning.pdf.

Denson, Nida. "Do Curricular and Co-curricular Activities Influence Racial Bias? A Meta-Analysis." *Review of Educational Resources* 79, no. 2 (2009): 805–38.

Djikic, Maja, Keith Oatley, and Mihnea C. Moldoveanu. "Reading Other Minds: Effects of Literature on Empathy." *Scientific Study of Literature* 3 (2013): 28–47.

English, Cathie. "Finding a Voice in a Threaded Discussion Group: Talking about Literature Online." *English Journal* 97, no. 1 (2007): 56–61.

Fierros, Cindy O., and Dolores Delgado Bernal. "Vamos a Pláticar: The Contours of Platicas as Chicana/Latina Feminist Methodology." *Chicana/Latina Studies: The Journal of Mujeres Activas en Letras y Cambia Social* 15, no. 2 (2016): 98–121.

González, Juan Carlos, and Edwardo L. Portillos. "Teaching from a Critical Perspective/ Enseñado de una Perspectiva Crítica: Conceptualization, Reflection, and Application of Chicana/o Pedagogy." *International Journal of Critical Pedagogy* 4, no. 1 (2012): 18–34.

Haraway, Donna. *Simians, Cyborgs, and Women: The Reinvention of Nature*. New York: Routledge, 1991.

Ho, Jennifer. "When the Political Is Personal: Life on the Multiethnic Margins." In *Race in the College Classroom: Pedagogy and Politics*, edited by Bonnie

TuSmith and Maureen T. Reddy, 62–70. New Brunswick, NJ: Rutgers University Press, 2002.

Hu-DeHart, Evelyn. "Ethnic Studies in U.S. Higher Education: History Development and Goals." In *Handbook of Research on Multicultural Education*, 2nd ed., edited by James A. Banks and Cherry A. McGee Banks, 869–81. San Francisco: Jossey-Bass, 2004.

June, Audrey Williams. "The Invisible Labor of Minority Professors." *Chronicle of Higher Education*, November 8, 2015.

Kidd, David Comer, and Emanuele Castano. "Reading Literary Fiction Improves Theory of Mind." *Science* 18 (2013): 377–80.

Meacham, Rebecca. "The Entanglements of Teaching *Nappy Hair*." In *Race in the College Classroom: Pedagogy and Politics*, edited by Bonnie TuSmith and Maureen T. Reddy, 71–83. New Brunswick, NJ: Rutgers University Press, 2002.

Oatley, Keith. "Fiction: Simulation of Social Worlds." *Trends in Cognitive Science* 20, no. 8 (August 2016): 618–28.

Peñalosa, Fernando. "Toward an Operational Definition of the Mexican American." *Aztlán: A Journal of Chicano Studies* 1, no. 1 (1970): 1–12.

Pérez-Torres, Rafael. "Chicano Culture Reclaiming Our America: Coyotes at the Border." *American Literature: A Journal of Literary History, Criticism, and Bibliography* 67, no. 4 (December 1995): 815–24.

Powers, Peter Kerry. "The Ghost in the Collaborative Machine: The White Male Teacher in the Multicultural Classroom." In *Race in the College Classroom: Pedagogy and Politics*, edited by Bonnie TuSmith and Maureen T. Reddy, 28–39. New Brunswick, NJ: Rutgers University Press, 2002.

Sándoval, Chela. "New Sciences: Cyborg Feminism and the Methodology of the Oppressed." In *The Cyber Cultures Reader*, edited by David Bell and Barbara M. Kennedy, 374–89. New York: Routledge, 2000.

Sleeter, Christine E. *The Academic and Social Value of Ethnic Studies: A Research Review.* Washington, DC: National Education Association, 2011. www.nea.org/assets/docs/NBI-2010-3-value-of-ethnic-studies.pdf.

Social Sciences Feminist Network Research Interest Group. "The Burden of Invisible Work in Academia: Social Inequalities and Time Use in Five University Departments." *Humboldt Journal of Social Relations* 39 (2017): 228–45.

Strauss, Valerie. "Texas GOP Rejects 'Critical Thinking' Skills. Really." *Washington Post*, July 9, 2012. https://www.washingtonpost.com/blogs/answer-sheet/post/texas-gop-rejects-critical-thinking-skillsreally/2012/07/08/gJQAHNpFXW_blog.html.

Totenberg, Nina. "Trump Presses Case that 'Mexican' Judge Curiel Is Biased Against Him." NPR, June 4, 2016. https://www.npr.org/2016/06/04/480714972/trump-presses-case-that-mexican-judge-curiel-is-biased-against-him.

Valk, Frank Vander. "Identity, Power, and Representation in Virtual Environments." *Journal of Online Learning and Teaching* 4, no. 2 (2008): 205–11.

Voithofer, Rick. "Nomadic Epistemologies and Performative Pedagogies in Online Education." *Educational Theory* 52, no. 4 (2002): 479–94.

Wray, Amanda. "Race, Region, and Ethos." *Pedagogy: Critical Approaches to Teaching Literature, Language, Composition, and Culture* 17, no. 1 (2017): 59–76.

PART IV

HISTORICIZING THE MOMENT, HISTORICIZING THE CURRICULUM

CHAPTER 13

A DU BOISIAN APPROACH TO MAKING BLACK LIVES MATTER IN THE CLASSROOM (AND BEYOND)

DERRICK R. BROOMS AND DARRYL A. BRICE

In this chapter, we interrogate and reflect critically on our experiences as Black male professors who teach sociology courses focused on race, racism, diversity, and urban experiences. In these courses, we use a critical race pedagogy approach informed by W. E. B. Du Bois's pioneering work to incorporate some of the ongoing experiences and perspectives from the Black Lives Matter movement in our teaching. Du Bois's work has a particular appeal to us as his work was rooted firmly in Black communities. As Wright offered, "Du Bois desired to establish a long term program of research on Blacks to offset the biased and unscientific car window sociology studies littering the existing sociological and social science literature at the turn of the twentieth century."[1] As sociologists have argued, there is both a need to center race in our teaching and a clear need to "reposition" race in our research in the "post-racial Obama age."[2] Given the landscape of national politics and policies, such as relegating some Black activists to the category of "extremists" and akin to a "terrorist group," how we teach about race (and racism) is not just a teaching exercise but, as we see it in the case discussed in this chapter, an effort aimed at affirming Black humanity.[3]

In particular, we explicate discussions and learning of *how* Black lives matter through three primary means: (a) grounding our teaching within a historical approach; (b) engaging students in critical conversations regarding contemporary issues and experiences of Black lives in Black communities and across the US; and (c) developing assignments that ask students to make connections between past and current realities (e.g., from Dred Scott to Ferguson). We draw on lessons from events in places like Ferguson (Michael Brown), Chicago (Laquan McDonald and Rekia Boyd), and Baltimore (Freddie Gray) as specific cases in which to interrogate our lives, roles, and responsibilities as educators in teaching for change and engaging students through a critical race pedagogy. In the next section, we offer a brief discussion of our teaching approach, primarily centered on Du Bois's work and critical race pedagogy; in the second half of the chapter, we turn attention to a specific discussion of our classroom teaching efforts. We conclude by discussing several pedagogical strategies that educators can adopt in their teaching praxis.

TEACHING APPROACH

Given our aim of centering Black lives and Black experiences in our teaching, we engage a Du Boisian approach to our teaching, which is informed by critical race pedagogy (CRP). Teaching from a CRP lens works well when teaching the aforementioned subject matter because Du Bois was one of the first people to employ this pedagogical strategy. With a relentless pursuit, Du Bois researched and studied the lives of Black people well before it was fashionable to do so or supported by white academicians. Further, with his well-established Atlanta School of Sociology, Du Bois was able to educate and train myriad Black scholars, and he incorporated the community into his efforts as well. As Black male professors who teach sociology, we are indebted to and privileged to model our teaching approach after Du Bois and take intentional efforts to engage the Black community in our work.

A DU BOISIAN APPROACH TO TEACHING

Postman and Weingartner start their book *Teaching as a Subversive Activity* with two assumptions. First, they note that the survival of our society "is threatened by an increasing number of unprecedented and, to date, insoluble problems." Second, they urge us to take action; they assert, "If you do not know which of these is indisputable and which is questionable, you have just finished reading this book."[4] In other words, they suggest that if teachers are not willing to confront, grapple with, and address societal ills affecting Black communities in the classroom, then their chapters will be of little use to you. We echo this statement for ourselves and our current chapter: let us understand teaching as a central action involved not only in CRP, but also in that teaching affects the formation and nurturing of Black communities in the classroom and beyond. Further, knowing these problems exist presents a more confounding predicament for educators because you must choose to act or remain complicit with the oppressive status quo. As Black educators, we understand our teaching charge and responsibilities; additionally, we vehemently reject nihilistic notions about extrajudicial killings of Black people in the United States. For us, teaching about the importance and value of Black lives and communities, as well as the Black Lives Matter (BLM) movement in our classrooms, is not just a pedagogical strategy to make a grand statement about a social problem. We are teaching for our lives and the lives of other Black people and Black communities. As professors, we believe and know that we can and do make a difference in the lives of our students by considering what we teach, how we teach, and why we teach.

Within a sociological perspective, one of the ways that we engage students with a historical perspective informed by past and current realities in our classes is to link our teaching of Black lives and communities to the work of Dr. W. E. B. Du Bois. Du Bois's contributions to the field of sociology are too voluminous to catalog here and yet, ironically, his work is largely omitted by mainstream academics. To paraphrase noted historian Howard Zinn (himself paraphrasing St. Augustine), omission is worse than lying because if we omit something (such as people and community members or particular historical facts) it is as if they never existed. However, if we lie about something (e.g., regarding their presence, role, or contribution), then at least others have a basis to interrogate our work and check the accuracy of our information. A good example of this omission occurred during our doctoral training. Both authors received doctorate degrees from the same graduate program where the works of Du Bois, and other Black scholar-activists like Ida B. Wells and Joyce Ladner, were never required reading in any of our sociology classes. Therefore, it is imperative to us that our students, regardless of their discipline or area of study, are aware of Du Bois's legacy as well as how much his works directly relate to sociology, race, history, teaching, research, and even Black Lives Matter (BLM)—both historically and contemporarily.

A brief glance at the titles of three of his more popular books displays his deep concern for Black lives: *The Philadelphia Negro* (1896), *The Souls of Black Folk* (1903 [1969]), and *Black Reconstruction in America* (1935). In *The Souls of Black Folk*, Du Bois stated, "Daily the Negro is coming more and more to look upon law and justice, not as protecting safeguards, but as sources of humiliation and oppression. The laws are made by men who have little interest in him; they are executed by men who have absolutely no motive for treating the black people with courtesy or consideration; and, finally, the accused law-breaker is tried, not by his peers, but too often by men who would rather punish ten innocent Negroes than let one guilty one escape."[5] Over a half century later, this prophetic quote is applicable still when addressing the extrajudicial killings of unarmed Black people in America. And, to be sure, we also hold concerns for all Black lives, regardless of age, status, sexuality, or other social identities.

ENACTING CRITICAL RACE PEDAGOGY

Given the ways that whiteness is privileged in academia and across wider society, we also engage critical race pedagogy into our teaching to complement our Du Boisian approach. Lynn defined CRP as "an analysis of racial, ethnic, and gender subordination in education that relies mostly on the perceptions, experiences, and counterhegemonic practices of educators of color."[6] Most importantly, this approach leads to a broad interpretation of emancipatory and pedagogical strategies aimed at honoring the humanity of all students.[7] Three tenets of a liberatory pedagogy are useful here: (a) teaching from a multicultural perspective, (b) encouraging and supporting cross-cultural dialogue in the classroom, and (c) affirming students and the diverse histories that they bring to the learning community.

Giroux theorized teachers as transformative intellectuals; in this capacity, he stressed that teachers take active responsibility for raising critical questions about their subject matter and pedagogical approach in conjunction with their goals. We grounded our lives in developing our teaching philosophies; that is, we interrogated our cities, neighborhoods, learning, miseducation, and the institutions that filled these to gain greater clarity on how our teaching can matter to our students. We believe that centering Black lives (and Blackness) in our teaching disrupts the status quo, resists dominant and deficit narratives of Black life, and rejects hegemonic teaching praxis. We use our Du Boisian and CRP approach without apologies, especially given the ways that Black bodies continue to be under assault daily and the pervasive nature of anti-Blackness in the US (and beyond). Thus, we can interrogate how Blackness is regarded and how Black lives are treated across a range of social institutions—such as schools and the criminal justice system—as well as within wider society. All too often, many of these sites and institutions are places for Black suffering.[8] Thus, making Black lives matter in the classroom is also aimed at elevating our students' critical consciousness and critical awareness. Additionally, our own experiences as Black men not only inform our teaching but also the ways in which we see our work as a scaffolding for our students' experiences; in effect, we are teaching for change, lifting them up, and inviting them to be co-creators of knowledge. In the following sections, we provide a few examples of our teaching praxis. In the main, we speak collectively from the "I" perspective.

HISTORICALLY GROUNDED CONTEXTS FOR TEACHING

Students often enroll in my (Dr. Brice) Introduction to Sociology courses expecting to take a "regular" sociology class. By "regular" I mean "white" sociology. "White sociology refers to those aspects of sociology designed more for the justification of racist institutions and practices than objective analysis of human institutions and behavior."[9] Consequently, students expect to embark on an academic journey that is like most of their other classes where contributions of dead white men dominate the discipline and people of color are rarely mentioned. Grounding my teaching in a historical context allows me to elevate and talk about how much people of color like Du Bois contributed to American sociology. This historical lens helps introduce students to sociology as a discipline and can help students map their learning across the curriculum. Also, this historical lens can help enhance students' foundation for future and complementary courses. Additionally, this approach legitimates teaching about the Black Lives Matter movement by showing how past events influence contemporary phenomena.

I start off my Introduction to Sociology classes by covering some of the leading theorists in the textbook chosen for the course. When addressing this topic, it would almost be blasphemous not to mention Karl Marx,

Emile Durkheim, and Max Weber. These men are usually referred to as the "Big 3" in the field of sociology. It would be quite rare for an individual to take an introductory-level course in sociology and not hear these three people mentioned. However, it is not uncommon for W. E. B. Du Bois to be left out of these courses entirely. For this reason, I teach about the "Big 4" instead of the "Big 3." By learning about Du Bois alongside these other figures, students can start to realize and appreciate how significant Du Bois was in and to sociology.[10] Further, as I explain why his legacy is/was omitted, students start to process how race and politics influence how people are treated and perceived in society.

Furthermore, once students are introduced to Du Bois as a key figure in the history and development of sociological work on race, I use some of his works to engage them on deeper levels about contemporary race relations in the United States. Wortham stated, "*The Philadelphia Negro* is a treatise on empirical sociology and stratification as much of the book is devoted to documenting racial inequality as it relates to living conditions, occupational opportunities, and education."[11] This book allows students to see how long research on racial inequality has been conducted and how we can apply some of the findings to our lives today. Du Bois rigorously researched Black lives and used various qualitative and quantitative methods to do so. I also pose questions to the class that originate from *Souls of Black Folk*. For instance, I engage the class in a discussion about what they think Du Bois meant when he quipped, "The problem of the twentieth century is the problem of the color-line,—the relation of the darker to the lighter races of men in Asia and Africa, in America and the islands of the sea."[12] This quote alone has led some students to bring up the extrajudicial killings of Black people in the US as an example of problems that exist today as a result of the color line. I have used this quote to frame discussions about BLM directly, but often students make the connection themselves. This approach is also helpful in class because there is often division between students on how they feel about race relations in the United States, especially about BLM. When I begin discussions by pointing to Du Bois's work at the turn of the twentieth century (and even some of his later work), the class has a clear example of the racial divide created by the color line.

As a sociologist, I have often heard from colleagues that I am lucky because I get to "teach the fun stuff." There is some truth to this statement, but ultimately what is implied is that unlike the "hard" sciences, I get to teach subjects that students enjoy. My response to statements such as these is that it is not fun teaching sexism to men, racism to white students, or homophobia to heterosexual students. The point here is that in a collegiate setting the professor has the choice to teach difficult subject matter; one has the choice to teach through a critical pedagogical lens as well. As a professor, I do not shy away from topics because they might be difficult to teach or because students might have a negative reaction. Instead, I have found ways to engage students in difficult topics like BLM (difficult because of the lack of understanding about what BLM is and the broad differences in thought about BLM) by weaving them into the content of the course. In other words, I do not have to depart from the scheduled lesson plan to take time out of the class to teach about BLM. I have found ways to make BLM a part of the curriculum. There are two areas specifically where I have used BLM to help students process and understand course content: C. Wright Mills's sociological imagination and Max Weber's inconvenient facts.

The sociological imagination, as articulated by C. Wright Mills, encourages students to think about how personal troubles can be influenced by larger social forces in society. This concept pushes students to see how biography and history intersect. Students struggle with this abstract concept if they do not have tangible examples of how this applies to society. Knowing this, I use the opportunity to insert BLM, police brutality, and extrajudicial killings of Blacks as prime examples of the larger social structure and the intersection of biography and history. First, we address data so they can begin to see trends emerge around race and policing. For example, from 2007 to 2013, "80 percent of the people Philadelphia police officers had shot were African American, even though less than half of the city's population is African American."[13] I purposefully use Philadelphia data because it coincides with Du Bois's work. Furthermore, I use these types of data to help students think about how structures and institutions impact individuals. Next, I incorporate some of the individuals who have been victims of police brutality and police shootings, like Michael Brown, Eric Garner, and Rekia Boyd, to name a few. I explain the circumstances under which they encountered police and, when available, I show videos of the incident—or of peoples' responses to the incidents and events. Students very quickly start to apply Mills's concept to these events. Many students easily make the connection that these individuals and their lives are part of a larger historical context of aggressive policing in Black communities.

Max Weber's concept of inconvenient facts fits well with this type of historical analysis. While Mills's sociological imagination is useful in helping students see how BLM is rooted in a larger historical context, Weber's analysis is important because students who are resistant to learning about BLM can start to process why they have aversions to it. Weber asserted that sociologists should teach their students to become comfortable with dealing with inconvenient facts. Inconvenient facts are "those pieces of evidence that contradict what you have always believed and/or want to believe about the social world."[14] Students come to class armed with several misconceptions about society. For instance, there are always students who believe that we live in a "post-racial" society. However, after presenting them with studies that show white-sounding names on résumés get more callbacks than résumés with Black-sounding names and that whites with a criminal record fare better in the job market than college-educated Blacks without a criminal record, students start to understand this Weberian concept.[15] Moreover, as the class processes this information, I encourage them to think about the racial inequities that Du Bois addressed in the 1900s and how relevant they still are today. BLM and disparate policing of Blacks is a major inconvenient fact for many students. Further, video footage where students see unarmed Blacks being chased, harassed, assaulted, and shot is oftentimes an inconvenient fact and an affront to students' visual and auditory senses.[16]

Not all students respond positively to this lesson. Some still argue that the shootings or assaults might be justified. For instance, as Douglas Julien's chapter in this volume similarly remarks, some students use a color-blind ideological approach to minimize racism or even, sometimes unintentionally, to engage cultural racism in justifying the actions by suggesting that the Black victims' actions jeopardized their own lives.[17] I incorporate a number of strategies to help students connect the dots, such as using a variety of news sources, connecting their viewing to assigned readings, giving writing assignments, and engaging in critical dialogue about past and current events. Our overarching goal and the most important aspect of teaching this way is that it can force students to confront these incidents from a sociohistorical intellectual point of view. This runs counter to the myopic view that most media outlets show in reference to these events.

Teaching from this Du Boisian historical framework is important because many students come to class with blind spots, given their lack of critical historical knowledge.[18] Loewen connects this lack of historical knowledge to the lack of understanding around the impact that historical events and social structures have on individuals in the present. He coined the term *soclexia* to represent this lack of understanding that plagues many of our students. Additionally, as mentioned, grounding classes within a sociological imagination keeps the intersections of biography and history at the fore of students' consciousness. It is important to keep our students aware of the role that past events play in the present and help them to avoid soclexia. Thus, teaching about a social movement like BLM from a historical perspective is vital because it helps students avoid the aforementioned pitfalls. More importantly, it forces students to address the fact that their present actions or inactions in regard to BLM will affect the future of students to come.

Lastly, teaching about Black lives and communities from a Du Boisian context gives students the opportunity to learn about other omissions in the field of sociology, namely Black women and their manifold contributions, from Ida B. Wells and Anna Julia Cooper to Joyce Ladner and Jacquelyn Johnson Jackson. Ida B. Wells was a founding member of the National Association for the Advancement of Colored People (NAACP), and her work on lynchings and her international anti-lynching campaign are paramount to current studies of Black social movement writ large and the Black Lives Matter movement more particularly. The contributions of Black women also must be brought from the margins to the center in teaching, given the prominent roles they continue to play in Black families and communities as well as in larger society. To point, in what ways can our students appreciate the contemporary movement for Black lives, co-founded by Alicia Garza, Opal Tometi, and Patrisse Cullors, absent from centering the contributions of Black women?

Du Bois concludes, "But what of black women? . . . I most sincerely doubt if any other race of women could have brought its fineness up through so devilish a fire."[19] This quote is fitting given Black women's contributions to sociology and the "devilish fire" that students in sociology need to address police brutality and human rights. Further, using Du Bois in this context allows the opportunity to bring in the work of civil rights activist Joyce Ladner, who challenged the validity of the field of "white sociology." Ladner stated, "But sociology, like history, economics and psychology, exists in a domain where color, ethnicity and social class are of primary importance. And, as long as this holds true, it is impossible for sociology to claim it maintains value neutrality in its approach."[20] This perspective helps students learn that identity characteristics impact how institutions interact with individuals in society. Equally important, it gives students the intellectual freedom to question their commonly held assumptions about BLM and disparate policing practices.

CONNECTING THE CURRENT TO THE PAST: BLACK LIVES IN PERSPECTIVE

In considering the possibilities of connecting the current to the past, I (Dr. Brooms) focus on my teaching of Race in the U.S. In this course, I help students connect current events and realities to past events.[21] Thus, this teaching approach serves as a bridge to the historical foundations used in teaching Introduction to Sociology. Here, the primary goal is to help students see the continuation and continuities of our social world—across time and space and across various social institutions as well.

I use my race and ethnicity course as a general introduction to the sociology of race and ethnic relations, with a particular emphasis on the situations and experiences of Black and Latinx people. I inform students that we begin the course from the basis that race and ethnicity are socially and politically constructed phenomena: that is, they are phenomena that vary significantly across time and place, and that ultimately rest on supra-individual processes of group boundary formation, segregation, and the creation of inter-group (racial) hierarchies. On the syllabus, I inform students that the two basic objectives of the course are to understand: 1) the social, political, and historical conditions under which segregation, racial hierarchies, and racial conflict emerge; and 2) the institutions through which racial boundaries and hierarchies are produced and reproduced in the United States. Two of our early readings include a selection from Dr. Du Bois's *Souls of Black Folk* and his 1944 piece, "The Prospect of a World without Racial Conflict." These two readings, among a number of others, help ground the students' understanding of race as a social construct and the ways that it can vary across time.

One way that I approach reaching these goals is by examining a variety of viewpoints on the criminal justice system. During the fall 2016 semester, I assigned students to read selections from Angela Davis on the "prison industrial complex" and Michelle Alexander's work on mass incarceration. By using these scholars' work, I engage students in conversations about intersectionality, policing, and the criminal justice system as a significant social organizing institution. I offer a variety of readings in different semesters, so that students can read from different viewpoints. In addition to Davis and Alexander, I also assigned students to watch Ava Duvernay's documentary *13TH*. Using the readings and the documentary, students could sharpen their historical perspective and begin to connect current realities to past laws, practices, and events.

Perhaps tragically, these readings and documentary complement current events as well, such as the recent shooting deaths of Philando Castile and Alton Sterling.[22] The current (and ongoing) events allow students to situate terms, concepts, theories, and other research within a contemporary perspective. My aim is to push students to understand that people's lives, families, and communities are connected to the research, reporting, and readings I share. By providing local and national stories, and by tapping into current events, I hope that students see the connections of our class to the real world. Some of the written work I engage students in includes reflection and analytic papers. In the reflection papers, I provide students with a prompt and they are required to write a two- to three-page response. For instance, I ask students to respond to writing prompts such as: How can we use Du Bois's writing to analyze some of our current realities? Or, more explicitly, use a passage from chapter 1 ("Of Our Spiritual Strivings") of *The Souls of Black Folk* and make an argument about the impact and meaning of race across a social institution of your choosing. I request that students incorporate at least three textual references in their paper and allow them to use evidence and support from any recent news in the matter as well.

I also use statistical data to help students "see" how race plays out within the criminal justice system and in police/policing activities. In particular, I use "stop-and-frisk" data from the New York Civil Liberties Union.[23] As one of my teaching files, I created a document that details stop-and-frisk data from 2002 through 2013 and distribute this to each student at the beginning of a class period focused on the criminal justice system. The document includes the NYCLU website where I pulled the data from and a description of what is documented in the data. I then provide students with two instructions. The first is aimed at critical thinking; I ask them to read the document and think about what these data show. The second instruction is intended to generate discussion; I ask students to discuss their thoughts about the data with a classmate (or two)—for the sake of ease, I ask them to discuss it with a classmate who is in close proximity. I inform students that they have five minutes for their conversations. I want the conversation to be brief, and my goal is to use this short conversation to springboard the class into a larger discussion about the implications of police data for social (in)justice. In an effort to provide variance, some semesters, after providing students with time to reflect on their own, I have given them six or seven minutes to jot down their thoughts through a free writing assignment (asking students to "think" on paper without censoring or editing themselves even before they have had a chance to formulate their responses).

In the class-wide conversations that follow from the initial writing and small group discussion, the stop-and-frisk data provide an opportunity to discuss policing practices at both the local level (in New York City or within our own city) and national level. In addition, these conversations also point us to specific events that continue to demand our attention, such as the uprisings and protests in Baltimore, Maryland (Freddie Gray); Ferguson, Missouri (Michael Brown); Oakland, California (Oscar Grant), and Chicago, Illinois (Rekia Boyd, Laquan McDonald, and a number of others). As professors, given our familiarity with cities such as Baltimore and Chicago and our experiences in traveling to Ferguson (and other local sites), we also are able to share with students our own insights from sociological and personal points of view. Our initial goals thus complicate some of the dominant narratives that often surround these events—such as engaging students in conversations about why particular images are used repeatedly and circulated within the media when discussing or reporting about individuals connected to some of these events (like the image of Trayvon Martin using hand symbols in a photograph, which was used to devalue his humanity and criminalize him posthumously). Our further goals, moreover, push students beyond their own peripheries, perspectives, and ways of thinking. Even more explicitly, I can engage students in a discussion (either through class conversation or through written assignments) about how the Black Lives Matter movement matters to our learning or even what we can learn from this movement.

In this course, the cumulative effect of connecting the current to the past creates a range of potential conversations and discussion opportunities. During one semester, in an assignment near the end of the course, I asked students to write a four- to five-page analytic paper about the contemporary practices of the criminal justice system within a historical perspective (e.g., using their sociological imagination). In this assignment, students have connected their analyses of contemporary phenomena to such historical contexts as the Dred Scott decision, convict leasing, the vestiges of African enslavement, and other practices that have devalued and denigrated Black life. The selection of readings for the topic area work in combination with our previous in-class discussions, writing assignments, and visual data (i.e., the stop-and-frisk data and appropriate video selections) to help students begin to see these events beyond the scope of isolated incidents.

As an example, a number of students responded that viewing the video for Joe Budden's 2016 song "Freedom" that I showed in class was quite informative and helped synthesize some of the major points of our discussion—such as Du Bois's writings about how Blackness is problematized in US society and how society is racially stratified by the color line. The video begins with images from inside the car of the shooting death of Philando Castile and quickly switches to images from the Jim Crow era, showing a Confederate flag and an image from Elizabeth Eckford's walk to Central High School in Little Rock, Arkansas. Overwhelmingly, the video footage overlays some of the current events (e.g., activists in Missouri with their hands in the air—from the popularized "hands up, don't shoot" rallies—and footage of Walter Scott running away from a police officer in North Charleston, South Carolina) with historical images of civil rights movement (e.g., civil rights marchers peacefully demonstrating, civil rights activists being physically and openly attacked by police officers, and the Black Panthers). Powerful, also, are Budden's lyrics throughout the song; in providing a counter-narrative about the value of Black lives and the permanence of racism, he invites listeners to consider the historical legacies of police malfeasance and violence perpetrated against Black bodies.

In one verse, Budden makes reference to "dangers" that Black bodies pose to themselves; in a succession of lines, he specifically cites Sandra Bland's death (while imprisoned at Waller County Jail in Hempstead, Texas) and the killings of Tamir Rice (on a playground in Cleveland, Ohio) and Eric Garner (on a public street in New York City). I also have used Janelle Monáe's "Hell You Talmbout" (2013) and Public Enemy's "Fight the Power" (1990) as songs for discussion. I find that using songs can be effective to convey a range of messages, providing pictorial and lyrical representations, and, particularly, they are germane in teaching about Black life and Black lives. As can be imagined, instructors can choose from a wide variety of music genres—primarily based on their own interests and also on the messages conveyed. The appeal and benefits of hip-hop, especially as related to teaching about race and social realities, are that a number of songs center on and stem from the lives and livelihoods of youth in urban environments and are focused on social issues, such as racial inequality. Clearly, in considering classes that focus on race, not only does race matter in how people experience the social world but also it helps unravel how race matters.

CONCLUDING THOUGHTS

The heart of this chapter is situated in showing how a Du Boisian approach to teaching can be incorporated in many different ways. Although we discussed different classes in this chapter, we do not see teaching from one class to another as distinctly different. Instead, we think about our teaching within a continuum that connects students' early learning experiences to future and complementary courses. Understandably, we see Introduction to Sociology and Race in the U.S. as foundation courses from which students can build their sociological acumen and understand how situating "community" in teaching can have important pedagogical and learning outcomes.

As we have shown, the structure of classroom discussions and lectures, including inquiry-based pedagogy, serves as an important tool to encourage student engagement and learning; these pedagogical tools can allow students to become partners in the learning process and deepen their understanding of content knowledge.[24] In addition, building relationships with students throughout the course can allow for more robust in-class experiences for students and can help develop the classroom into a collective learning environment.[25] Given the importance of Du Bois's work and Black Lives Matter, the following are critical pedagogical strategies that we use in our classes to build a dynamic classroom.

TEACH WHO YOU ARE, FROM THE "I" PERSPECTIVE, AND FOR THE COMMUNITY

A central component of our teaching praxis is teaching from and through a communal perspective. This strategy has the potential to create environments where students share because we as professors allow our communities and ourselves to be seen in more transparent ways. In sharing stories and speaking from the "I" perspective, we model the behaviors that we want our students to engage in. For instance, as we discern our connections to communities in our classes, we acknowledge the triumphs and struggles in our home cities and our communities. Our main goal is to help students bring down their walls and be willing to share, learn, and grow through the sharing and self-reflective processes. As we share our own lived experiences, as well as our research and racial justice interests and experiences, we hope to deepen some of the topics that we cover in class.

For instance, Dr. Brooms traveled to Ferguson, Missouri, the day after the verdict regarding the killing of Michael Brown to support the community. During this trip, I engaged in community with many people in Ferguson, talked with community members (local and from afar), and talked with reporters. I share some of the stories and images from my trip with students to provide them with another perspective regarding the events and responses. We have found that students are more willing to engage in learning, discussion, and sharing as we model these behaviors and interaction styles. We do not try to hide who we are and where we are from. We are Black male professors who grew up on the South Side of Chicago and in West Baltimore, respectively, and we explain how these experiences have shaped our lives, perspectives, and critical lenses. It is important to let students know who we are if we expect them to reveal who they are, their knowledge gaps, and their cultural wealth.

DEVELOP AND USE STUDENT-CENTERED ASSIGNMENTS

It is important that our students question their feelings and beliefs about various communities, social phenomena, and current realities. We take this approach in teaching students about Black Lives Matter so that they better understand and appreciate it as a movement and not a moment.[26] One of the ways we do this is *to engage students where they are*, and a key strategy we employ is using student-centered assignments. In these assignments, we require students to engage in critical self-reflection about their own ideas, assumptions, stereotypes, beliefs, and identity development. The assignments require students to write their racial narratives, take on the role of the other, and "do" sociology to help build awareness and understanding. As an example, Dr. Brooms required students to interview two individuals from different generations about various lived experiences with race and/or racism. Students not only learned from their own interviews (self-generated knowledge) but also learned from their peers' interviews. In a class of thirty-five students, this assignment allowed us to bring in voices and narratives of seventy additional people to expand our perspectives.

Similarly, Dr. Brice also required students to conduct intergenerational interviews with a relative who was involved in their socialization process. This type of interview positioned students as co-creators of knowledge by asking tough questions about racial ideologies and experiences.

Students then analyzed their interview data and interrogated how their racial ideologies aligned with or diverged from those of the interviewee. Consequently, both of our interview assignments, as well as other types of student-centered assignments, provide ample opportunities to help sharpen students' sociological eye by incorporating a Du Boisian approach. Not only does this approach help students better understand their own individual development; it also shows how students are connected to communities and how communities inform our socialization, individual and collective perspectives, and connectedness.

NOTES

1. Earl Wright II, *The First American School of Sociology: W. E. B. Du Bois and the Atlanta Sociological Laboratory* (Surrey, UK: Ashgate, 2016), 17.

2. See Derrick R. Brooms and Darryl A. Brice, "Bring the Noise: Black Men Teaching (Race and) White Privilege," *Race and Justice* 7, no. 2 (2017): 144–59; and Sandra L. Barnes, Zandria F. Robinson, and Earl Wright II, eds., *Repositioning Race: Prophetic Research in a Postracial Obama Age* (Albany: SUNY Press, 2014).

3. Jana Winter and Sharon Weinberger, "The FBI's New U.S. Terrorist Threat: 'Black Identity Extremists,'" *Foreign Policy*, October 6, 2017, http://foreignpolicy.com/2017/10/06/the-fbi-has-identified-a-new-domestic-terrorist-threat-and-its-black-identity-extremists. According to the FBI Report published August 3, 2017, "The FBI assesses it is very likely Black Identity Extremist (BIE) perceptions of police brutality against African Americans spurred an increase in premeditated, retaliatory lethal violence against law enforcement and will very likely serve as justification for such violence." Ironically, this report was issued less than two weeks before a group of white nationalists descended upon Charlottesville, Virginia, for a "Unite the Right" rally. The rally clashed with anti-racist protestors and resulted in one death and injuries to nearly three dozen people. Importantly, these events, and others, reveal how new (and old) forms of racism continue their persistence in the US. See also Eduardo Bonilla-Silva, "'*Hilando Fino*': American Racism after Charlottesville," *Contexts* 17, no. 1 (February 2018): 16–27, https://doi.org/10.1177/1536504218766539. Additionally, Charlottesville offered a glimpse into the ways that white-centric and white supremacist ideologies persist.

4. Neil Postman and Charles Weingartner, *Teaching a Subversive Activity* (New York: Delacorte, 1969), xi.

5. W. E. B. Du Bois, *The Souls of Black Folk* (1903; repr., New York: NAL Penguin, 1969), 198.

6. Marvin Lynn, "Toward a Critical Race Pedagogy: A Research Note," *Urban Education* 33, no. 5 (1999): 615.

7. See Paulo Freire, *Pedagogy of the Oppressed* (1970; repr., New York: Bloomsbury Academic, 2003); Henry A. Giroux, "Teachers as Transformative Intellectuals," *Social Education* 49, no. 5 (1985): 376–79; Lynn, "Toward a Critical Race Pedagogy"; Beverly D. Tatum, *Why Are All the Black Kids Sitting Together in the Cafeteria? And Other Conversations about Race* (New York: Basic Books, 1997).

8. For example, see Michael J. Dumas, "Losing an Arm: Schooling as a Site of Black Suffering," *Race, Ethnicity and Education* 17, no. 1 (2014): 1–29.

9. Robert Staples, "What Is Black Sociology? Toward a Sociology of Liberation," in *The Death of White Sociology*, ed. Joyce A. Ladner (Baltimore, MD: Black Classic, 1998), 162.

10. For instance, see Wright, "First American School of Sociology."

11. Robert A. Wortham, *W. E. B. Du Bois and the Sociological Imagination* (Waco, TX: Baylor University Press, 2009), 5.

12. Du Bois, *Souls of Black Folk*, 54.

13. Keeanga-Yamahtta Taylor, *From #BlackLivesMatter to Black Liberation* (Chicago: Haymarket, 2016), 3.

14. Lisa J. McIntyre, *The Practical Skeptic* (New York: McGraw-Hill Education, 2014), 50.

15. Marianne Bertrand and Sendhil Mullainathan, "Are Emily and Greg More Employable Than Lakisha and Jamal? A Field Experiment on Labor Market Discrimination," *American Economic Review* 94, no. 4 (2004): 991–1013; Devah Pager, "The Mark of a Criminal Record," *American Journal of Sociology* 108, no. 5 (2003): 937–75.

16. See Brooms and Brice, "Bring the Noise."

17. See Eduardo Bonilla-Silva, *Racism without Racists: Color-Blind Racism and the Persistence of Racial Inequality in America*, 5th ed. (Lanham, MD: Rowman and Littlefield, 2017).

18. See James Loewen, *Teaching What Really Happened: How to Avoid the Tyranny of Textbooks and Get Students Excited about Doing History* (New York: Teachers College Press, 2010); Jessica C. Nelson, Glenn Adams, and Phia S. Salter, "The Marley Hypothesis: Denial of Racism Reflects Ignorance of History," *Psychological Science* 24, no. 2 (2013): 213–18.

19. W. E. B. Du Bois, *Darkwater: Voices from Within the Veil* (New York: Kraus-Thomson, 1975), 171.

20. Joyce A. Ladner, introduction to *The Death of White Sociology: Essays on Race and Culture*, ed. Joyce A. Ladner (1973; repr., Baltimore, MD: Black Classic, 1998), xix.

21. See Theresa Rajack-Talley and Derrick R. Brooms, *Living Racism: Through the Barrel of the Book* (New York: Lexington, 2018).

22. At the time of this writing, Jeronimo Yánez, a St. Anthony, Minnesota, police officer, was acquitted of all charges in the shooting death of Philando Castile on July 6, 2016. The vehicle that Castile was traveling in as a passenger,

operated by Diamond Reynolds (his girlfriend) with his toddler daughter in the backseat, was pulled over by Officer Yanez in Falcon Heights, Minnesota. Reynolds captured the fatal shooting via Facebook Live video. Officer Yanez was found not guilty of second-degree manslaughter on June 16, 2017; he also was acquitted of two counts of intentional discharge of a firearm that endangered the safety of others. This ruling joins the throng of others that continue to diminish and degrade Black life, even posthumously.

23. See New York Civil Liberties Union, "Stop-and-Frisk Data," 2016, accessed September 5, 2016, https://www.nyclu.org/en/stop-and-frisk-data.

24. See also Derrick R. Brooms, "Developing Your Teaching Craft: Observations from the Classroom," in *Beginning a Career in Academia: A Guide for Graduate Students of Color*, ed. Dwayne A. Mack, Elwood Watson, and Michelle Madsen Camacho (New York: Routledge, 2014), 160–69.

25. See Darryl A. Brice and Derrick R. Brooms, "Relationships Precede Learning: Reflections on Being and Teaching Students of Color," in *Reflections on Academic Lives: Identities, Struggles, and Triumphs in Graduate School and Beyond*, ed. Staci M. Zavattaro and Shannon K. Orr (New York: Palgrave Macmillan, 2017), 128–30.

26. See Taylor, *From #BlackLivesMatter*.

BIBLIOGRAPHY

Barnes, Sandra L., Zandria F. Robinson, and Earl Wright II, eds. Repositioning Race: Prophetic Research in a Postracial Obama Age. Albany: SUNY Press, 2014.

Bertrand, Marianne, and Sendhil Mullainathan. "Are Emily and Greg More Employable Than Lakisha and Jamal? A Field Experiment on Labor Market Discrimination." American Economic Review 94, no. 4 (2004): 991–1013.

Bonilla-Silva, Eduardo. "'Hilando Fino': American Racism after Charlottesville." Contexts 17, no. 1 (February 2018): 16–27. https://doi.org/10.1177/1536504218766539.

———. Racism without Racists: Color-Blind Racism and the Persistence of Racial Inequality in America. 5th ed. Lanham, MD: Rowman and Littlefield, 2017.

Brice, Darryl A., and Derrick R. Brooms. "Relationships Precede Learning: Reflections on Being and Teaching Students of Color." In Reflections on Academic Lives: Identities, Struggles, and Triumphs in Graduate School and Beyond, edited by Staci M. Zavattaro and Shannon K. Orr, 128–30. New York: Palgrave Macmillan, 2017.

Brooms, Derrick R. "Developing Your Teaching Craft: Observations from the Classroom." In Beginning a Career in Academia: A Guide for Graduate Students of Color, edited by Dwayne A. Mack, Elwood Watson, and Michelle Madsen Camacho, 160–69. New York: Routledge, 2014.

Brooms, Derrick R., and Darryl A. Brice. "Bring the Noise: Black Men Teaching (Race and) White Privilege." Race and Justice 7, no. 2 (2017): 144–59.

Coates, Ta-Nehisi. Between the World and Me. New York: Spiegel and Grau, 2015.

Du Bois, W. E. B. Darkwater: Voices from Within the Veil. New York: Kraus-Thomson, 1975.

———. The Souls of Black Folk. 1903. Reprint, New York: NAL Penguin, 1969.

Dumas, Michael J. "Losing an Arm: Schooling as a Site of Black Suffering." Race, Ethnicity and Education 17, no. 1 (2014): 1–29.

Freire, Paulo. Pedagogy of the Oppressed. 1970. Reprint, New York: Bloomsbury Academic, 2003.

Giroux, Henry A. "Teachers as Transformative Intellectuals." Social Education 49, no. 5 (1985): 376–79.

Ladner, Joyce A., ed. The Death of White Sociology: Essays on Race and Culture. 1973. Reprint, Baltimore, MD: Black Classic, 1998.

Loewen, James. Teaching What Really Happened: How to Avoid the Tyranny of Textbooks and Get Students Excited about Doing History. New York: Teachers College Press, 2010.

Lynn, Marvin. "Toward a Critical Race Pedagogy: A Research Note." Urban Education 33, no. 5 (1999): 606–26.

McIntyre, Lisa J. The Practical Skeptic. New York: McGraw-Hill Education, 2014.

Mills, C. Wright. The Sociological Imagination. New York: Oxford University Press, 1959.

Nelson, Jessica C., Glenn Adams, and Phia S. Salter. "The Marley Hypothesis: Denial of Racism Reflects Ignorance of History." Psychological Science 24, no. 2 (2013): 213–18.

New York Civil Liberties Union. "Stop-and-Frisk Data." 2016. Accessed September 5, 2016. https://www.nyclu.org/en/stop-and-frisk-data.

Pager, Devah. "The Mark of a Criminal Record." American Journal of Sociology 108, no. 5 (2003): 937–75.

Postman, Neil, and Charles Weingartner. Teaching as a Subversive Activity. New York: Delacorte, 1969.

Rajack-Talley, Theresa, and Derrick R. Brooms, eds. Living Racism: Through the Barrel of the Book. New York: Lexington, 2018.

Staples, Robert. "What Is Black Sociology? Toward a Sociology of Liberation." In The Death of White Sociology, edited by Joyce A. Ladner, 161–72. Baltimore, MD: Black Classic, 1998.

Tatum, Beverly D. Why Are All the Black Kids Sitting Together in the Cafeteria? And Other Conversations about Race. New York: Basic Books, 1997.

Taylor, Keeanga-Yamahtta. From #BlackLivesMatter to Black Liberation. Chicago: Haymarket, 2016.

Winter, Jana, and Sharon Weinberger. "The FBI's New U.S. Terrorist Threat: 'Black Identity Extremists.'" Foreign Policy, October 6, 2017. http://foreignpolicy.

com/2017/10/06/the-fbi-has-identified-a-new-domestic-terrorist-threat-and-its-black-identity-extremists.

Wortham, Robert A. W. E. B. Du Bois and the Sociological Imagination. Waco, TX: Baylor University Press, 2009.

Wright, Earl II. The First American School of Sociology: W. E. B. Du Bois and the Atlanta Sociological Laboratory. Surrey, UK: Ashgate, 2016.

Zinn, Howard. A People's History of the United States. 1980. Reprint, New York: Harpers, 2015.

CHAPTER 14

THE RACIAL ORACLE HAS A HISTORY

MARK WILLIAM WESTMORELAND

Whether I am teaching my Philosophy of Race and Racism course or raising concerns about race in any of my other courses, I am met with a curious phenomenon, namely, a lack of historical awareness regarding, first, how the concept of race developed over the last few hundred years and, second, how racism has been embedded in this development. No doubt, students have some vague sense of slavery, lynching, and segregation. Perhaps a few know about Jim Crow laws and the one-drop rule. One or two may even be able describe one of more of the following: *Dred Scott v. Sandford* (1857), *Plessy v. Ferguson* (1896), *Korematsu v. United States* (1944), *Brown v. Board of Education* (1954), or *Loving v. Virginia* (1967). Regardless of their knowledge of the history of race and racism, the overwhelming majority of my students share the perspective, unfortunately, that widespread personal and institutional racism are things that came to an end sometime in the 1960s—synchronous with or shortly following the Civil Rights Act of 1964. They would admit that racism still exists but only as an occasional, accidental episode within a more racially equal society, that racism is, for the most part, exhibited by white supremacist groups, for which this volume's introduction provides a brief overview and context for understanding these moments specifically as *racial* episodes. I do not blame my students. Their failure to understand the historical thread that ties slavery to, for example, contemporary police brutality is not their own fault. Even while I aim to turn that faultlessness into a motivation to take responsibility for a better awareness, their lack of knowledge with regard to eugenics, unfair housing discrimination and loan practices, and racist state violence is not their fault to bear alone. Most of us, their teachers, discuss race in an ahistorical manner, simply talking about current events as if they occur in a vacuum. Even if there is a historical dimension in our discussion, it is often shortsighted or lacking nuance.

I want my students to see themselves as participants within a larger story of humanity, a story that conditions them but also allows them to write its future. A critical pedagogy takes as its starting point the sociohistorical context of people. An individual does not enter the room as a deracialized tabula rasa waiting to have information etched into the walls of their mind. Students enter having already participated in the world. They are already actors within a social matrix and, as such, are continually trying to negotiate their way through racialized quotidian spaces. Therefore, our classrooms ought to be both sites in which students grasp the stakes of the material as it relates to their own lives and sites in which they can practice inclusion and collaboration with their peers. I want them to have the courage to imagine a world of possibilities, to not stop asking questions, to cultivate the tools useful for addressing those questions, to have compassion, and to listen and understand others who form differing opinions on those same pressing questions.

In this chapter, I want to offer some encouragement to fellow teachers by explaining some practices that have worked for me and by providing an example of how to navigate the vicissitudes of classroom pedagogy using a four-pronged strategy that makes conversations about race a productive experience of rupture. Rupture in this context is my way of describing what happens when the white epistemic coding of the typical classroom is problematized, how the dispossession of white epistemic certainty and white mental safety opens up a space for allowing the students to make a personal decision about how they will see their racialized reality. My starting point for talking about race is for students to reflect on the racial dynamics of their own biographies. I want students to tarry with the thought of how race and racism have conditioned their lives. Next, I ask students to take an excursion through a genealogy of the modern concept of race so that they become more aware of the historical development that has led to a reality of racial formation. Third, I have students consider a set of examples of how race and racism are sedimented within the foundation and architecture of sociopolitical life. After considering this issue on the institutional front, my students and I turn to an investigation of illustrations from racialized interpersonal encounters of everyday life.

Two traps should be avoided. First, we ought not quickly move to discussions of horrors of slavery, Native American genocide, or Jim Crow laws. Twenty-first-century students too easily respond, "That's in the past. The civil rights movement from my grandparents' day fixed that stuff." Second, we ought not naively raise (unreflective) stories of interpersonal encounters. Students can easily dismiss the conversation with claims like "I don't do anything racist" or "I never experience racism." In my experience, whenever the personal stories are publicly shared before the heavy lifting of historical and theoretical work has been done, conflicting narratives result because white students assert, often unconsciously, their epistemic privilege. Put differently, while I ask students to journal, for instance, about their own experiences of race and racism, I make the tactical decision of delaying the moment when students share their stories primarily because I have observed that, earlier in the semester, white students do not hear the truth of what peers who are People of Color have to say. I act from a base condition that recognizes how ideas particularly about race have consequences that may often elude students.

IDEAS HAVE (RACIAL) CONSEQUENCES

Many scholars of race argue that it was not until the late eighteenth century that the modern concept of race began to develop any sense of consistency, albeit one that arose as a form of pseudoscience.[1] This modern conception, often exemplified by variations in human phenotypes, assumed that races referred to distinct biological groups of human beings, each with essential characteristics. Members of such groups did not belong to the same family or nation but rather shared inherited physical and cultural traits that differ from those belonging to members of other racial groups.

The association of whiteness with purity is not a new phenomenon. In many European travel journals throughout the early modern and modern eras, we can find accounts of non-whites described as barbarous monsters—as cannibals, those who practice human sacrifice, those who summon evil spirits, and those who commit other transgressions against civilization and decorum; race has been used as a shibboleth for cultural belonging since the sixteenth century.[2] At a later moment in the emergence of a specifically American modernity, one can look at the first entry for "negro" in the first American edition of the *Encyclopedia Britannica* (1798), which describes negroes as ugly, unhappy, vicious, without conscience, and corrupt: "vices the most notorious seem to be the portion of this unhappy race. [Negroes] are strangers to every sentiment of compassion, and are an awful example of the corruption of man when left to himself."[3] These sources, from allegedly objective, rational voices, falsely and dangerously portrayed Black persons as deviant and threatening. Such a voice also appeared in, for example, South Carolina's An Act for the Better Ordering and Governing of Negroes and Slaves (1712) and the Fugitive Slave Act (1850), where individual whites were conditioned to see all Black persons as criminal and potentially dangerous. Such monstrous Calibans from Shakespeare's moment forward needed to be segregated from good, virtuous, white society, which was later unjustly, yet legally, sanctioned in racial zoning statutes that followed *Plessy v. Ferguson*'s central "separate but equal" provision that fostered segregation. White spaces were meant to be kept pure, and the presence of a non-white body was marked as a threat.

Fast-forward to the last few decades and one sees how stop-and-frisk and racial profiling carry on this same logic. The Black person, under the white gaze, is already coded as criminal. "White gazing," George Yancy writes, "is a specific historical practice, socially collective and intersubjective, a process that is dutifully maintained."[4] The white gaze, which maintains the transcendental normativity of whiteness, is the lens and action through which whiteness views Blackness as irrevocably other. This view relates to Sharon D. Raynor's chapter in this volume, "'Survival Is Not an Academic Skill': Life behind the Mask," in which she provides an in-depth discussion about Frantz Fanon's concept of "the other." Under the white gaze, Black *persons* are invisible, that is, they are stripped of their personhood. Their humanity is not seen. At the same time, the Black *body* is hypervisible, which means that the body is already charged with meaning. The hypervisible Black body is known ahead of any particular encounter as something already coded as deviant, criminal, or evil vis-à-vis whiteness as pure and virtuous. Twelve-year-old Tamir Rice can play with his toy on a playground alone in daylight and be killed immediately by a police officer who discharged his weapon before his partner could finish exiting the vehicle and before any words were ever spoken to the child.[5] None of this is simply a matter of one police officer engaging in racism. Such blatant disregard for human life is predicated on social histories that exceed the particularity of any one act of racism. Put differently, the individual acts are part of a larger historical social matrix in which whites are conditioned, most often implicitly, to view Black people suspiciously. Let us not forget that while Black people are dehumanized, whiteness passes through social space uninterrogated and unchallenged due solely to their epidermal hue and having nothing to do with their virtue.

Most white students do not seem to think racism like this occurs with any regularity, and they showcase their assumed epistemic privilege by downplaying or being indifferent to the reality that most Black people experience. So I ask my students to once again reflect on their biographies and consider how race has affected their lives, either by providing them with an unearned advantage or by daily devaluing their existence. There are perfect examples in this volume by Jason E. Cohen, Stephen W. Sheps, and Kerri-Ann M. Smith and Paul M. Buckley in which biographical reflection and analysis are used within their teaching pedagogy. Journals are a key component of what makes my course successful in this regard. Some journal assignments ask students to reflect on specific readings. Others are reflective of their own lives. Throughout the remainder of this chapter, readers will find a few examples of journal assignments that coincide with specific course content. While most educators will not be spending several weeks focused on race and racism, perhaps a few of the examples throughout this chapter will be useful.

The first journal entry helps students understand the various understandings of racism and inconsistencies with how the term *racism* is used. It serves as a nonconfrontational way of introducing approaches to defining racism in terms of its ideological, behavioral, and affective aspects.

> Journal: Conduct an interview. Ask ten people total, five people under 50 years old and five people over 50 years old, to define racism. Were people willing or hesitant to respond? What similarities and differences did you find among the answers? Did age and race seem to affect the answers? Did answers focus more on motives/intentions, actions/beliefs, or consequences of actions?

The second entry is not shared with the class but prepares students for taking stock of their own racialized experiences and helps them personally connect with the material of the course:

> Journal: What was your first experience of being the victim of racism? What was your most recent experience of being the

> victim of racism? What was your first experience of being the perpetrator of racism? What was your most recent experience of being the perpetrator of racism? Is there a racist thought that you repeatedly have? Is there a specific experience that conditioned that thought?

This journal also challenges any assumption that racism is more or less a thing of the past.

EARLY MODERN RACE-THINKING

Ideas have consequences. The idea of race and the phenomenon of racism coexist. In fact, race, Charles W. Mills writes, is "sociopolitical rather than biological."[6] In order to explain this to students, I borrow Paul Taylor's three "stages of modern racialism."[7] Taylor divides modernity into three eras (early modern, high modern, and late modern), each with its own ideology. First, early modern race-thinking in the sixteenth century demonstrated a shift in terms. "Race" in the medieval period most often referred to horse breeds or various threads of cloth. Being raced in the late sixteenth and early seventeenth centuries held only a negative connotation. By 1611, there is an additional referent: "Race in lineage is understood to be bad, as to have some Moorish or Jewish race."[8] (It is worth noting that, in this usage, "race" does not apply to all human beings and is, consequently, not aligned with how the word functions today.) With the rise of global trade and colonization, Europeans debated the status of non-European populations. For instance, in 1550, in the Spanish city of Valladolid, the city where Christopher Columbus died, theologians Juan Ginés de Sepúlveda (1494–1573) and Bartolomé de Las Casas (1484–1566) debated the status and moral worth of those indigenous to the so-called new world whom Columbus had described as being either childlike and friendly or beastly and cannibalistic. For Sepúlveda, the Ameri-Indians were non-rational and naturally fit for slavery; whereas for Las Casas, they were like Europeans to the extent that they were fully human and governed by reason.[9] This debate, while acknowledging human differences, did not utilize the concept of race even while it engaged in ethical questions about the relationships among agency, nationality, and ethnicity.

Before exploring a genealogy of the concept of race, I ask students to consider what they know about racial classification. Because race seems obvious to students, they usually meet the following journal assignment with a degree of confusion. They each think that the questions are straightforward, that is, until we collectively share our responses. They realize that some think of race solely in terms of skin color or phenotypes while others also associate it with culture, religion, and language.

> Journal: How do you know to which race you belong? What race do you think a stranger would ascribe to you upon meeting you for the first time? Why? Is there a chance that such a stranger might also find some of your racial features belonging to a member of a different race? Indeed, can you think of any feature that all members of your race possess that no member of any other race possesses?

The fluidity of the classifications that emerged among the entries within this journal assignment allows us to better see the stakes of genealogical work.

Early modern race-thinking tended to naturalize race insofar as "race" referred to human variations (of one single species); that is, sociocultural and national differences were mapped onto inheritable bodily differences. This is most clearly seen in the centuries-long shift from anti-Judaism to anti-Semitism.[10] As George Fredrickson explains, "Anti-Judaism became antisemitism whenever it turned into a consuming hatred that made getting rid of Jews seem preferable to trying to convert them, and antisemitism became racism when the belief took hold that Jews were intrinsically and organically evil rather than merely having false beliefs and wrong dispositions."[11] Certain varieties of human beings were prone to artifice while others were disposed to honesty and order. Taylor claims that "on the theoretical level [naturalizing social difference] meant dividing humankind into deeply distinct but still related varieties, and on the practical level it meant turning social and cultural differences into elaborate and far-reaching relations of privilege and domination."[12]

A key transitional piece in the genealogy of the concept of race was Carl Linnaeus's *The System of Nature* (1735). Linnaeus (1707–78), a lifelong naturalist and the so-called father of modern taxonomy, established a way of classifying organisms that was theological and scientific. His classification system, which established the use of binomial nomenclature, placed human beings within the natural hierarchy of flora and fauna and, by doing so, attempted to demonstrate how the order and laws of nature were a reflection of a God who values structure, order, laws, and purpose:

1. Copper-coloured, choleric, erect. *American.*

   Hair black, straight, thick; *nostrils* wide; *face* harsh; *beard* scanty; obstinate, content, free. *Paints* himself with fine red lines. *Regulated* by customs.

2. Fair, sanguine, brawny. *European.*

   Hair yellow, brown, flowing; *eyes* blue; gentle, acute, inventive. *Covered* with close vestments. *Governed* by laws.

3. Sooty, melancholy, rigid. [*Asian*]

   Hair black; *eyes* dark; *fevere*, haughty, covetous. *Covered* with loose garments. *Governed* by opinions.

4. Black, phlegmatic, relaxed. [*African*]

   Hair black, frizzled; *skin* silky; *nose* flat; *lips* tumid; crafty, indolent, negligent. *Anoints* himself with grease. *Governed* by caprice.[13]

Epidermal hue and geography are related, according to Linnaeus, with each human variety having its own set of unique bodily features, personality traits, and social characteristics. Moreover, the relation between mind and body is racialized insofar as temperament corresponds with physical qualities. Linnaeus's system is not without bias: he puts the starkest contrast between the African and the European. The former is marked by a lack of law and order, that is, caprice, whereas the latter is the most godlike, having governed itself by laws. The journal assignments help students better understand that they may have their own preconceived system by which they classify race.

HIGH MODERN RACE-THINKING

In Taylor's second stage, the high modern era, classical race-thinking emerged, in which race referred to human types and the ideology was one of rationalizing race. High modern race-thinking, Taylor writes, "theorized, and thereby widened, the gaps between races, treating them not as provisionally differentiated varieties but as essentially distinct types. And it refined and expanded the techniques of racial domination and mechanisms for disseminating the new racial 'knowledge.'"[14] Rather than being matters of degree, differences began to illustrate profoundly distinct human types, which arose due to the inheritably of (racial) features that could be plainly and hierarchically ranked. President Thomas Jefferson (1743–1826) exemplifies this mode of race-thinking in *Notes on the State of Virginia* (1787): "The first difference which strikes us is that of colour . . . [Blacks have] a very strong and disagreeable odour . . . Their existence appears to participate more of sensation than reflection . . . I advance it . . . that the blacks, whether originally a distinct race, or made distinct by time and circumstances, are inferior to the whites in the endowments both of body and mind."[15] Classical race-thinking, like that of Jefferson, justified white domination by establishing and maintaining a social order that segregated and controlled races through norms, laws, and institutional policies and practices. Races were understood to be natural, discrete types, fundamentally different in body and mind. Human difference was essentialized: for example, one is violent because one is Black. One's whiteness indicates one's capacity for virtue and harmonious living. Put differently, one's racial qualities were innate and immutable—unchanging due to the natural inheritability of one's racial essence.

By this time, racial classifications were explicitly evaluative and racial prejudice and discrimination were overt. Immanuel Kant (1724–1804) is arguably the first theorist of race to give a rigorous and scientific account of race. A defender of monogenesis, Kant claims that the races emerged in response to environmental conditions and that the four human races all descend from an original root genus, which is no longer extant. Nevertheless, Kant describes that origin as proximate to white skin and brunette hair. For Kant, the white race is closest to the lineal root genus and is also superior to the others. "Humanity is at its greatest perfection," he suggests, "in the race of the whites. The yellow Indians do have a meagre talent. The Negroes are far below them and at the lower point are a part of the [Native] American peoples."[16] Within a century of Kant, the pseudoscientific accounts of race, illustrated, for example, by Robert Knox (1793–1862) and Arthur de Gobineau (1816–82), would lead to overtly racist policies: rationalizing race as distinct types undergirding the rationalizing of racial sterilization and extermination projects. In the United States, the nineteenth-century expansion westward required the continual management (i.e., genocidal exploitation) of Native Americans by provoking violence, forcing migration onto reservations, and coercing into assimilation—the latter exemplified by the use of harsh boarding schools such as the Carlisle Indian Industrial School in Pennsylvania. Scott Manning Stevens's chapter in this volume, "On Native American Erasure in the Classroom," may provide a bit more insight on this subject. The Chinese Exclusion Act of 1882 fostered anti-Asian sentiment and established the so-called threat of yellow peril.[17] In the twentieth century, eugenics, first developed by English scientist Francis Galton (1822–1911), was practiced in the United States. In *Essays in Eugenics* (1909), Galton writes, "While most barbarous races disappear, some, like the negro, do not. . . . What nature does blindly, slowly, and ruthlessly, man may do providently, quickly, and kindly. [It is] his duty to work in that direction [for] the improvement of our stock seems to me one of the highest objects that we can reasonably attempt."[18] The removal of Black persons from society, whether via eugenics or today through mass incarceration, was seen by dominant white culture as necessary for the flourishing of civil society.[19]

The transitional moment between early modern, high modern, and late modern race-thinking is the Jim Crow era in US history. Like the "black codes" of the 1860s, Jim Crow laws restricted the mobility, prospects, and rights of Black people. Taking on a caste mentality, white people stigmatized the sharing of quotidian social space with non-whites. In other words, the white gaze upon Black bodies rendered those bodies as a problem for the alleged purity of white civilization. Jim Crow laws prevented races from sharing, including but not limited to, the same (sections of) hospitals and public transport, water fountains and restrooms, swimming pools and parks, and even the same neighborhoods. Moreover, they deprived People of Color the right to vote and denied them any parity of participation in public life. These laws also prohibited interracial marriage.

These laws were not divorced from interpersonal instantiations of the white gaze. In *Sister Outsider*, Audre Lorde recalls a scene from her childhood near the end of Jim Crow when she and her mother were riding a train after shopping. There was a vacant seat next to a white woman and Lorde's mother told her to sit there. The white woman attempted to distance herself from Lorde and pulled her overcoat away. Making eye contact, Lorde watched as the white woman looked down at her with obvious disgust. She thought that there must be an insect somewhere on herself or the seat that the woman was avoiding. Lorde writes, "When I look up the woman is still staring at me, her nose holes and eyes huge. And suddenly I realize there is nothing crawling up the seat between us; it is me she doesn't want her coat to touch."[20] Realizing the white woman's disgust was directed at her Black body, Lorde experiences the white gaze as a violation of her sense of worth, a harm against her body, and a violence against her personhood. As we saw in Raynor's chapter in this collection, Lorde's *Sister Outsider* deeply examines the racial relationships between black and white women to make visible the presumptive power of the white gaze that underscores racial difference and social inequality. Lorde's body was ultimately not the problem; rather, the problem resides in the assumption of a white audience that carries an anti-Black ideology aiming to perpetuate the myth of white purity. What a white woman feared was a figment of her own imagination.

LATE MODERN RACE-THINKING

In our third era, late modern race-thinking, according to Taylor, "rejects the thought that racial difference and social inequality must necessarily and automatically be linked."[21] In this era, social-constructivist approaches to race receive more attention, gains are made in the area of civil rights, and overtly racist regimes, like the Jim Crow South, Nazi Germany, or apartheid South Africa, collapse. Scientific accounts of race were waning. Anthropologist Ashley Montagu (1905–98) argues, "Physical anthropologists directed their attention principally toward the task of establishing criteria by means of which races of humankind might be defined . . . By arbitrarily selecting the criteria one could nearly always make the races come out exactly as one thought they should . . . Most physical anthropologists took completely for granted the one thing required to be proved, namely, that the concept of race corresponded to a reality that could actually be measured and verified and descriptively set out so that it could be seen to be a fact."[22] Montagu claims that the entire history of the idea has been an intellectual failure. For a few centuries, scholars have tried to establish what demarcates one race from another and what criteria a person must have in order to be a member of a particular race; and yet, they have failed even to justify that race as a natural category exists at all.

Late modernity is the era when students often think there was a full repudiation of racism since full equality (in a formal sense) was granted in 1964. However, evident in this historical moment is the rise of neo-racism, exemplified by nativism and xenophobia; covert racism, often manifested in, for example, personal microaggressions; and racial hegemony and institutional racism, illustrated by the reduction of legal protections.

For example, the "war on drugs," which arguably started with the Nixon administration and continues today, directly targets Black people and gives them harsher punitive sentences compared to their white counterparts. In 2013, the Supreme Court struck down key elements on the Voting Rights Act of 1965 that had protected the voting rights of Black people.

The ideology of this third era is one of "politicizing difference instead of naturalizing or rationalizing it in the manner of earlier periods."[23] This does not mean that the older ideologies have died out; rather, the ideologies of the older regimes are less dominant today. One rarely hears of someone defending slavery or lynching or arguing that People of Color are naturally inferior.[24] Nevertheless, whiteness remains property, as Cheryl Harris critically describes it, and, according to the ideology of politicizing race, it must be defended against the Other.[25] "Whiteness," Mills suggests, "is not really a color at all, but a set of power relations."[26]

Three episodes are illustrative of the early years of the late modern era and the extent to which race and racism continue to be about domination. The following journal assignment, which students share with the class, supports their understanding of how racist policies and practices of the past have consequences that reverberate into the future. It also challenges any opinion that racism is merely a thing of the past or that if we were "color-blind" then racism would disappear.

> Journal: Research one of the following topics: the Tuskegee Syphilis Experiment, Robert Moses's racist civil engineering, or segregation/integration in Levittown, NY. Write a short story describing how these practices negatively affect people today.

The overwhelming majority of white people do not view their default social position as one of active racism: that word is too often relegated to only the most explicit and direct instantiations of racism, like those espoused by members of the Ku Klux Klan. Many whites tend to think that racism remains with us only because we talk about it too much and that the solution is to ignore racial differences. However, we ought to reject the oft-heard prescription for a color-blind approach to race relations, that is, the method of allegedly alleviating racial discrimination by ignoring (i.e., being "blind" to) racial differences or treating racial differences as if they were invisible. "The very notion of blindness about color," Patricia Williams writes, "constitutes an ideological confusion at best, and denial at its very worst."[27] To recognize the humanity of all persons, one must recognize the ways in which individuals are conditioned by racist institutions and by systems of oppression. Color-blindness obfuscates the extent to which persons are differentially affected by racist structures and policies within society. Additionally, color-blindness denies the historical legacy of oppression and glosses over an individual's identity.

What can we learn from these three episodes? Given the value of white life, in order to study syphilis, scientists experimented on poor, ill-informed, Black sharecroppers. The notorious Tuskegee Experiment, which lasted from 1932 to 1972 and was conducted by Public Health Services, observed the effects of syphilis when left untreated in Black males. The "patients" were subject to this experiment for many years despite the emergence of penicillin as a standard medical practice by 1947. Our second example is that of Robert Moses's civil engineering throughout New York from the 1930s to the 1960s. Moses (1888–1981), a New York City parks commissioner, was the father of urban "redlining" policies and is now known widely for his disregard of Black life. He designed a series of roads that racially segregated the city as well as highways that cut through and destroyed poor and Black neighborhoods. Likewise, Moses had bridges constructed that were too low for public busing, thereby keeping Black people out of white areas, including newly created city parks.[28] The third example was a national phenomenon whose racial consequences we continue to experience, namely, the housing discrimination and redlining promoted by the Federal Housing Administration (FHA). Established in 1934, the FHA, Richard Rothstein explains,

> subsidized mass-production builders of entire subdivisions, entire suburbs. And it did so with a requirement that no homes be sold to African-Americans and that every home in these subdivisions had a clause in the deed that prohibited resale to African-Americans . . . [African-Americans] were prohibited [from moving into white suburbs] because the developers of these suburbs got bank loans on condition that they sell no homes to African-Americans . . . It was written out in the [FHA's] manuals that they gave to underwriters who were appraising properties for possible mortgage insurance . . . [Redlined maps] were designed to indicate where it was safe to insure mortgages. [African-American neighborhoods] were colored red to indicate to appraisers that these neighborhoods were too risky to insure mortgages.[29]

The systemic refusal to provide mortgage loans due to race significantly affected the vast majority of Black people, including veterans, who, even as beneficiaries of the GI Bill, were excluded from receiving loans since Veterans Affairs assumed all of the FHA stipulations regarding redlining. By the time the Fair Housing Act was passed in 1968, the damage had been done. Homes in the white suburbs, then formally available to Black folk, remained practically out of reach due to their unaffordability, that is, the drastic increase in property values. Over three decades, whites were able to send their children to better-equipped public schools, secure access to sufficient health care, and accrue equity in their real estate, which in turn generated wealth that would eventually lead to providing their children with the means for higher education. While the FHA lifted many whites into the middle class, providing them with the means to accumulate wealth and to educate and secure jobs for their children, Black people were disenfranchised, kept in poverty, and consigned to a world with a scarcity of resources (e.g., jobs). By the time they were legally able to pursue the middle-class dream, their white counterparts were already well ahead, which leads directly to the discussion about post-racial spaces.

POST-RACIAL QUOTIDIEN SPACES? NOT EVEN CLOSE

As the class discussion transitions from institutional racism to interpersonal acts of racism, I ask students to share their thoughts on the recent debate around Confederate statues and the effects of symbols of white supremacy. This assists us in rethinking how racism can be viewed from the perspectives of beliefs, actions, and ill will:

> Journal: Write a dialogue that addresses the following question: Should statues and monuments honoring Confederate soldiers of the Civil War be removed from public spaces such as parks and government buildings? What is the purpose of these statues (research the permit applications and speeches given for some of these instead of merely speculating)? Do they teach history? Does removing them imply that one is erasing history? If so, is it erasing the history of what is being honored (i.e., the Civil War) or the history of the monument's particular history (white nationalism and/or supremacy)?

I facilitate a conversation with my students that engages them on multiple levels, namely, their understanding of the history of sociocultural spaces, ideas, practices, and institutions, their current awareness of their own thrownness into a world already conditioned by race-thinking, and their imagination of a world otherwise. Thinking practically, we ought not be surprised if our students avoid discussing race. Like many of us, they try to keep a distance from conflict, particularly if that conflict involves self-examination and dealing with the mess we/they find. Rarely, if ever, will we find the white student who is a classical, overt racist; but frequently will we face the goodwill white student. Janine Jones claims that "goodwill whites define racism simply as racial prejudice. By not understanding racism as a system of advantage based on race, the goodwill white avoids the considerable pain, guilt, and shame that might be elicited by a definition of racism that clarifies how she benefits from racism and perhaps serves as an active, intentional though unconscious, participant in it,"[30] which is the focus of the next journal assignment.

> Journal: Write a poem or song lyric based on the following prompt: Why do you think racial slurs are offensive? Do you ever use racial slurs (publicly or only in your head)? When quoting lyrics or a movie line that contains racist words, do you still sing or say the slurs? Why or why not might this be problematic?

By restricting racism only to the beliefs and actions of the overt racist who harbors a sense of both racial superiority and racial antipathy, goodwill whites claim ignorance of their being implicated within a white normative, white supremacist society.[31] And, furthermore, they deny any participation in microaggressions such as using racialized code words (e.g., "thug" as the new n-word) or characterizing Black poverty as if it is pathology.

It is predominantly, but not exclusively, white students who want to escape any obligation to talk about race and racism. While students of various races might say some of the following, these are more commonly attributed to white students. One hears, "We're post-racial. Former president Barack Obama is Black." Or: "Oprah—white people love Oprah, and she's super rich." Or: "We fixed the race issue back in the '60s. There might be racism sometimes, but it's not something that applies to me." In addition to hearing denials such as these, I have also witnessed students become noticeably uneasy and avoid "the race talk" to the extent that they have a visceral reaction when asked to join the conversation. Avoidance is likely due to their lack of experience with racial settings, their anxiety due to ignorance of other racial groups, or their fear of exposing their own racial biases or racist beliefs. Some students might agree to talk about race but participate in the conversation with a strong dose of hesitation to say what is really on their mind. This often stems from a desire to not offend others, to all get along. But this glosses over the actual disparate experiences among racial groups. I have found that the attempt to avoid offense is regularly linked with color-blindness. Students may even misappropriate King's "I Have a Dream" speech—judge others by the content of their character—without realizing the extent to which, by reducing everyone to sameness, they have imposed standards of whiteness upon People of Color, thereby robbing of them of part of their identities and their historical and quotidian experiences. "The refusal to see race," Arnold Farr suggests, "is the refusal to see the long-term effects of racism on Black people. It is a refusal to see the social, institutional, legal, and economic mechanisms that are in place to keep a large portion of the Black population from achieving the same optimal form of life as their White peers."[32] In order to redirect students, I have them explore a constellation of episodes in which we discern indirect racism, unintentional racism, and implicit bias.

Linda Martín Alcoff reminds us that "although all communities of color have shared the experience of political and economic disenfranchisement in the United States, there are significant differences between the *causes* and the *forms* of disenfranchisement."[33] On the one hand, it would be inaccurate to paint the picture that all races experience racism in the same way, that the causes, forms, and content of racism are universalizable. On the other hand, there does seem to be a common feature, namely the supremacy of whiteness. It is more accurate, but more difficult to convince the skeptics, to speak of "white supremacy" or "whiteness as a system" rather than "white privilege." In the US, these structures of domination buttress whiteness. US society is not merely one that privileges white people; additionally, it includes white normativity and white domination. According to Mills, "The dominant interpretation of white racism in the white population is probably individual beliefs about innate nonwhite (particularly black) biological inferiority, and individual hostility toward people of color (especially blacks). Given this conception, most whites think of themselves as nonracist . . . while continuing to hold antiblack stereotypes. [However,] the real issue for a long time has not been individual racism but, far more important, the reproduction of white advantage and black disadvantage through the workings of racialized social structures."[34] Consider the following. What is it that explains why all-white juries are 16 percent more likely to convict a Black defendant than a white defendant, but when the jury contains at least one Black juror, the conviction rates are the same?[35] Why are Black people looking for an apartment to rent shown fewer rental units and quoted higher payments than their white counterparts?[36] Why are white job applicants 50 percent more likely to receive a callback from a potential employer than a Black applicant even when their résumés are statistically identical except for the only notable difference being the applicant's name?[37]

In addition to discussing racist project and policies that preceded the Civil Rights Act of 1964 (e.g., phenomena like slavery, Jim Crow laws, and redlining), I have my students consider how the logics that undergird those phenomena remain intact in the examples of job application discrepancies, unequal treatment when searching for rental properties, and racial profiling.[38] Driving while Black, shopping while Black, breathing while Black—these are a few of the things that affect the everyday lives of Black people. As a way of concluding, I want to return to the thought of Tamir Rice and the culture of profiling that covers the American landscape. Sociologist Joe Feagin claims that "more than half of all African Americans killed by whites were killed by white [police] officers [between 1920 to 1932]. Police were regularly implicated in the estimated 6,000 bloody lynching of black men and women from the 1870s to the 1960s."[39] A more recent study done by the New York Civil Liberties Union shows that 90 percent of those stopped and frisked by officers are innocent. In New York, Black people are five times more likely to be stopped than their white peers.[40] This means, first, many white criminals are overlooked because the focus is on the salience of the Black body and, second, innocent life is met with the presumption of guilt—being Black means being criminal. Moreover, arrests for drug possession reveal an institutional bias against Black people. For example, whites and Blacks equally use drugs. However, the latter are five to six times more likely to be arrested for drug possession and more likely to receive harsher sentences. Naomi Zack gives a unique perspective on this: "If 14 out of 15 or more than 93 percent of African American men are not 'in' the criminal justice system, compared to more than 97 percent of Hispanic men and 99 percent of white men, then racial profiling that relies on the racial proportions of convicted criminals ignores the rights of the overwhelming majority who are law-abiding—in all races."[41] By viewing Black lives through the white gaze, innocence is lost. Well-known professor Cornel West was pulled over for driving while Black, accused of trafficking cocaine, and called "nigger" by the officer while on his way to Harvard's campus.[42] Even on the playground, a Black child like Tamir Rice can be seen not as a child but as an imminent danger deserving execution: "Black boys are really Black men; they have forfeited their innocence from birth."[43] How could officer Jonathan Aledda, who in July 2016 fired three rounds at innocent Black life, not understand that mental health therapist Charles Kinsey was helping a patient?[44] I do not think the answer is simply "because he's a racist." Regardless of his heart, his actions and their consequences were racist. Furthermore, what I take to be the lesson for us is how we are to best understand the process of racialization that fuels white supremacy and its tool of the white gaze.

Used within white supremacist society to dehumanize Black people, the white gaze is both the epistemic filter through which whites (or whiteness) view(s) Black persons. White people act as "seer" or "knower" (i.e., bearer of epistemic privilege) while Black humanity is objectified. It is not a two-step process of first seeing the Black body and then making a value judgment. Rather, the white gaze, at the same moment, constructs an image that Black equals deviant, Black equals lazy, Black equals criminal. One's personhood is rendered invisible while the Black body is seen as hypervisible. The blackness of the body becomes the only salient feature, and this body's blackness is formed within a sociohistorical matrix that preceded any of us and will outlive us as well. My hope is for students to recognize how they are conditioned by this history, how they currently participate in it, and how that might affect the narrative of the future.

NOTES

1. See Robert Bernasconi, "Who Invented the Concept of Race? Kant's Role in the Enlightenment Construction of Race," in *Race*, ed. Robert Bernasconi (Malden, MA: Blackwell, 2001), 11–36.

2. See, for an early example, the "itineraries" or travel narratives of Jan Huygen van Linschoten, *His discours of voyages into ye East and West Indies D[i] vided into Four Bookes* (London: John Wolfe, 1598).

3. "Negro," *Encyclopaedia Britannica*, in *Race and the Enlightenment*, ed. Emmanuel Chukwudi Eze (Malden, MA: Blackwell, 1997), 94. A recent computational approach to the *Encyclopaedia Britannica* has revealed the continuity of racial bias across its hundred-year publication history. See the project at https://generalknowledgeproject.network/racialclassifier.

4. George Yancy, *Black Bodies, White Gazes: The Continuing Significance of Race in America*, 2nd ed. (Lanham, MD: Rowman and Littlefield, 2017), 243.

5. See Emma G. Fitzsimmons, "12-Year-Old Boy Dies after Police in Cleveland Shoot Him," *New York Times*, November 23, 2014.

6. Charles W. Mills, *The Racial Contract* (Ithaca, NY: Cornell University Press, 1997), 126.

7. Paul Taylor, *Race: A Philosophical Introduction*, 2nd ed. (Malden, MA: Polity, 2013).

8. "Raza, en los linages se toma en mala parte, como tener alguna raza de moro o judio." Sebastián de Covarrubias Horozco, *Tesoro de la lengua castellana* (1611), the first Spanish monolingual dictionary in Europe. Quoted in Kathryn Burns, "Unfixing Race," in *Histories of Race and Racism: The Andes and Mesoamerica from Colonial Times to the Present*, ed. Laura Gotkowitz (Durham, NC: Duke University Press, 2011), 57.

9. See Anthony Pagden, *The Fall of Natural Man: The American Indian and the Origins of Comparative Ethnology* (Cambridge: Cambridge University Press, 1982), 109–44.

10. See David Nirenberg, *Anti-Judaism: The Western Tradition* (New York: Norton, 2014).

11. George M. Fredrickson, *Racism: A Short History* (Princeton, NJ: Princeton University Press, 2015), 19.

12. Taylor, *Race*, 41.

13. Carl von Linné, quoted in "The God-Given Order of Nature," in Eze, *Race and the Enlightenment*, 13.

14. Taylor, *Race*, 41.

15. Thomas Jefferson, "The Difference Is Fixed in Nature," in Eze, *Race and the Enlightenment*, 102.

16. Immanuel Kant, from *Physical Geography*, in Eze, *Race and the Enlightenment*, 63.

17. See Scott Kurashige explain both "yellow peril" and the "myth of the model minority": "Professor Kurashige on the Yellow Peril and Model Minority Stereotypes of Asians in the U.S," YouTube, March 9, 2011, https://www.youtube.com/watch?v=LOB0VCCEUa4&t=4s.

18. Francis Galton, "Eugenics: Its Definition, Scope and Aims," in Bernasconi and Lott, *The Idea of Race*, 81, 83.

19. See chapter four of Stefan Kühl, *The Nazi Connection: Eugenics, American Racism, and German National Socialism* (New York: Oxford University Press, 1994).

20. Audre Lorde, *Sister Outsider: Essays and Speeches* (Berkeley, CA: Crossing Press, 1984), 147–48.

21. Taylor, *Race*, 71.

22. Ashley Montagu, *Man's Most Dangerous Myth: The Fallacy of Race*, 6th ed. (Lanham, MD: Rowman and Littlefield, 1997), 102.

23. Taylor, *Race*, 71.

24. See Gary Younge interview Richard Spencer, who claims that Black people benefited from slavery: Gary Younge, “Why Interviewing Richard Spencer Was a Risk Worth Taking,” *Guardian*, November 8, 2017, https://www.theguardian.com/commentisfree/2017/nov/08/interviewing-richard-spencer-white-supremacist.

25. Cheryl L. Harris, “Whiteness as Property,” *Harvard Law Review* 106, no. 8 (1996): 1709–91.

26. Mills, *Racial Contract*, 127.

27. Patricia Williams, *Seeing a Color-Blind Future: The Paradox of Race* (New York: Farrar, Straus, and Giroux, 1997), 4.

28. See Langdon Winner, “Do Artifacts Have Politics?,” *Daedalus* 109, no. 1 (1980): 121–36; Robert A. Caro, *The Power Broker: Robert Moses and the Fall of New York* (New York: Vintage, 1975); and for an opposing view, see Bernward Joerges, “Do Politics Have Artefacts?,” *Social Studies of Science* 29, no. 3 (1999): 411–31.

29. Richard Rothstein and Terry Gross, “A ‘Forgotten History’ of How the U.S. Government Segregated America,” NPR, May 3, 2017, https://www.npr.org/2017/05/03/526655831/a-forgotten-history-of-how-the-u-s-government-segregated-america. See Richard Rothstein, *The Color of Law: A Forgotten History of How Our Government Segregated America* (New York: Liveright, 2017).

30. Janine Jones, “The Impairment of Empathy in Goodwill Whites for African Americans,” in *What White Looks Like: African-American Philosophers on the Whiteness Question*, ed. George Yancy (New York: Routledge, 2004), 69.

31. See Lawrence Blum, “Racism: What It Is and What It Isn't,” *Studies in Philosophy and Education* 21 (2002): 203–18.

32. Arnold Farr, “Racialized Consciousness and Learned Ignorance: Trying to Help White People Understand,” in *Exploring Race in Predominantly White Classrooms: Scholars of Color Reflect*, ed. George Yancy and Maria del Guadalupe Davidson (New York: Routledge, 2014), 102.

33. Linda Martín Alcoff, *Visible Identities: Race, Gender, and the Self* (New York: Oxford University Press, 2006), 253. See this chapter for a critique of the Black/white paradigm of race relations in the US.

34. Charles W. Mills, “Racial Exploitation and the Wages of Whiteness,” in *What White Looks Like*, 33.

35. Shamena Anwar, Patrick Bayer, and Randi Hjalmarsson, “The Impact of Jury Race in Criminal Trials,” *Quarterly Journal of Economics* 127, no. 2 (2012): 1017–55.

36. US Department of Housing and Urban Development, *Housing Discrimination against Racial and Ethnic Minorities 2012*, June 2013, https://www.huduser.gov/portal/Publications/pdf/HUD-514_HDS2012.pdf.

37. Marianne Bertrand and Sendhil Mullainathan, “Are Emily and Greg More Employable Than Lakisha and Jamal? A Field Experiment on Labor Market Discrimination,” *American Economic Review* 94, no. 4 (2004): 991–1013. See also Devah Pager, Bart Bonikowski, and Bruce Western, “Discrimination in a

Low-Wage Labor Market: A Field Experiment," *American Sociological Review* 74 (2009): 777–99.

38. See Ta-Nehisi Coates and Chris Hayes, "Ta-Nehisi Coates: The Case for Reparations," YouTube, June 18, 2015, https://www.youtube.com/watch?v=Kk63XQwix28; and Ta-Nehisi Coates, "The Case for Reparations," *The Atlantic*, June 2014, https://www.theatlantic.com/magazine/archive/2014/06/the-case-for-reparations/361631.

39. Joe R. Feagin, *Racist America: Roots, Current Realities, and Future Reparations*, 3rd ed. (New York: Routledge, 2014), 156.

40. New York Civil Liberties Union, "Stop-and-Frisk Data," accessed November 27, 2019, http://www.nyclu.org/content/stop-and-frisk-data.

41. Naomi Zack, *White Privilege and Black Rights: The Injustice of U.S. Police Racial Profiling and Homicide* (Lanham, MD: Rowman and Littlefield, 2015), 55. See also chapter five of Albert Atkin, *The Philosophy of Race* (Durham, NC: Acumen, 2012).

42. Cornel West, *Race Matters* (New York: Beacon, 2001), xii.

43. Yancy, *Black Bodies, White Gazes*, 6.

44. See Charles Rabin, "Cop Shoots Caretaker of Autistic Man Playing in the Street with a Toy Truck," *Miami Herald*, July 20, 2016.

BIBLIOGRAPHY

Alcoff, Linda Martín. *Visible Identities: Race, Gender, and the Self.* New York: Oxford University Press, 2006.

Anwar, Shamena, Patrick Bayer, and Randi Hjalmarsson. "The Impact of Jury Race in Criminal Trials." *Quarterly Journal of Economics* 127, no. 2 (2012): 1017–55.

Atkin, Albert. *The Philosophy of Race*. Durham, NC: Acumen, 2012.

Bernasconi, Robert. "Who Invented the Concept of Race? Kant's Role in the Enlightenment Construction of Race." In *Race*, edited by Robert Bernasconi, 11–36. Malden, MA: Blackwell, 2001.

Bernasconi, Robert, and Tommy L. Lott, eds. *The Idea of Race*. Indianapolis: Hackett, 2000.

Bertrand, Marianne, and Sendhil Mullainathan. "Are Emily and Greg More Employable Than Lakisha and Jamal? A Field Experiment on Labor Market Discrimination." *American Economic Review* 94, no. 4 (2004): 991–1013.

Blum, Lawrence. "Racism: What It Is and What It Isn't." *Studies in Philosophy and Education* 21 (2002): 203–18.

Burns, Kathryn. "Unfixing Race." In *Histories of Race and Racism: The Andes and Mesoamerica from Colonial Times to the Present*, edited by Laura Gotkowitz, 57–71. Durham, NC: Duke University Press, 2011.

Caro, Robert A. *The Power Broker: Robert Moses and the Fall of New York*. New York: Vintage, 1975.

Coates, Ta-Nehisi. "The Case for Reparations." *The Atlantic*, June 2014. https://www.theatlantic.com/magazine/archive/2014/06/the-case-for-reparations/361631.

Coates, Ta-Nehisi, and Chris Hayes. "Ta-Nehisi Coates: The Case for Reparations." YouTube, June 18, 2015. https://www.youtube.com/watch?v=Kk63XQwix28.

Eze, Emmanuel Chukwudi, ed. *Race and the Enlightenment*. Malden, MA: Blackwell, 1997.

Farr, Arnold. "Racialized Consciousness and Learned Ignorance: Trying to Help White People Understand." In *Exploring Race in Predominantly White Classrooms: Scholars of Color Reflect*, edited by George Yancy and Maria del Guadalupe Davidson, 102–9. New York: Routledge, 2014.

Feagin, Joe R. *Racist America: Roots, Current Realities, and Future Reparations*. 3rd ed. New York: Routledge, 2014.

Fitzsimmons, Emma G. "12-Year-Old Boy Dies after Police in Cleveland Shoot Him." *New York Times*, November 23, 2014.

Fredrickson, George M. *Racism: A Short History*. Princeton, NJ: Princeton University Press, 2015.

Galton, Francis. "Eugenics: Its Definition, Scope and Aims." In Bernasconi and Lott, *The Idea of Race*, 81–83.

Gotkowitz, Laura, ed. *Histories of Race and Racism: The Andes and Mesoamerica from Colonial Times to the Present*. Durham, NC: Duke University Press, 2011.

Harris, Cheryl L. "Whiteness as Property." *Harvard Law Review* 106, no. 8 (1996): 1709–91.

Joerges, Bernward. "Do Politics Have Artefacts?" *Social Studies of Science* 29, no. 3 (1999): 411–31.

Jones, Janine. "The Impairment of Empathy in Goodwill Whites for African Americans." In Yancy, *What White Looks Like*, 65–86.

Kühl, Stefan. *The Nazi Connection: Eugenics, American Racism, and German National Socialism*. New York: Oxford University Press, 1994.

Kurashige, Scott. "Professor Kurashige on the Yellow Peril and Model Minority Stereotypes of Asians in the U.S." YouTube, March 9, 2011. https://www.youtube.com/watch?v=LOB0VCCEUa4&t=4s.

Lorde, Audre. *Sister Outsider: Essays and Speeches*. Berkeley, CA: Crossing Press, 1984.

Mills, Charles W. *The Racial Contract*. Ithaca, NY: Cornell University Press, 1997.

———. "Racial Exploitation and the Wages of Whiteness." In Yancy, *What White Looks Like*, 25–54.

Montagu, Ashley. *Man's Most Dangerous Myth: The Fallacy of Race*. 6th ed. Lanham, MD: Rowman and Littlefield, 1997.

New York Civil Liberties Union. "Stop-and-Frisk Data." Accessed November 27, 2019. http://www.nyclu.org/content/stop-and-frisk-data.

Nirenberg, David. *Anti-Judaism: The Western Tradition*. New York: Norton, 2014.

Pagden, Anthony. *The Fall of Natural Man: The American Indian and the Origins of Comparative Ethnology*. Cambridge: Cambridge University Press, 1982.

Pager, Devah, Bart Bonikowski, and Bruce Western. "Discrimination in a Low-Wage Labor Market: A Field Experiment." *American Sociological Review* 74 (2009): 777–99.

Rabin, Charles. "Cop Shoots Caretaker of Autistic Man Playing in the Street with a Toy Truck." *Miami Herald*, July 20, 2016.

Rothstein, Richard. *The Color of Law: A Forgotten History of How Our Government Segregated America*. New York: Liveright, 2017.

Rothstein, Richard, and Terry Gross. "A 'Forgotten History' of How the U.S. Government Segregated America." NPR, May 3, 2017. https://www.npr.org/2017/05/03/526655831/a-forgotten-history-of-how-the-u-s-government-segregated-america.

Taylor, Paul. *Race: A Philosophical Introduction*. 2nd ed. Malden, MA: Polity, 2013.

U.S. Department of Housing and Urban Development. *Housing Discrimination against Racial and Ethnic Minorities 2012*. June 2013. https://www.huduser.gov/portal/Publications/pdf/HUD-514_HDS2012.pdf.

West, Cornel. *Race Matters*. New York: Beacon, 2001.

Williams, Patricia. *Seeing a Color-Blind Future: The Paradox of Race*. New York: Farrar, Straus, and Giroux, 1997.

Winner, Langdon. "Do Artifacts Have Politics?" *Daedalus* 109, no. 1 (1980): 121–36.

Yancy, George. *Black Bodies, White Gazes: The Continuing Significance of Race in America*. 2nd ed. Lanham, MD: Rowman and Littlefield, 2017.

———, ed. *What White Looks Like: African-American Philosophers on the Whiteness Question*. New York: Routledge, 2004.

Yancy, George, and Maria del Guadalupe Davidson, eds. *Exploring Race in Predominantly White Classrooms: Scholars of Color Reflect*. New York: Routledge, 2014.

Younge, Gary. "Why Interviewing Richard Spencer Was a Risk Worth Taking." *Guardian*, November 8, 2017. https://www.theguardian.com/commentisfree/2017/nov/08/interviewing-richard-spencer-white-supremacist.

Zack, Naomi. *White Privilege and Black Rights: The Injustice of U.S. Police Racial Profiling and Homicide*. Lanham, MD: Rowman and Littlefield, 2015.

CHAPTER 15

THE DEATH OF THE BLACK CHILD

TASHA M. HAWTHORNE

> The paradox of education is precisely this—that as one begins to become conscious one begins to examine the society in which he is being educated.
>
> —James Baldwin, "A Talk to the Teachers"

The year 2017 was a watershed year in American politics. I started writing this chapter a few months after Donald Trump was inaugurated as the 45th president of the United States, while a white nationalist rally was held in Thomas Jefferson's beloved city of Charlottesville, Virginia, and many unarmed Black people continued to be murdered by the police. The Black Lives Matter movement (#BLM) that has catapulted the deaths of Black people into the media spotlight has also raised a new level of awareness for the nation. #BLM is a phenomenon that far exceeds its original intent. Originally a grassroots social justice movement cohering around online activism by a trans-positive, queer, Black woman, Alicia Garza, who was, to borrow the famous line from Fannie Lou Hamer, "sick and tired of being sick and tired" of witnessing police violence against Black people, #BLM, much like the Occupy movement, "eschews hierarchy and centralized leadership" and instead focuses on a "horizontal ethic of organizing, which favors democratic inclusion at the grassroots level. [#BLM] emerged as a modern distinction of Ella Baker's thinking—a preference for ten thousand candles rather than a single spotlight."[1] When we say #BLM we are also saying that race and racism are alive and well in the United States in 2020 that movement reveals how race and politics are the central dynamic in America at this time.

Despite the national attention that Michael Brown's and Trayvon Martin's cases[2] have garnered over the last few years, America's preoccupation with—and misrepresentation of—Black death is long-standing. From Ida B. Wells's *Red Record* (in 1892), which chronicles the lynching of Blacks throughout the South, to Emmett Till's horrifying murder (in 1955) for whistling at a white woman (Carolyn Bryant) while visiting his family in Mississippi, to Aiyana Stanley-Jones's atrocious death (in 2010), Black bodies have long been offered up for public consumption. In practical terms, this chapter chronicles the strategies that I have developed in the context of teaching African American literature, contemporary politics, and activism by exploring how I help students understand how, when, and to whom "Black Lives Matter." In more philosophical ways, this chapter is an exploration of how a Black academic can read Black suffering with her students. What happens when we place the concerns of Black students, or, dare I say, Black people, at the center of one's teaching? To be clear, I am *not* suggesting that I do not value the learning and growth that I hope and expect for all of my students; rather, what happens when we "move [Black students' needs] from the margin to the center," to borrow from bell hooks?[3] Do we have a shared responsibility to educate strategically so that we can affirm, inform, and reeducate all students as we are explicit in our affirmation of the value of Black life? Composed of five parts—Part I: Personal and Pedagogical Imperatives, Part II: Black Texts Matter, Part III: A Day in the Life (We Read Together), Part IV: The Sacred and the Profane: Reading Classic and Modern Texts, and the Conclusion—this chapter argues that when we make space to explore contemporary issues, we must consider the ways that those moments are always already informed by a historical past that is mired in racism, violence, and Black pain.

Each section coheres around reciprocity between instructor and student and between students and the texts at hand. How might one facilitate honest engagement with difficult subjects? How do we acknowledge our histories so that we are not fated to act out the same solipsistic notions about each other? How do we work toward proper exchange of ideas rather than unidirectional modes of communication? Fundamentally, the contemporary must feed from the historical material needs and vice versa.

This chapter attempts to show that when we defer to the fecund narratives, theories, and experiences we find in African American literature, we might be able to teach our students to understand better these fraught sociopolitical moments. Ultimately, my hope is that this chapter recasts Black students' needs as particular, while simultaneously exploring their universality because Black death concerns us all.

PART I: PERSONAL AND PEDAGOGICAL IMPERATIVES

This course—Death of the Black Child—grew out of a space of deep concern and love for my students. I write these words not for their sentimentality or overly dramatic flair, but rather from a deep desire to ensure that my students were armed with knowledge, born out of a commitment to their safety, despair, anger, or confusion, as well as a commitment to their intellects. Prior to teaching at my current institution, Berea College, I honed my teaching skills at an elite New England boarding school where the students were precocious, young, overwhelmingly white, and excessively privileged. Many had been baptized, unknowingly, in the false-flag American church of fairness and meritocracy. So, in response to the horror that my few students of color were contending with amid the daily onslaught on the national news about the shooting of unarmed African American citizens, I decided to alter my plans for the final term of my senior elective in African American literature. I threw out my original syllabus and instead decided to teach a course that required that all of my students confront, learn from, commiserate with, and share in these contemporary moments of Black American life and death. During this era, we must make the space and create the time in our classrooms to transform them in response to current events. Our students are not ignorant—they see what is going on beyond the confines of the hallowed classroom walls. Teaching and learning do not stop once the bells chime from the clock tower. Critical race pedagogy—the impact of race and historical race relations alongside practices of teaching and learning—must be pressing and present.[4]

Because of Berea College's noteworthy history and continued mission—founded in 1855 by a Presbyterian minister abolitionist, the first interracial and coeducational school in the South, and its refusal to charge admission since the late nineteenth century—the course necessarily had a unique valence with my students in Kentucky. Most, if not all, come from economically disadvantaged regions of the United States or abroad, most notably the South. Many have not been required to read complex, multifaceted prose—and certainly not that written by African Americans. Some are not accustomed to reading literature or history at all. However, they are hungry and believe wholeheartedly, as do I, in the college's mission to democratize education for all. As a result, I'm learning that to succeed with my Berea students I need to understand—and feel—the specific constellation of educational and emotional challenges they bring to the classroom each day. Oftentimes, their needs and emotions mirror those of the characters and people about whom we are reading.

I begin the first day of all of my classes by asking students: What brings you to the table? What do you hope to learn by exploring African American literature? At times, the questions seem to disarm them. Silence comes first. On the one hand, for many students, they have not considered what their learning means to them beyond a grade, a checkbox amid a sea of requirements, or the inevitable hoop they need to jump through in order to take the courses they most want. On the other hand, the question puts my discipline and me, a dark-skinned, natural-haired, African American woman, front and center in their learning experience. My presence at the head of their learning table is an altogether foreign one for most, if not all, of my students. I never take those moments lightly. The key is to move my students from this destabilized position into receptivity to my invitation. I do this by offering a clear—and mutable—roadmap through our days, our weeks, and our semester together. But I also give them another disclaimer: I want us to attend to the text. Let us contend with what is in front of us, unless I ask otherwise. All white students have a story about the racist grandfather to whom you can't let your Brown friends talk. Or the parent of whom one is never quite sure about what is going to come out of her mouth, so you wait with bated breath until they make their off-color joke about some current event. If we can agree to attend to the text, by acknowledging these ugly episodes but not being locked into a cycle of shame about them, typically, my students and I can make good progress. Introductions completed, expectations set, we can turn to the texts.

Because I have been struck by my students' inabilities to make clear connections between our contemporary moments and historical ones, my first goal is to decide upon which texts should make up the syllabus.[5] The core texts for the class have included Ida B. Wells's *Southern Horrors and Other Writings: The Anti-Lynching Campaign of Ida B.*

Wells, 1892–1900, James Baldwin's *The Evidence of Things Not Seen*, and Toni Cade Bambara's *Those Bones Are Not My Child*. This combination of texts—journalistic exposé, extended essay, and novel—are historical compendiums of responses to anti-Black rhetoric, but also, and read together, the texts provide students with an understanding of various kinds of Black activism. They trace how Black writers and intellectuals have responded directly to racism and violence. One of the many things that I want my students to consider is how these texts are linked, not simply in terms of their specific subject matter, but also in how they convey information about African American life and culture as well as their articulation of and engagement with various kinds of Black activism. Ultimately, I want my students to understand that advocating for change can come in many different forms. Importantly, these texts reveal also how Black people continue to live robust lives.

Pedagogically, I have found the most success in teaching these texts chronologically. Each text urgently attends to Black death as a matter of rightful, national concern—much in the same way that students are seemingly bombarded with Black Lives Matter posters, articles, and news feeds. As a result, they can begin to see how these new-to-them but old stories prefigure the now. My criteria for texts has included the following: (1) Time period—How much history will the students know? How much of a crash course in specific moments in American history will the students need? In African American history, specifically? Will they look up keywords and events in appropriate sources? How much time will they need to spend looking up information on Wikipedia? (2) Medium and mode of the text—Is the piece a historical document, novel, poem, documentary, newspaper article, song, or video? How much will our reading strategies change based on the medium? And, finally, (3) length and composition of the reading(s)—Realistically, how long will it take my students to read thoughtfully, and how, or in what ways, are readings in conversation with one another? I have found that the pacing and structure of the class requires that we move back and forth between older, more historical texts and contemporary texts or moments in history. Often, I will try to pair a foundational text with a more contemporary one. Sometimes I will do this in small doses. The first few weeks of the course are meant to provide the students with some basic articulations of key terms. These include race, racism, Black, double-consciousness, sexism, racial profiling, lynching, and intersectional, so the syllabus is replete with foundational ideas and texts. I'm interested in helping the students articulate what it means to be Black in 2018, but what it meant to be Black in the late nineteenth century, too, because I want to ensure that we all have a shared, working vocabulary by which we might discuss our texts. The course offers them an opportunity to learn to see historically situated throughlines.

PART II: BLACK TEXTS MATTER

When I set out to create this course, I kept returning to three important texts. The first is Elizabeth Alexander's essay "Can You Be Black and Look at This? Reading the Rodney King Videotape(s)" in *The Black Interior*.[6] The second is Saidiya Hartman's *Scenes of Subjection: Terror, Slavery, and Self-Making in Nineteenth-Century America*.[7] And the third is W. E. B. Du Bois's *The Souls of Black Folk*.[8] Alexander outlines a history of Black bodies in pain that have been offered up for public consumption as she tries to articulate the vexed nature of being Black in America while at the same time belonging to "a people." Alexander struggles to create a language that makes clear the irrefutable truth of Blackness as both a state of being and a state of mind. She asks, "What do black people say to each other to describe their relationship to their racial group, when that relationship is crucially forged by incidents of physical and psychic violence that boil down to the 'fact' of abject blackness?"[9] Even though her essay is culturally pegged to its moment (2004) and she's focused on Rodney King's very public beating, I understand her query to be poignant and still timely. Alexander rightfully insists upon an understanding of blackness that is rooted in its corporeality. When she writes, "if any one aphorism can characterize the experience of black people in this country, it might be that the white-authored national narrative deliberately contradicts the histories our bodies know,"[10] she's speaking to a specific history that knows no boundaries, and certainly sees no end in sight. I both hear and understand Alexander, and for the purposes of my classroom and this chapter, I'm interested in exploring how we can acknowledge and value these significant and different histories while we gain knowledge in a way that is honest and respectful and lacks condescension as we teach in predominantly mixed-race classrooms.

To address race, particularly Black suffering, in the mixed-race classroom, I draw on Saidiya Hartman's *Scenes of Subjection: Terror, Slavery, and Self-Making in Nineteenth-Century America*, a text that explores both the quotidian terrors of racial subjugation during and after slavery and how such treatment engendered Black identity formation. Hartman begins with a stunning close reading of one of the most famous beatings in any slave narrative—Frederick Douglass's account of the beating of his Aunt Hester. Yet she leaves out the actual recounting of the beating itself. Douglass's explicit text is absent from Hartman's narrative. Instead, she writes the following:

> I have chosen not to reproduce Douglass's account of the beating of Aunt Hester in order to call attention to the ease with which such scenes are usually reiterated, the casualness with which they are circulated, and the consequences of this routine display of the slave's ravaged body. Rather than inciting indignation, too often they immure us to pain by virtue of their familiarity—the oft-repeated or restored character of these accounts and our distance from them are signaled by the theatrical language usually resorted to in describing these instances—and especially because they reinforce the spectacular character of black suffering.[11]

Unfortunately, one need only watch the nightly news to understand that Hartman's position is accurate. Tamir Rice, Sandra Bland, Philando Castile, Eric Garner, Michael Brown—their deaths and the deaths of so many other Black people have circulated effortlessly in the news and on social media. So much so that I might easily substitute their names for the unnamed "slave's ravaged body" Hartman describes from the nineteenth century. Because I acknowledge the danger in teaching this course that has an overabundance of readily available visual representations of Black suffering and Black death, specifically, and which has inured us to Black pain, I believe Hartman's framework is useful. In following her lead, I do not use such representations. Instead, I ask my students to defer to texts—mostly written, some audible, a few newspaper stills, or visual art. I refuse to view or display graphic photographs of contemporary slain victims or watch police body cam videos out of respect for those victims and so as not to perpetuate a cycle of lurid violence against Black bodies. African American literature well reminds us of our continuing saga with and our responses to state-sanctioned violence and racism, despite varied news outlets' reporting on the distinct nature of these un-racially motivated crimes. These crimes are part and parcel of a larger narrative about African American citizens' responses to systems of oppression, be they racism, sexism, or other.

To ensure that the class has a shared understanding and vocabulary to discuss race and racism, I turn to W. E. B. Du Bois's foundational and prescient *The Souls of Black Folk*. In spite of the fact that he penned his text in 1903, his words that "the problem of the twentieth century is the problem of the color line" still ring true.[12] His interrelated concepts of *double-consciousness* and *the veil* are quintessential to the Black experience in the United States and, as such, ones that I discuss in several class periods and ones to which we refer continually. Du Bois describes *double-consciousness* as the "sense of always looking at one's self through the eyes of others, or measuring one's soul by the tape of a world that looks on in amused contempt and pity."[13] Put another way, double-consciousness describes the internal conflict experienced by an subordinated group (African Americans) in an oppressive and dominant society (white America). For Du Bois, *the veil* is both literal and figurative and refers to four states. Du Bois describes these conditions as follows: "After the Egyptian and Indian the Greek and the Roman, the Teuton and Mongolian, the Negro is a sort of seventh son, born with a veil, and gifted with second-sight in this American world,—a world which yields him no true self-consciousness, but only lets him see himself through the revelation of the other world. It is a peculiar sensation, this double-consciousness."[14]

To begin, *the veil* describes the literal darker skin tones of Black people, which physically mark us as different from white Americans. But it is also white Americans' inability to see Black people as bona fide Americans with all of the same privileges accorded to white citizens. In addition, *the veil* refers to Black peoples' inability to see themselves outside of what white America describes and prescribes for them. Considering the demographics of my current Berea College students, when I ask them to imagine the kinds of emotional, psychological, physical, and psychic tolls living under and within the veil might engender, it is not difficult for them. Finally, while many scholarly readings of the veil meditate on its debilitating effects, I remind my students to read closely, because Du Bois notes that the Negro is "gifted with second-sight." While such giftedness is ironic for Du Bois, it does nonetheless afford Black Americans to this day an ability to see this country in all of its naked beauty, shame, and promise, a state in which most white Americans cannot perceive it. Ultimately, these texts help me to frame both the content and the ethics of the course.

PART III: A DAY IN THE LIFE (WE READ TOGETHER)

Typically, I begin the day with a song, a poem, a word, a quotation, or a portion of a podcast that is our way of opening up a conversation about Black pain and suffering; this practice also affords me and the students an opportunity to incorporate a low-stakes writing component. For example, one day I presented the class with Rita Dove's poem "Trayvon Redux."[15] Penned soon after George Zimmerman's acquittal in the murder of Trayvon Martin, it is Doves meditation on that deadly interaction.[16] I asked them to read the poem and write about it for 7–10 minutes. I then led the class in a discussion about the media, ideology, and race. The following are potential questions I might ask: For what occasion was the poem written? These various responses help to frame the specific context of the poem but also how we understand Dove's perspective and what we know of the case. How do we understand the title? What does *redux* intimate? From whose perspective(s)? How do we make sense of Dove's use of italics? Might we speculate about the insertion of William Carlos Williams's "Asphodel the Greenery Flower" after the first stanza? In what ways is broadcast television (the news, *Matlock*, etc.) invoked? Is there a change in tempo between the first and fourth stanzas? If so, why? Is there a shift in perspective between the first and fourth stanzas? If so, why? How do we understand Dove's use of the words "rights," "law," "vigilante," and "enforcers"? Who is enforcing what? Dove's poem is an opportunity to remind my students not only of the topic of the class—Black death, as rendered in this horrifyingly public assault and death of young Trayvon Martin—but also of how this specific literary form "helps us slow down, observe and think more deeply, and better understand each other and our world."[17]

Then I'll shift to the reading for the day, such as "The Whites of Their Eyes: Racist Ideologies and the Media" by Stuart Hall.[18] Generation Z's voracious capacity for consuming popular culture allows me to include videos and other media alongside written texts. Hall's essay is a useful starting point when I want to screen anything media-related, because it challenges the students to think about the ways in which cultural representations are always already saturated in particular ideologies. In clear and precise language, Hall theorizes how we come to understand what it is we see and how such understanding upholds various systems of domination and inequity. As a way of framing Hall's discussion about ideology, in addition to foregrounding our sustained conversations about the death of

Black children, I ask the students to conduct a series of academic searches comparing news-related articles about the JonBenét Ramsey murder case and the Atlanta child murders.[19] Overall, I want the students to explore the differences in representation of these two particular cases. Here I am asking the students to think about the following questions: Who frames which narrative? How it is framed? What news outlets run which stories and can you speculate why? I want them to consider seriously what Hall means when he writes, "The media are not only a powerful source of ideas about race. They are also one place where these ideas are articulated, worked on, transformed, and elaborated."[20] In terms of photographic representation, how are we meant to understand the flat, black-and-white photos of nameless Black children when we compare them to the glossy, manicured images of a little white girl beauty queen (JonBenét)? Clearly, race and class play major factors in how these cases were reported.

Dividing the students into small groups, I asked each group to explore one particular database.[21] For the purposes of our search, we explored four distinct electronic databases: Access World News, Academic Search Complete, Ethnic News Watch, and Historic New York Times. We hypothesized what we *should* find and then what we *might* find when we compared the representations of the cases. Considering the fact that the Atlanta child murders happened almost a decade and a half before the JonBenét Ramsey case, we surmised that with the passage of time there would be more written about the Atlanta child murders. Also, because of the sheer number of victims (approximately twenty-nine) in the Atlanta child murders, we presumed that the higher number would predominate the coverage. What we found was not shocking, but it did confirm some of our initial suspicions: there is an overabundance of reporting on the Ramsey case.

Much of our class discussion cohered around issues of reporting. How do we access information? Who is reporting what? For whom? To whom? Does the proportion of results hold across all of the databases we are searching? What specific work does each database do? With what perspective are the various databases interested? Can we make a broader assertion about what news organizations do and do not do?

Not only does this exercise encourage the students to read sources critically, but also it demands that we ask questions about what stories get excised from our cultural imagination when specific news stories do not gain traction or garner public attention.[22] And how that dynamic may or may not alter how we understand history.[23] The points here are that teaching students discernment with respect to source development and evaluation is critical, as is the explicit critique of shifts in news cycles and their political machinations. What we see here is the Black body emerging time and time again as the *sine qua non* of American inequity. While race remains implicit in this comparison, these moments in class make race explicit as a term for comparison. As James Baldwin so powerfully asserts in *The Evidence of Things Not Seen*, "for the children came, mainly, from Atlanta's lowest economic stratum. This means that they were strangers to safety, for, in the brutal generality, only the poor watch over the poor. The poor do not exist for others, except as an inconvenience or a threat or an economic or sometimes missionary or sometimes genuinely moral opportunity. *The poor ye have with you always;* indeed, but never, in the main, to be seen, and never, certainly, as we should know by now, to be heard."[24]

PART IV: THE SACRED AND THE PROFANE: READING CLASSIC AND MODERN TEXTS

Because popular culture is rife with opportunities that allow students to explore and reflect upon historical texts, I welcome any new opportunities to bridge the gaps between the past and the present explicitly. W. E. B. Du Bois's *Souls*, as previously mentioned, is one of those texts to which I always return in class. After discussing the text for several days in class and assigning an essay wherein the students were required to write a new version of any one of Du Bois's chapters by putting it into a new genre, one of my students asked, offhandedly, if I had heard the rapper T.I.'s most recent song, "Warzone."[25] The student sheepishly suggested that "maybe T.I. is talking about what Du Bois is talking about?" As soon as I left class, I listened to the song and watched the video. Not only was my student correct—and we needed to read closely this song and its accompanying video—but he was linking T.I., an Atlanta-based, contemporary, Black rapper to African American literature and theory, as well as its contemporary imperative. This moment was another occasion to bridge the then and the now.

During the next class period, I asked the other students if we might do as my student suggested—explore how and if "Warzone" affirms some of the philosophical articulations/claims Du Bois makes about the veil and double-consciousness in his famous "Forethought" and "Of Our Spiritual Strivings." I focused on those chapters in particular because they establish the parameters of his overall argument. Building upon my student's observations, I asked: How is T.I. signifying upon Du Bois and our contemporary moment? What does he have to say? And why is it important? The result was one of the most lively and fruitful class discussions we ever had together.

The dual juxtaposition of a T.I. video production and the white characters on the screen, as well as the initial melodic organ music, contrasts starkly with T.I.'s voice as he raps loudly, "Can't you see we livin' in a war zone."[26] From the onset of the song and its accompanying video, the viewer/listener is on notice that our ocular experience and ideological frame regarding race and racism will be challenged. One might ask of the music video, "Where are the Black people?" T.I. continues,

> Like every weekend it's a man down.
> Ain't got no pity for the innocent.
> So I'm a represent it.
> Dedicated tell 'em.
> Hands up. Can't Breathe.
> Hands up. Can't Breathe.
> Hands up. Can't Breathe.
> Hands up. Can't you see we livin' in a war zone?[27]

Placing us squarely within the language of the rallying cry for #BLM, T.I.'s hands raised high image counterposes the boy's walking.[28] Soon other details in the video emerge—T.I. has recast all of the modern-day male victims of police brutality as white citizens, and all of the unflappable and aloof onlookers in the video are Black citizens. Subsequently, the listener/viewer watches reenactments of Tamir Rice's murder, Eric Garner's murder, and Philando Castile's murder.[29]

Screening this music video allows me to engage my students in a robust discussion about the contemporaneity of Du Bois's argument. Do we have a visceral reaction to the reenactments of these crimes? With white bodies? What about when the bodies are Brown? What does it mean that T.I. closes his video with the voice of Jane Elliot?[30] To what history is he alluding by using her voice? After discussing T.I.'s "Warzone" we return to Du Bois's final chapter, the short story "Of the Coming of John," to rethink how Du Bois is using doubles, allegory, and signification, as well as to explore his articulation of "second sight" by refashioning violence onto the lives of alternative bodies.

Most significantly, I became aware that my students' reflections were shifting as we were learning together. By not assuming textual supremacy based on medium and in response to my students' curiosity, I opened up space for exploration. This move allowed them to think critically about what they read, saw, heard, and felt. In some ways, popular culture allowed us to explore and learn on equal standing, because certainly my knowledge of contemporary rap pales in comparison to my students', just as their understanding of African American history and literature pales compared to my own. This moment recalled the teachings of educator and philosopher Paulo Freire, specifically his "banking concept of education" wherein "knowledge is a gift bestowed by those who consider themselves knowledgeable upon those whom they consider to know nothing. Projecting an absolute ignorance onto others, a characteristic of the ideology of oppression, negated education and knowledge as processes of inquiry."[31] Together, my students and I were able to work through their nascent understanding of Du Bois's work at the same time that I was developing my nascent understanding of contemporary rap.

Moreover, that examination allowed me to reframe Frantz Fanon's theories regarding race and interpellation in terms that account for gender.[32] Whereas Fanon's theories of interpellation are decidedly gendered male, when I introduce Ida B. Wells and her anti-lynching campaign, I am able to begin the class with a device modeled after an exercise that Kimberlé Crenshaw employs that offers a corrective.[33] First, I ask my students to stand. Their instructions are simple: sit down when they recognize any of the names I read from a list. I then begin to read a list of the many Black men who have been brutalized or murdered by the police.[34] After several minutes, it becomes clear that most of the class is seated. Then I ask them to repeat the process. This time, I read the names of the many Black women and trans women of color who have been brutalized or murdered by the police: Kayla Moore, Rekia Boyd, Shelly Frey, Shantel Davis, Kyam Livingston, Aiyana Stanley-Jones, and too many others. When it becomes clear that few have heard about these victims and the heinous crimes committed against them, they are aghast. Oftentimes my students will ask why they haven't heard about these cases. Immediately, this moment leads us into a discussion wherein we can talk about how "although Black women are routinely killed, raped, and beaten by the police, their experiences are rarely foregrounded in popular narratives of police brutality."[35] We explore Crenshaw's #SayHerName campaign and the ways that Black people, Black women in particular, have advocated historically for themselves and protested against state-sanctioned violence against them and their communities.[36]

While Kimberlé Crenshaw's activist work with the Say Her Name movement is certainly new for the students, it does have historical antecedents in a figure like Ida B. Wells.[37] Here, I make clear that I am connecting both the individual work of these activists and these women's understanding of the cultural violence aimed at the subjugation of Black people through violence. After our early discussions of Ida B. Wells's personal history, we examine how the risks that Wells takes in her writings were unprecedented coming from a Black woman in the nineteenth century—and, subsequently, how those risks amplified the failings of Reconstruction. As Jacqueline Goldsby writes in *A Spectacular Secret: Lynching in American Life and Literature*, the "social transformations that made her career in journalism possible—the emancipation of African Americans from slavery, the liberation of women from Victorian-era gender roles, and the ascendance of American newspapers as central arbiters of historical knowledge in public life—allow us to examine how those modes of secularized progress paradoxically helped create the milieu in which lynching thrived before World War I."[38] I ask the students to think about how Wells deploys language and rhetorical strategies. In what ways do we see Wells using her own subject position within the narrative? If we compare her narrative to other texts (narrative or otherwise) that we have read, what does her positioning afford her? Why? I might ask them to speculate on the very nature of activism and compare it to the activism they see in Kimberlé Crenshaw and even Zala Spencer, the fictionalized mother in *Those Bones Are Not My Child*. Ultimately, I want the students to explore what happens when gender is a critical mode of inquiry used to combat racialized state violence.

Not all of my lesson plans require several sessions, nor are they all carried out in class. When we are grappling with a particularly difficult text, like James Baldwin's *The Evidence of Things Not Seen*, for example, and I want them to write about it, I'll shift the focus for a moment and we will read random, sample book reviews from diverse sources: the *New Yorker*, *People*, *Elle Magazine*, the *Economist*, *Cosmopolitan*, or *African American Review*. To be clear, I have found that reviewing different genres from a wide range of book reviews—academic presses, celebrity gossip news magazines, even cultural magazines—lessens my students' anxieties about how they write, as well as what they write. For example, when we critique Michael Winerup's 1999 review in the *New York Times* of J. K. Rowling's *Harry Potter and the Sorcerer's Stone*,[39] the students are taken aback that we are reading a serious review of children's literature. But then we begin. We consider the tone, the effect, grammar, style, and the overall composition of the piece. I articulate verbally and in writing how looking at these specific book reviews, critiquing their contents, and asking explicit questions is both the same rubric by which I will measure their subsequent book reviews and part and parcel of a larger system of skills that we are developing in their overall writing processes. Then I ask my students to put pen to paper and begin to write book reviews about Baldwin's *The Evidence of Things Not Seen*.[40] Their prose is sharper, their ability to identify and articulate his thesis clearer, their understanding of how and why Baldwin is using history as it pertains to racism and classism comes into focus. Modeling clear, concise prose strengthens their writing, boosts their confidence, and generates their nascent voices too.

CONCLUSION

In the final chapters of *From #BlackLivesMatter to Black Liberation*, Keeanga-Yamahtta Taylor takes stock of how Black lives have been devalued and lost historically while simultaneously articulating a nascent political action plan that demands solidarity. "Solidarity is standing in unity with people," she writes "even when you have not personally experienced their particular oppression."[41] While I agree wholeheartedly with Taylor's clarion call, I cannot help but think that in this particularly divisive political moment a preliminary step is needed; courses like Death of the Black Child is one such step. I would like to think that in the construction and design of my course I'm careful to remain honest and forthright in my responses to students. Every time I teach this course, I conjure the images of my first set of adolescent students who asked me those necessary, pressing, and prevailing questions. In response, I offer historical precedence, rigor, candor, and care, but also a space where listening, sympathy, solidarity, and a sense of urgency is paramount because "Black liberation is bound up with the project of human liberation and social transformation."[42] We create communities of solidarity and *in* solidarity in the classroom. My goal in teaching this course and contributing to this volume on teaching race and ethnicity is to explore the hows and whys of my pedagogy. Through this examination, I offer different ways to frame national conversation(s) while historicizing contemporary politics through Black literature.

NOTES

1. Jelani Cobb, "The Matter of Black Lives," *New Yorker*, March 7, 2016, https://www.newyorker.com/magazine/2016/03/14/where-is-black-lives-matter-headed. The most recent scholarly publication that historicizes #BLM is Keeanga-Yamahtta Taylor's timely book, *From #BlackLivesMatter to Black Liberation* (Chicago: Haymarket, 2016). Also, Jelani Cobb's reporting in the *New Yorker* regarding #BLM has been informative and historically grounded, including "The Matter of Black Lives," "Old Questions but No New Answers in the Philando Castile Verdict," "The Walter Scott Case Mistrial and the Crisis of Facts," "Creating 'Luke Cage,' the First Woke Black-Superhero Show," "Inside the Trial of Dylan Roof," and "After Dallas, the Future of Black Lives Matter."

2. Michael Brown was an unarmed Black teenager shot by Ferguson, Missouri, police officer Darren Wilson. His death and the subsequent outrage gave rise to the Black Lives Matter movement (#BLM). Trayvon Martin was an unarmed Black teenage boy who was tracked and shot by vigilante George Zimmerman. Zimmerman mistook the Skittles in Martin's pocket for a weapon. He accosted the boy and ultimately killed Martin. Zimmerman was later acquitted of murder charges.

3. bell hooks, *Feminist Theory from Margin to Center* (Boston: South End Press, 1984). Here I am borrowing from the title of bell hooks's second book, which articulates a radical feminist politics wherein hooks charges all to reconstitute the center of political discussions as women-focused and feminist learning.

4. The late legal theorist Derrick Bell's formative work in critical race theory in jurisprudence paved the way for a number of scholars to think about the ways in which race and pedagogy intersect in the classroom. Derrick Bell, *Faces at the Bottom of the Well* (New York: Perseus Books, 1992). Edward Taylor, David Gillborn, and Gloria Ladson-Billings, eds., *Foundations of Critical Race Theory in Education* (New York: Routledge, 2011). Here I'm grateful to Dr. Jamiella Brooks for reminding me that what I am describing is critical race pedagogy.

5. They cannot see how young Emmett Till's murder is linked to Rodney King's beating in Los Angeles in 1991. They cannot see because they do not know this history. They are not, however, responsible for said ignorance. I can no longer count the number of times my students have told me that they haven't learned anything about Black history, as if that history is not categorically *American* history. Putting specific literary and historical texts alongside popular culture and the news demands that students learn more history and read critically.

6. Elizabeth Alexander, *The Black Interior* (Minneapolis: Graywolf, 2004).

7. Saidiya Hartman, *Scenes of Subjection: Terror, Slavery, and Self-Making in Nineteenth-Century America* (New York: Oxford University Press, 1997).

8. W. E. B. Du Bois, *The Souls of Black Folk*, ed. Henry Louis Gates Jr. and Terri Hume Oliver (New York: W. W. Norton, 1999).

9. Alexander, *Black Interior*, 176.

10. Alexander, *Black Interior*, 179.

11. Hartman, *Scenes of Subjection*, 3.

12. Du Bois, *Souls of Black Folk*, 7.

13. Du Bois, *Souls of Black Folk*, 11.

14. Du Bois, *Souls of Black Folk*, 11.

15. Rita Dove, "Trayvon, Redux," in *Killing Trayvons: An Anthology of American Violence*, ed. Kevin Alexander Gray, Jeffrey St. Clair, and JoAnn Wypijewski (Petrolia: CounterPunch, 2014), 63–65.

16. Trayvon Martin was an unarmed Black teenage boy who was tracked and shot by vigilante George Zimmerman. Zimmerman was acquitted of murder charges. Zimmerman mistook the Skittles in Martin's pocket for a weapon. He accosted the teenage boy and ultimately killed Martin. Rita Dove is the commonwealth professor at the University of Virginia as well as the former poet laureate of the United States.

17. Tracy K. Smith, "Coming Soon: The Slowdown," *The Slowdown*, podcast audio, October 1, 2018, https://www.slowdownshow.org.

18. Stuart Hall, "The Whites of Their Eyes: Racist Ideologies and the Media," in *Gender, Race and Class in Media: A Text-Reader*, ed. Gail Dines and Jean M. Humez (Thousand Oaks, CA: Sage, 1995), 18–22.

19. JonBenét Ramsey was a six-year-old child beauty pageant winner who was found murdered in the basement of her home on Christmas Day 1996. Despite the fact that her parents and her brother were home, none were convicted of her murder. Her unsolved death and murder predominated national news for years. Even after all these years, several television shows, documentaries, and miniseries have been based on Ramsey's death. The Atlanta child murders were a series of murders committed in the city of Atlanta from 1978 to 1981. Throughout that time, twenty-nine adolescents and adults were kidnapped and subsequently found murdered. Wayne Williams, a twenty-three-year-old Black native of Atlanta, was convicted of two of the murders. He was arrested and sentenced with two consecutive life terms. In a bizarre turn of events, however, the police attributed a number of murders to Williams and closed the cases, even though the individual cases of all of the victims were never brought to trial. Sources vary about the many missing and murdered children. Scant national or historical attention has been paid to these heinous crimes. I am grateful to my reference librarian friends, Amanda Peach at the Hutchison Library at Berea College and Liza Oldham at the Oliver Wendell Holmes Library at Phillips Academy at Andover, for their help with these searches and their thoughts about these particular cases.

20. Hall, "Whites of Their Eyes," 22. A more contemporary example of this phenomenon is the reporting on the Brock Turner rape case. Brock Turner assaulted an unresponsive, intoxicated women after a Stanford fraternity party. As he attempted to flee the scene of the attack a few Swedish exchange students

witnessed the assault and tackled him to the ground, thus preventing him from fleeing.

21. There are a few ground rules, however, to establish and some caveats to highlight before the students begin this exercise. To begin, in order to complete the activity, the students need to be competent users of their institution's library and its electronic resources. To ensure basic library literacy, I invite a reference librarian to my class for guided instruction or I will sign up my class for a day of research with a reference librarian. Evaluating sources is key. One must, as reference librarian Amanda Peach states, "evaluate sources via the CRAAP criteria." The acronym CRAAP stands for C=currency, R=relevancy, A=authority, A=accuracy, and P=purpose. (Amanda Peach, email message to Tasha M. Hawthorne, October 27, 2017.) I also remind the students that we need to think about these points: "1) CNN's 24 hour news cycle program was in its beginnings in the early 1980s. As a result, media saturation was impossible in the late 1970s and early 1980s. 2) It is harder to do comparable searches for the Atlanta child murders since there were multiple victims, and the name 'Atlanta child murders' is a more contemporary shorthand" (Liza Oldham, email message to Tasha M. Hawthorne, February 12, 2018.). 3) Students must remember to use the same exact search terms each time they conduct a search. 4) Students should limit their searches to specific databases.

22. As an aside, I shift immediately back in time to explore why and for what purposes Mamie Till Bradley, mother of slain teenager Emmett Till, would demand to expose her son's murdered body in an open coffin. For the images that galvanized the civil rights movement, see *Jet* magazine's September 15, 1955, issue.

23. For example, the spotty coverage of the Atlanta child murders has opened up space for a new true crime podcast, *Atlanta Monster*. In the podcast liner notes on iTunes the podcast is described as follows: "From the producers of *Up and Vanished* and *HowStuffWorks*, *Atlanta Monster* aims to tell the true story of one of Atlanta's darkest secrets, almost 40 years later." For more on *Atlanta Monster*, listen to Mary Louise Kelly's NPR interview: "'Atlanta Monster' Podcast Hopes to 'Close the Door' on 1970s Child Murders," NPR, https://www.npr.org/2018/02/08/584085035/atlanta-monster-podcast-hopes-to-close-the-door-on-1970s-child-murders; Sarah Larson's article, "'Atlanta Monster': In Pursuit of Justice and a Hit Podcast," *New Yorker*, https://www.newyorker.com/culture/podcast-dept/atlanta-monster-in-pursuit-of-justice-and-a-hit-podcast, Nicholas Quah's review, "*Atlanta Monster* Is a Different Kind of True-Crime Podcast," *Vulture*, http://www.vulture.com/2018/01/atlanta-monster-podcast-review.html.

24. Baldwin, *Evidence of Things Not Seen*, 62.

25. "Warzone," performed by T.I., on *Us or Else*, Grand Hustle Records and Roc Nation, 2016. I'm grateful to Gerardo Soto, Berea College class of 2020, for sharing this song with me.

26. "Warzone."

27. "Warzone."

28. Tamir Rice is the twelve-year-old African American boy who was playing with a toy gun in a public park and killed by the Cleveland police. For more on Rice's death, see Sean Flynn, "The Tamir Rice Story: How to Make a Police Shooting Disappear," *GQ*, July 14, 2016, https://www.gq.com/story/tamir-rice-story; Starla Muhammed, "Outrage Brews in Police Shooting of 12-Year-Old," *Louisiana Weekly*, December 15, 2014; and J. Wade, "Clevelanders 'Up in Arms' Over the Shooting of 12-Year-Old Tamir Rice," *Call & Post*, December 3, 2014.

29. Eric Garner is the African American man who was put into an illegal chokehold by the New York City police and died of asphyxiation. For more on Eric Garner's death, see Matt Taibbi's *I Can't Breathe: A Killing on Bay Street* (New York: Spiegel and Grau, 2017).

30. Jane Elliott is an educator and cultural critic. Dismayed and horrified by Dr. Martin Luther King Jr.'s assassination, third-grade teacher Elliott felt as if she had to do something to teach her young Iowa students about discrimination. She created and conducted the blue eyes/brown eyes exercise in 1968. In short, Elliott separated her students by the color of their eyes—blue eyes vs. brown or green eyes—and either provided them with privileges or took away their privileges based on their eye color. To this day, the exercise continues to create controversy.

31. Paulo Freire, *Pedagogy of the Oppressed* (New York: Continuum, 1994), 53.

32. Frantz Fanon, *Black Skin, White Masks* (New York: Grove, 2008).

33. Homa Khaleeli describes this exercise in her article in the *Guardian*. Khaleeli, "#SayHerName: Why Kimberlé Crenshaw Is Fighting for Forgotten Women," *Guardian*, May 30, 2016, https://www.theguardian.com/lifeandstyle/2016/may/30/sayhername-why-kimberle-crenshaw-is-fighting-for-forgotten-women.

34. Gawker ran a harrowing story, replete with color photos, of a litany of Brown folk killed by the police from 1994 to 2014. Rich Juzwiak and Aleksander Chan, "Unarmed People of Color Killed by Police, 1994–2014," *Gawker*, December 8, 2014, http://gawker.com/unarmed-people-of-color-killed-by-police-1999-2014-1666672349.

35. Kimberlé Crenshaw, *#SayHerName: Resisting Police Brutality against Black Women*, African American Policy Forum, July 16, 2015, https://aapf.org/sayhernamereport.

36. I will also use this occasion to introduce Crenshaw's important work regarding intersectionality. For more on Crenshaw's use of "intersectionality," see Kimberlé Crenshaw, "Mapping the Margins: Intersectionality, Identity Politics, and Violence against Women of Color," *Stanford Law Review* 43, no. 6 (1991): 1241–99, *JSTOR*, www.jstor.org/stable/1229039.

37. This is another opportunity to have students read and explore different texts about Black death through different mediums. Crenshaw and her team at the African American Policy Forum, which is "an innovative think tank that connects academics, activists, and policy-makers to promote efforts to dismantle structural inequality," have built a veritable treasure-trove website replete with initiatives,

campaigns, blogs, reports, and a host of resources. Specifically, Crenshaw has an initiative dedicated to her work surrounding Black women and violence. Oftentimes I will ask the students to peruse their work through this website. For more, see the African American Policy Forum, www.aapf.org.

38. Jacqueline Goldsby, *A Spectacular Secret: Lynching in American Life and Literature* (Chicago: University of Chicago Press, 2006).

39. Michael Winerup, review of *Harry Potter and the Sorcerer's Stone*, by J. K. Rowling, *New York Times*, February 14, 1999.

40. I use James Baldwin's 1985 reissued *The Evidence of Things Not Seen* as a bridge text. It is the link between Wells's older and seemingly distant *Southern Horrors* and the more contemporary, palatable novel form we read in Bambara. After living in France for several years, Baldwin was contacted by Walter Lowe, an editor at *Playboy*, to fly to Atlanta to report about the Atlanta child murders. Sources vary about the many missing and murdered children. Scant national or historical attention has been paid to these heinous crimes. I call students' attention to the medium and mode of Baldwin's atypical reporting. The facts of the actual case are sparse, the objectivity absent, and the prose more homily than newspaper-speak. Additionally, I ask the students to first read Derrick Bell and Janet Derrick Bell's foreword and Baldwin's preface, because they function as primers on the case, Baldwin's prose, and his commitment to the civil rights movement. I have found that this text is difficult for the students to read, not because of Baldwin's writing style but rather because of his insistence upon the reader's knowledge base. Baldwin's unwieldy text is about more than the case against Wayne Williams—it is about our country's inability to have an honest, national dialogue about race that attends to history, the false promises of democracy, and racism.

41. Taylor, *From #BlackLivesMatter*, 215.

42. Taylor, *From #BlackLivesMatter*, 194.

BIBLIOGRAPHY

Alexander, Elizabeth. *The Black Interior*. Minneapolis: Graywolf, 2004.

Baldwin, James. *The Evidence of Things Not Seen*. New York: Henry Holt, 1985.

Bambara, Toni Cade. *Those Bones Are Not My Child*. New York: Random House, 1999.

Cobb, Jelani. "The Matter of Black Lives." *New Yorker*, March 7, 2016. https://www.newyorker.com/magazine/2016/03/14/where-is-black-lives-matter-headed.

Crenshaw, Kimberlé. *#SayHerName: Resisting Police Brutality against Black Women*. African American Policy Forum, July 16, 2015. https://aapf.org/sayhernamereport.

Dove, Rita. "Trayvon, Redux." In *Killing Trayvons: An Anthology of American Literature*, edited by Kevin Alexander Gray, Jeffrey St. Clair, and JoAnn Wypijewski, 63–65. Petrolia, CA: CounterPunch, 2014.

Du Bois, W. E. B. *The Souls of Black Folk.* Edited by Henry Louis Gates Jr. and Terri Hume Oliver. New York: W. W. Norton, 1999.

Fanon, Frantz. *Black Skin, White Masks*. New York: Grove, 2008.

Freire, Paulo. *Pedagogy of the Oppressed*. New York: Continuum, 1994.

Goldsby, Jacqueline. *A Spectacular Secret: Lynching in American Life and Literature*. Chicago: University of Chicago Press, 2006.

Hall, Stuart. "The Whites of Their Eyes: Racist Ideologies and the Media." In *Gender, Race and Class in Media: A Text-Reader*, edited by Gail Dines and Jean M. Humez, 18–22. Thousand Oaks, CA: Sage, 1995.

Hartman, Saidiya. *Scenes of Subjection: Terror, Slavery, and Self-Making in Nineteenth-Century America*. New York: Oxford University Press, 1997.

hooks, bell. *Feminist Theory from Margin to Center*. Boston: South End Press, 1984.

Khaleeli, Homa. "#SayHerName: Why Kimberlé Crenshaw Is Fighting for Forgotten Women." *Guardian*, May 30, 2016. https://www.theguardian.com/lifeandstyle/2016/may/30/sayhername-why-kimberle-crenshaw-is-fighting-for-forgotten-women.

Taylor, Edward, David Gillborn, and Gloria Ladson-Billings, eds. *Foundations of Critical Race Theory in Education*. New York: Routledge, 2011.

Taylor, Keeanga-Yamahtta. *From #BlackLivesMatter to Black Liberation*. Chicago: Haymarket, 2016.

Wells, Ida B., *Southern Horrors and Other Writings: The Anti-Lynching Campaign of Ida B. Wells, 1892–1900*. Edited by Jacqueline Jones Royster. Boston: Bedford/St. Martin's, 1997.

Winerup, Michael. Review of *Harry Potter and the Sorcerer's Stone*, by J. K. Rowling. *New York Times*, February 14, 1999.

AFTERWORD

Teaching Race within Criminal Justice

CHYNA CRAWFORD

Over the past several years, incidents involving police officers who have killed people of color, purportedly in the line of duty, have been shockingly on the rise. It is dimly comforting to see, in response, that those incidents have begun to raise a greater public awareness, and in cities like Minneapolis, Minnesota, some have called for the defunding of entire police forces in response to the systemically enabled killing of black and brown bodies. Nevertheless, and as of the time of this writing most forcefully seen in the denial of police culpability for the police shooting that caused the death of Breonna Taylor, police officers are too often not indicted and, when charged, not convicted; far too often, those officers escape even the most basic level of internal reprimand or probationary oversight. When brought to trial, these cases often hinge on the character of the actors, circumstances surrounding the death, perceived threats, and environmental factors influencing the actions rather than the fact of the wrongful death of an innocent citizen that was caused by a police officer's gun. In response to national conversations about race and policing, and during this emerging era of the Black Lives Matter movement, scholarly attention has turned to violence perpetrated by police on civilians and the racial and organizational context of this violence.[1]

Born and raised in Charlottesville, Virginia, I have witnessed how police violence and systemic racism can stifle students, from elementary school onward, from academic success. The Unite the Right rally (and the larger movement it represents) in Charlottesville was responding directly to a local black teenager who was incensed that race was ignored in the city's public schools and, further, that a racist Confederate history was openly endorsed and celebrated by the city's monuments. She called for the removal of those monuments while speakers for Unite the Right supported keeping the statues. The protests ultimately resulted in a deadly scene when a twenty-year-old Ohio man drove his car into a crowd of counter protesters, killing one counter protester and leaving nineteen others injured.[2] Incidents such as this are why teaching race is not only important but it is necessary. Within the field of criminal justice, this imperative has become all the more urgent as the topic has become a matter of life and death: "To understand crime fully . . . [teaching race] must become an integral part of the discussion about who is criminal, and which public policies will best control crime."[3]

As an undergraduate at Longwood University in Farmville, Virginia, and later as a graduate student, my exposure to race-centered topics was initially nourished at home. My family educated me on the significance of Farmville and its place in the history of racial politics and resistance. Farmville and Prince Edward County students' protests resulted in a court case included in the joint case of *Brown v. Board of Education*, the landmark Supreme Court decision that ended school segregation nationwide. The local school system countered punitively, closing the public-school system (and at the same time, a private white-only school opened to absorb the white student population) for five years, from 1959 to 1964, rather than permitting school desegregation. Many of the area's white students, particularly those from more affluent families, still attend that private school to this day.[4]

However, my first institutional lesson regarding race occurred at the doctoral level. At Prairie View A&M University, I was introduced to a book that came to shape my career: *African American Classics in Criminology and Criminal Justice*. These readings contextualized race within a legal and criminal justice framework and answered long-harbored questions regarding the criminal justice system and the disproportionate responses to black and brown citizens. During those same years in graduate study, I encountered one specific incident that reinforced my determination to teach race within the field of criminal justice studies: the case of Sandra Bland. In 2015, Bland was pulled over for failure to signal a lane change. A confrontation with the officer occurred, and she was taken into custody and detained on a charge of assaulting an officer; she was found hanging in her jail cell with a plastic trash bag around her neck. Her death, although ruled a suicide, has been highly debated because of lasting suspicions over police officers' actions in the circumstances surrounding her death.[5] This incident took place just yards from the front entrance of Prairie View A&M University, the institution that sparked the flame of interest in and knowledge about race and criminal justice.

As history repeats itself, I have come to teach the materials I once studied, including the protests against police violence and the underlying systemic racism embedded in our institutions that are once again underway across the United States. I teach criminal justice within a social and historical context, and my Introduction to Criminology course provides an overview of the system before digging into the topics that have become hot-button issues for my students, especially as these many incidents play out as though stuck on repeat across media outlets. Within the classroom, there are seven cases that I use as examples that act as mirror images of actions that keep repeating, and my class examines them as reflections of these cycles: the Central Park Five/New York Stop and Frisk, Trayvon Martin/Renisha McBride, Michael Brown/George Floyd, and I include readings from W. E. B. Du Bois forward in order to help students understand the founding, shifting legal and social contexts and present the evolution of the US criminal justice system.

Since the start of 2020, the United States has not only been faced with a global health crisis but has experienced civil and racial upheaval that echoes past decades' turmoil. Recent protests call for deep-seated modifications to US policing. This awareness has refocused the much-needed attention to the systemic racism within our criminal justice system. The modern criminal justice system, emerging from the post–Civil War conception of justice, has facilitated preserving a racialized order within the United States. Given this, it should not, at this point in United States history, surprise anyone to hear that there are still dramatic racial disparities in the enforcement of laws, judiciary proceedings, and treatment within and beyond the criminal justice system. Since 2014, some prominent fatalities include Eric Garner (2014), Michael Brown (2014), Tamir Rice (2014), Laquan McDonald (2014), John Crawford (2014), Freddie Gray (2015), Sandra Bland (2015), Walter Scott (2015), Alton Sterling (2016), Philando Castile (2016), Terence Crutcher (2016), Antwon Rose (2018), Atatiana Jefferson (2019), and Breonna Taylor (2020), among many others.

Because these cases have brought about a wide range of emotions, conversations, policy proposals, protests, and actions that often spill into college classroom, we must now ask ourselves again: How do we address our students' concerns about race, violence, and policing and their understanding of procedural justice? Within the more traditional criminal justice classroom, resources such as research, teaching, service learning, and other outreach activities focus on innovative empirical applications. Traditionally, these techniques allow for trends in law enforcement decision-making, the relationship between policy and policing influence, and the role of civilian demographics in the likelihood of experiencing a police shooting. However, in a race-centered classroom or course, many deeply held views and assumptions about self and society are challenged. Courses related to racial justice can have several objectives: to spread knowledge, increase empathy, confront misconceptions, develop viewpoints, improve analytic proficiency, or develop tools for creative/constructive discourse.

At the beginning of the course, I always encounter some pushback from students who believe that they know about the foundations of the criminal justice system and the purposes, goals, and effectiveness of that system. My classes' demographics include students from varied backgrounds—from urban areas to rural areas, including those who have had negative experiences with law enforcement. I will also have students who come from communities who have very positive experiences with local law enforcement. Many of the students come from backgrounds where their ties to the criminal justice system are rooted in familial relations. Many may not have been exposed to race in the context of learning, and many may not be aware of the systemic issues that exist. Within the criminal justice discipline, many students come into the classroom with preconceived notions of law enforcement and the criminal justice system based on family ties, peripherical interactions, or awareness of generally upheld myths.

I have found that, although my voice and experiences have shaped my views and why I teach race, those experiences are not the first thing that I expose students to when I am in front of them in class. One of the first assignments I ask students to complete is a self-awareness essay, a kind of a racially attuned autobiography. I ask them to reflect upon their own identities; family, education, social groups, and environments; their assumptions about the institution of policing; and what they believe the course will be about. I use this self-reflective technique at intervals throughout the course. After each chapter or significant case is addressed, students are then required to make connections between the course content and their lived experiences. Often, we have to buck common language and assumptions about learning and dealing with race-based issues. Terms such as *safe spaces* are not used in my classrooms because teaching and learning about race is often uncomfortable, and this space of discomfort is also where growth happens. Students learn early that they will not always agree but that they need to actively listen to opposing viewpoints and provide evidence to support their opinions.

My course is organized into modules that address the areas of the criminal justice system: police, law, courts, corrections, juvenile justice, and critical issues in criminal justice. In the policing module, I provide students a historical overview of policing strategies and systems. One of the first cases we discuss in that context centers on the Central Park Five. The details fit the historically disproportionate pattern of targeting, arresting, and convicting minorities. As you may recall, while other people were in that park that night, five young black and brown boys, later deemed the "Central Park Five," were suspected and charged of the assault and rape of a white woman purely based on a fit between the racial profiles of the defendants and the discriminatory assumptions held by the prosecution. The defendants were all still juveniles, aged fourteen to sixteen years old. News media was used to try these juveniles in the court of public opinion and vilify them prior to defending the case that was taking place in court. In fact, a young Donald Trump spent approximately $85,000 on a campaign to bring back the death penalty in 1989, referring explicitly to the Central Park case in full-page advertisements that appeared in four New York City newspapers. Trump's advertisement, then, adopts the same racist perspective of policies and practices he has endorsed and expanded while in office, including the increase of discretionary use of lethal force, militarized police munitions and vehicles, surveillance and no-knock search warrants, dangerous chokes and physical submissions, and other direct and indirect applications of police power. Together, these steps have emboldened many law enforcement officers to ignore or sweep under the rug claims of police brutality.

After reading the text and discussing the case, students are asked: Do racial and ethnic minority police officers make a difference in situations like this? Discussion questions that grow from the study of the Central Park Five case permit students to examine racial disparities in the criminal justice system and, in addition, reflect upon how different racial and ethnic groups have diverse experiences about law enforcement along with many of the actors within the criminal justice system. I have had students come into these discussions with firmly held beliefs that if an innocent suspect would be quiet and follow instructions that the investigatory process imbedded in the criminal justice system would find the correct offender. This does not always happen. With respect to the Central Park Five, students ask questions like this: If there were officers who were aware of the culture, would these juveniles have been labeled suspects? This student-led discussion enables a more open dialogue about cultural perceptions, communication styles, and how being an outsider can shape how you view a group of people. Some of those same students, including some who previously held adamant views about offenders and law enforcement, leave the course with a different viewpoint, arguing in favor of the opposite, that African Americans and minorities of color have and continue to be arrested, detained, and convicted at higher rates than their white counterparts.

In the parallel cases of Trayvon Martin, in Florida, and Renisha McBride, in Detroit, students in this discussion analyze the role of self-defense and racial profiling. When discussing Martin and McBride's cases, students tend to feel some semblance of connection to the victim because undergraduate students may be out late at night visiting service stations and mom-and-pop shops to break up the mundane routines of campus life. These twin cases spark discussions about the implicit social contract that US society is built upon. This unspoken contract includes the basic assumption that citizens have agreed to sacrifice some degree of individual freedom for community and state protection. This debate hinges on whether the freedoms we cede to the state are fairly and equitably given. Some say they are. Some, on another side of the debate, believe in the context of sentencing and court that a community member or a neighborhood-watch member can or should be allowed to seize the authority to take a life with no consequence. This position is troubling to the majority of students in my classes. This debate sparks a realization in some students that they may come from a privileged background and may unconsciously benefit from living in a society that accommodates them rather than alienating them.

Finally, I introduce students to the case of Michael Brown, in Ferguson, Missouri, and then draw connections to the more recent developments with George Floyd, an African American man who was killed while being arrested by the police in Minneapolis, Minnesota. This case is used as a tie-in for a cumulative discussion of the criminal justice system and the issues of police brutality and the lack of accountability that have become critical over the evolution of the system. These two cases force students to contend with their views, feelings, and judgments about not only these incidents but how they exist in relation to their beliefs about how the criminal justice system should function. As tensions escalated in both cases, reports of police using tear gas and rubber bullets on protesters and protests becoming violent emerged. Local police officers were replaced with the state highway patrol, state National Guard soldiers, and ultimately included federal reinforcements. The deaths of both Michael Brown and George Floyd and the conditions surrounding them raise questions about the disparity of power. It brought to bear what happens when local police lose contact with the communities they serve. Concerns over the loss of social and economic justice also come into play when we look at how the costs (human, social, and economic) of controlling those protests escalate in the face of federal interventions. This pair of cases enables a sustained conversation with students about the police's militarization on the one hand and the social-justice activism that has garnered high levels of attention and responsiveness to effect change on the other. As the police have become more militarized, the emphasis has changed from the older views in which the police protect and serve local communities to a more modern neoliberal view of law enforcement as the primary street-level tool to suppress social dissent and unrest. This is an important difference in how police interact with suspected offenders. Some students believe that militarization efforts are needed to keep the peace within these communities, while other students are adamant that more de-escalation techniques and withdrawal of heavy artillery are more helpful. This ideological shift in the function of police and the impacts on certain demographics cannot be denied. This discussion is, perhaps not surprisingly, often polarizing. To account for these opposing viewpoints, and to ensure that these conversations are constructive and civil, students submit their reflective essays prior to the in-class discussions. Students are asked to bring a colored pen or pencil and annotate during the in-class discussion about counterpoints or things that they may view differently after the in-class discussions. Students then submit the annotated reflection for credit. The classroom discussions mirror the national debate surrounding defunding, abolition, and retraining.

Our classroom exchanges must continue to focus on power and privilege issues and the consequences that unearned privilege has on marginalized groups. Students need to learn about racial disparities in the criminal justice system and reflect on how whites and people of color have different law enforcement experiences. It is integral that stereotypes are addressed and that academics and students can identify situations in which they have been stereotyped and have stereotyped others. Our criminal justice system continues to mirror a long-standing set of policies and laws that reflect bias, such as when some racial/ethnic groups are deemed "of a criminal nature" and need to be left to civilize themselves. In contrast, others are "redeemable" and worthy of investment through equitable education, housing, and health care, among other structural investments. To form a deeper understanding of the foundation of our nation's highly racialized and inequitable criminal justice system, students might imagine more equitable goals and opportunities for change. Although some may believe issues of race are improving in the United States, this collection supports the argument that we are mostly unwilling to engage in difficult conversations about race as a nation. These authors understand the importance of race and making connections to their students. While teaching race is difficult, we must encourage teachers and professors to talk about race not only for their scholarship and growth but also for their students' education and improvement. Because those who cannot remember the past are condemned to repeat it.

NOTES

1. Kim Fridkin, Amanda Wintersieck, Jillian Courey, and Joshua Thompson, "Race and Police Brutality: The Importance of Media Framing," *International Journal of Communication* 11 (January 2017): 3394–14.

2. Meghan Keneally, "What to Know about the Violent Charlottesville Protests and Anniversary Rallies," ABC News, August 8, 2018, https://abcnews.go.com/US/happen-charlottesville-protest-anniversary-weekend/story?id=57107500.

3. Shaun L. Gabbidon, Helen Taylor Greene, Vernetta D. Young, and Anne T. Sulton, preface, *African American Classics in Criminology & Criminal Justice* (Thousand Oaks, CA: Sage, 2002), ix–x.

4. Gregory S. Schneider, "A Small Town That Has Wrestled with Big Issues," *Washington Post*, October 3, 2016.

5. Adeel Hassan, "The Sandra Bland Video: What We Know," New York Times, May 7, 2019.

6. Shaun L. Gabbidon, Helen Taylor Greene, and Vernetta D. Young, *African American Classics in Criminology & Criminal Justice* (Thousand Oaks, CA: Sage, 2002).

CONTRIBUTORS

Darryl A. Brice, Instructor, Highline College

Dr. Darryl A. Brice was born and raised in Baltimore, Maryland. He attended Frostburg State University in Frostburg, Maryland, where he received his BS in political science and justice studies. He received his MA and PhD in sociology from Loyola University Chicago. Dr. Brice is currently an instructor of sociology and diversity and globalism studies at Highline College, where he has taught since 2003 and where he was awarded tenure in 2007. The next year, Highline College recognized him as Faculty Member of the Year. In 2009 he was the recipient of the NISOD (National Institute for Staff and Development) Excellence Award. In addition, Dr. Brice has appeared in Who's Who Among America's Teachers.

Derrick R. Brooms, Associate Professor, University of Cincinnati

Derrick R. Brooms is faculty in sociology and Africana studies at the University of Cincinnati and serves as a youth worker as well. His research and activism focus on educational equity, race and racism, diversity and inequality, and identity. Dr. Brooms is an educator, activist, practitioner, and mentor. He recently received both the Presidential Exemplary Multicultural Teaching Award (2016) and the Diversity Champion Award (2016) from the University of Louisville and was acknowledged with the Jacquelyn Johnson Jackson Early Career Scholar Award (2019) from the Association of Black Sociologists. Dr. Brooms is the author of *Being Black, Being Male on Campus: Understanding and Confronting Black Male Collegiate Experiences* (2017), coauthor of *Empowering Men of Color on Campus: Building Student Community in Higher Education* (2018), and coeditor of *Living Racism: Through the Barrel of the Book* (2018).

Dr. Paul M. Buckley, Director of Diversity Equity and Inclusion, Fred Hutchinson Cancer Research Center

Dr. Paul M. Buckley is a diversity consultant and anti-oppression worker. His most recent post in higher education was as the inaugural director of the Butler Center and assistant vice president at Colorado College. Dr. Buckley is committed to institutional transformation through inclusion, diversity, and equity-conscious approaches and rigorous anti-racist work at predominantly white and white-centered institutions. His research interests focus on discourse theory of race and racism, community and coalition building among people of color, student development and retention, and organizational resistance to tactics that dismantle manifestations of oppression. Dr. Buckley leads diversity equity and inclusion work at the Fred Hutchinson Cancer Research Center in Seattle, Washington.

Emerald L. Christopher-Byrd, Assistant Professor, University of Delaware

Dr. Christopher-Byrd serves as a faculty member in the Department of Women and Gender Studies at the University of Delaware. She received her PhD in language, literacy, and culture from the University of Maryland, Baltimore County. Across her research, Dr. Christopher-Byrd explores the translation of social and cultural representations of Black women into political institutions, policies, and practices. Her current research focuses on racialized gendered borders of Black womanhood that lead to institutional and sociocultural violence against Black women.

Jason E. Cohen, Associate Professor, Berea College

Jason E. Cohen is an associate professor of English at Berea College, where he is a Whiting Foundation Public Engagement Fellow for 2019–21. His early modern scholarship has appeared in the *International Journal of Humanities and Computing*, *The Library*, and elsewhere. He leads digital and computational humanities initiatives at Berea, and his work has been supported by the NEH and the Andrew W. Mellon Foundation. Currently, he is working on *Disrupting the Peace: Transformational Practices and Enduring Concerns in Public Humanism*, which situates institutions of higher education in relation to civic engagement in the public humanities. In addition, he is coauthoring a cultural history of dimensional lumber, titled *2x4*.

Daniel J. Delgado, Associate Professor, Texas A&M University–San Antonio

Daniel is an associate professor at Texas A&M University–San Antonio. His research is focused on three areas: Latino/a student experiences in higher education, middle-class Latinx experiences with processes of racialization, and understanding how race and new urbanism intersect in the Southwest. He is working on a book addressing the everyday racial politics experienced by middle-class Mexican-ancestry Latinx people. He has published in several edited volumes and journals; his most current article is in *Sociology of Race and Ethnicity*. Recently he published an edited book on Latinx experiences in the US titled *Latino Peoples in the New America: Racialization and Resistance*. He lives in his hometown of San Antonio, Texas.

Felicia L. Harris, Assistant Professor, University of Houston–Downtown
Dr. Felicia L. Harris is an assistant professor of communication studies and assistant director for the Center for Critical Race Studies at the University of Houston–Downtown. In her research, Harris explores the intersections of race, gender, power, and privilege within the contexts of mass media, popular culture, and college campuses and classrooms. Prior to joining the faculty at UHD, Harris worked in student affairs for four years while spearheading social media initiatives for university housing at the University of Georgia, including the award-winning diversity-focused social media campaign, #OneUGA. In addition to scholarly publications in academic journals such as *The Black Scholar* and *FIRE!!! The Multimedia Journal of Black Studies*, Harris is an engaged public intellectual with articles published in *Chronicle Vitae* and *HuffPost*.

Tasha M. Hawthorne, Assistant Professor, Berea College
Tasha M. Hawthorne is an assistant professor of English at Berea College who specializes in twentieth-century African American literature. Currently, she's working on her first book manuscript, which explores how the transgressive and salacious black pulp fiction of the mid-twentieth century represented a popular challenge to the normative aesthetic and moral assumptions underpinning both the formation of an African American literary canon and the maintenance of a pragmatic but conservative politics of black respectability.

Dr. Douglas Eli Julien, Associate Professor of English, Texas A&M–Texarkana
Dr. Douglas Eli Julien is an associate professor of English at Texas A&M–Texarkana and currently the department chair of the Department of Literature, Composition, Media, and Communication. He received his doctoral degree for comparative studies in discourse and society in 2005 from the

University of Minnesota. Prior to his PhD, he earned a master's degree from Western Illinois University in literature and a bachelor's degree from Eastern Illinois University. His areas of expertise include world literature (especially postcolonial literature and theory), literary theory (especially continental philosophy and critical theory), and the study of popular music. Guiding his research in all three of these areas is the study of race.

Dwayne A. Mack, Vice President for Diversity, Equity, and Inclusion, Professor of History, and the Carter G. Woodson Chair in African American History at Berea College

Dwayne A. Mack, PhD, is the vice president for diversity, equity, and inclusion, a professor of history, and the Carter G. Woodson Chair in African American History at Berea College. His research focuses on the Black West, the civil rights movement, policing in America, and equity, inclusion, and diversity in academia. He is the lead editor of *Beginning a Career in Academia: A Guide for Graduate Students of Color* (2015) and *Mentoring Faculty of Color: Essays on Professional Advancement in Colleges and Universities* (2013); coeditor of *Violence Against Black Bodies: An Intersectional Analysis of How Black Lives Continue to Matter* (2017), *Law Enforcement in the Age of Black Lives Matter: Policing Black and Brown Bodies* (2018), and *Freedom's Racial Frontier: The African American West in Twentieth- and Twentieth-First-Century History*; and author of *Black Spokane: The Civil Rights Struggle in the Inland Northwest* (2014).

Shane A. McCoy, Lecturer, Middle Tennessee State University

Dr. Shane A. McCoy (they/them/theirs) is a lecturer in the Department of English at Middle Tennessee State University. Dr. McCoy's research focuses on Africana women's literature, critical and feminist pedagogies, social justice, and pedagogies of empowerment. Their courses have focused on contemporary transnational literature, women of color and black feminisms, Hurricane Katrina, and comedy as social and cultural critique. Dr. McCoy is currently at work on a book manuscript that weds contemporary Africana women's literature to feminist affect studies.

Erin Murrah-Mandril, Assistant Professor, University of Texas at Arlington

Erin Murrah-Mandril is an assistant professor of English at the University of Texas at Arlington. Her book, *In the Mean Time: Temporal Colonization and the Mexican American Literary Tradition*, focuses on Mexican

American authors' use of time to navigate US colonization in the late nineteenth and early twentieth centuries. Dr. Murrah-Mandril is a core faculty member for the Center for Mexican American Studies (CMAS) at UTA. She regularly teaches courses in Chicana/o literature, Latina/o/x literature, literature of the US West, Mexican American studies, literary history, and theory.

Sharon D. Raynor, Professor of English and Dean—School of Humanities and Social Sciences, Elizabeth City State University (North Carolina)

Sharon D. Raynor is the dean of the School of Humanities and Social Sciences and a professor of English at Elizabeth City State University (ECSU). She has a forthcoming book, *Practicing Oral History with Military and War Veterans*, that focuses on trauma and the special issues involved with conducting oral history interviews with military and war veterans. Her scholarly work focuses on trauma, conflict, loss, and silence and has appeared in the *Oral History Review*, *Word and Text: A Journal of Literary Studies and Linguistics*, *Comparative Literature and Culture*, *(In)Scribing Gender: International Female Writers and the Creative Process*, *Australian Feminist Review*, *A Journal of Social Theory*, *We Wear the Mask: Paul Laurence Dunbar Collection*, *Cultural Studies/Critical Methodologies*, *Zadie Smith: Critical Essays*, and more.

Rachel Roegman, Assistant Professor, University of Illinois, Urbana-Champaign

Rachel Roegman is an assistant professor of educational leadership in the Department of Education Policy, Organization and Leadership at the University of Illinois, Urbana-Champaign. Her research interests examine the interconnections of equity, contexts, and leadership, and her teaching focuses on the development and support of equity-focused leaders.

Serena J. Salloum, Associate Professor, Ball State University

Serena J. Salloum is interested in how school context promotes educational outcomes. In particular, she focuses on how organizational culture and structure promotes equity in high-poverty schools. Current projects include studies of how early-career teachers' planning and enactment of mathematics instruction are influenced by their social network members and social context. In addition, she is investigating the instructional resources state educational agencies endorse for Common Core implementation and implications for classroom instruction. She teaches courses on educational policy and research methods.

Stephen W. Sheps, Lecturer, Ryerson University

Stephen W. Sheps is a sessional lecturer at Ryerson University who specializes in both sport sociology and the sociology of education. Stephen has recently published in *Critical Studies in Education* and the *International Review for the Sociology of Sport* and is currently working on a book exploring the intersection of national narratives, multiculturalism, and the lack of diversity in Canadian hockey. Stephen regularly teaches sport sociology, popular culture, and introductory sociology at Ryerson, despite his precarious employment. Prior to Ryerson, he worked as a visiting assistant professor in the US at the University of the South and at Trent University in Peterborough, Ontario.

Kerri-Ann M. Smith, EdD, Assistant Professor, Queensborough Community College (CUNY)

Kerri-Ann M. Smith is an assistant professor of English at Queensborough Community College. She has done professional development and research in Ghana, Nigeria, and Senegal and has taught several courses in English and education on both community college and university levels. Her research focuses on curriculum and instruction, with emphasis on culturally responsive pedagogy. She serves on the Faculty Diversity Strategic Plan Advisory Committee at her campus and is very engaged with issues concerning diversity and social justice. She is the coauthor of the textbook *Writing Identities: A Guide to Writing through Reading* (2012).

Scott Manning Stevens, Associate Professor of Native American and Indigenous Studies, Syracuse University

Dr. Stevens is a citizen of the Akwesasne Mohawk nation and holds the position of associate professor and director of the Native American and Indigenous Studies Program at Syracuse University. He earned his PhD in English and is also a tenured member of the English faculty at Syracuse. His research and publications focus on Indigenous material literary and visual culture, as well as museum studies, and have appeared in journals such as the *American Indian Culture and Research Journal*, *Northwest Review*, and *Early American Literature*. He is a coauthor of *The Art of the American West* and *Home Front: Daily Life in the Civil War North*, as well as coeditor and contributor to the collection *Why You Can't Teach*

United States History without American Indians. Dr. Stevens is particularly interested in how Native American history is frequently ignored in high school and college curricula and otherwise marginalized in national cultural institutions. His research has been funded by the Mellon Foundation, the National Endowment for the Humanities, and the Ford Foundation.

Keja Valens, Professor, Salem State University
Keja Valens is a professor of English at Salem State University, where she also serves as co-faculty fellow for Diversity, Power Dynamics, and Social Justice. She teaches and writes on literatures of the Americas and queer theory. Her recent books are the coedited volumes *Querying Consent: Beyond Permission and Refusal* (2018) and *The Barbara Johnson Reader* (2014) and the monograph *Desire between Women in Caribbean Literature* (2013). Her next book project is a study of cookbooks, national culture, and independence movements in the Caribbean.

Mark William Westmoreland, Doctoral Candidate, Villanova University
Westmoreland is a doctoral candidate in philosophy at Villanova University, where he received the John G. Tich Award in Research Excellence. He works in political philosophy and philosophy of race and also publishes on pedagogy. He recently published "Bergson, Colonialism, and Race" in *Interpreting Bergson: Critical Essays* (2020). Westmoreland coedited with Andrea J. Pitts *Beyond Bergson: Examining Race and Colonialism through the Writings of Henri Bergson* (SUNY, 2019), guest-edited a special issue on Bergson for the *Journal of French and Francophone Philosophy* 24, no. 2 (2016), and curated "Bergson(-ism) Remembered" in the same issue.

INDEX

Adichie, Chimamanda Ngozi, 184, 187–88, 189; *Americanah*, 187–88, 192
affect, 5, 8, 10, 66–67, 73, 185, 191–93, 323; affective relationship, 12, 185, 189. *See also* Black rage; guilt, feelings of
African American literature, 238–39, 345–47, 349
African American Policy Forum, 67, 361n37
African Americans, 71–73, 239–40, 247, 314n3, 331, 335, 349–50. *See also* Black people
Alexander, Elizabeth, *The Black Interior*, 348
Alexander, Michelle, 308
algorithms, 106–109, 114, 126n16
alienation, 31, 207, 234
antiblackness, 105, 114–15, 117, 303, 329, 334, 347
anti-racist, 241, 249; classroom, 166, 283; discourse, 281. *See also under* pedagogy
assimilation, 31, 33–34, 327–28
autobiography, 67, 206, 258; racial, 160, 368
autoethnography, 14, 157, 257–58; collaborative, 157; performative, 257
Baker, Quenton, 247
Baldwin, James, 1–2, 6, 8, 343, 353, 357, 362n40
Ball State University, 159
Baum, Bruce, *The Rise and Fall of the Caucasian Race*, 244
Beck, Koa, 236
Bell, Lee Anne, 138
belonging, 13, 235–36, 348; cultural, 279, 321
blackness, 44, 124, 244, 303, 322, 336, 348
Black Panthers, 311
Black people, 69–70, 88, 114, 234, 241, 244, 300–302, 323, 328, 330–32, 334–36, 343–44, 347–50, 355–56; Black Identity Extremists, 314n3. *See also* African Americans; Women of Color
Black Power movement, 53
Black rage, 64–65, 68–69, 71–75
Bland, Sandra, 7, 74, 311, 349, 366–67
BLM (Black Lives Matter) movement, 73–75, 205, 299–307 passim, 312–13, 343–44, 354, 358n2; and women, 65, 67
Boyce Davies, Carole, 244
Boyd, Rekia, 7, 300, 305, 310, 355
Bracero History Archive, 286, 288

Brown, Michael, 7, 72, 300, 305, 310, 313, 344, 349, 358n2, 367, 370–71
Bruner, Jerome, 185, 197n7
Budden, Joe, 311

Cannon, Katie, 247
Castile, Philando, 309, 311, 315n22, 349, 354, 367
Charlottesville, Virginia, 102, 314n3, 343, 365–66
class. *See* socio-economic class
classroom(s), 3, 5–15, 25–26, 41–45, 47–51, 55–57, 183–87; intergenerational, 47, 50, 53–54
colonialism, 26–27; settler, 26–28, 32, 257, 266
colonization, 27–28, 234, 324; relationship between colonizer and colonized, 234
colorblindness, 11, 85–89, 89, 96n9, 124, 192, 209, 281, 306, 330–31, 334; color-neutral, 170. *See also* post-racial
Cooper, Anna Julia, 307
courageous conversations, 164
criminal justice system, 303, 308–10, 335, 366–72
critical race theory, 5, 160, 358n4. *See also under* pedagogy
Cullors, Patrisse, 307
culturally responsive school leadership, 165–67, 168, 172–73
curriculum, 146, 183–87, 196, 206–12, 215–18, 226n25, 261–62, 305; design of, 190, 194

DACA (Deferred Action for Childhood Arrivals), 286
Davies, Lynn, 264–65
Davis, Angela, 308
decolonization, 234, 266, 282
deficit view(s), 162, 167, 169. *See also under* narrative
DeVos, Betsy, 240
discrimination, 14, 72, 103–104, 120, 239, 241, 275, 327, 361n30; effects of, 88; technologies of, 103, 106, 113. *See also* redlining
diversity, 29, 43, 47–48, 193, 205–22, 224n4, 225n14, 226n15, 227n32, 245–46, 283; initiatives, 140, 208–209; requirements, 12–13, 208, 214–15, 217, 219, 223n2, 226n15
Diversity, Power Dynamics, and Social Justice (DPDS) requirement, 208–21; implementation of, 207–208, 215, 227n32
double-consciousness, 232–33, 247, 350
Dred Scott (decision), 300, 310, 319
Du Bois, W. E. B., 5, 206–207, 232–33, 247, 299–302, 304–307, 311, 350, 353–55; *Black Reconstruction in America*, 302; *The Philadelphia Negro*, 302, 304; *The Souls of Black Folk*, 302, 304, 308–309, 348, 350, 353.
Dunbar, Paul Laurence, 231–32, 247; "We Wear the Mask," 231, 247, 249
Duvernay, Ava, 308

Eckford, Elizabeth, 311
education: graduate, 194–96; higher, 24, 103, 114, 183, 196, 222, 232, 259–60 (*see also names of colleges/universities*); K-12, 33, 157–58, 161–62, 282; of teachers, 161, 166, 261 (*see also under* pedagogy). *See also* general education
embodiment, 5, 66, 276–78, 287, 289
equity audit, 160–61

faculty support, 171–72, 221–22; lack of, 242–43, 256
Fanon, Frantz 114, 125n13, 233–34, 250, 266, 322, 355; *Black Skin,*

White Masks, 234; *The Wretched of the Earth*, 234.
feminism, 49, 65–67, 217–18, 224n4, 290, 358n3; Black, 183–86, 191–93; Chicana, 275; intersectional, 186, 191, 193–94, 265
Ferguson, Missouri, 71–72, 300, 310, 313, 358n2, 370–71
Foucault, Michel, 123, 214, 225n9, 234, 265

Garner, Eric, 7, 305, 311, 349, 354, 361n29, 367
Garza, Alicia, 307, 343
Gasman, Marybeth, 239, 245
gender, 186–88 passim, 217–18, 236, 243–44, 287–88; and colonization, 27, 31; cross-gender solidarity, 191–92; and race, 17n10, 63–68, 70, 124, 247, 355–56. *See also* Women of Color
general education, 9, 183–85, 193–94, 208, 210–16, 220–21, 226n15, 226n25; requirements, 205, 208, 210–11, 216–17. *See also under* diversity
Ginsburg, Michal, 233
Giroux, Henry, 260, 302
Grant, Oscar, 310
Gray, Freddie, 7, 72, 74, 300, 310, 367
guilt, feelings of, 10, 24, 26, 164, 333; presumption of, 335

hailing, 123, 284–85. *See also* interpellation
Hartman, Saidiya, 348–49
HBCU (Historically Black Colleges and Universities), 236, 239–40, 244, 246
Hill Collins, Patricia, 130n52, 186, 191–93
Hitchcock, Peter, 248; *Dialogics of the Oppressed*, 248
hooks, bell, 6, 49, 51, 55–56, 68–69, 71, 72, 102, 107, 137, 139, 208–209, 213, 215–17, 220–21, 233, 241, 243, 249, 344, 358n3
horror, 243–44
Husserl, Edmund, 234

identity, 67, 149, 234, 236–37, 282–85, 287; cultural, 32, 48; digital, 114, 276; fluidity of, 274; formation of, 232, 274, 349; Indigenous, 32, 284; Latina/o/x, 204–85, 288–89; national, 274, 279; politics, 6–9, 94, 101, 107, 116, 215; racial, 92–94, 105, 107–108, 216, 234–35, 274, 285 (*see also under* Black people); shared, 278; white, 282–84
inconvenient: facts, 305–306; truths, 24
Indigenous 10, 24–36, 324; pedagogical practices, 265–66. *See also* land acknowledgements; mestizaje; Native Americans
interpellation, 355. *See also* hailing
intersectionality, 65–67, 141, 149, 183–86, 190–91, 193–94, 361n36. *See also* Women of Color
inferiority, beliefs about, 327, 334; feelings of, 234
institutional: politics, 101–102; racism, 64, 87, 113, 266, 319, 329–30, 332, 334–35; structures, 25, 103, 105, 109, 119–20, 123–24, 209, 214–16, 220–22

Jim Crow: era, 52, 54, 70–71, 240, 311, 328–29; laws, 319, 328

knowledge transfer, 138, 189, 190

Latina/o/x, 206–207, 222, 275, 278–79, 281, 284–89
Ladner, Joyce, 301, 307

land acknowledgments, 24
land-grant universities. *See* Purdue University; University of Minnesota
Lee, Barbara, 240
librotraficantes, 281
LMS (Learning Management Systems), 276, 279, 287. *See also* online instruction
Loewen, James, 306
Lorde, Audre, 75, 101, 105, 208, 211, 215, 232–33, 237, 246–47, 249, 328–29
Lynn, Marvin, 302

Manufactured Crisis, 163
mask(s), 44, 231–37, 246–50; masking, 232–33, 237, 246–47, 249–50
marginalization, 88, 140–41, 195, 236, 244–45, 248, 250
marginalized: communities, 74; voices, 186, 192, 267 (*see also* silencing)
McDonald, Laquan, 7, 300, 310, 367
#MeToo, 74
mestizaje, 285. *See also under* identity
Mills, Charles W., 72, 324, 330, 334
Mills, C. Wright, 266, 305–306
Monáe, Janelle, 311
Morrison, Toni, 88, 92–94, 233–35, 243–44; *The Origins of Others*, 235; "Recitatif," 88–89, 92–94
museums, 25–26. *See also* National Museum of the American Indian

NAACP (National Association for the Advancement of Colored People), 75n1, 307
narrative(s), 65–68, 107–108, 110, 127n21, 257–58, 313, 348, 352, 355–56; deficit, 303; national, 25–27, 259, 348; racist, 163–64, 171–72, 310; of survival, 233–34
National Museum of the American Indian, 26, 35–36
Nation at Risk, A, 163
Native Americans, 10, 25–26, 28–36, 241, 324, 327–28. *See also* Indigenous; mestizaje
neoliberalism, 163, 183, 188, 259–60, 263, 281
netiquette, 276
NYCLU (New York Civil Liberties Union), 309, 335

online instruction, 161, 290: asynchronous, 158, 168–70; hybrid, 158, 168–70; synchronous, 158, 168–70. *See also* LMS; pedagogy: online
oppression, 65, 68, 75, 159–60, 186, 219, 240, 248, 249, 331, 355; and power, 139, 277–78; structures/systems of, 141–42, 331, 350; systemic, 136–37, 148. *See also* intersectionality; institutional: racism; power
Other, 4–5, 47, 234, 235, 241, 246; Othering (process), 234–35, 239, 242–44, 249; Otherness, 43, 44, 51, 95n4, 237
outsider within, 184–86, 191–94

passing, 46, 75n1, 236–37, 274
patriarchy, 218, 243, 246; capitalist, 72–73, 107. *See also under* white supremacy
pedagogy, 48, 138–39, 142, 184, 195; anti-racist, 282–83; critical, 184, 194, 320; critical race, 184, 194, 299–303, 345, 358n4; culturally relevant/responsive, 48, 140, 148, 165, 198n23; disciplinary, 64–65; of discomfort, 193; of empowerment, 193; ethnic studies, 278, 286;

intersectional feminist, 186, 191, 193–94; online, 284; radical, 51, 209, 215–16, 226n25; reality, 48; of risk, 195. *See also under* education
People of Color, 206, 220, 241, 245, 282–84, 303, 328, 334. *See also* African Americans; Black people; Indigenous; Latina/o/x; Women of Color
police brutality, 64, 67, 305, 307, 314n3, 319, 335, 354–55, 369–70. *See also* stop-and-frisk
post-racial, 11, 70, 72, 82, 103, 107, 299, 306, 332–33. *See also* colorblindness
power, 31–32, 84, 102, 112, 137–38, 148, 193, 211–16, 224n4, 235, 237, 244–45, 284, 330; racialized, 102, 106; structures/systems of, 44, 139, 276–77, 281, 290
Predominantly White Institution (PWI), 43, 185, 236, 246
privilege, 166–67, 236–37, 241, 246–47, 361n30, 370; epistemic, 321, 323, 336; white, 54–55, 163, 191, 193, 236, 238, 242, 247, 283–84, 334, 384
protocols, 161, 164, 168, 186, 191, 196
Public Enemy, 311
Purdue University, 159

race: history of, 319–22, 324–30; and leadership, 156, 159–60, 167–68, 173; as medium, 103, 110, 112–13, 122–24; as metaphor, 244; myth of, 90; and racism, 96n12, 183–96, 334, 350; as social construct, 5–9, 93, 237; teaching of, 2–3, 42, 48–50, 57, 80, 104, 161–62, 190, 194–97, 233, 308–309, 366–69. *See also under* gender; intersectionality
racist(s), 83–87, 95n3, 242, 243, 246, 281, 321, 323–24, 333–34, 336; narratives, 171–72; policies, 327, 329–31; words, 4, 104–107, 115–16, 170
redlining, 331–32, 335
Rice, Tamir, 7, 311, 335, 336, 349, 354, 361n28, 367

Said, Edward, 234
Salem State University, 207–11, 217, 220–23, 225n14
scaffolding, 187, 189, 197n6–7, 264, 303; for justice, 139, 183–86, 188, 191–92, 264
segregation, 69–70, 83–86, 167, 240, 308, 319, 322; school desegregation, 55, 366. *See also* Jim Crow
sequencing, 142, 184–85, 197n8
silence, 90, 96n17, 124, 160, 191, 242; and black women, 65; as erasure, 36, 63
silencing, 26, 139, 166, 171–72, 232–33, 235–36, 241–42, 249. *See also* marginalized: voices; oppression
Sleeter, Christine, 280, 282
social justice, 28, 32, 64, 137–44, 147–49, 160–62, 183–85, 193–94, 196, 209–14, 216, 220. *See also under* scaffolding
social media, 4, 15, 24, 35, 64, 72, 101–102, 106–108, 110–24, 126n16, 141, 144–45, 148, 287, 349. *See also* algorithms
socio-economic class, 45, 57, 212–13, 244
sociological imagination, 256, 266, 305, 307, 310
sovereignty, 29–32, 109; tribal, 29–30
Sterling, Alton, 309, 367
stop-and-frisk, 309–10, 322, 367. *See also* police brutality

stranger(s), 4, 235, 322, 325, 353
students: first-generation, 52, 140, 210, 256, 275; indigenous, 25; majority-society, 26, 30, 32; non-traditional, 9, 53–54, 57, 139, 257; transfer, 190
survival, 232–33, 236, 246–50, 261, 279, 300. *See also under* narrative

T. I., 353–54
Tometi, Opal, 307
Trump, Donald J., 51, 64, 75, 79, 80–85, 87–88, 94, 106, 157, 183, 192, 194–95, 198n21, 244, 274, 280–81, 286, 343, 369
Trump University, 275

"Unite the Right" rally, 314n3, 365–66. *See also* Charlottesville, Virginia
University of Minnesota, 81

Vygotsky, Lev, 185, 197n7

wage gap, 92
Weber, Max, 304–306
Wells, Ida B., 301, 307, 355–56; *Red Record*, 344; *Southern Horrors and Other Writings*, 346–47, 362n40
white: fragility, 6, 164, 166–67, 192–93, 283; gaze, 322, 328–29, 336; representation, 232. *See also* whiteness; white supremacy
whiteness, 51, 114, 124, 130n51, 167, 185, 237, 241, 283, 302, 321–23, 327, 330, 334; critical, 167; studies, 220, 282–83. *See also* power
white supremacy, 67–68, 70–72, 75, 192–93, 220, 247–48, 336; and patriarchy, 51, 65, 72; symbols of, 332. *See also under* privilege
Women of Color, 64–68, 237, 241, 245, 247, 250, 307, 355. *See also* African Americans; Black people; People of Color

Zinn, Howard, 301

www.ingramcontent.com/pod-product-compliance
Lightning Source LLC
LaVergne TN
LVHW040201080826
844660LV00001B/69

* 9 7 8 1 4 3 8 4 8 2 2 5 5 *